Larkin, Ideology and Critical Violence

Larkin, Ideology and Critical Violence

A Case of Wrongful Conviction

John Osborne

First published 2008 by
PALGRAVE MACMILLAN
Houndmills, Basingstoke, Hampshire RG21 6XS and
175 Fifth Avenue, New York, N.Y. 10010
Companies and representatives throughout the world

PALGRAVE MACMILLAN is the global academic imprint of the Palgrave Macmillan division of St. Martin's Press, LLC and of Palgrave Macmilla Macmillan® is a registered trademark in the United States, United King and other countries. Palgrave is a registered trademark in the Europea Union and other countries.

ISBN-13: 978–1–4039–3706–3   hardback
ISBN-10: 1–4039–3706–0   hardback

This book is printed on paper suitable for recycling and made from ful managed and sustained forest sources. Logging, pulping and manufact processes are expected to conform to the environmental regulations country of origin.

A catalogue record for this book is available from the British Library.

A catalog record for this book is available from the Library of Congress

10   9   8   7   6   5   4   3   2   1
17   16   15   14   13   12   11   10   09   08

Transferred to Digital Printing in 2009

Contents

Acknowledgements

I am deeply grateful to the Arts and Humanities Research Council for a Research Leave Award that made the writing of this book possible.

I would also like to thank Professors Robert Crawford and Barbara Everett for supporting my application for the AHRC grant; Judy Burg and the staff of the Brynmor Jones Library for guidance in the consultation of Larkin manuscripts; the Philip Larkin Society for providing a laboratory in which to road-test my ideas; Sylvia Tynan, Smitha Manoj and the staff of Macmillan India Ltd for invaluable assistance in preparing the typescript; the Society of Authors as the Literary Representative of the Estate of Philip Larkin; Jane Thomas for personal and scholarly support; and Rhiannon, Aeronwy and Carys for their forbearance.

Although this book was written in an isolating spirit of contestation, there are two intellectual debts I would like to specify: first, to Larkin's friend Ted Tarling, who died before he had the chance to comment on my ideas but who shaped them anyway, in an act of unaccountable generosity, by bequeathing me his library; and, second, to Jim Orwin, the world authority on musical settings of Larkin's poems, who has repeatedly given me the benefit of his researches.

I dedicate this book to my mother: whatever virtues it displays, I learned from her; the vices are all my own.

The author and publishers acknowledge the following permissions to reprint copyright material: Faber and Faber Ltd and Farrar, Straus and Giroux, LLC, for quotations from *Collected Poems* (1988) by Philip Larkin; excerpts from *Selected Letters of Philip Larkin, 1940–1985*; and excerpts from *Required Writing* by Philip Larkin. Faber and Faber Ltd for excerpts from *Jill, A Girl in Winter, All What Jazz, Further Requirements, Larkin's Jazz* and *Early Poems and Juvenilia* by Philip Larkin. The foregoing are all copyright the Estate of Philip Larkin. Marvell Press, England and Australia, for quotations from 'Whatever Happened', 'Born Yesterday', 'Poetry of Departures', 'Wants', 'Arrivals, Departures', 'At Grass', 'Skin', 'Dry-Point', 'Next, Please', 'Latest Face', 'Maiden Name', 'Church Going', 'Places, Loved Ones', 'If, My Darling', 'Lines on a Young Lady's

Photograph Album', 'Reasons for Attendance' and 'Toads', reprinted from *The Less Deceived*. Faber and Faber Ltd and Farrar, Straus and Giroux, LLC, for excerpts from Collected Poems by Thom Gunn. Faber and Faber Ltd and Harcourt, Inc., for quotations from Collected Poems by T.S. Eliot. Peterloo Poets for an excerpt from *Love is a Four-Letter World* by Maurice Rutherford. Excerpts from Siegfried Sassoon's *Collected Poems, 1908–1956*, copyright Siegfried Sassoon, by kind permission of the Estate of George Sassoon. Every effort has been made to trace copyright holders, but if any have been inadvertently overlooked, the author and publishers will be pleased to make the necessary arrangements at the first opportunity.

Abbreviations

All references to the works of Philip Larkin are incorporated in the
using the following abbreviations:

AWJ   *All What Jazz*
CP   *Collected Poems* (1988)
EPJ   *Early Poems and Juvenilia*
FR   *Further Requirements*
GW   *A Girl in Winter*
J   *Jill*
LJ   *Larkin's Jazz*
RW   *Required Writing*
SL   *Selected Letters*
TWG   *Trouble at Willow Gables and other fictions*

All other citations may be found in the notes.

Introduction: Radical Larkin and the Late Millennial Bowdler

I The original Bowdler

For three centuries after his death, Shakespeare was regarded as a major poet so wanting in taste that even his greatest works were marred by regrettable moral and linguistic lapses. On hearing Shakespeare's boast that he never blotted out a line, Ben Jonson rejoined: 'Would he had blotted out a thousand'. Dr Johnson concurred: 'Shakespeare never has six lines together without a fault'. John Dryden claimed that Shakespeare 'is the very Janus of poets; he wears almost everywhere two faces; and you have scarce begun to admire the one ere you despise the other'. While Voltaire loftily declared that 'Shakespeare is a drunken savage ... whose plays can please only in London and Canada'.[1]

One solution to the problem of Shakespeare's unevenness was to improve his plays by rewriting them. 'Tate rewrote *King Lear* to give it a happy ending; the Honorable James Howard, Dryden's brother-in-law, rewrote *Romeo and Juliet*' marrying the young lovers; and Poet Laureate 'Sir William Davenant did a jolly production of *Macbeth*, complete with singing and dancing'.[2] In all such instances, not only were offending passages excised from Shakespeare's original but new material was added by the subsequent, more judicious author.

In 1807, the approach changed, Hannah Bowdler published *The Family Shakespeare*, which in an unsigned preface pledged to remove 'everything that can raise a blush on the cheek of modesty'. (In a nice case of the Bowdler bowdlerized, Hannah wielded her scalpel anonymously 'to avoid the odium of admitting that she, an unmarried gentlewoman of fifty, understood Shakespeare's obscenity' well enough to expertly remove it!)[3] Hannah's volume was far from comprehensive, some plays being omitted in their entirety; however, eleven years later

1

her brother Dr Thomas Bowdler published the revised and enlarged edition that, in ten volumes, became the best-selling Shakespeare of the nineteenth century. Dr Bowdler surgically removed from Shakespeare's text 'whatever is unfit to be read by a gentleman in a company of ladies' or 'which may not with propriety be read aloud in a family'.[4] In practice, this meant suppressing all overt sexual allusions and many religious ones. This in turn entailed greatly diminished roles for the likes of Hamlet, Macbeth, Falstaff and the Nurse, and the total elimination of reprehensible characters like Doll Tearsheet. 'True to his medical training', the good doctor 'neatly stitched the loose ends across' the cut to 'avoid scars. He substituted very few words of his own', and he neither paraphrased 'nor (with rare exceptions) added commentary'.[5]

Such was the success of *The Family Shakespeare* that Bowdler went on to expurgate Edward Gibbon's *The History of the Decline and Fall of the Roman Empire*. He also set a trend for what as early as 1836 became known as 'bowdlerizing'; distinguished text-cutters who followed in his footsteps including the great dictionnarian Noah Webster, William Cullen Bryant, W.M. Rossetti, the novelist Charlotte Yonge, Palgrave of *The Golden Treasury* (though not in that volume), Bulfinch of the *Mythology*, Lewis Carroll, Justice Brewer of the Supreme Court, Quiller-Couch of Oxford and the Poet Laureate John Masefield.[6] Thanks to the sterling efforts of these guardians of taste, three or four generations of anglophone readers grew up with an inaccurate idea of their own literary inheritance. With the First World War, the assumptions underpinning bowdlerism seemed to lose their legitimacy. The cultural tide turned in the direction of ever-greater deregulation and the artistic licence to challenge rather than endorse polite taste. When bowdlerism re-emerged in the second half of the twentieth century, it took a very different form and Larkin was a principal victim.

II   The late millennial Bowdler and the biographical fallacy

Dr Bowdler was very clear that in expurgating the indecent and blasphemous passages 'he was conferring a benefit not only on the reader but on Shakespeare as well'. Whenever you erase improper material from the plays, he observed, you do so 'not only without injury, but with manifest advantage ... to the sense of the passage and to the spirit of the author'.[7] With the late millennial Bowdler, by contrast, expurgation moves from the *textual* to the *interpretative* plane; and the effect is often, though not necessarily, such as to diminish rather than enhance the reputation of the chosen author.

Unlike Dr Bowdler and his sister, who were fully cognizant of what they were doing and declared their objectives to the reader, their late millennial counterparts appear to work without a conscious methodology. Nonetheless, their procedure is systematic and can therefore be explicated. The first vital step is to discuss literary texts as though they were spoken, not written; listened to, not read; received by ear, not by eye. The language employed by the text may be described as a 'tongue', the narrative referred to in terms of 'speech', the narrator described as an authorial 'mouthpiece', the author's career made to pivot on the discovery of a 'voice' of his or her own. This might be defended as an innocent use of metaphor, not intended to be taken seriously. In practice, the act of writing – with all its implications of inscriptedness or redrafting, its potential for variable rereading, its scribal sensitivity to the texture of text, to the way words can flow, granulate, chafe or caress – is evaporated in favour of the supposed immediacy of oral exchange.

This first move facilitates an exegetical simplification in which authors are perceived as 'speaking' more or less direct to the audience. In the case of poetry, for example, the narrators of all the individual poems in a collection will be conflated with the actual author. This conflation not only involves vanquishing the individualized narrators – the expurgation process is by now well under way – but also suppressing intertextual references of the sort that draw attention to the textuality of the text and the constructedness of its narration. In old-fashioned parlance, for the critic to admit the presence in the poem of 'voices' other than the author's own risks acknowledging that the narrator's 'speech' differs from that of the author by being compounded with non-authorial elements.

These deletions are hidden from the reader (usually from the bowdlerizer too) by wadding the resultant interpretative *lacunae* with biographical information. Typically, the critic will identify locations in poems that are non-site specific, gender the narrators and addressees in poems that are non-gender specific, and date events in poems that are temporally unhoused. A favourite tactic in accomplishing this feat is to refer the text back to the biographical incident that the critic believes prompted it. The hermeneutical quest for textual meaning is replaced by a biographical quest for the moment of origination.

Finally, it is worth remarking the frequency with which our contemporary bowdlers compensate for any shortage of biographical fact by essentializing the author's life in relation to the categories of nationality, race, class, sex and gender. In this schema, a poet like Larkin might be described as quintessentially English (i.e., xenophobic, repressed,

middle-class), Dylan Thomas or Brendan Behan as typical Celts (in
perate, romantic, *drunk*), Sylvia Plath as archetypically female (
tional, possessive, hysterical), Ted Hughes as Yorkshire person
(wind-swept, taciturn, brutal) or Allen Ginsberg as flamboyantly
(oedipal, promiscuous, attention-seeking). The precipitate of ideol
so familiar as to pass notice, these types and their defining traits re
neither justification nor analysis; they have been 'naturalized', an
appealed to as obvious truths. Their role is not to aid different
thinking but to thwart it.

This, then, is the sequence of displacements that constitute
methodology, no less systematic for being unconscious (it is when
ology is unawares that it is most pervasively at work), of the late
lennial Bowdler: text is equated with speech; all narrators are colla
into one and conflated with the author; the life of the author is us
the key to the work, so that literature is displaced onto biography
author's life is displaced onto the template of a group identity of w
he or she is perceived as representative; and that group identi
defined in relation to a few symbolic traits so stereotypical as to
self-evident, so self-evident as to deter interrogation. This redu
hermeneutics became hegemonic in the literary journalism of the
ond half of the twentieth century and spread from there to certair
tors of academic criticism. Nowhere were its effects more ubiquito
obliterative than in the domain of poetry.

III   Bowdlerizing the Beats

Two literary movements of the 1950s and 1960s fell victim to his
raphical essentialism, though both might be accused of having bro
down that fate upon their own heads. The first group, the Beats, m
be so accused in relation to subject matter. For example, Jack Kero
novels are heavily fictionalized chronicles of the antics of him an
pals – Allen Ginsberg becoming the Alvah Goldbook of *The Dh*
Bums, Lawrence Ferlinghetti becoming the Lorenzo Monsanto o
Sur, William Burroughs being pseudonymized as Old Bull Lee in *O*
Road and Gregory Corso appearing as Raphael Urso in *Desolation An*
thereby creating the misleading impression that the reader might p
the text in order to grasp an originatory autobiographical 'truth'.

This misleading impression is entrenched at the aesthetic level
Beats adopting an expressivist poetics in which it is proposed tha
should aim for the heart rather than the head, the best way of affe
the reader's emotions being to speak directly from one's own ('I an

substance of my poetry', Corso claimed). With regard to the act of composition, this entailed a privileging of the spontaneous, the inspirational, the epiphanous, over the considered and premeditated: see Ginsberg's poem 'On Improvised Poetics', whose axiom 'First thought best thought' might be translated as 'First draft, best draft' and might, as Dennis O'Driscoll has pointed out, 'evoke a "First reading, last reading" reproach from his readership'.[8] It is with unbashed pride that Kerouac claimed to have written *The Subterraneans* in three nights and Ginsberg boasted of having composed 'Sunflower Sutra' in twenty minutes and the long first section of 'Howl' in an afternoon.

The reality is very different. The major works in the Beat canon are almost invariably those which benefited from arduous crafting while the genuinely impromptu pieces are usually the most disposable. This is not to say that the masterpieces exude laboriousness, but that their spontaneity has been hard won. Ginsberg's 'Howl' is the poem that is usually thought to epitomize Beat aesthetics. When a facsimile edition was published in 1986 it reprinted five drafts of Part I, eighteen of Part II, five of Part III and seven of Part IV – though it makes no mention of a fifth part which Ferlinghetti persuaded Ginsberg to drop entire.[9] Other versions, now lost, are alluded to in the commentary. The variants that are included demonstrate the dramatic revisions the poem underwent before assuming its final form. In Part I, for instance, what is now the seventh strophe began as the fiftieth; similarly, the present twenty-second, twenty-third, twenty-seventh and thirtieth strophes all moved fifty or more places in the sequence, often undergoing extensive rewording in the process. Moreover, the facsimile edition concentrates on the period 1955–6, whereas Ginsberg actually met the poem's dedicatee Carl Solomon in 1949, jotting down at the time many of the latter's anecdotes and aphorisms which subsequently found their way into the poem. So 'Howl' was composed over a seven-year period, some parts of it undergoing at least twenty rehearsals before arriving at a persuasively 'improvised' discourse. To put it another way, it took protracted effort to get this text to masquerade as speech.

Also contrary to the authors' propaganda regarding spontaneity and improvization is the dense palimpsestic multi-layering of quotes and allusions that mediates any autobiographical disclosures in the Beat text. James Campbell has remarked the extraordinary literary pedigree of Kerouac's title *On the Road*, citing as evidence works of the same name by Douglas Goldring (1910), Gwen John (1920), Langston Hughes (1935) and Cyril Campion (1954).[10] As for Ginsberg, many of his best poems are written over the top of previous works by earlier authors: 'Malest Cornifici Tuo

Catullo' translates and adapts a poem by Catullus; 'A Supermarke
California' rewrites Lorca's 'Ode to Walt Whitman'; 'Sunflower Sutr
modelled on Blake's 'Ah, Sunflower!'; while 'Kaddish' leans heavily
Edward Marshall's 'Leave the Word Alone'. In 'Howl' the layers multi
for instance, Ginsberg took Christ's agonized cry 'eli eli lamma lan
sabachthani' – 'My God, my God, why has thou forsaken me?' – not f
its New Testament source in Matthew 27.46, but via Tristan Corbi
'Cris d'Aveugle', so that both anterior texts are in play in the pertin
passage towards the end of Part I. Whatever such works do provide, t
clearly do not offer unmediated authorial speech.

Paradoxically, even the most urgently personal aspects of this bod
literature serve to demonstrate the fictiveness of the Beat text and
absurdity of trying to take its measure in biographical terms. A
Ginsberg met Carl Solomon in the Columbia Presbyterian Psychia
Institute in 1949 when Ginsberg became a voluntary patient in orde
escape imprisonment for possession of stolen goods. Ginsberg regar
Solomon as 'an intuitive Bronx Dadaist and prose-poet', noted dowr
more memorable anecdotes and turns of phrase, picked up from
Artaud's concept of the artist as a mad (i.e., sane) person in a sane t
mad) world, and six years later brought all these elements together
poem whose full title is 'Howl for Carl Solomon'.[11] The piece famo
begins

> I saw the best minds of my generation destroyed by madness,
>   starving hysterical naked,
> dragging themselves through the negro streets at dawn looking
>   for an angry fix[12]

and Solomon is presented as the prime example, a lunatic saint cru
incarcerated by an uncomprehending society. The pivotal momen
the long first section of the poem begins with a passage particul
reliant on Solomon's stories –

> who threw potato salad at CCNY lecturers on Dadaism and
>   subsequently presented themselves on the granite steps of
>   the madhouse with shaven heads and harlequin speech of
>   suicide, demanding instantaneous lobotomy
> and who were given instead the concrete void of insulin,
>   Metrazol electricity
> hydrotherapy psychotherapy occupational therapy pingpong
>   & amnesia[13]

– and culminates in the direct address: 'ah, Carl, while you are not safe I am not safe'. The third part of 'Howl' opens with a variant of the address – 'Carl Solomon I'm with you in Rockland' – the last five words of this line thereafter being repeated eighteen times as a refrain (Rockland was the hospital in which Solomon was held after a mental breakdown in 1955). In short, Solomon is the poem's dedicatee, addressee, inspiration and hero-victim. He is to 'Howl' as Neal Cassady is to *On the Road*, the real person whose life the work celebrates.

Once again, however, the case is not what it seems. Not only does Ginsberg's poem meld Solomon incarcerations from two different geographical locations and two different decades, but as the latter admitted the wild escapades he had earlier recounted to the poet, and which provide 'Howl' with much of its vivacity, were largely bogus:

> I gave Allen an apocryphal history of my adventures and pseudo-intellectual deeds of daring, He meticulously took note of everything I said. ... [H]e published all of the data, compounded partly of truth, but for the most [part] raving self-justification, crypto-bohemian boasting a la Rimbaud, effeminate prancing, and esoteric aphorisms plagiarized from Kierkegaard and others – in the form of *Howl*. Thus he enshrined falsehood as truth and raving as common sense for future generations to ponder and be misled.[14]

In making this disclosure, Solomon gleefully supposes that he has exposed the poem as worthless whereas what he has actually proven is that the autobiographical 'truth' of Beat literature is most plausible when the product of fictive means. Ginsberg probably thought he was 'telling it like it is', complete with Solomon's eye-witness testimony; but by persuading the poet of the truth of his fabricated life, Solomon released him from the treadmill of the biographical into a larger realm of linguistic and imaginative play. And this, in turn, made the fiction real in the only place that matters, not at the level of the life lived but at the level of the words on the page. To put it another way, the success of Beat literature stems from the fact that even when the authors were trying to be autobiographical they signally failed in the endeavour.

Alas, the forgoing complexities have largely eluded the movement's commentators: in *The Penguin Book of the Beats*, their leading light Ann Charters repeatedly asserts that 'Beat literature is predominantly autobiographical' and that 'the Beats insisted on writing directly about events in their own lives', while her biography of Kerouac preposterously recycles episodes from his novels as though they were transcripts

of actual events.[15] As a result of this late millennial obsession with
biographical, the individual Beat writers enjoy celebrity status while
critical discussion of their work is more rudimentary and misgu
than anything stemming from Bowdler's deletions.

IV Bowdlerizing the Confessional poets

Much the same holds true with those authors commonly ident
with M.L. Rosenthal's term 'the Confessional Poets': Robert Lov
John Berryman, Sylvia Plath and Anne Sexton – what Larkin joki
called 'the-look-at-me-I'm-round-the-bend school'. Once again it c
be claimed that the writers were complicitous with biographical
cism, the very fact that their verse was characterized by the public '
fession' of transgressions which would formerly have been admi
only in private to a priest or analyst seeming to necessitate aut
centred interpretation. Typical Confessional themes include fraught
tions with parents, personal accounts of infidelity and divorce, nerv
breakdown, incarceration in mental institutions and suicidalism
infatuation consummated in the cases of Berryman, Plath and Sext
As with the Beats, the best books on the subject tend to be biograph
the literary critics bowdlerizing the poetry of interpretative complex
that do not reflect the tabloid sensationalism of the author's lives.

Sylvia Plath is a case in point, her most famous poems contai
strong enough hints of the autobiographical to lure her critics into
shallows. All remark the similarities between Plath and her narra
fewer remark the dissimilarities (for instance, that Plath did not have
Nazi father or the Jewish-Gypsy mother of the protagonist of 'Daddy',
did she attempt suicide at the age of ten like the narrator of 'L
Lazarus'). None remark the dense interweave of allusions that consti
what they like to call the narrative 'voice', attributing directly to P
lines quoted from other authors. In one particularly vexed case, Am
Jewish and American-Jewish critics have divided over the legitimac
Plath's use of Holocaust imagery. Irving Howe, Marjorie Perloff and L
Wieseltier argue that she was a gentile who did not earn the righ
address the catastrophe, while George Steiner and Jacqueline Rose def
her against the charge. At the centre of the controversy is the use of
first person singular in such lines as the following from 'Daddy' –

> I began to talk like a Jew.
> I think I may well be a Jew ...
>
> I may be a bit of a Jew.[16]

– a personalization that hostile commentators view as an unwarranted appropriation of other people's suffering. What neither side pauses long enough to notice is that Plath's lines are a reworking of passages such as the following from Henry Miller's *Tropic of Cancer*: 'I too would become a Jew. ... I already speak like a Jew. And I am as ugly as a Jew.'[17]

This denial of the literarity, the constructedness, of Plath's narration extends to her other masterpieces. No one seems to have noticed that the magnificent ending of 'Lady Lazarus' –

> Herr God, Herr Lucifer
> Beware
> Beware
>
> Out of the ash
> I rise with my red hair
> And I eat men like air.[18]

– comes from the end of Coleridge's 'Kubla Khan' –

> And all who heard should see them there,
> And all should cry, Beware! Beware!
> His flashing eyes, his floating hair![19]

– possibly by way of Longfellow's 'Beware':

> I know a maiden fair to see,
> Take care!
> She can both false and friendly be,
> Beware! Beware![20]

What Plath gains by this perpetual if unremarked paralleling of male-authored texts might be broached by a glance at these lines from 'The Applicant':

> Now your head, excuse is empty.
> I have the ticket for that.
> Come here, sweetie, out of the closet.
> Well, what do you think of *that*?
> Naked as paper to start.
>
> But in twenty-five years she'll be silver,
> In fifty, gold.

> A living doll, everywhere you look.
> It can sew, it can cook,
> It can talk, talk, talk.[21]

The poem explicitly uses an interview in a marriage bureau to crit
the way in which mid-century marital values demean women. How
not a single commentator appears to have noticed that it simult
ously mocks the institutionalized sexism of several decades of pop
music. The immediate target is Cliff Richard's international hit reco
1959, 'Living Doll', which is mimicked throughout the poem
directly invoked in the second stanza quoted above. That song was
a rewrite of the Johnny Black standard, 'Paper Doll' (1915), which
enjoyed particular success in a Mills Brothers recording of 1943. 'T
Doll' subsequently resurfaced in the 1955 play *A View from the Brid*
Arthur Miller, a favourite Plath dramatist. In the wake of both num
come all those pop lyrics whose diction of doll, baby and child sys
atically infantilizes the woman addressed. (On the *With the Be*
album released in the year of Plath's premature death, even Lennon
McCartney succumbed to the near paedophilia of 'Little child,
child, / Little child won't you dance with me, / I'm so sad and lonely /
take a chance with me ...'.) In effect, the poem is positing that
bring to the marriage contract the sorts of expectation they have
trained to by the popular culture of their teenage years.

Robert Lowell characterized Plath's work as 'womanish'; D
Holbrook approached it as clinical evidence of her schizophrenia;
many of her feminist champions viewed her as a victim of patria
whose special significance lay in the vehemence with which she von
anguished feeling direct upon the page (not so much the word made
as the flesh made word). In their various ways, all these commentato
personalize Plath's narratology that they are blinded to her skills at
tiche, intertextual reference, collage, narrative transvestism and g
subversion. The truth is that Plath's gift for rewriting male-dominate
erary genres so as to render them woman-centred has given permissic
several generations of feminist Postmodernists to do likewise. *The*
Girl and *The Book of Mrs Noah* by Michèle Roberts, Jeanette Winter
Boating for Beginners, and such Carol Ann Duffy poems as 'Pilate's V
'Queen Herod' and 'Mrs Lazarus' all follow the example of 'Lady Laz
in re-gendering parts of the *Bible*. Angela Carter's *Fireworks* rew
Gothic after the manner of the closing verses of 'Daddy', which re
Bram Stoker's *Dracula*. 'Elvis's Twin Sister' by Carol Ann Duffy

'The Applicant' in mocking pop's machismo. While Joyce Carol Oates in *Cybele*, Christine Brooke-Rose in *Amalgamemnon*, Christa Wolf in *Cassandra*, and Carol Ann Duffy of many of the poems in *The World's Wife* (including one called 'Medusa') revisit ancient Greek myth as Plath had already done in 'Medusa'. Other contemporary women writers have extended this strategy to male genres Plath did not live long enough to tackle: desert island adventures (*Crusoe's Daughter* by Jane Gardam); pornography (*Fanny* by Erica Jong); science fiction (*The Female Man* by Joanna Russ); and 'on the road' buddy fictions, whether novels or movies (Callie Khourie's script of *Thelma and Louise*).

None of the foregoing denies that Plath made poems out of her life; but as with the Irish, who make whiskey out of potatoes, everything depends upon the quality of the fermentation. The complaint against our contemporary Bowdlers is that they discuss Plath's precious malt as though it were a plate of King Edwards. The disproportion between their ceaseless chatter about Plath's marriage to Ted Hughes and their total silence about her crucial role in the formation of feminist Postmodernism is just one example of the vulgarity of this approach.

V The biographical fallacy and critical theory

One of many ironies of this situation is that the fashion for biographical interpretation runs counter to almost everything twentieth-century critical theory has tried to instil. From T.S. Eliot's landmark essay 'Tradition and the Individual Talent' (1919) via Wimsatt and Beardsley's 'The Intentional Fallacy' (1946) to Roland Barthes's Poststructuralist classic 'The Death of the Author' (1968), theoreticians have deplored the fact that

> The image of literature to be found in ordinary culture is tyrannically centred on the author, his person, his life, his tastes, his passions, while criticism still consists for the most part in saying that Baudelaire's work is the failure of Baudelaire the man, Van Gogh's his madness, Tchaikovsky's his vice. The *explanation* of a work is always sought in the man or woman who produced it, as if it were always in the end, through the more or less transparent allegory of the fiction, the voice of a single person, the *author* 'confiding' in us.[22]

Different theorists give different reasons for claiming that (in T.S. Eliot's words) 'divert[ing] interest from the poet to the poetry ... would conduce

to a juster estimation of actual poetry, good and bad'. For Eliot
because the *'significant* emotion' is that 'which has its life in the p
and not in the history of the poet'. Indeed, as far as the artist is
cerned, 'poetry is not a turning loose of emotion, but an escape f
emotion; it is not the expression of personality, but an escape from
sonality'.[23] James Joyce's fictional character Stephen Dedalus, echo
Flaubert, sums up in the following words this Modernist belief in
'impersonality' of the artist: 'The artist, like the god of creation, rem
within or behind or beyond or above his handiwork, invisible, refi
out of existence, indifferent, paring his fingernails'.[24]

For Wimsatt and Beardsley, the biographical approach is invari
reductive since it involves interpreting a text, every word of whic
available for scrutiny and delectation, through speculation about
author who one has usually not met, knows next to nothing about
whose intentions were probably hidden from him or herself let alo
third party. Consequently, 'the design or intention of the author is
ther available nor desirable as a standard for judging the success
work of literary art'.[25]

Barthes, perhaps, offers the most sophisticated argument. For hin
for Bakhtin, what really prevents the author's life or intentions f
completely determining the written work is the fact that languag
communally constructed over centuries by a succession of contenc
culture groups, so that at any given moment a particular lexis is a
location of deposits from across its historical development. This
only means that language is always in process of concretion, n
finally arrived, but also that it is inherently dialogic rather t
monologic, heterogeneous rather than homogeneous, mutual
unprivatizable. As a result of the *'stereographic plurality'* of, say,
English language, any text written in it is 'woven entirely with citati
references, echoes, cultural languages ..., antecedent or contempor
which cut across it through and through, in a vast stereophony'.
overwhelming mass of 'the citations which go to make up a text
anonymous, untraceable, and yet *already read*: they are quotations w
out inverted commas'.[26]

For Barthes, what distinguishes avant-garde writing is not that
polyphonic, for in so far as the foregoing propositions are true they
true of all linguistic acts, but that it is particularly adept at calling at
tion to this often suppressed characteristic. In this view, the literary
of intertextual reference is not so much (as Wimsatt and Beardsley fea
a biographical trace, a record of the author's private reading, as a ges

out towards the communal and citational nature of language itself. And it is this surplus of meaning over authorial intentionality that biographical readings seek to deny:

> To give a text an Author is to impose a limit on that text, to furnish it with a final signified, to close the writing. Such a conception suits criticism very well, the latter then allotting itself the important task of discovering the Author ... beneath the work: when the Author has been found, the text is 'explained' – victory to the critic.[27]

When Barthes made the next step and proposed that 'The Death of the Author' was a prerequisite for reading, he drew a deal of amused contempt from critics in the British empirical tradition who gaily pointed out that without Shakespeare *Hamlet* would not exist. However, what Barthes was attempting to dispense with was the absurd formula that the reader is confined to 'getting out' of a text precisely what the author 'put in', a formula that submits the text to authorial bondage and displaces the study of literature onto the realm of biography. In practice, the fact that we know nothing about Homer, whose historicity many scholars doubt, does not disable us from reading *The Odyssey*. Nor does the superfluity of our knowledge of Jeffrey Archer replenish the bare cupboard of his fiction. Once the impediment of the author is removed, once we stop approaching a text as 'a line of words releasing a single "theological" meaning', the message of the God-like creator, then we can start to enjoy a literary artefact for the profusion of its communicability, its inexhaustible renewals.[28] It is in this sense that the birth of the reader must be at the cost of the death of the author.

VI   Bowdlerizing Larkin

During his lifetime, Philip Larkin was regarded as having pulled off a unique double-whammy, writing poems that were equally admired by academics and the general reading public. W.H. Auden called him 'a master of the English language', Donald Davie described him as 'the best-loved poet of his generation'. Anthony Thwaite referred to 'the affection in which Larkin's readers hold him, and the remarkable sense of privilege which they feel at knowing his work. I can think of very few British (or American) poets whose poems are so substantially known by heart and quoted.'[29] If anything, this extraordinary status was enhanced in the immediate aftermath of Larkin's premature death from cancer,

the poet Peter Levi's obituary catching the note of love in the w
spread sense of public grief:

> Philip Larkin, until his death on 2nd December 1985, was the fu
> est and most intelligent English writer of the day, and the gre
> living poet in our language.
>   It is possible to feel about him, as people felt about Eliot, tha
> was the last great poet. His life was led privately and in the provir
> ... Yet no one was more loved, no poet I ever met was so entertair
> so generously witty, or such an enhancer of life to his friends ...[3]

Of course, there had been occasional dissenters, such as Ch
Tomlinson and Al Alvarez; but as both were unexceptional poets it
possible to regard their niggardly, carping judgements as proof of
adage that weak talents console themselves by trying to detect flav
strong ones. Certainly, nothing in their guarded responses prepared
for the avalanche of moral outrage, invective and censure that b
over Larkin's reputation in the 1990s.

The storm of hostility was keyed to a series of publications, r
notably Anthony Thwaite's *The Selected Letters of Philip Larkin* (19
Andrew Motion's biography *Philip Larkin: A Writer's Life* (1993) an
a lesser extent, James Booth's edition of *Trouble at Willow Gables*
other Fictions (2002). The posthumous revelation that the man p
ously characterized as 'decent' and 'shy' harboured opinions that w
racist, sexist and boorish provoked what Clive James has termed 'a
of dunces,' literary critics and journalists greeting each new disclo
with the glee of cannibals spicing a baby.[31] The very name La
engendered a mini lexicon, every declension of which was pejora
A new verb appeared, to *Larkinize*, meaning to demolish an artist's
utation on the basis of his or her private opinions, as in Anthony La
remark that 'there is every danger that Eliot is now in the proces
being Larkinized'.[32] The term *Larkinesque*, which formerly meant
self-deprecating and undeluded, came to signify some obscure but
perversion; one would not have been surprised to find it in Krafft-Eb
As for *Larkinalia*, that presumably indicated the paraphernalia of
Larkinesque – lesbian pornography, perhaps, or spanking equipmer

In the gadarene rush to judgement, commentators committed e
methodological sin associated with late millennial bowdler
Reviewing the biography, Peter Ackroyd moved seamlessly from
appallingly partial assessment of the man (Larkin was 'rancid and ir
ious', 'a foul-mouthed bigot') to the deduction that he was 'essent

a minor poet who for purely local and temporary reasons has acquired a large reputation'.[33] Bryan Appleyard dismissed Larkin as a 'provincial grotesque'.[34] Germaine Greer smeared Larkin's verse as 'anti-intellectual, racist, sexist, and rotten with class-consciousness'.[35] Tom Paulin combined the vehemence and vituperation of his colleagues with a degree of unfairness all his own, describing the *Selected Letters* as a 'revolting compilation which imperfectly reveals and conceals the sewer under the national monument Larkin became'.[36] This is the same Tom Paulin who praises Ted Hughes without mentioning the suicides of his wife and lover and the murder of his daughter, and who is equally lavish in his appreciation of Elizabeth Bishop (especially when he detects satirical echoes of Larkin) both of whose lesbian lovers committed suicide. I am opposing, not advocating, the use of lurid biographical detail in the evaluation of literature; however, if Paulin is going to blacken Larkin's poetic reputation on the basis of a minority of his private letters, he ought, in all conscience, to do the same with those eminent writers whose hands are besmirched with something stronger than ink.[37]

The personalized assault on Larkin's reputation continues in the present century: Jonathan Bate used a review of *Trouble at Willow Gables* to insinuate that Larkin was a homosexual paedophile; Andrew Duncan claimed that he was 'depressing', 'frigid', 'boring', 'had no literary talent' and 'never managed to write a good poem'; while as recently as 2005, in the arts section of *The Telegraph*, Christopher Bray added 'sadism' to the litany of Larkin's moral misdemeanors.[38] Dámaso López Garcia noted that at a recent eBay auction Motion's biography was advertised under the following key words: 'Homosexual Pornography Poet PHILIP LARKIN Nazi'.[39]

It is alarming that Larkin should be such a conspicuous victim of this biographical fallacy for, as he was wont to bemoan, his life lacked the 'Technicolor' of other candidates: the wife-murdering heroin addict William Burroughs; the alcoholic serial-adulterer and suicidalist Anne Sexton; the Italian writer and film director Pier Paolo Pasolini, who was sacked from his teaching post for 'corrupting' an underage male pupil, and who was murdered in 1975 by being repeatedly driven over by his own car; the Japanese novelist Yukio Mishima, who ritually disembowelled himself after the failure of his military *coup*; or Gunter Grass, the conscience of modern Germany, who for sixty years conveniently forgot fighting in the Waffen-SS. The worst that anyone has discovered about Larkin are some crass letters and a taste for porn softer than what passes for mainstream entertainment in contemporary cinema or television (let alone the internet). In their prosecutorial zeal, critics forgot

the Larkin who a young Indian pupil at King Henry VIII, Cove
found the most solicitous of schoolmates; who as the Holocaust r
cocked a snook at his father's Fascist sympathies by putting a St
David next to his signature in war-time letters to his pal Jim Su
who enthusiastically supported Robindra K Biswas' application fc
English lectureship at the University of Leicester; who on *Desert Is*
Discs declared that he would be unable to save his life by fishing s
the practice was too cruel; and who Monica Jones described as how
with grief when he accidentally killed the hedgehog memorialize
'The Mower'; who built up library holdings of a distinctly socialist
including the archive of the National Council for Civil Liberties; wl
Arts Council meetings argued passionately on behalf of postcolonia
erature; who was the first to champion neglected women writers
Stevie Smith or Barbara Pym; and whose friends and acquaintar
myself included, regard as the wittiest person they ever met.

The purpose of this biographical excursion is to demonstrate
before the aforementioned critics proceed to travesty the work,
first travesty the life: the effect is doubly detestable. As this is a wo
literary criticism, not a biography, the aspect of this debate I wis
emphasize is a chilling readiness to censor. Writing in the normally se
pages of the Library Association *Record*, an unnamed columnist pse
nymized as 'the Commoner' compared Larkin to David Irving,
Holocaust denier, and concluded that Larkin's books 'should be banne
Calling attention to the 'steady stream of casual obscenity, throwa
derogatory remarks about women, and arrogant disdain for those of
ferent skin colour or nationality' in the *Selected Letters*, Lisa Jardine n
the ultimate Bowdler's transition from condemnation of the private
respondence to suppression of the public art: 'we don't teach Larkin n
now in my Department of English. The Little Englandism he celebrate
uneasily with our revised curriculum'.[41] By the mid-1990s, Larkin's pc
had disappeared from the school syllabus.

VII   The complicity of Larkin's admirers

Jonathan Bate, Lisa Jardine, Germaine Greer and Tom Paulin (we s
shortly have cause to extend this list to the likes of Terry Eagleton,
Smith, John Lucas and Neil Corcoran) are distinguished professo
English. They ought to be more than usually aware that if aske
choose between perfection of the life or of the work, the true artist
for the latter. They more than most ought to be aware that the func
of criticism is to facilitate appreciation of literature, not depreciatio

its creators. It is tempting to adduce their dereliction of duty as evidence that critics hate great poets as clergymen hate saints. This temptation should be resisted on the grounds that the way had been prepared for the vitriolic critical reductionism of the 1990s by the pro-Larkin criticism that preceded it. This is not just a matter of claiming that the reaction against Larkin was the more extreme because of the extraordinarily high regard in which he was held before the biographical disclosures. It is also a matter of acknowledging that the pro-Larkin lobby has been (and continues to be) dominated by a well-meaning but conservative adherence to biographical interpretation of the kind we have identified with late millennial bowdlerism.

The first monograph and in that sense the founding text for Larkin studies was *Philip Larkin* (1973) by David Timms. An admirably diligent and perceptive work that can still illuminate thirty years after its original publication, the Timms monograph nonetheless sets in place many of the exegetical vices that would be used much less responsibly by Larkin's detractors. His starting point is that Larkin 'writes his poetry not from a preconceived set of principles, but as a direct and personal response to particular experiences'.[42] This view was echoed twenty years later when James Booth, the doyen of Larkin critics, wrote: 'Larkin has no programme to fulfil, no Byzantium to seek out, no "still point of the turning world" to which all his experiences must be related'. And just as Booth a paragraph later asserts that 'All Larkin's work is fundamentally autobiographical', so Timms takes the short but lethal step towards rolling into one the narrators of separate poems and then conflating that composite figure with the author.[43]

Hence, of poem 'XII' in *The North Ship* it is said: 'Larkin sits in a railway carriage, watching a Polish air girl speaking incomprehensively to her companion'. The analysis of poem 'XX' begins: 'Out walking in Winter, Larkin sees a young girl'. A little later we are told, 'The poet in poem "XXXII" has spent the night with a girl and he stands looking out of the hotel window while she brushes her hair'. Moving on to *The Less Deceived*, Timms describes 'Dockery and Son' as 'the reminiscence of the poet on his journey home, having visited his old college'; while the plot of 'Church Going' is summarized as follows: 'Out for a bicycle ride, the poet stops at a church, and goes in to look round'. Not only are the differences between the various protagonists minimized on the assumption that they are all Larkin but, conversely, and yet more damagingly, these narrators are repeatedly referred to as 'the poet' when in not a single case is it vouchsafed that they pursue that singular vocation. Nor is it enough to rejoin that they must be poets because their narration is versified: the semi-literate truant schoolboy Huckleberry Finn narrates in the first person the novel that takes his name, but it would be an hermeneutical absurdity to describe Huck as a 'novelist' or to otherwise elide the distinction between Huck and Mark Twain. Worse follows. Of 'Reference Back', Timms says 'the speaker' (there it is again, that efface-ment of the difference between speech and text that facilitates the effacement of the difference between narrator and author) 'is a man in his thirties visiting his parents' home. Mother and son have little in common. ...'[44] Since Timms this has become the *donnée* for all interpre-tations of this poem: approximately twenty years later, Professor Trevor Tolley asserts that 'In "Reference Back" ... Larkin recalls an attempt by his mother to reach out to him emotionally in the "time at home" that she "Looked so much forward to"';[45] a further six years on, Warren Hope's *Student guide to Philip Larkin* unequivocally asserts that '"Love Songs in Age" and "Reference Back" deal with Larkin's loyal but strained rela-tionship with his mother'.[46] In point of fact, we are not told that the narrator is Philip Larkin and the addressee Eva Larkin; nor is it certain that a son is visiting his mother, for the relationship is not specified; we are not even told that the one is male and the other female. Sooner than explore these interpretative *lacunae*, our critics plug those gaps with biographical data.

Similarly, Timms writes of 'Reasons for Attendance': 'Larkin plays the academic university librarian, just old enough to feel out of touch with the students with whom he deals. Invited to a student dance, he approaches cautiously, and peering through a window, sees that this is not the place for him'.[47] John Whitehead later supplemented this account with a precise geographical location: 'the *persona* peers through a window watching couples at a student dance (in fact at Queen's University, Belfast)'.[48] Nowhere does the poem state that the narrator is male: we may exercise a heterosexist presumption and infer as much from the reference to 'the wonderful feel of girls', though the vulnera-bility of such a reading strategy has been highlighted by the recent pub-lication of *Trouble At Willow Gables*, with its evidence of Larkin's fascination with lesbian perspectives. More particularly, the poem tells us nothing whatsoever about the narrator's profession, certainly not specifying that 'he' is a librarian, nor that the dancers are students, nor that the latter issued the former with an invitation to the party, nor that the events are located on or near a university campus, nor that the set-ting is the capital city of Northern Ireland. These are all details that Timms and Whitehead have invented on the basis of what they know of Larkin's life and they are being deployed, one assumes unconsciously, so as to render certain everything that is ambiguous in the poetry. This is a good example of what Barthes meant when he wrote that 'to give a text an Author is to impose a limit on the text, to furnish it with a final signified, to close the writing'. It also illustrates my argument that with this sort of reading strategy *the hermeneutical quest for textual meaning is replaced by a biographical quest for the moment of origination*.

We are now in a position to see that early affirmative critics like Timms not only established the methodological malpractices that Larkin's detractors would later use to wantonly denigrate the work, but that in the process they already started to carve a poet of autobiographical directness out of highly ambiguous verse. The simple truth is that literary narrators do not construct their stories as speech but are constructed by them as text, and what sort of narrator a specific work constructs is a key question for the reader to contemplate, probably with a limited plurality of plausible answers, rather than the foregone conclusion of the late millennial Bowdler. By combining the biographical approach of critics like Timms with the undeniably offensive remarks contained in his private correspondence, Larkin's detractors converted him from what he is, the greatest poet of doubt since Hardy, into a poet of certitude, often to the point of bigotry

VIII The biographical fallacy and Larkin's critical prose

Larkin's defenders and detractors might alike claim to be adopting a biographical reading strategy which he had endorsed in the essays and reviews he preserved in *Required Writing* (1983). Discussing Wilfred Owen, for example, he had thrown out the general principle that 'a writer's reputation is twofold: what we think of his work, and what we think of him. What's more, we expect the two halves to relate: if they don't, then one or other of our opinions alters until they do' (*RW*, 228).

Further Requirements (2001), Thwaite's gathering of the previously uncollected non-fiction prose, contains more comments in a similar vein – as when Larkin claims that 'novels are about other people and poetry is about yourself' (*FR*, 24, 33, 114). However, Larkin lacked the predictability of small minds, and this volume elsewhere shows him struggling to develop a more sophisticated theoretical position and one more consonant with his verse practice, which was not essentially autobiographical. In an interview he said, apropos of 'An Arundel Tomb': 'I was delighted when a friend asked me if I knew a poem ending "What will survive of us is love". It suggests the poem was making its way in the world without me. I like them to do that' (*FR*, 58). In approving his interlocutor's ignorance

of the fact that he was the author of the poem in question, Larkin ass
to non-biographical readings of his work. He went still further in a
broadcast for the overseas service when he said:

> I suppose the kind of response I am seeking from the reader is, ****
> know what you mean, life *is* like that; and for readers to say it
> only now but in the future, and not only in England but anyw
> in the world.
>
> (*FR*

At the very least, this aspiration to address our common huma
regardless of sex, gender, race, creed, continent or historical epoch r
severely qualify the earlier author-centred approach, limiting the a
biographical content of the poems to those areas of subjectivity sh
by all.

Even more remarkable are those passages in which he comes clos
the theory of impersonality Eliot had outlined in 'Tradition and
Individual Talent', an essay Larkin sometimes affected to despise ('\
does [Charles Tomlinson] assume I haven't read Tradition and the
I have, and think it piss') (*SL*, 274). Writing of the poem 'Absen
which ends 'Such attics cleared of me! Such absences!' Larkin declare

> I suppose I like 'Absences' (a) because of its subject-matter – I am al\
> thrilled by the thought of what places look like when I am not there
> because I fancy it sounds like a different, better poet rather than my
> The last line, for instance, sounds like a slightly unconvincing tra\
> tion from a French symbolist. I wish I could write like this more of
>
> (*FR,*

Ten years later, on a BBC Radio Three programme, he prefaced a r
ing of 'The Explosion' with the words:

> What I should like to do is to write different kinds of poems
> might be by different people. Someone once said that the great tl
> is not to be different from other people but to be different from y
> self. That's why I've chosen to read now a poem that isn't espec
> like me, or like what I fancy I'm supposed to be like.
>
> (*FR,*

These are wonderfully arresting formulations, profoundly at odds \
biographical interpretations. We have the dizzying paradox of La

trying to imagine himself present at scenes from which he relishes his absence. We have the celebrated xenophobe (*'Foreign* poetry? *No!'*) wishing to resemble a French symbolist in translation (*FR*, 25). We have the supposedly autobiographical poet trying to make each poem seem the product, not just of a separate narrator, but of a separate author. In their idiosyncratic way these statements share the Modernist ethos of Rimbaud's famous seer's letter of 1871 ('I is Another'); Fernando Pessoa's multiple heteronyms; the aforementioned 1919 essay by Eliot ('poetry ... is not the expression of personality, but an escape from personality'); Stephen Dedalus' 'I am other I now' in Joyce's *Ulysses* (1922); and Auden's statement – alluded to in Larkin's radio talk – that 'The problem of every man and writer is at all times essentially the same, namely first to learn to be himself and then to learn to be not himself'.[49]

There are many other aspects of Larkin's critical practice that work against the view that he was a naively autobiographical poet untroubled by narratological complexities. For instance, not one of his nine articles devoted to John Betjeman's verse draws upon the subject's complicated sex life (about which Larkin must have known) or his private correspondence (of which Larkin must have been a recipient). Conversely, Larkin's scintillating memoir of his Coventry childhood, 'Not The Place's Fault', shows him to have much fonder memories of the place than the narrator of his great anti-roots poem 'I Remember, I Remember'. The stark truth is that the overwhelming majority of the poems tell one nothing about the gender, race, class or nationality of either their narrators or their addressees, but that both the poet's champions and detractors fill in the missing information by jumping to the conclusion that the protagonist is always and only a white, male, middle-class Englishman named Philip Larkin.

IX The biographical fallacy and Larkin's poetry

One of Larkin's most important prose statements on autobiographical literature came in a private letter to a friend in 1978. Virginia Peace, wife of the professor of Russian at the University of Hull, had shown him a novel she had written about her experience of losing a son in a tragic accident. Larkin's reply strikes at a central predicate of biographical criticism:

> You have done amazingly well to describe what happened in so dispassionate and calm a way, but for you this is enough, the events speak for themselves. Unfortunately for the reader it isn't: the reader

wants that impure thing, literature – plot, suspense, characters, ups, downs, laughter, tears, all the rest of it. ... Now I can quite see that to 'play about' with the kind of subject matter you have taken would seem heartless, frivolous, even untrue, an offense against decency or decent feelings, something you couldn't do, and yet in literature it somehow has to be done – one might almost say that it's the mixture of truth and untruth that makes literature.

(SL, 593)

Biographical criticism assumes that the truth of literature resides in its fidelity to the lived experience of the author. Larkin disagrees: the true artist is ready to 'play about' with experience, to shape it, edit it, fictionalize it, to render it 'impure', even 'untrue', if such enhances the quality of the artefact. Peace's novel is too true to its originatory tragedy to be artistically true: 'Your narrative isn't a story, it's a frieze of misery'.

This same position is articulated in the verse. Larkin was an excellent photographer but in 'Lines on a Young Lady's Photograph Album' suggests that photography is too true to experience to be considered an art of form:

> But o, photography! as no art is,
> Faithful and disappointing! that records
> Dull days as dull, and hold-it smiles as frauds,
> And will not censor blemishes ...

(CP, 71)

The camera 'overwhelmingly persuades' us 'That this is a real girl in a real place, // In every sense empirically true!' (*CP*, 71–2). But realism and empiricism are not enough: art is constitutive as well as reflective; it does not just copy, it transfigures and invents. And it is an unavoidable corollary of the foregoing that a narrator of invented experiences is not to be confused with an actual author and real ones.

'Fiction and the Reading Public' was written in February 1950 as Larkin embarked upon a succession of breakthrough poems: 'At Grass', 'Deceptions', 'If, My Darling', 'Wants', 'No Road', 'Wires', 'Absences'. The title is taken from Q.D. Leavis's 1932 study *Fiction and the Reading Public* which posits that the rise of popular culture and the attendant commodification of literature have seduced the reading public away from significant contemporary writing. Leavis quotes a self-help guide to *Journalism for Profit* as sounding 'a representative note':

> ... the next business in hand is getting on the right side of the Great British Public. ... Amuse it. Cheer it up. Chat to it. Confide in it. Give it, now and again, a good old cry. It loves that. But don't, for your success's sake, come the superior highbrow over it.[50]

Leavis claims that when the commercial policy of 'Giving the Public what it wants' is extended to the novel, this journalistic compact between writer and reader is debasing. The modern bestseller no longer 'keeps the reader at arm's length' so as to provide a critical distance on the subject matter, but instead becomes a receptacle into which 'the author has poured his own day dreams, hot and hot'. As a result, 'the author [is] identified with the leading character, and the reader is invited to share the debauch'.[51] Larkin's poem paraphrases this thesis in a way that may be read as a satire on biographicalism.

The poem opens with 'the reader' demanding of the writer 'Give me a thrill'. Judging by the rather specialized knowledge that follows ('I pay your screw, / Write reviews and the bull on the jacket'), this is a *publisher's reader*, though one who claims to speak for the *general reader*, Queenie Leavis's debased literary punter. The ensuing poem consists of this compound reader's advice to a prospective author as to what the trade considers marketable. The tone is set in the first verse in which the standard writing school precept, begin from personal experience, swiftly mutates into a demand for flagrant autobiographical disclosure:

> Choose something you know all about
> That'll sound like real life:
> Your childhood, your Dad pegging out,
> How you sleep with your wife.
>
> (*CP*, 34)

The second verse concentrates on the imperative 'make me feel good'. (According to the *Dictionary of Twentieth Century Words*, the term 'feel-good factor' was coined in 1984, but Larkin has anticipated its meaning by thirty-four years.) The 'reader' suggests developing the God concept so that any narrative unhappiness can be made to seem 'for the best' and the audience 'may lie quiet' in their beds 'And not be "depressed"'. This is a brilliant act of foresight on Larkin's part: after his death he would be arraigned by critics like Terry Eagleton ('few poets of stature have been so remorselessly concerned to negate rather affirm') and James Wood (for whom Larkin is 'a minor registr disappointment, a bureaucrat of frustration') who seem to regard li ture as a moral bra providing spiritual uplift.[52]

After a little muscle-flexing ('I call the tune in this racket'), the re returns in the third and last stanza to the confessionalist demands which the poem began:

> ... start serving up your sensations
> Before it's too late;
> Just please me for two generations –
> You'll be 'truly great'.

The vicariousness, the emotional cannibalism of this (the writer ser up personal sensations like a waiter serving up food), is even more nounced in 'Round the Point', one of Larkin's imaginary dialogue 'Débats', in which the same poem ends –

> And let me suck up your sensations,
> Laugh, weep, masturbate:
> Just please me for two generations –
> You'll be 'truly great'.
>
> (*TWG*, 472)

The biographical formula that the reader can only get out of a p what the author puts in, the text evaporating in a direct emoti encounter between living persons, is viciously lampooned, the rang responses in the last stanza perhaps being keyed to the subjects item in the first: let me 'Laugh' at 'Your childhood' yarns; 'weep' at 'your pegging out'; 'masturbate' at graphic accounts of 'How you sleep your wife'. The 'truly great' of the last line is savagely ironical (*The (Tradition* by Queenie's husband, F.R. Leavis, was published two years lier), art being reduced to lurid self-exposure – like pornography – reading to a species of Pavlovian response.

X Prospectus

As will already be evident from this introduction, the present volun as much about critical methodology as it is about a specific write the twenty to thirty critical books and sixty or so worthwhile essay

Larkin, well over ninety per cent employ the biographical approach. My primary objective is to revolutionize Larkin studies by releasing the poems from this hegemonic methodology, and to do so in a manner applicable to innumerable other authors. Wherever possible, the merits of the orthodox approach will be acknowledged as a prelude to excavating the substantial areas of meaning it represses in Larkin's *oeuvre*. My purpose is not so much to annihilate biographicalism (it has its uses) as to dislodge it from a monopoly position; or, at the very least, to mount such a challenge as will oblige its defenders to rethink their positions in order to retrench them. This will necessitate quarrelling with most of the recognized authorities on Larkin – so much so, indeed, that I can scarcely imagine who might review my labours favourably – though I have repeatedly drawn strength from a clutch of brilliant essays by Barbara Everett, Steve Clark, Robert Crawford and others. The contestation will be justified to the extent that there emerges from these pages a Larkin more compellingly rich in meanings than the one we know from the critical consensus.

The first two chapters investigate the Himalayan range of Larkin's knowledge of and indebtedness to the Modernist movement he publicly excoriated. Chapter One proposes that Larkin found in jazz examples of popular Modernism, sexual deinhibition and diasporic experience which he could learn from. Chapter Two draws particular attention to the way his use of Eliotic citationality declares the constructedness of his narrators, foregrounding their distance from the author. These same chapters initiate an argument, continued throughout the book, to the effect that Larkin is as much critiquing as assimilating Modernism, not least for backsliding from its own revolutionary ideology (as when artists like Eliot, Epstein, David Jones and Auden revert to a pre-Nietzschean religiosity).

Chapters Three and Four, on Larkin and philosophy, are perhaps the most surprising – if only because he is commonly perceived as a hopelessly naïve thinker best consigned to a British empirical tradition suspicious of continental abstraction: in Roger Day's words, 'his thinking had a very "English" cast to it in that he seemed uninterested in, perhaps mistrustful of, ideas'.[53] These chapters propose that Larkin's focus upon doubt, alterity and undecidability is so drastic in its implications as to anticipate Deconstructionism. They then go on to analyse a variety of techniques with which he instantiated unfixity in the very fabric of his verse. These techniques (ellipses, split similes, double negatives, oxymora, paronomasia, asymmetrical stanza length and rhyme schemes, etc.) are the implements of Larkin's home-grown Deconstructionism.

The next four chapters examine how this deconstructive appr
was applied by Larkin to the subjects of nationality, gender, po
and identitarianism. The effect in every case is such as to de-natur
de-essentialize and de-stabilize the discourses of power – somet
with gratifyingly unexpected results. Hence, Larkin's political de
tors see him as reprehensibly Tory; but the only poem he wrot
commission for the Conservative Party was so little to their liking
they brutally censored it before publication. Similarly, the misei
racism of Larkin's private correspondence has lured certain biogra
cal critics into smearing his poetry (see Greer, above). Yet as ever
titles of his poems attest ('Going', 'Strangers', 'Arrivals, Departi
'Home is so Sad', 'The Importance of Elsewhere'), Larkin's sense of (
cination, exile and incomplete belonging is more akin to that of et
minorities and immigrants – such as the heroine of his finest ni
A Girl in Winter – than to Powellite tribalism or Norman Tebbit's i
rious cricket analogy.

The Conclusion proposes that Larkin responded to fifty yeai
unparalleled slaughter, much of it in the name of utopian certitude
creating at the mid-century a literature of radical scepsis. Not onl
his novels and poems sabotage conventional pieties regarding chi
state, nationality, marriage, gender, race and capital, but in the pro
they play a central role in the cultural transition to Postmodernist i
terminacy. This proposition is endorsed in two ways. First, by expli
Larkin's ideological affinities with Postmodernist gurus like Der
Baudrillard, Jameson and Lyotard. Derrida's undermining of bi
opposites and Lyotard's injunction to 'wage war on totality' wi
found especially close to Larkin's corrosive scepticism. More topic
Larkin's utility to new millennial writing is demonstrated by brief
cussion of the admiring references to his work that garnish such
temporary classics as Julian Barnes's *Flaubert's Parrot*; Adeline Yen N
Watching The Tree; David Mitchell's *Cloud Atlas*; John Banville's *Th*
(winner of the 2005 Booker prize); Ian McEwan's *Saturday*; Zadie Sm
On Beauty (winner of the Orange Prize for 2006): and recent volumi
verse by Alan Jenkins, Kathryn Gray, Paul Farley and Nick Laird. Th
Chinese writer like Yen Mah, experimentalist like Mitchell, Irish
like Banville and black woman writer like Smith should find Larki
enabling influence is inexplicable in terms of the conventional vie
the poet but entirely understandable in terms of the revisionist m
proposed herewith.

1
Larkin and Modernism: Jazz[1]

I The modernity of jazz

In the riotous introduction to *All What Jazz*, Larkin argued that in the mid-century period, with the generations of Charlie Parker, Dizzy Gillespie, Miles Davis and John Coltrane, jazz lost (or wilfully squandered) its high communicability, becoming as obscure, experimental and culturally elitist as the poetry of Ezra Pound or the painting of Pablo Picasso. Having made this alliterative triangulation between Parker, Pound and Picasso, he then breaks over the heads of all three an oceanic tirade against Modernism:

> I dislike such things not because they are new, but because they are irresponsible exploitations of technique in contradiction of human life as we know it. This is my essential criticism of modernism, whether perpetrated by Parker, Pound or Picasso: it helps us neither to enjoy nor endure. It will divert us as long as we are prepared to be mystified or outraged, but maintains its hold only by being more mystifying and more outrageous: it has no lasting power. Hence the compulsion of every modernist to wade deeper and deeper into violence and obscenity ...
>
> (*AWJ*, 17)

One can hardly be more categorical than that: Larkin hates Modernism; jazz becomes Modernist in the 1940s; therefore the history of jazz fits a lapsarian model being divisible into pre-Parker (good) and post-Parker (bad) eras.

Alarmingly, even when they disagree with his view that it represents a qualitative decline, most commentators tacitly accept Larkin's assumptions

27

that jazz becomes Modernist with Charlie Parker.[2] The truth, of course, is quite otherwise, and such as to destabilize Larkin's cod absolutes. For if Modernism is characterized by radical stylistic innovation, then jazz was from its inception Modernist music *par excellence* – and was recognized as such at the time. As early as 1922, F. Scott Fitzgerald designated the 1920s, the high point of Modernism, as 'the jazz age'. The poets of the day sought to incorporate staccato rhythms, blues idioms or descriptions of jazz records and gramophones as earnest of their modernity: think of Eliot in *The Waste Land* ('O O O O that Shakespeherian Rag'); Joseph Moncure March in *The Wild Party* ('the melody began to float / From a saxophone's low-pitched, husky throat'); Langston Hughes in 'The Weary Blues'; E.E. Cummings's syncopated lyrics; or William Carlos Williams's inclusion in *Paterson* of a chunk of the jazz clarinetist Mezz Mezzrow's autobiography, *Really the Blues* – forerunners, all of them, of 'For Sidney Bechet' ('Oh, play that thing!') and 'Reference Back' ('Oliver's *Riverside Blues*, it was').

The great Modernist composers in the classical tradition also recognized the peculiar contemporaneity of jazz and swiftly moved to assimilate certain of its features. One thinks of the Stravinsky of *The Soldier's Tale*, *Ragtime for Eleven Instruments* and *Piano-Rag Music*, all composed scarcely a year after that momentous day, 26 February 1917, when the Original Dixieland Jass Band went into the Victor Studios in New York City and made the very first jazz record. One might also mention the Kurt Weill of *The Rise and Fall of the City of Mahagonny*; George Antheil's *Jazz Symphony*; the Shostakovitch of the *Jazz Suites* and of *Tahiti Trot*; Darius Milhaud's 'ballet nègre' *The Creation of the World*; and the Ravel of the *Piano Concerto in G* and the *Violin Sonata* (the slow movement of which is called, simply, *Blues*). Béla Bartók, Aaron Copland, Morton Gould, Alex North and Paul Hindemith all wrote extended compositions for Benny Goodman; Igor Stravinsky and Leonard Bernstein did the same for Goodman's fellow jazz clarinetist Woody Herman; while Arnold Schoenberg nominated George Gershwin the greatest composer of the century for his ability to amalgamate classical, showbiz and jazz components in works like *Rhapsody in Blue* and *Porgy and Bess*. And this is to ignore jazz musicians like Duke Ellington, who were crossing the line from the other side, expanding jazz's horizons to almost symphonic proportions.[3]

The modernity of jazz lay only in part with its formal innovations – its emphasis on improvisation, its complex and insistent percussiveness, the use of the so-called blue notes, its occasional syncopation and, above all, its conception of performance as creative rather than merely interpretative. Though, indeed, no Modernist art has shown less respect for the received truths about itself than has jazz, topping up its modernity by undergoing (in Larkin's words) 'a radical upheaval every twenty years' (*LJ*, 75). For deeper than this is the way in which the black American experience is central to and constitutive of modernity because of its catastrophic exposure to enforced diaspora, genocide, exile, alienation, cultural mutation and hybridity, and fractured or doubled selfhood. The sheer scale and iniquity of the slave experience marked out blacks as the first truly modern people by obliging them to confront in the eighteenth century horrors which only became the substance of everyday life in Europe in the era of Stalin and Hitler. Elements of this argument were propounded decades ago by W.E.B. DuBois in *Black Reconstruction* and C.L.R. James in *The Black Jacobins*, but have been taken up and amplified by such contemporary cultural historians as Paul Gilroy in *The Black Atlantic: Modernity and Double Consciousness* (1993).

Some of these critics – most notably Ann Douglas in *Terrible Honesty: Mongrel Manhattan in the 1920s* (1994) and Francis Davis in *The History of the Blues* (1995) – have stressed the fact that jazz itself was the product of the cultural hybridity that resulted from the slaves' exposure to a wealth of musical influences in the United States. On different occasions, Larkin himself described jazz as 'this musical border-country between Africa and the New World' (*AWJ*, 25) and a 'multi-racial, Afro-European musical stew' (*LJ*, 37). Trying to account for the universal appeal of jazz, he suggested that it had 'something to do with the hybrid nature of the music, no doubt, the union of Europe and Africa, the waltzes and hymns' (*LJ*, 140–1). One such influence derived from religious conversion, the enforced Christianization of slaves having the unlooked-for effect of the Africanization of the hymn book in an uprush of creativity that eventually gave rise to the Spiritual, Gospel and Soul. Other influences included plantation work songs; Irish folk music; Western orchestral instrumentation and the band line-up; the legacy of minstrelsy, coon shows and vaudeville; and the Jewish-American input of New York's Tin Pan Alley.[4] There was even a distinct contribution from musicians of Native American ancestry, such as the trombonist Kid Ory; saxophonist Frankie Trumbauer; trumpeters Bubber Miley and Art Farmer; guitarist Jim Hall; and pianists Duke Ellington, John Lewis, Dave Brubeck and Horace Silver (every one of whom is praised in *All What Jazz*). Hence, jazz is at once the historical repository of the black experience in the United States and an art form characterized by its cosmopolitanism, pluralism and mutability. Not so much jungle music as mongrel music. Not so much roots music as routes music. Which is also to say that the really distinguished thing about jazz is that here was a rare example of popular Modernism, Modernism with street credibility, Modernism rising from the bottom up not percolating down from a cultural elite.

Larkin responded to all of this wholeheartedly and in full consciousness of the socio-political implications of the dispossessed being the creators of 'the unique emotional language of our century' (*LJ*, 40):

> It is ironical that the first American music to catch world attention should have originated among the nation's most despised section – the Negroes, who well within living memory had been regarded as a species of farm animal ('nobody killed, just a mule and a couple of niggers'). It must have been galling for Europe-orientated concert-goers of Boston and Philadelphia when Dvorak proclaimed 'in the Negro melodies of America I discover all that is needed for a great and noble school of music'; when Ravel insisted on going to The Nest in Chicago to hear Jimmy Noone; when Milhaud and Honegger used jazz rhythms as if they took them seriously. For this jazz was not only a hideous cacophony played on old tins and saxophones, it was the very language of the brothels and speakeasies where it was played, and constituted a direct incitement to immorality, so menacing the entire fabric of society.
>
> (*LJ*, 57)

The last point is worth emphasizing: jazz was intimately connected with the sex industry – the word itself (like 'rock 'n' roll' later) means sexual intercourse or orgasm, and many key practitioners had been pimps (Jelly Roll Morton), prostitutes (Billie Holiday) and bordello entertainers (the titular venue of Louis Armstrong's 'Mahogany Hall stomp' was an up-market New Orleans brothel). The innuendo of George Formby's 'With my little stick of Blackpool rock' was as nothing compared with the culinary metaphors jazz employed to escape the blue pencil: 'Does anybody here want to try my cabbage?', 'Nobody in town can bake a sweet Jelly Roll like mine', 'Who's gonna chop your suey when I'm gone?' and 'Another man's been cookin' in my lady's pan'. Jazz was at the forefront of a sexual as well as a musical revolution: John Reith, first director general of the BBC, recognized as much in praising the Nazis for banning it, his only regret being that 'we should be behind in dealing with this filthy product of modernity'.[5]

Whatever his claims to the contrary, then, Larkin's real critique of the Parker generation is not that it renders jazz threateningly Modernistic, but that it renders the jazz which had always been Modernistic less accessible, converting it into a minority cult and relinquishing the mass audience to the genuine but rhythmically less sophisticated pleasures of rock 'n' roll (he was an admirer of Bob Dylan and the Beatles):

> It doesn't take much imagination to see that this is where the jazz impulse, the jazz following, has migrated. This is where the jazz public has gone, and even where jazz has gone, for this music, rock and roll, rhythm and blues, or just plain beat, is for all its tedious vulgarity nearer jazz than the rebarbative astringencies of Coleman, Coltrane and the late Eric Dolphy.
>
> (*LJ*, 142)

'Jazz is a popular art no longer' (*LJ*, 140), Larkin moaned, for the Western world that formerly boogied to Benny Goodman, Count Basie and Artie Shaw now jived to Elvis, Little Richard or the Rolling Stones. The likes of Archie Shepp and Ornette Coleman had managed the seemingly impossible: they had produced a form of jazz that could not be danced to.

Whatever its rights and wrongs, this position is radically different from and more plausible than the one Larkin pretends to adopt. So why does he do it? Because his love of jazz directly contradicts his anti-Modernist stance, shifting one of his already decideds towards undecidability; by pretending that jazz only became Modernist in the 1940s he is able, at a cosmetic level, to square his love of the former with his supposed loathing of the latter. Larkin loved many aspects of Modernist music but lied about it, and when we move to Modernist poetry we find that once again he was attracted to the liberating heresy of that which he publicly excoriated.

II 'For Sidney Bechet' and Modernist aesthetics

One way we might consolidate this claim is by looking at 'For Sidney Bechet', Larkin's most direct address in verse to the subject of jazz, and a poem one of whose principal themes is the endorsement of Modernist aesthetics. This last may seem a perverse interpretation when so many of Larkin's reviews and interviews positively relish the assertion of Realist dogmas. What Realist dogmas? That art should be representational, objectively copying what the eye sees ('Poetry is an affair of sanity, of seeing things as they are.' *RW*, 197). That the concept of authorial intentionality is valid, readers' interpretations deviating from those of the author being wrong ('Interviewer: *But what if a critic construes a poem in a way you felt you didn't mean?* Larkin: I should think he was talking balls.' *FR*, 50). That modern critical theory is misguided in its preoccupation with the multiplicity of a text's meanings and the relativity of the readerly responses elicited (hence Larkin's sarcasm about the desire of 'twentieth-century criticism … to demonstrate that what looks simple is in fact complicated, that what seems to have one meaning has in fact three or four'. *RW*, 247). That art should not only tell the truth, but should do so in a style so lucid as to obviate critical explication ('I may flatter myself, but I think … there's not much to say about my work. When you've read a poem, that's it, it's all quite clear what it means.' *RW*, 53–4). That one of the virtues of this transparency of style is that it makes no demands upon the reader. Larkin ended his essay on 'The Pleasure Principle' – a title appropriated from Freud – by endorsing the sentiments of Samuel Butler: 'I should like to like Schumann's music better than I do; I dare say I could make myself like it better if I tried; but I do not like having to try to make myself like things; I like things that make me like them at once and no trying at all' (*RW*, 82). That radical stylistic experimentation ('irresponsible exploitations of technique in contradiction of human life as we know it', *AWJ*, 17) is therefore to be condemned, especially when it involves alluding to other art works instead of conveying experience direct ('Poems don't come from other poems, they come from being oneself in life', *FR*, 54). That this depiction of the indisputably true in a language of utter transparency elicits immediate assent from the reader because if he or she had the requisite skill they would have described the experience in exactly the same way. Hence Larkin's comment on 'The Whitsun Weddings': 'It was just the transcription of a very happy afternoon. I didn't change a thing. … It only needed writing down. Anybody could have done it' (*FR*, 57).

Each of these points, so passionately advocated in Larkin's prose, is directly contradicted by 'For Sidney Bechet', which discusses and approves an alternative Modernist agenda. It is a cardinal principle of Modernism that the reality of the artwork takes precedence over any reality depicted in it. So much so, indeed, that Modernism is in part characterized by a long infatuation, sometimes consummated, with complete abstraction. One small symptom of this in literature, the most referential of the arts, was the adoption of musical titles in deference to the most abstract of art forms. The most famous example is that of Eliot, with such poems as the 'Preludes', 'Rhapsody on a Windy Night', 'The Love Song of J. Alfred Prufrock' and *Four Quartets*. Larkin's poem affiliates itself to this Modernist tradition to the extent that it is based not directly upon life, as the Realist credo demands, but upon a prior art form, the most abstract of the arts (music), and the most experimental of modes within that art (jazz).

This acknowledgement of the autonomy of art is accompanied by its corollary, that the concept of intentionality is a chimera, the author no longer being treated as the source and arbiter of meaning. This is affirmed at two levels: the poem resolutely declines to conflate its narrator with Larkin, disclosing little or nothing about the age, race, gender, marital status, sexual orientation or religion of its narrator; and just as the author is erased (or at least decentred) from his poem, so Bechet's music is described from a number of perspectives, none of them biographical. This approach is congruent with Eliot's notion of the impersonality of the artist and with the words of Stephen Dedalus in *A Portrait of the Artist as a Young Man*: 'The artist, like the God of creation, remains within or behind or above his handiwork, invisible, refined out of existence, indifferent, paring his nails'.

Once the meaning of an artefact is no longer regarded as having been nailed to the floor of the author's intentions, a limited plurality of interpretations is generated relative to different reading perspectives; for, as Eliot averred, 'to understand anything is to understand from a point of view'.[6] This is precisely the aesthetic theory dramatized in 'For Sidney Bechet'. The poem opens by comparing Bechet's famous vibrato to the rippling of New Orleans reflected in the waters of the Mississippi river:

> That note you hold, narrowing and rising, shakes
> Like New Orleans reflected on the water ...
>
> (*CP*, 88)

The simile is decidedly strained, even factitious, and serves from the very start to alert us to the fact that what we are discussing is the *image* (inverted, inconstant, written on water) of New Orleans and not the place itself. The next line extends this idea by suggesting that jazz – like the other arts – belongs to the realm of imagination rather than fact, and that therefore the sensations it gives rise to, however apposite or profound, are in a sense fictitious or false:

> That note you hold, narrowing and rising, shakes
> Like New Orleans reflected on the water,
> And in all ears appropriate falsehood wakes ...

At one level the meaning of that phrase 'appropriate falsehood' might be thought to accord with Picasso's view that art is a lie that helps one see the truth more clearly. At another level something more precise may be inferred, as in this gloss from *All What Jazz*:

> Every age has its romantic city and ours is New Orleans. ... In its way, it was a kind of Cockaigne: parades, picnics, funerals, all had their brass bands, and every citizen, shoeblack, cigarmaker, bricklayer, was half a musician. Their music has become synonymous with a particularly buoyant kind of jazz that seems to grow from a spontaneous enjoyment of living.
>
> *(AWJ, 45)*

Cockaigne was the utopian country of medieval poetry and of a famous painting by Pieter Bruegel the Elder, an abode of luxury, idleness and gluttony. The fabulatory nature of the reference is confirmed when Larkin adds that the joyousness of New Orleans jazz was ever a triumph of optimism over experience, the actuality of the place, certainly for its black residents, being 'an appallingly vicious squalor' (*AWJ*, 45). Bechet's music may especially be considered a source of 'appropriate falsehood' in that, although he was one of the two greatest exponents of the New Orleans sound (the other being Louis Armstrong), he left the city in 1919, scarcely out of his teens, and apart from two fleeting visits in 1944 he never went back. At the time of Larkin's birth, Bechet was resident in England, and by the time of the poem's composition he was a citizen of France. The New Orleans of his recordings was at best a distant memory, irradiated perhaps by the golden glow of nostalgia, and may actually have been no more than a particular way of doing music that required no anchorage in the original topography.

The conviction that we have moved beyond the reflective metaphor of the first two lines of the poem (art as a mirror held up to nature) towards a constructivist theory of art is confirmed by the first word of the fourth line, 'Building', with its suggestion that jazz has invented New Orleans rather than the other way round. This key word simultaneously pivots the argument towards reader reception, the rest of the poem enumerating (with no suggestion that the list is exhaustive) four 'appropriate falsehoods', four different versions or facets of New Orleans conjured up by Bechet's performance. The first of these is the historic French quarter of the city, subsequently a major tourist attraction, not least for its jazz museum:

> And in all ears appropriate falsehood wakes,
> Building for some a legendary Quarter

> Of balconies, flower-baskets and quadrilles,
> Everyone making love and going shares –
>
> Oh, play that thing!

The second is Storyville, a particular segment of the French quarter that constituted the red light district and whose partial closure in 1917 (one of the reasons the district is now 'mute') contributed to the diaspora of New Orleans jazz players like Bechet:

> Mute glorious Storyvilles
> Others may license, grouping round their chairs
> Sporting-house girls ...

A third response is the archival one of a certain sort of jazz fanatic who gets all wrapped up, as though in a travel-rug or plaid (these days the simile would be that of an anorak), with the precise membership of particular bands:

> ... scholars *manqués* nod around unnoticed
> Wrapped up in personnels like old plaids.

As it happens, personnels *were* fluid in New Orleans bands of all sizes, not least because club managers might reduce their costs by the temporary laying-off of members on nights when the paying audience was small. When it came to recordings the problem was yet more complex, even major artists like Bechet feeling it necessary to break contract and supplement their meagre earnings by participating in studio sessions anonymously or pseudonymously. Plenty of material here for what Larkin disparagingly referred to as 'discographical train-spotters' (*LJ*, 55).

The fourth and final response, that of the narrator, is the most emotional of them all and seems the more so coming immediately after the rather fusty antiquarian approach:

> On me your voice falls as they say love should,
> Like an enormous yes. My Crescent City
> Is where your speech alone is understood,
>
> And greeted as the natural noise of good,
> Scattering long-haired grief and scored pity.

Here Bechet's sound seems almost God-like, his 'voice' falling from above, like manna from heaven, the epitome of 'love', of yea-saying and of 'good'; in other words, the very antithesis of another American voice from above, that of the bogus Evangelist in 'Faith Healing', the poem immediately preceding 'For Sidney Bechet' in *The Whitsun Weddings*. It is also worth underlining the fact that this benign, almost sacramental interpretation of Bechet necessitates an Eliotic acceptance that 'the more perfect the artist, the more completely separate in him will be the man who suffers and the mind which creates', for in art the only '*significant* emotion' is that 'which has its life in the poem and not in the history of the poet'.[7] Bechet, of whose 'fits of temperament' Larkin was indulgently aware (*LJ*, 45), was first imprisoned and then deported from Britain for assaulting a London prostitute, and was later imprisoned and then deported from France for starting a gun fight in which three innocent people, one man and two women, were seriously wounded. As drummer Zutty Singleton said: 'He was a hell of a cat. He could be mean. He could be sweet. He could be in between.'[8] Would that some of Larkin's commentators could keep in mind the distinction between the art and the artist of 'For Sidney Bechet', which takes it as axiomatic that a man may be a bit of a devil but still play the sax like an angel.

Thus far we have seen how our poem uses jazz to underline the autonomy of art, to emphasize that art is constitutive rather than merely reflective of reality, to discredit author-centred interpretations, and to demonstrate the multiplicity of meanings to which even music of two or three minutes' duration gives rise relative to the viewpoints of different audients. Many of these values are entrenched on the plane of the poem itself. Thus, not only does 'For Sidney Bechet' attribute to jazz a multiplicity and relativity of meaning, but it too is open to a variety of sometimes mutually exclusive interpretations.

One small, teasing example is that of the polysemic wordplay contained in the phrase 'Mute glorious Storyvilles'. The line invokes 'Elegy Written in a Country Churchyard' by Thomas Gray, which was composed two hundred years earlier and which speculates of the eponymous burial ground, 'Some mute inglorious Milton here may rest'. Gray's words in turn derive from the following passage of the *Aeneid* (Book XII, lines 395–7):

> ... ille ut depositi proferret fata parentis,
> scire potestates herbarum usumque medendi
> maluit et mutas agitare inglorius artis.

In contravention of Larkin's professed Realism ('Poems don't come from other poems ...'), we already have art (Larkin's poem) about art

(Bechet's jazz) about art (Gray's 'Elegy') about art (the poet John Milton) about art (Virgil's *Aeneid*). This palimpsestic multi-layering is later supplemented by invocations of the end of James Joyce's *Ulysses* in the phrase 'an enormous yes' and of the *Book* of *Proverbs* (xxxi, 10) in the words 'priced/Far above rubies'. Equally dizzying are the puns. We have already remarked that 'mute', as well as helping to recall Thomas Gray, may be taken to refer to the silencing of Storyville in 1917. More obviously, it is an attachment, much favoured by jazz musicians, used to soften the sound of brass instruments in an orchestra. As for Storyville, that not only refers to the New Orleans bordello district, named after alderman Joseph Story who sponsored the legislation that created it, but has also lent its name to a jazz magazine and two different jazz labels, both of which Bechet was associated with.[9] We could go on piling up the puns and citations in this three-word unit: the point is that not only will different readers catch or miss different levels of signification, but that even those who register the identical shades of meaning might assign them different places in the hierarchy of value, thereby altering (if ever so slightly) the overall purport of the poem.

Narratologically, the clause 'Oh, play that thing!' is quite as vertiginous. Whose words are they? Is the imprecation to be read as Philip Larkin's, as the biographical criticism he sometimes espoused would have us believe ('novels are about other people and poetry is about yourself', *FR*, 24)? Is it uttered by a representative of the first of the four reading positions enumerated above, within whose section of the poem it appears to fall? Or does the fact that it follows a dash and a stanza break indicate that it is an excited interjection by the narrator, momentarily endorsing the equation between Bechet's colossal energy and the vitality of the French Quarter before going on to offer a rather different perspective of his or her own ('On *me* your voice falls ...')?

The difficulty in deciding who utters the words is compounded by the knowledge that they constitute a quotation in search of an originatory source. From within the realms of literature the best candidate is probably 'Jazz Band in a Parisian Cabaret' by the African-American jazz poet Langston Hughes, the very first words of which are 'Play that thing ...!'[10] From the realm of Bechet recordings, the most likely contender is his sensational 1932 version of *Maple Leaf Rag* in the background to which a voice (possibly Bechet's own) can be heard shouting 'Play it, man, play it!' during Hank Duncan's piano solo.[11] By that date, however, the expression already had a considerable discological history so that any use of it came within several sets of quote marks. For instance, when the Fletcher Henderson Orchestra headhunted the rising star Louis Armstrong from

King Oliver's Creole Jazz Band they reworked the latter's 1923 *Dippermouth Blues* as *Sugar Foot Stomp* (1925), an unnamed vocalist repeating in parodic falsetto the earlier disc's urgent 'Oh, play that thing!' And when later that same year Armstrong left Henderson to form the celebrated Hot Five, he used the new outfit's recording of *Gut Bucket Blues* to introduce each member of the band in turn: 'Oh, play that thing Mr St Cyr', 'Oh, whip that thing Miss Lil', 'Oh, blow it Kid Ory, blow it Kid', etc. Anterior to all these scribal and recorded usages by the artists themselves are the countless exhortations of anonymous members of the jazz public: Jelly Roll Morton could remember the whores of the Monarch Saloon in Memphis (real 'Sporting-house girls') urging on the resident pianist with the shout 'O play it, Benny, play it!' in the period before the invention of the gramophone.[12] We began by asking whose are these words: is Larkin quoting Hughes quoting Jelly Roll Morton; or the narrator quoting Bechet quoting Armstrong quoting Henderson quoting King Oliver? No doubt a true jazz buff could quickly multiply the citations and demonstrate yet more forcibly the exegetical complexity of these four, misleadingly transparent monosyllables.

A larger, even more vexatious instance of the poem's susceptibility to interpretative variety such as it attributes to jazz pertains to the issue of whether or not the narrator's view of Bechet is definitive, or at least the most 'appropriate falsehood'. Certainly, V. Penelope Pelizzon takes that line in what is thus far one of the two most sustained critical analyses of the poem.[13] She bases this judgement on two factors: first, that the other interpretations relate Bechet's music to particular precincts of the city (the French Quarter, Storyville), suggesting a limited or partial perspective, whereas the narrator's view comprehends the whole of New Orleans; second, she takes the opening of the final sentence – 'My Crescent City/Is where your speech alone is understood' – to mean 'My view of New Orleans alone correctly represents what you are saying'.

For the present writer, by contrast, the 'all' in line three ('And in *all* ears appropriate falsehood wakes') is authoritative, encompassing the narrator's vision of New Orleans as surely as the others. Moreover, I parse the opening of the concluding sentence to mean 'In my New Orleans the only *lingua franca* is your jazz'. It is true that the simile 'Like an enormous yes' is so arresting that it lends the narrator's account of Bechet's jazz great weight. However, it is also true that this account is rendered less than decisive by its retinue of qualifiers ('as they say', 'should', 'like'). Besides, for all their differences, the four views are too complementary to leave much room for self-aggrandizement on the part of the narrator. After all, the first version of New Orleans depicts a French Quarter characterized by *joie de vivre*, communality and sexual licence; the second concentrates exclusively on an image of commodified sex such as one finds in the 1912 Storyville photographs of E.J. Bellocq; the third on the obsessional dedication of the fanatic; and the fourth on a more expansive, affirmative love – nearer to *agapé* than *eros*. The fact that the four interpretations, although perceptibly different one from another, are all variants on the theme of love suggests that Larkin's poem is less an assertion of the narrator's viewpoint at the expense of the others, as Pelizzon claims, than a demonstration that Bechet's art is rich enough to sustain a plurality of overlapping readings. Such an assessment has the gratifying side effect of rescuing the narrator from the charge of big-headedness.

This last may be just as well since, whether or not Larkin intended it, his narrator is unreliable. The narrator ends the poem by crediting Bechet with the capacity to scatter 'long-haired grief and scored pity'. The opposing of a music of joy to one of sorrow is predicated on a deeper opposition between jazz and classical music – the latter traditionally being associated with hirsute maestros such as Toscanini, the most famous conductor of the day, and with a puctilious attention to the score. Bechet, by contrast, was a magisterial exponent of improvization who never learned to read music (according to Jelly Roll Morton, 'he plays more music than you can put down on paper').[14] Yet the opposition is bogus – an 'appropriate falsehood' of the narrator's, perhaps. Bechet loved classical music: he kept a portrait of Beethoven on his wall; likened his own use of vibrato to that of his beloved Caruso; and with the aid of amenuenses composed extended works such as *The Negro Rhapsody*, the ballet suite *La nuit est un sorcière* and the operetta *New Orleans*. In the case of the celebrated 1939 recording of 'Summertime', which Larkin described as a demonstration of 'full-throated felicity' that 'made even the accompanists clap' (*AWJ*, 29), Bechet wittily inserted between the first and second choruses a quotation from a favourite opera, Leoncavallo's *I Pagliacci*. When we remember that the influence was reciprocal, Bechet sometimes being credited with a direct effect upon Stravinsky, the closing opposition seems simplistic and divisive.[15] Once again the narrator's view is found to be more fallible and less conclusive than Pelizzon suggests, leaving the reader with a limited plurality of viable interpretations to consider and adjudicate between.

There are other grounds for quarrelling with Pelizzon's essay: for example, she assumes that the music described is played on a clarinet when the poem does not specify the instrument and Bechet's preference was for the soprano sax; and she sees the depiction of the 'scholars *manqués*' as a wry self-caricature by Larkin when his copious writings on jazz adopt the opposite of their dusty approach ('A.E. Housman said he could reco[?] poetry because it made his throat tighten and his eyes water: I can [?] nise jazz because it makes me tap my foot, grunt affirmative exhorta[?] or even get up and caper round the room.' *AWJ*, 197). Yet the crucia[?] is not the superiority (or otherwise) of my view as compared with he[?] rather the ambiguity and complexity of a poem which offers more [?] one hermeneutical route through it. Hence, the concluding senter[?] 'For Sidney Bechet' is forever open to Pelizzon's reading and to mir[?] disagree as to which meaning has primacy but neither of us can u[?] choice to vanquish the other and bring the poem to closure. This ir[?] illustrates how Larkin's poem demands active readership rather tha[?] sive consumption, refusing to offer itself up in a state of self-eviden[?] 'at once and no trying at all'. Such dissensus, whether between dif[?] readers of Larkin or different listeners to Bechet, also puts paid t[?] Realist belief in a consensual, self-explanatory world that is somehov[?] there' waiting to be xeroxed. ('It was just the transcription of a very [?] afternoon. It only needed writing down.') Instead, the emphasis o[?] Sidney Bechet' is entirely upon the power of art to generate differen[?] ities, the power of readers to generate different versions of that art ar[?] singularity of those art works which are particularly plenitudinous i[?] production of meanings (not so much 'anybody could have done[?] only Bechet – or Larkin – could have). Above all, the explanatory r[?] adopted by the poem is one which accepts that pre-Parker jazz such a[?] of Sidney Bechet was already the epitome of Modernist aesthetics.

Of course, it might be rejoined that while Larkin accepts Modernis[?] thetics in theory, his verse forms are largely regular and unadventur[?] that he is, at most, a Realist with a Modernist sensibility. There is cc[?] erable truth in this, Larkin's contribution to an emergent Postmode[?] stemming in part from his forging of new amalgams from the [?] tional and the Modernist inheritances. Nonetheless, 'For Sidney Be[?] is formally far less predictable and far more dislocated than mig[?] thought. At seventeen lines, it is three lines too many for a sonnet[?] lines too few for a villanelle, one line too many to be divisible into [?] rains and one line too few for tercets. Larkin's thoroughly idiosyn[?] solution appears to combine the worst of both worlds by dividin[?] poem into tercets, with a last stanza that is one line deficient, and[?] superimposing an abab rhyme scheme more appropriate to the [?] rain, the penultimate line of the poem breaking the rhyme patte[?] being supplementary to it. The resulting hybrid approximates but congeals into a number of traditional forms: the Shakespearian sonnet (with its abab cdcd efef gg rhyme scheme); the *quatorzain* of Shelley's *Ode to the West Wind* (aba bcb cdc ded ee); *terza rima*, a three-line stanza form rhyming aba bcb cdc and usually ending with a single line (xyx y); the villanelle (with its three-line stanzas and opening aba rhyme scheme); and the Caudate sonnet (from the Latin word *cauda*, meaning a tail or coda), in which the usual fourteen-line form is augmented by an extra couplet preceded by an introductory half line. At sixteen and a half lines, this last is very close in duration to Larkin's model, but the version of the sonnet usually adopted when adding 'tails' is the Petrarchan, which has a totally different rhyme scheme (*octave:* abbaa bba: *sestet:* cdecde or cdcdcd).

The same calculated frustrating of expectations takes place at the level of line-length and rhythm. What at first appears to be pentametric is in practice quite irregular, with one line of nine syllables, seven of ten syllables, eight of eleven syllables and one of twelve syllables. The inconsistent addition and subtraction of syllables to or from the anticipated row of ten works to vary time and pitch, delaying stresses and modulating the residually iambic rhythm. As William Harmon has pointed out, there is even a hint of 'ragging' in 'the finely syncopated rhythm in the last line – trochee, iamb, spondee, iamb, trochee – where the scazon [the substitution of a trochee for the concluding iamb] delivers the final rhyme a syllable sooner than our ear expects'.[16] Such deviations from the norm may be modest compared to the free verse fireworks of Modernists like Cummings, Apollinaire, Mayakovsky and Marinetti, but they accord very well with the views T.S. Eliot expressed in his 1942 essay 'The Music of Poetry':

> As for 'free verse', I expressed my view twenty-five years ago by saying that no verse is free for the man who wants to do a good job. ... Only a bad poet could welcome free verse as a liberation from form. It was a revolt against dead form, and a preparation for new form or the renewal of the old; it has an insistence upon the inner unity which is unique to every poem, against the outer unity which is typical.[17]

The reference back a quarter of a century with which this quotation begins is to Eliot's 1917 essay 'Reflections on *Vers Libre*' in which he again anticipates some aspects of Larkin's practice. The proposition that 'the ghost of some simple metre should lurk behind the arras in even the "freest" verse' is very close to the way in which iambic pentameters and a variety of sonnet structures shadow 'For Sidney Bechet'. The following passage is also peculiarly pertinent:

> And this liberation from rhyme might as well be a liberation *of* rhyme. Freed from its exacting task of supporting lame verse, it could be applied with greater effect where it is most needed. There are often passages in an unrhymed poem where rhyme is wanted for some special effect, for a sudden tightening-up, for a cumulative insistence, or for an abrupt change of mood.

'For Sidney Bechet' is neither 'lame verse' nor 'an unrhymed poem', but it does liberate rhyme, set it loose, in pursuit of 'some special effect' specific to the task at hand. Consider, for example, the terrific spinal column of syllables ending in 'd' that, vertebra by vertebra, provides the poem with its hidden backbone: hold – [false]hood – quad[rilles] – fad[s] – nod – plaid[s] – should – [under]stood – good; all, perhaps, deriving from Sid[ney] in the title. Notice the musical pattern created by the superabundance of present participles: narrowing – rising – Building – making – going – grouping – Sporting – scattering. Two smaller series of pararhymes, the shake[s] – wake[s] – mak[ing] and the play – may – *manqués* – they – say sequences, combine to produce an extended assonantal chain based on the shared 'a' sound, possibly sparked off by the second syllable (pronounced 'shay') of Bechet's surname. We could go on to list many more uses of internal rhyme (the Sidney – balconie[s] – on me – City – pity sequence, for instance), as well as quite other effects such as alliteration ('natural noise', etc.) and a plethoric use of sibilants (license, circus, priced, yes, Crescent). What is already apparent is that the prosody, the total sound-system of the poem, is much more densely orchestrated than usual – so much so that I gave up marking the melodic effects in my own copy for fear of completely obliterating the text. This is a poem that endeavours not just to describe music but to enact it, in the process achieving an aural richness that, if not exactly experimental, does have affinities with the more sonorous Modernists such as Hopkins, Yeats, Eliot and Dylan Thomas. As early as 1942, in a letter to James Sutton, Larkin had written: 'Jazz and poetry are my life, my life'.[18] Twelve years later, in 'For Sidney Bechet', he brings the two arts together in a shared relation to Modernist aesthetics that thoroughly confounds his own Realist propaganda.

III   Larkin's racial ideology

At the time of the poem's composition, Sidney Bechet was alive and living in France as a fifty-six-year-old exile from American racism. Back in 1910, when the precocious thirteen-year-old Bechet first started playing in adult jazz bands, twenty-one Negroes were lynched because the white American heavyweight boxer Jim Jeffries lost a world title fight with the black American champion Jack Johnson. In 1918, the year before Bechet joined the northward migration of New Orleans jazz musicians, seventy-eight African-Americans were lynched, in part as a warning to black soldiers returning from the First World War that they should not expect at home the freedoms they had enjoyed while fighting abroad for their country. Throughout the inter-war period, Bechet and his fellow black musicians had to enter by the back door the venues in which they were starring, had trouble booking hotel rooms, were refused food at public diners, were ignored by taxi drivers and, when it came to cutting discs, were paid a small recording fee with no royalties. In 1933, Bechet and trumpeter Tommy Ladnier opened a tailor's shop in Harlem in an endeavour to make ends meet, Bechet pressing clothes and Ladnier doing shoeshine. Nor did things improve much after the Second World War: in 1946 a jazz concert in the Constitutional Hall of Washington D.C., the nation's capital, was banned on the grounds that one of the performers – Sidney Bechet – was black. In 1950, after many previous visits, some of them protracted, he emigrated to Europe. In 1954, the year in which Larkin completed 'For Sidney Bechet', the United States Supreme Court pronounced that separate educational facilities for black and white children were 'inherently unequal', and the following year schools were ordered to proceed to desegregation with 'all deliberate speed'. It was not until the end of the following year, on 1 December 1955, in Montgomery, Alabama, that Mrs Rosa L. Parks, a forty-three-year-old seamstress, refused a bus driver's order to vacate her seat to a white man and was arrested, charged and fined. The ensuing Montgomery bus boycott was the spark that ignited the Civil Rights Movement and brought to the fore leaders of the distinction of Martin Luther King. Three years later, Sidney Bechet was dead from cancer.

Meanwhile, back in 1941 a bespectacled, stammering, English teenager named Philip Larkin, whose father was an admirer of Hitler, was writing to his pal Jim Sutton: 'I rushed out on Monday and bought "Nobody Knows The Way I Feel This Morning". Fucking, cunting, bloody good! Bechet is a great artist. As soon as he starts playing you automatically stop thinking about anything else and listen. Power and glory.'[19] In 1952 this same Larkin, who had a pathological fear of foreign travel and preferred listening to jazz on record than in live performance, was visiting a Parisian night club under the misapprehension that the Claude Luter band would that night be featuring its regular star guest, Sidney Bechet.[20] Throughout the rest of his life in numerous reviews of jazz records and books Larkin reiterated his admiration for the 'irreplaceable vitality' (*AWJ*, 205) of 'the incomparable master of the soprano sax' (*AWJ*, 82), the 'Roi Soleil of jazz' (*AWJ*, 221). In one representative passage, Larkin rapturously enthuses about

> ... the marvelous 'Blue Horizon', six choruses of slow blues in which Bechet climbs without interruption or hurry from lower to upper register, his clarinet tone at first thick and throbbing, then soaring like Melba in an extraordinary blend of lyricism and power that constituted the unique Bechet voice, commanding attention the instant it sounded.
>
> (*AWJ*, 29)

This piece was played at the memorial service for Philip Larkin which was held in Westminster Abbey on, appropriately enough, St Valentine's Day, 1986. The love affair had continued beyond the grave.

One of the functions of this historical excursion is to foreground Larkin's cognizance that the contemporaneity of jazz ultimately derived from black Americans' uniquely unpleasant exposure to the acids of modernity. He constantly reminded his readers that 'It is an irony almost too enormous to be noticed that the thorough penetration of Anglo-Saxon civilization by Afro-American culture by means of popular music is a direct, though long term, result of the abominable slave trade' (*LJ*, 83). He knew that in embracing this music whites were tacitly acknowledging historical guilt: 'there is a curious logic in the world's enthusiastic response to the music of the Negro, as if in some gigantic Jungian case-history where salvation is shown to lie in whatever is most feared and despised' (*LJ*, 41). He also recognized that this secular redemption or catharsis only worked because certain black artists had the creative genius necessary for 'this achieved paradox of turning suffering, misery and injustice into a new kind of music' (*LJ*, 44). In the process, these artists provided the best available role model for Larkin's own poetic project of transfiguring suffering into aesthetic pleasure, pain into beauty. Hence, his tendency to equate jazz with the blues and to choose his musical heroes accordingly: 'There are not many perfect things in jazz, but Bechet playing the Blues could be one of them' (*LJ*, 45).[21] His position, then, is anti-essentialist, refusing to *naturalize* jazz by attributing it to an inherent Africanness on a racial model: 'The Negro did not have the blues because he was naturally melancholy. He had them because he was cheated and bullied and starved' (*AWJ*, 87). He was also finely aware that to see jazz as biologically black would not only belittle great white practitioners like Bix Beiderbecke, Pee Wee Russell and Eddie Condon, but would also incur 'the resentment felt by Negro musicians at the idea that jazz is "natural" to them, and that they therefore deserve no great applause for playing it' (*AWJ*, 63). In this regard, Larkin's position was identical with Bechet's, for as the latter's biographer records: 'Sidney always fidgetted when [the clarinetist Mezz] Mezzrow said that, although he had a white skin, he was really a Negro at heart. Years later Bechet told a Scandinavian friend, Dr Terkild Winding: "Mezz should know that race does not matter – it is hitting the notes right that counts."'[22]

The brouhaha that greeted the miserable racism of the later entries in Larkin's *Selected Letters* and the drunken tapes he made with Monica Jones in his declining years has not been matched by a comparable attention to the radicalism and cosmopolitanism of the racial ideology of his jazz writings, whether in verse or prose. 'For Sidney Bechet' was written at a time when children's literature (from Enid Blyton to the *Beano*) was replete with patronizing racial stereotypes, when leading British statesmen routinely expressed the view that Africans were too childlike to govern their own affairs,[23] when the top-grossing 1955 film *The Dam Busters* could unblushingly depict its anti-Nazi hero Guy Gibson with a pet dog called Nigger, and when blackface coonery was perfectly acceptable on BBC television (the most notorious example, *The Black and White Minstrel Show*, was not launched until four years *after* Larkin's poem and was discontinued as recently as 1978).[24] For a quarter of a century, Larkin was ahead of the dominant culture; by the time it caught up with him, his poetic gift had evaporated and in his private misery he sometimes lapsed into the very racism his muse had deplored.

That the poetry is indeed racially progressive can be confirmed by a cursory reconsideration of the issue of narratology. We have already demonstrated that the narrator of 'For Sidney Bechet' subsumes into the prevailing discourse a limited plurality of alternative viewpoints or reading positions (see Figure 1.1). We have also remarked that the four-word unit 'Oh, play that thing!' parades before the reader a dizzying array of possible 'authors'. We can now add that this extraordinary polyphony (and Larkin's poems are far less monological than is commonly acknowledged) works to unhouse racial certitudes.[25] Hence, of the nine putative

For Sidney Bechet

Everyone who responds to New Orleans jazz pictures the city differently.	That note you hold, narrowing and rising, shakes Like New Orleans reflected on the water, And in all ears appropriate falsehood wakes,
1. Some think of the French Quarter.	Building for some a legendary Quarter Of balconies, flower-baskets and quadrilles, Everyone making love and going shares—
2. Some think of Storyville.	Oh, play that thing! Mute glorious Storyvilles Others may license, grouping around their chairs Sporting-house girls like circus tigers (priced
3. Some become obsessed with the personnel of the jazz bands.	Far above rubies) to pretend their fads, While scholars *manqués* nod around unnoticed Wrapped up in personnels like old plaids.
4. Our narrator responds to the New Orleans sound as "'the natural noise of good", "Like an enormous yes'".	On me your voice falls as they say love should, Like an enormous yes. My Crescent City Is where your speech alone is understood, And greeted as the natural noise of good, Scattering long-haired grief and scored pity.

Figure 1.1

authors we ascribed to 'Oh, play that thing!' in a list that was far from exhaustive, only one is assuredly white (Philip Larkin); three are racially unspecified (the narrator, the representative of the first reading position and the Memphis whores); while five are black (Langston Hughes, Sidney Bechet, Louis Armstrong, Fletcher Henderson and King Oliver).

Even if the reader of 'For Sidney Bechet' after due consideration decides that the predominant narrative idiom is British, perhaps specifically English, its enormous yes of love is still international, indeed transcontinental. If the reader goes further and perceives the prevailing narrative to carry a 'white' inflection, then the enormous yes of love it describes is a cross-racial one. If the reader feels that the narrative is gendered 'male', then the enormous yes of love is a cross-racial but same-sex one. And whatever the reader feels, the poem indisputably articulates a high art love for popular culture that transgresses the critical orthodoxy of the day as established and policed by the likes of F.R. Leavis and Clement Greenberg. (In the very year the poem was begun Greenberg was complaining that 'our culture, on its lower and popular levels, has plumbed abysses of vulgarity and falsehood unknown in the discoverable past'; to which Larkin's 'I can live a week without poetry but not a day without jazz' forms the perfect riposte).[26] In short, 'For Sidney Bechet' displays more audacity, transgressivity and sophistication regarding racial, sexual and cultural politics than any of its commentators has recognized or Larkin would have cared to admit.

One last shaft of ideological awareness we might note concerns the tidal flow of the love in question, which is from the jazz musician to the grateful fan. If the narrator shares the author's race, then the love flows from black to white, making the narrator's position the very opposite of the self-aggrandizement of those whites who flaunt political correctness by adopting a black pal as a kind of accessory ('some of my best friends ...'). Rather, the enormous yes of Bechet's jazz comes like the undeserved but enabling benediction described in 'Faith Healing', the poem that immediately precedes this one in *The Whitsun Weddings*:

> In everyone there sleeps
> A sense of life lived according to love.
> To some it means the difference they could make
> By loving others, but across most it sweeps
> As all they might have done had they been loved.
> (*CP*, 126)

The expression 'On me your voice falls *as they say love should'* (my emphasis) suggests that our narrator is affirmed by the jazz as never by God, parents, spouse or lover; in the words of 'Faith Healing', Bechet vouchsafes our narrator 'A sense of life lived according to love'.

The significance of this is lost on B.J. Leggett, whose *Larkin's Blues* provides what is thus far the most extended analysis of the poem. Leggett takes as his predicate Eric Hobsbawm's observation that 'the jazz fan, however knowledgeable, is fundamentally a lover. While old-style pop music ... crystallized and preserved the relation of human beings in love ("They're playing our song"), jazz, more often than not, is itself the love object for its devotees'. Leggett adds: 'The convention of the jazz "lover" – jazz as the love object rather than the background music for love – is crucial to readings of two of Larkin's later jazz poems, "Reasons For Attendance" and "For Sidney Bechet."'[27] In point of fact, 'Reasons For Attendance' does not disclose that the dance music involved is jazz.[28] More pressingly, while Leggett registers that 'For Sidney Bechet' is essentially a love poem, he misses its closing reversal of the jazz fan as lover convention. This may seem a minor distinction, but in terms of racial politics it is vital: our narrator is the humbled recipient of black love rather than the proud dispenser of white love to the ethnically inferiorized. Larkin's emphasis on the jazz exponent as the lover grants Bechet an agency that Leggett's emphasis on the fan as lover would deny. This is, indeed, the most direct expression in Larkin's *oeuvre* of what it feels like to be illuminated by another's love. Here as elsewhere, the poet's radicalism eludes even his best explicators.

We began with Larkin's notorious proposition that Charlie Parker is the Picasso of jazz, the man whose undeniable genius rendered the art form Modernist and in the process replaced its massive popular following with a minority audience of academics and *aficionados*. This essay has sought to demonstrate that Larkin always knew this argument to be specious and reductive, his writings on Sidney Bechet showing a lively appreciation of the fact that the jazz of this earlier era was already Modernist and in ways he sometimes wished to emulate. Let us end with a brief reference to Louis Armstrong, that other giant of the New Orleans style and arguably the only jazz musician Larkin ranked above Bechet. Eighteen months after the publication of *All What Jazz*, with its tabloid caricature of the Cubist artist who 'painted portraits with both eyes on the same side of the nose' (*AWJ*, 11), Larkin wrote in the following terms to Charles Monteith commending the idea of Faber publishing a critical study of Armstrong: 'it is already accepted – or if it isn't, it soon will be – that Louis Armstrong was an enormously important cultural figure of our century, more important than Picasso in my opinion, but certainly quite comparable ...' (*SL*, 443). Even by Larkin's standards this is an almost farcical *volte-face*: in 1971, Armstrong is lauded for that which in 1970 Parker was abominated – namely, his comparability to Picasso! And unless Euclid was very much mistaken in the belief that if A and B are equal to C then A and B are equal to each other, it follows that if Armstrong and Parker are comparable to Picasso, then they are comparable to each other; and that if Picasso and Parker are Modernist, so must Armstrong be. In other words, not only does Larkin's artistic practice confound his own propaganda, but the propaganda is so riddled with contradiction as frequently to confound itself. The time has passed when responsible critics can predicate a literary evaluation upon Larkin's curmudgeonly persona and fitful anti-Modernist ravings. As we said at the start, he loved and learned from many aspects of Modernist music and litera-ture, but lied about it: the proof is to be found in the only place that matters, in the poems.

2
Larkin and Modernism: Poetry

I   On the excellence of Barbara Everett

Barbara Everett's essay 'Philip Larkin: After Symbolism' (1980) marks the *anno domini* of Larkin studies.[1] Before her intervention the critical lexicon – largely, but not exclusively, the creation of Larkin detractors – had been dominated by descriptors like 'middlebrow', 'suburban', 'provincial', 'genteel', 'middle-class' and 'defeatist'. Charles Tomlinson began his 1961 essay 'Poetry Today', in the seventh volume of the highly influential *Pelican Guide to English Literature*:

> Over forty years ago two Americans and an Irishman attempted to put English poetry back into the mainstream of European Culture. The effect of those generations who have succeeded to the heritage of Eliot, Pound and Yeats has been largely to squander the awareness these three gave us of our place in world literature, and to retreat into a self-congratulatory parochialism.[2]

Linking Larkin's statement that he had 'no belief in "tradition" or a common myth-kitty or casual allusions in poems to other poems or poets' with his 'dislike of Mozart' and his 'mild xenophobia', Tomlinson concludes:

> His subject-matter is largely his own inadequacy, but it requires the technical capacity of a Laforgue or a Corbière to convince us that such a subject is worthwhile. One can only deplore ... Larkin's refusal to note what had been done by the French before 1890 in the ironic self-deprecatory mode.[3]

So, Larkin hates Modernism because its intertextual rigours ('allusions in poems to other poems or poets') challenge a cosy middlebrow consensus and because his Little Englandism is affronted by a movement that was launched by the French and imported by the Irish and Americans.

Tomlinson's equation proved extremely tenacious: a quarter of a century later, Andrew Swarbrick was still blithely referring to Larkin's 'parochialism' and his 'xenophobic reluctance to look beyond the shores of England';[4] while the brilliant American celebrant of literary Modernism, Hugh Kenner, was utterly deceived by Larkin's mock Francophobia:

> 'I think foreign languages irrelevant': indeed, 'I don't see how one can ever know a foreign language well enough to make reading poems in it worthwhile'. For one thing, 'if that glass thing over there is a window, then it isn't a *Fenster* or fenêtre or whatever'. Lord ... From England's unofficial post-war laureate such plain-guy platitudes are pretty dismaying.[5]

Kenner, who exudes the air of having read *everything*, had not read 'Philip Larkin: After Symbolism'.

Everett's exquisite essay simply ignored the blimpishness with which Larkin misled interviewers and concentrated on excavating the French substrate of his supposedly Anglocentric poems. As early as *The Less Deceived*, 'Arrivals, Departures' offered 'a beautiful imitation' of Baudelaire's prose poem 'Le Port', while the 'wonderfully English "Toads" ... have a strong resemblance to the Chimeras carried on the shoulders of men' in the same poet's 'Chacun sa Chimère'. By the time of *High Windows*, Larkin is showing a 'boldly individual use of French Symbolist poetry, a use that makes new poems, rather than merely "alluding" or imitating'.[6] The title poem itself is shadowed by Mallarmé's 'Les Fenêtres' and two prose poems of Baudelaire, one of which shares the Mallarmé title. (Kenner's discomfiture is complete!)

As for 'Sympathy in White Major', that could 'be called a learned poem, even an esoteric one, precisely in the way in which we expect a modernistic poem to be'.[7] The title calls into play Théophile Gautier's 'Symphonie en blanc májeure' while the opening stanza parallels Mallarmé's 'Salut'. Moreover, such citations carry further references in their wake: for instance, Gautier's title was adopted by the expatriate American artist Whistler for a mini-series of 'Symphony in White' paintings, one of which inspired Swinburne's poem 'Before the Mirror'. Larkin's genius is to orchestrate these intertextual references in a way that mobilizes and challenges the cultural history entailed.

> He makes use of, and very consistent use of, that species of literary idealism which symbolism implies, *only* in order to record its unavailability. Thus 'Sympathy in White Major' is not a *'Symphony* in White Major' – its title implies parody.[8]

Larkin's incorporation of 'modernistic' elements simultaneously exploits Modernism and announces its supersession: 'Symbolism is being used negatively, in a post- or even anti-Symbolist fashion'.[9]

Critics like David Lodge (1977), Blake Morrison (1980), Wilfred Mellers and Rupert Hildyard (1989), Neil Corcoran (1993), Ian Gregson (1996), Andrew Duncan (2003) and Randall Stevenson (2004) continue to endorse Tomlinson's charge that Larkin is 'anti-Modernist'. Since Everett's decisive intervention, however, a growing minority of revisionist critics, led by Seamus Heaney and Andrew Motion, has taken issue with this reductive orthodoxy, finding in Larkin's verse an abiding fascination with Yeats. In particular, Motion and Heaney have done sterling work in demonstrating that Larkin's moments of transcendence, and their accompanying rhetoric ('the moon thinned / To an air-sharpened blade', *CP*, 181), owe much to Yeats. So effective have they been in this that there will be no necessity to pursue the point in the present volume. Instead, our consideration of that relation in the next chapter will focus upon Yeats's development of a capacious verse paragraph that facilitates sustained argumentation: ratiocinative Larkin, like transcendent Larkin, learned much from the great Irishman.

Despite these triumphs, Heaney and Motion represent a perceptible shrinkage from Everett's expansive lucidities. Where she ranges freely across languages and nations (Gautier, Whistler, Swinburne), opening one vista after another, like a recession of 'windows' on a computer screen, they collapse Symbolism into a single anglophone 'mentor'. In the process they squander her appreciation of the profundity of Larkin's acquaintance with the French (as a young man he translated Villon, Verlaine and Baudelaire; he was familiar with Proust; and to the end of his life he retained an unillusioned affection for the brilliantly disagreeable Henri de Montherlant). Equally, they obscure

Everett's recognition that the poet who offered the most utile model for assimilating French Symbolism was not Yeats, but Eliot. Deft indications of Larkin's debts to Eliot, from 'Saint Narcissus' to *Four Quartets*, permit Everett to make the larger point that having acquired the art of intertextual reference from the Modernists Larkin used it to plunder their works as audaciously as they had pillaged Homer, Dante and Shakespeare. She further appreciates that this Eliotic citationality desiderates a text-centred rather than an author-centred methodology, the incorporation of elements by other hands generating a problematics of multiplicity, heterogeneity and exteriority that challenges the author's sovereignty.[10] Hence her resistance to the intentionalist virus befuddling Kenner and Tomlinson.

Lastly, Everett is finely aware that in raiding poets like Eliot, Larkin is viewing Modernism retrospectively, as a defunct movement ready for asset-stripping: 'his poems appear to have profited from a kind of heroic struggle *not to* be modernistic ... they have wished to be, not merely after, but *well* after Eliot'.[11] She thereby opened the door to an entirely revisionist prospectus in which Larkin is, in a precise sense, a Postmodernist, absorbing and moving on from Modernism – rather than, like Betjeman, pretending it had never happened.

II   Larkin and intertextuality

'Poets in our civilization, as it exists at present, must be difficult', wrote Eliot.[12] As we saw in the previous chapter, Larkin's favourite debating ploy was to oppose the pleasure principle to this Modernist concept of difficulty: 'I have been most influenced by the poetry that I've enjoyed – and this poetry has not been Eliot or Pound or anybody who is normally regarded as "modern"' (*FR*, 19). He was particularly scathing about Modernist intertextuality:

> This American idea – it is American, isn't it? started with Pound and Eliot? – that somehow every new poem has to be the sum of all old poems, like the latest Ford, well, it's the sort of idea lecturers get, if you'll excuse my saying so. Makes sense and so on: only it's not how poetry works.
>
> (*FR*, 54)

Not the least of his objections was that it required poet and reader 'to be terribly educated, you have to have read everything to know these things' (*FR*, 19).[13]

Part of the fun of the game is that the Larkin interviews from wh꜠ these remarks are drawn are themselves replete with the types of allꜱ being disparaged. In the *Observer* interview he provocatively declare꜠

> I count it as one of the great moments of my life when I first rea꜠ one could actually walk out of the theatre. I don't mean offensiv꜠ but go to the bar at the interval and not come back. I did it fiꜱ Oxford: I was watching *Playboy of the Western World* and wher bell rang at the interval I asked myself: 'Am I enjoying myself?' I've never watched such stupid balls.' So I just had another drink walked out into the evening sunshine.
>
> (*RW*

This is an unacknowledged prose reworking of Hilaire Belloc's world's a stage' which Larkin had included in *The Oxford Boc Twentieth-Century English Verse*. (It only goes to thicken the plot Belloc's title is itself a quotation from Jaques's 'All the world's a sꜱ speech from Shakespeare's *As You Like It*, II.vii.139.) Sometime꜠ lobbed misquotes and false attributions at his interviewers as thc testing their fitness for the job. In conversation with John Haffende꜠ credited Hardy with the proposition that 'life was a comedy to t who think, but a tragedy to those who feel' (*FR*, 51), though it is ꜳ ally drawn from a letter of Horace Walpole. To the American corres dent of *Paris Review* he hilariously reversed the meaning of ꜰ Donne's most famous line. Neither interlocutor noticed.

Of course, it might be claimed that by applying Modernist allu ness to Shakespeare, Donne, Walpole, Belloc and Hardy, Larkin anglicizing the technique so as to situate his poems in a national ra than an international continuity. Some such chronology as the fo꜠ ing might be adduced in support. *Sixteenth Century*: Sir Philip Sidꜱ *Astrophel and Stella* provides the title of 'Sad Steps'. *Late Sixteenth–c Seventeenth Century*: Lorenzo's refrain 'In such a night as this' ꜰ *The Merchant of Venice* is quoted in 'Midsummer Night, 1940' w title invokes another Shakespeare play, *A Midsummer Night's Dream* *Tempest* is quoted in Larkin's poem 'Toads' ('that's the stuff / dreams are made on') while K. Narayama Chandran finds 'remꜱ cences' of *As You Like It*, *Macbeth* and *King Lear* in 'The Old Foo *Seventeenth Century*: 'The Mower' invokes four poems of that n꜠ by an earlier Hull poet, Andrew Marvell. *Eighteenth Century*: a have seen, Gray's 'Elegy' is alluded to in 'For Sidney Bechet' while same poet's 'Ode on the Spring' provides the 'Luminously peoplec of 'Here'.[15] ***Early Nineteenth Century***: Keats' letter to Benjamin Bailey, 22 November 1817, provides the title 'Essential Beauty'. ***Victorian Period***: the 'sweet girl graduate' of 'Lines on a Young Lady's Photograph Album' is appropriated from Tennyson's 'The Princess'; 'This Be the Verse' mockingly plucks its title from Robert Louis Stevenson's sentimental elegy 'Requiem'; 'Next, Please' is a wholesale and brilliant rewrite of W.W.M. Hunt's commonplace 'Someday';[16] while the 'and not to come again' motif of 'Night in the Plague', 'An April Sunday ...' and 'Sad Steps' derives from two of the poems in Housman's *A Shropshire Lad*, 'Loveliest of Trees' and (to a lesser extent) 'Into My Heart an Air That Kills', both included in Larkin's Oxford anthology. ***Early Twentieth Century***: the end of 'Toads Revisited' calls into play Kenneth Grahame's Edwardian classic *The Wind in the Willows* ('"Here's old Toad!" cried the Mole ... Mole drew his arm through Toad's'); Hardy's poignant 'The Oxen' underwrites the close of 'Climbing the hill within the deafening wind'; Somerset Maugham's novel *The Moon and Sixpence* provides much of the spirit and certain of the motifs ('*He chucked up everything*', 'Stubbly with goodness') for 'Poetry of Departures'; Larkin's friend Ted Tarling thought he could detect an echo of Siegfried Sassoon's 'The Heart's Journey', part XI, in 'Best Society' and of Shaw's *Man and Superman* ('We do the World's will, not our own') in the last stanza of 'The Life with a Hole in It';[17] while Evelyn Waugh's first novel, *Decline and Fall*, provided the punch line for 'Having Grown Up in Shade of Church and State'.

Even from within the confines of the English tradition, then, the palimpsestic range and density of Larkin's referencing is such as to render his *oeuvre* a Palgrave or Quiller-Couch atomized into radiant piths and gists.[18] Consequently, Larkin's allusions to English literature cannot be opposed to international Modernism since their frequency is only explicable in relation to Modernist aesthetics. Besides, as Everett intimated, Modernism not only provided the technique but also much of the substance of Larkin's citations. His notorious diaries attest as much, for though their contents were destroyed in accordance with the terms of his will, their covers survive. Larkin's own paste-ups of photos, newsclippings and typescripts, these collages largely consist of quotations, often in French, from such moderns as Wilde, Hardy, Edward Thomas, Baron Corvo, Proust, Lawrence, Yeats, Joyce, Flann O'Brien, de Montherlant and jazz giant Pee Wee Russell.[19] The same holds true when we turn to Larkin's poems.

The last stanza of 'Days' ('Ah, solving that question / Brings the priest and the doctor / In their long coats / Running over the fields', *CP*, 67)

seems a deliberate reversal of section 40 of Whitman's 'Song of M
('To anyone dying, thither I speed ... / Let the physician and the
go home').[20] That favourite mannerism of a short double exclama
frequently inaugurated by the word 'O', such as one finds in 'Gath
Wood' ('O short, still days! / O burrow fires!', *CP*, 91), 'Absences',
Steps', 'The Card-Players', 'Livings' II and 'Long Lion Days', is picke
from Rimbaud, most Modernist of nineteenth-century Symbolists,
even employs it in his titles – 'O Venus, o Déeesse!' 'O saison
châteaux'. The last verse of Larkin's most patriotic poem, 'MCM.
with its refrain of 'Never such innocence again' (*CP*, 127–8), is renc
somewhat less patriotic by its origins in part four of that anti-nationa
poem *Hugh Selwyn Mauberley* by the high priest of Modernism, Pou
the very man Larkin had anathematized in his introduction to *All*
Jazz. The nail-paring image in 'Unfinished Poem' invokes the pas
from Joyce's *A Portrait of the Artist* quoted in our previous chapter; v
the 'lame girl' of 'Negative Indicative' (*CP*, 79) recalls the limping C
McDowell, object of Leopold Bloom's masturbatory voyeurism
Ulysses. The 'Home is so Sad', 'We all hate home' ('Poetry of Departu
CP, 85) vein of invective may have been fuelled by such Lawrence es
as 'Nottingham and the Mining Country' ('I believe in their hea
hearts all Englishmen loathe their little homes'). The beautiful wo
'in a trilby hat' of 'Lines on a Young Lady's Photograph Album'
reminded several commentators of Lady Brett Ashley in Hemingw
The Sun Also Rises. The last line of 'The Trees' is anticipated by Virg
Woolf's *To the Lighthouse* ('Get that and start afresh; get that and
afresh ...'). The last line of 'None of the books have time' was alr
certainly prompted by a great favourite of Larkin's, *At Swim-Two-E
by Flann O' Brien ('There will be whisky and porter for furt
orders'). The 'spectacled schoolteaching sod' in 'The Life with a F
in It' (*CP*, 202) derives from the 'spectacled sod' of Auden's 'Sho
the latter's sonnet 'A.E. Housman' providing the 'Something to
with violence' formula of 'Love Again' (*CP*, 215). Henry Miller's criti
of his native United States in *The Air-Conditioned Nightmare* is ligh
(but pertinently) invoked in Jake Balokowsky's 'the air-conditio
cell' (*CP*, 170).

As for Eliot, his influence is so pervasive that it is possible to de
echoes of his work in nearly forty Larkin poems. The influence is app
ent at the levels of diction, of phrasing and tone, and of metrics. I
briefly consider each of these before using a direct comparison of
Waste Land and 'The Whitsun Weddings' to explore more comp
corollaries of this citational practice.

III   Larkin and Eliot

Although private property in the sphere of language does not exist,[21] the question of diction arises from Larkin's readiness to recycle vocabulary Eliot had made distinctive use of. The strikingly unusual 'vans' in the first part of *Ash Wednesday* ('Because these wings are no longer wings to fly / But merely vans to beat the air') is adopted in 'The horns of the morning'. The equally memorable use of 'carious' in Eliot's own favourite passage of *The Waste Land* ('Dead mountain mouth of carious teeth that cannot spit') is invoked by 'the stained unsightly breath / Of carious death' in Larkin's 'Under a splendid chestnut tree' (*CP*, 43–4), while the 'unreal' leitmotif of *The Waste Land* ('unreal city, / Under the brown fog of a winter dawn ...') is echoed in 'Nothing Significant Was Really Said', 'Schoolmaster', 'The Whitsun Weddings', 'The Large Cool Store' and 'The Building'.[22]

As for Eliot's influences on phrasing and tone, this is especially evident with regard to 'The Love Song of J. Alfred Prufrock', perhaps the single work by any author most often alluded to in Larkin. Even a short extract such as the following (and I quote it in abbreviated form) reverberates throughout Larkin's *oeuvre*:

> And indeed there will be time
> For the yellow smoke that slides along the street
> Rubbing its back upon the window-panes;
> There will be time, there will be time ...
> Time for you and time for me,
> And time yet for a hundred indecisions,
> And time for a hundred visions and revisions,
> Before the taking of a toast and tea.[23]

So much so, indeed, that one can partially reconstruct Eliot by juxtaposing phrases and clauses from half-a-dozen Larkin poems:

When night slinks, like a puma, down the sky   (*EPJ*, 22)

But none the less exists, at the back of the fog,
Bare earth, a lamp, scrapers. Then it will be time   (*CP*, 75)

I dread its indecision   (*CP*, 23)

That slows each impulse down to indecision   (*CP*, 209)

Surrounds us with its own decisions –
And yet spend all our life on imprecisions   (*CP*, 107)

And silently, in words of indecision   (*EPJ*, 322)

The shy Smith sat on the edge of a sofa
Taking tea ...   (*EPJ*, 322)

As Eliot is to Larkin, Laforgue is to Eliot: the interior monologue,
dithering male protagonist, the urban alienation, the irony that
once self-protecting and self-deprecating, the oneiric imagery, the p
dic identification with Hamlet – these are properties shared by all th
Despite his elaborate pretence of monolingualism ('If that c
Laforgue wants me to read him he'd better start writing in Englis
Larkin followed Eliot's lead in raiding the French precursor.[24] In
early 1950s he told Arthur Terry that Laforgue's 'L' Hiver qui vient'
'the poem I've been trying to write all my life', and two decades late
included Martin Bell's splendid imitation of it, 'Winter Coming On
The Oxford Book of Twentieth-Century English Verse.[25] When in s
poems of heterosexual male diffidence as 'Letter to a Friend about G
and 'The Dance' Larkin explicitly calls upon 'Prufrock', he simulta
ously but implicitly calls upon Laforgue too.[26] Tomlinson could scar
be more wrong.

Eliot's impact on Larkin's metrics may be demonstrated with regar
quatrains. Ezra Pound recalled that by 1918 he and Eliot, who had d
so much to revolutionize verse practice in this country, 'decided that
dilution of *vers libre* ... had gone too far' and that the antidote lay v
'Rhyme and regular stropes' modelled on Gautier's *Émaux et Cam*
(whence the 'Symphony in white major' so astutely discussed
Everett).[27] The principal fruits of this temporary reversion to strict me
were twofold: Pound's *Hugh Selwyn Mauberley* (1920) and Eliot's *Poe*
1920. As we have already intimated (and shall pursue in Chapter Sev
Larkin did learn from *Mauberley*; however, he was far more indebtec
Eliot's quatrain poems – 'Burbank with a Baedeker: Bleistein with
Cigar', 'Sweeney Erect', 'A Cooking Egg', 'The Hippopotamus', 'Whisp
of Immortality', 'Mr Eliot's Sunday Morning Service' and 'Swee

Among the Nightingales'. Trevor Tolley's edition of the *Early Poems and Juvenilia* (2005) shows the seventeen-year-old Larkin replicating these 'four-liners' (and their French model) in 'Stanley en Musique', 'À un ami qui aime', 'Stanley et la Glace', 'Erotic Play' and 'Evensong'. Just as Eliot's *homme moyen sensuel*, Sweeney, reappears in the fragmentary verse drama 'Sweeney Agonistes', so Larkin's pale equivalent, Stanley, pops up in 'Behind the Façade'.

What principally concerns us here is that this Eliotic vein continues into mature works like 'Naturally the Foundation will Bear Your Expenses' and 'Livings' III, though in both cases the regularly rhymed quatrains (abab // cdcd) are disguised by being bunched into eight-line stanzas. The ending of 'Livings' III –

> The fields around are cold and muddy,
> The cobbled streets close by are still,
> A sizar shivers at his study,
> The kitchen cat has made a kill;
> The bells discuss the hour's gradations,
> Dusty shelves hold prayers and proofs:
> Above, Chaldean constellations
> Sparkle over crowded roofs.
>
> (*CP*, 188)

– splices past and present, sacred and profane, in a manner highly reminiscent of the close of 'Sweeney Among the Nightingales':

> The host with someone indistinct
> Converses at the door apart,
> The nightingales are singing near
> The Convent of the Sacred Heart,
>
> And sang within the bloody wood
> When Agamemnon cried aloud
> And let their liquid siftings fall
> To stain the stiff dishonoured shroud.[28]

However, Larkin tends to alternate nine and eight syllable lines rather than observe Eliot's and Gautier's immaculate tetrameters.

The list of Eliotic traces will be augmented throughout the ensuing volume, though it is already long enough to suggest that Larkin's largely unremarked indebtedness to Eliot is as profound as that to

Yeats. The danger with this type of argument is that it risks swap
one absurdity (that Larkin owed nothing to Modernism) for anc
(that he owed everything to Modernism). The slowness and the ‹
pleteness with which he emerged as a great poet are due to the ten‹
with which he wrestled with one after another of the contempc
masters of the art – Hardy, Edward Thomas, Yeats, Eliot, Au‹
MacNeice, Frost and (to a lesser extent) Dylan Thomas. In this
stage of the debate a parallel will be drawn between *The Waste*
and 'The Whitsun Weddings' in exemplification of Everett's point
Larkin's relation to Modernism was not passive, but evaluative
contestatory.

Both poems begin with departures from the north, Eliot's 'I read, r‹
of the night, and go south in winter' becoming Larkin's 'slow
stopping curve southwards' (*CP*, 114). Both travel from heat
drought, with much play on the way shadows lengthen or contra‹
accord with the angle of the sun, to hints of regenerative rain.
describe major rivers, Eliot's 'Sweet Thames, run softly till I end my s
being a quotation from Edmund Spenser's 'Prothalamium', a poem
ten, like 'The Whitsun Weddings', to celebrate a multiple marriage.
poems complicate these wholesome riverine images with descriptio‹
industrial waterways, Eliot's seedy urban pastoral ('I was fishing ir
dull canal / On a winter evening round behind the gashouse') t
closely paralleled in Larkin's description of 'Canals with floatin‹
industrial froth'. Both move towards a close with references to to‹
London and polluted walls (*The Waste Land* describes 'a blackened ‹
'The Whitsun Weddings' has 'walls of blackened moss'; *CP*, 116).
end with the prospect of sexual regeneration – the restoration to pot‹
of the Fisher King in *The Waste Land*, the consummation of the marr‹
in 'The Whitsun Weddings' – alike symbolized by the yoking of the ‹
'rain' to a present participle (Eliot's 'bringing rain', Larkin's 'becor‹
rain'). Add the parallelings of word and phrase (Larkin's 'girls' marke‹
'unreally from the rest' invoking the previously mentioned 'unre‹
The Waste Land; or Eliot's 'She … nearly died of young George' becor‹
'*I nearly died*' in 'The Whitsun Weddings') and the analogies seem‹
close to be accidental.[29]

Technically, also, the two poems are more akin than has been n‹
in that both incorporate a mass of literary allusions along the
before climaxing in a kaleidoscopic tessellation of citations. Henc
addition to the running parallel with *The Waste Land*, 'The Whi‹
Weddings' orchestrates an array of echoes that effectively pricks o‹

though upon a map, the poem's geographical itinerary. The end of the first stanza

> The river's level drifting breadth began,
> Where sky and Lincolnshire and water meet.
>
> (*CP*, 114)

invokes the opening of 'The Lady of Shalott':

> On either side the river lie
> Long fields of barley and of rye,
> That clothe the wold and meet the sky.[30]

– all very appropriate as the train crosses the river Humber into Tennyson's county of Lincoln. If the 'reek' of the 'buttoned carriage-cloth' brings to mind Coriolanus' reference in the Shakespeare play to the 'reek o' the rotten fens' (III.iii.121), then the displaced epithet serves to remind us that the train journey from Hull to London skirts the fenland. The subliminal citation would also provide another cross-stitch with *The Waste Land* which more explicitly alludes to *Coriolanus*. As already noted, 'I nearly died' in stanza seven parallels 'She ... nearly died' in *The Waste Land*; now we can add that both may share a common source in 'Laugh! I thought I should 'ave died' from Albert Chevalier's music-hall hit 'Wot Cher' or 'Knocked 'em in the Old Kent Road' (the cockney accent of which reminds us that we have now reached the outskirts of London). In the penultimate stanza the clause 'An Odeon went past' (*CP*, 116) invokes 'An Odeon flashes fire' from Betjeman's 'The Metropolitan Railway', another apposite allusion since that poem too links London, trains and marriage.[31]

Even the poem's close may be read in this way, though unpacking its dense encryptings involves acknowledging that 'The Whitsun Weddings' encourages comparison with *The Waste Land* as a first step towards rejecting Eliotic values. Larkin told his publisher, Jean Hartley, that the arrow-shower simile derived from a scene in Laurence Olivier's film of *Henry V* (1944), permitting those who so wish to yoke the patriotic fervour of the English defeat of the French at Agincourt to the wartime context in which the film was made and seen by Larkin:[32]

> We slowed again,
> And as the tightened brakes took hold, there swelled

> A sense of falling, like an arrow-shower
> Sent out of sight, somewhere becoming rain.

That the narrator describes the arrows 'sent out of sight', not kno▨
where they will land but knowing they must land 'somewhere', r▨
'The Arrow and the Song' by Longfellow:

> I shot an arrow in the air,
> It fell to earth, I know not where.[33]

Longfellow had already suggested the title of Larkin's 'Under a sple▨
chestnut tree' and later supplied the *Hiawatha* metre of 'The Explo▨
(of which, more anon). However, as Andrew Motion remarked, 'Lar▨
arrows serve Cupid's purpose, not Mars'.[34] William Blake's 'arrow▨
desire' are superimposed upon Shakespeare and Longfellow. More▨
if we give this Roman god of love, Cupid, mentioned by Motion▨
original Greek name of Eros, we may descry a further subtextual r▨
ence in that arrow-shower 'aimed' at the heart of the metro▨
'becoming rain'. For in popular mythology the heart of London is▨
Eros fountain in Piccadilly Circus, a monument that combines fa▨
water, the god of love, and bow and arrows (for thus was Eros equi▨
from at least the time of Euripedes) and therefore wonderf▨
emblematizes the poem's purport. As it happens, the Eros fountain▨
erected as a memorial to the nineteenth-century philanthropist ▨
Shaftesbury, the sculpter Alfred Gilbert claiming that the nude wir▨
statue represented Anteros, the Greek god of selfless love, tho▨
Westminster City Council named it 'The Angel of Christian Char▨
Popular taste rejected both these pious associations, profane love▨
placing sacred love in a gesture Larkin would surely have appro▨
since that is what 'The Whitsun Weddings' effects in rewriting▨
Waste Land.[35]

Eliot's poem is in part an account of the emotional and spiritual ba▨
ruptcy of Western culture in the aftermath of the First World War▨
this composite metaphysical allegory, sexual malaise is a recurrent s▨
bol of spiritual impoverishment. Individual erotic episodes are uni▨
sally tawdry because unredeemed: from the aristocratic woman▨
'A Game of Chess', possibly at commode, whose opulent surroundi▨
have as their centrepiece a painting of a rape; via the garrulous cockn▨
in the pub with their unlovely obsession with extractions, whethe▨
rotten teeth ('You have them all out, Lil and get a new set') or unwan▨
foetuses ('It's them pills I took, to bring it off, she said. / [She's had ▨

already, and nearly died of young George.]'); to 'the young man car-
buncular' of 'The Fire Sermon', who takes his sexual pleasures without
regard for those of his 'lovely woman':

> Exploring hands encounter no defence;
> His vanity requires no response,
> And makes a welcome of indifference.[36]

A central function of Larkin's engagement with *The Waste Land* is the
secularizing and sexualizing of Eliot's religious discourse. It is noticeable, for instance, that Larkin's poem resolutely declines to exploit the
Whit connection. Whitsun, or 'White Sunday', falls on the seventh
Sunday after Easter and is celebrated in the Christian calendar as the day
of Pentecost when the Holy Spirit descended upon the disciples of Jesus
in Jerusalem empowering them to 'speak in tongues'. However, the reason so many marriages occurred at this time was not spiritual but fiscal:
the anomalous British tax laws of the 1950s granted a married man's tax
allowance for the previous year to couples who got married by the Whit
deadline. The narrator's observation that 'the girls' wear 'nylon gloves
and jewellery-substitutes' (*CP*, 115), so often cited as proof of Larkin's
middle-class condescension, is actually rather a delicate statement of an
economic reality, that the rush to meet the tax deadline was most conspicuous in lower-income groups for whom every penny counts (and
who go off on honeymoon by public transport).

It is true that the girls stare at their newly married friends as 'At a religious wounding', but this stigmatic imagery carries connotations of sexual penetration in the context of the train's ejaculatory 'gouts of steam'
and the glimpse of a phallic 'cooling tower'. The lexicon of feeling
'loaded', of 'what it held / Stood ready to be loosed', of 'swell [ing] and
'fall [ing]', and of an 'out of sight' (because vaginally enclosed?)
'shower' of 'rain', is the language of sexual arousal and release. By stripping the occasion of the religiosity the Whit connection affords, and in
the process mounting a critique of Eliot's moral repression and body
hatred, the poem celebrates the act of consummation, as though sexual
union has a consecration of its own requiring no theological blessing.

IV   Intertextuality and narratology

Narrators do not construct poems in speech but are constructed by
them as text. Any form of allusion draws attention to the textuality of
the text and the factitiousness of the narrator. It is true that Larkin's

echoes and accretions are more glancing than those of Eliot or I
unobtrusively enriching the poem's prosody and purport, like an
ground river that shapes the surface vegetation while itself rem
hidden. The beauty lies in the way that 'The Whitsun Weddin
more than *The Waste Land* or *The Cantos* may be appreciated by
who ken none of its citations. The fact remains that 'a poem, w
being dependent on our knowing certain things, may yet benefit
from our doing so'.[37] Certainly, one of the benefits of recog
Larkin's citations is a heightened awareness of the violence done
texts by biographical critics.

For example, it is striking how much more commentators know
the narrator of 'The Whitsun Weddings' than the poem does. Al
with Timms that the perceiving subject is 'a man'. From this
assumption rival exegetes are able to construct an identikit pictu
is a 'bachelor' (Lerner); a 'librarian' (Tolley); a 'poet' (Swarbric
'intellectual' (Regan) reading 'a book' (Whitehead); and a 'passiv
resentative of the 'middle-class' (Morrison). As the poem do
vouchsafe a single one of these details, one deduces that all these
cators believe what only Tolley is naïve enough to declare, that 't
is clearly Larkin'.[38]

Once author and narrator have been conflated, the way is cl
Larkin's detractors to explicate his texts by recourse to his privat
udices (real or assumed). The poetry described as 'classist' by Gre
by John Newsinger as 'gripped by class hatred' is characterized fc
Smith by 'condescension', for Sean O'Brien by an increasingly
snobbery' and for Corcoran by an ideology 'in which class is sup
to have no part, but in which in fact it sets the entire tone of
address'. 'The Whitsun Weddings' is regarded as a specimen case,
finding it plagued by 'class consciousness' while Gilbert Phelps c
'a distinct touch of hauteur' about the way 'Larkin puts a di
between ... himself' and 'the comical goings-on of the lower orde

This mode of interpretation is optative, critics like Regan, Phel
Smith using class as their hermeneutical key because they have, wit
or unwittingly, raced, sexed, aged, classed and nationalized the n
in accord with what they know about the author. The line 'r
Thought of the others they would never meet' (*CP*, 115) is repe
cited as an expression of class superiority. It *may* be a false note
does the narrator know what the other passengers are thinking? – t
the primary meaning is obvious: that being unaccompanied, the n
is free to comprehend the whole scene in a manner not true
participants, the marital partners only having eyes for each

Even then the narration is far from authoritative being subject to repeated double-takes and rethinks in a species of perceptual relativity.

Hence, the narrator admits that 'At first, I didn't notice what a noise / The weddings made', misreading the 'whoops and skirls' as evidence of the high spirits of the porters (*CP*, 114). Discovering the mistake –

> I leant
> More promptly out next time, more curiously,
> And saw it all again in different terms ...
>
> > (*CP*, 115)

Observation becomes a self-monitoring, self-correcting process, rather than the bourgeois judgementalism identified by hostile critics. To this extent, the narrator's position is comparable to those of the family and friends of the marriage partners, their observations also being relative to the point of view. The poem specifies, 'each face seemed to define / Just what it saw': for the children, 'something dull'; for the fathers, huge 'success'; for the women, 'a happy funeral'; and for the girls, 'a religious wounding'. Just as none of these positions can be said to be definitive, so the narrator's viewpoint, though it has the advantage of compre-hending theirs, is far from omniscient. As the last sentence admits, the young couples will disembark for destinations unknown, 'out of sight, somewhere' (*CP*, 116).

Once the elements of provisionality and fallibility in the narrative are acknowledged, it is possible to challenge the idea that 'The Whitsun Weddings' institutionalizes the power of the middle-class gaze, reducing the working class to the condition of anthropological exotics. That a degree of 'distancing' is involved is not under dispute, but rather to what we ascribe that partial detachment. The pronominal fluctuations usually parsed as the mixed identification and disdain of a socially supe-rior perceiving subject might as readily be taken as an index of racial, religious, ethnic, sexual or age-related outsiderdoom: *stanza one*, I-my-we; *stanza two, we; stanza three*, I-we-I-we-we-us; *stanza four*, I; *stanza five*, we; *stanza six*, we; *stanza seven*, I; *stanza eight*, we-we-we. Is this not the precise lexical register of a person caught with one foot inside the culture and the other foot outside? If we picture the narrator as black or Muslim or lesbian or gay – or simply imagine how such readers identify with the narrative (not a bizarre idea for critics in a multicultural soci-ety to entertain, especially when they habitually parade their political correctness in such matters) – does the poem not signify as powerfully, though differently, as when we employ class-based interpretations?

This is where the citations come into play, their cosmopoli‹
(Longfellow, Yeats, Eliot) encouraging hermeneutical speculation ‹
ing the narrator's alienation. Consider these lines from the sixth st

> Free at last,
> And loaded with the sum of all they saw,
> We hurried towards London ...
>
> (*CP*, 115)

In 1958, when the poem was completed, perhaps only Larkin's
jazz buffs and some members of the black community would
caught the echo of the African-American spiritual 'I Thank God I'‹
At Las'.[40] Five years later, but still a year before the poem was publ
the citation became world famous when Dr Martin Luther King in
the same source at the climax of his 'I have a dream' spee
Washington D.C., on 28 August 1963:

> ... when we allow freedom to ring ... from every village and
> hamlet, from every state and every city, we will be able to spe
> that day when all of God's children – black men and white mer
> and Gentiles, Protestants and Catholics, will be able to join
> and sing in the words of the old Negro spiritual: 'Free at last! ‹
> last! Thank god Almighty, we're free at last!'[41]

Though a more subliminal instance this might be placed alongsid‹
play that thing!' in 'For Sidney Bechet' as illustrations of Larkin's ‹
to infiltrate ethnically diverse citations into 'correct English' – ‹
tempted to say, like asylum seekers illegally entering the country.

The point is not that the narrator is black or Christian or a jazz
African-American. Rather, that the internationalism of such refe‹
chafes against the nationalism of the topography, unhousing the
tive from autobiographical belonging and legitimizing interpre
diversity. In short, the heterogeneity of the Larkin text undermin‹
narrative homogeneity imposed upon it by biographical critics.

V Intertextuality and qualitative analysis

The sheer perversity of the attempts to present Larkin as the epitc
Englishness, bourgeois or otherwise, may be demonstrated by ta‹
closer look at 'The Explosion', one of the poems most frequently
in this context. The ensuing discussion may act as an appetiz

Chapter Five while, more importantly, allowing us to explore the problematics of citationality. Larkin is as adept as any Modernist at orchestrating intertextual echoes, even if his are less attention-seeking than theirs; but his poems, like theirs, can be undone when the allusions refuse to cohere. 'The Explosion' is a case in point.

The critical agenda for discussion of this piece was set by two characteristically beautiful, characteristically misleading essays by Seamus Heaney. The first of these, symptomatically entitled 'Englands of the Mind', is the transcript of a 1976 lecture given in the United States on the subject of the different constructions of England in the poetries of Hughes, Hill and Larkin. According to Heaney, 'the loss of imperial power, the failure of economic nerve, the diminished influence of Britain inside Europe, all this has led to a new sense of the shires, a new valuing of the native English experience'. In the case of Larkin this yields 'an England of department stores, canals with floatings of industrial froth, explosions in mines, effigies in churches, secretaries in offices ...'. The mining disaster of 'The Explosion' thus takes its place in a list of what Heaney presents as representative English experiences. As for Larkin himself, 'he is a poet ... of composed and tempered English nationalism, and his voice is the not untrue, not unkind voice of post-war England'.[42]

Six years later, in 'The Main of Light', Heaney entrenched this argument by including 'The Explosion' among a selection of Larkin poems conjuring an ancient, idealized, sun-drenched vision of Albion:

> All these moments spring from the deepest strata of Larkin's poetic self, and they are connected with another kind of mood that pervades his work and which could be called Elysian: I am thinking in particular of poems like 'At Grass', 'MCMXIV', 'How Distant', and most recently, 'The Explosion'. To borrow Geoffrey Hill's borrowing from Coleridge, these are visions of 'the spiritual, Platonic old England', the light in them honeyed by attachment to a dream world that will not be denied because it is at the foundation of the poet's sensibility. It is the light that was on Langland's Malvern, 'in summer season, when soft was the sun', at once local and timeless. In 'The Explosion' the field full of folk has become a coalfield and something Larkin shares with his miners 'breaks ancestrally ... into / Regenerate union'.[43]

It is noticeable that in order to skew the poem into his meaning Heaney completes the last sentence by quoting, not 'The Explosion', but 'Show Saturday'. By such rhetorical skills Heaney set the tone for

the succeeding debate about the poem. While some praise and
damn him for it, critics like Whitehead, Corcoran, Draper and
see 'The Explosion' as an expression (in the latter's words) of 'La
intense and admitted Englishness'.[44] Frederick Grubb even treat
occlusion of the sun that results from the eponymous explosion a
of the national obsession with the weather saying, 'the sun "dim
in England it frequently does'.[45]

Some of these critics validate their emphatic *anglicizing* of
Explosion' by plausibly detecting in it echoes of the D.H. Lawren
the Nottinghamshire mining novels, especially *Sons and Lovers.*
acknowledge the much more blatant debt to Henry Wadsw
Longfellow, presumably because he was an American. Yet in his
day Longfellow was regarded as the American equivalent to Tenn
(he is commemorated in Poets' Corner, Westminster Abbey), an
works were as widely read and studied. It is true that by the turn o
century he had come to epitomize Victorian long-windedness
insipidity: the Imagist poet, Amy Lowell, declared it an aspect o
mission to rid the world of Longfellow. But even after his reputa
went into eclipse it enjoyed a sort of afterlife in anthologies and c
rooms. Certainly, a bookish child of Larkin's generation woul
familiar with such favourites as 'The Wreck of the Hesperus',
Village Blacksmith' (whence Larkin drew the title for his 'Und
splendid chestnut tree'), 'Paul Revere's Ride', 'The Arrow and the S
and *The Song of Hiawatha.*

An honourable exception to this critical blindness is I
Hollindale's essay 'Philip Larkin's "The Explosion"', the only analys
the poem which can be said to be indispensable. For Hollindale
poem is the successful amalgam of two disjunct literary inheritan
that of Longfellow's *The Song of Hiawatha* and that of the British ba
of industrial disaster. The latter provides the subject matter: 'in
nineteenth century the disaster ballads, as well as seeking commu
support for the bereaved, are expressing love, the grief of prema
loss, a stoic faith in God's mercy and a hope of eventual reunion bey
the grave'. What Longfellow provides is a rhythm and syntax appro
ate to this theme of life after death:

> The power of the *Hiawatha* metre is that it causes nothing to s
> condition merges with condition, like season with season, by aln
> imperceptible gradations, and in [the] closing section of Longfello
> poem ... it brings this quality of natural and muted transposition
> the change from life to death.[46]

Hollindale adds the 'the expression of smooth evolution from one condition to another, depends on the balance between verbs of impetus, placed in the past tense and betokening change, and verbs of stasis, present participles providing a continuous present tense'. He then goes on to argue that the first half of 'The Explosion' is dominated by verbs of impetus and the second by verbs of stasis so that, paradoxically, it is with the death of the miners that the poem moves from the past to the present tense. Thus, whereas earlier in the poem a living miner 'showed' the eggs, after his death he is witnessed '*showing* the eggs unbroken' (my italics).[47]

This is well said. Four years after this essay was published, Motion's biography established that the inspiration for the poem was a television documentary about the mining industry that Larkin watched during Christmas 1969. In an interview with Haffenden, Larkin confirmed that it was a disaster ballad featured on the documentary that provided the immediate impetus for 'The Explosion':

> I heard a song about a mine disaster; a ballad, a sort of folk song. I thought it very moving, and it produced the poem. It made me want to write the same thing, a mine disaster with a vision of immortality at the end – that's the point of the eggs.
>
> (*FR*, 61)

Typically, Larkin earlier in this same interview had contemptuously dismissed the very idea that a poem could derive from prior literary works: 'I don't think poetry is like that. Poems don't come from other poems, they come from being oneself, in life. Every man is an island, entire of himself, as Donne said' (*FR*, 54). It is amusing to note that in order to defend a position that directly contradicts his own account of the genesis of 'The Explosion' Larkin resorts to yet another literary allusion, badly mangling it in the process. What Donne actually said was '*No* man is an island, entire of it self; every man is a piece of the Continent, a part of the maine' (my italics).[48]

Hollindale did well to see through the smokescreen of Larkin's denials and situate 'The Explosion' in relation to its complex literary ancestry. However, even the excellent Hollindale minimizes the multicultural implications of Longfellow's contribution, and thereby allows the British *matière* too easy an assimilation of its alien metrics. This, in turn, not only permits those who so wish to recuperate the poem to a depthless Englishness, it also – wrongly in my opinion – credits the poem with a degree of unity and closure that underwrites

its theme of redemption. It therefore behoves us to take a closer
at *The Song of Hiawatha*.

Longfellow's readings of anthropologists like Catlin, Heckew
and, especially, Henry Rowe Schoolcraft gave him the idea for a
poem that would bring together in a loose unity a group of r
American tales centring upon a genuine culture hero. In Schoolcr.
came across an Algonkian demigod named Manabozho, whor
source had confused with the historical Iroquoian statesman, Hiaw
Native American tradition credits Hiawatha with the formation c
Iroquois League, a confederacy of five (later six) tribes within
Iroquois family of languages. In his miraculous character, especia
aggrandized by Schoolcraft's confusions, Hiawatha is the incarnati
human progress and civilization. He teaches agriculture, naviga
medicine, the arts, the abandonment of cannibalism, civil auth
and inter-tribal peace.

As for the structure and metrics of *The Song of Hiawatha*, Longf
modelled these on the *Kalevala*, the national epic of the Finns, whic
indeed provided the original inspiration for his project. The *Kaleva*
synthetic epic stitched together in the mid-nineteenth century by a
try doctor and amateur anthropologist named Elias Lonnrot fron
materials he gathered on eleven field trips. Although the number of
ing lines composed by him is negligible, the mass of material from v
the *Kalevala* was compiled has no unity of its own, Lonnrot invest
with epic form in accord with classical models like Homer. The basic
of the *Kalevala* is the trochaic tetrameter, but in Finnish this may be
ured quantitatively (so that the syllables alternate long and sho
accentually (stressed and unstressed). However, Longfellow came
the *Kalevala* in a German translation by Anton Schiefner which was
tently accentual and already characterized by the narcotic repetitiven
what anglophones call 'the *Hiawatha* metre'. It should by now be a
ent that wherever one drills into the textual surface of Larkin's poen
meets, not resistant English bedrock, but one exotic stratum after an
in a potentially infinite recession of layers. The point of proceedi
excavation is that, whether or not Larkin realized it (he claimed th
only became aware of having used the *Hiawatha* metre after comp
'The Explosion'), different of the features that constitute the geomor
ogy of the poem derive from different of these cultural sediments.

We have already remarked (*pace* Hollindale) that Larkin's combin
of the past tense and present participles derives from Longfellow.
many other effects, such as the row of two-syllable words separated

by commas – 'Fathers, brothers, nicknames, laughter' (*CP*, 175) – which has many precedents in *The Song of Hiawatha*:

> Warm and merry, eating, laughing ...
> Questioned, listened, waited, answered ...
> Forests, mountains, lakes, and rivers ...
> Restless, struggling, toiling, striving ...

On the other hand, Longfellow's use of parallelism derives, via Schoolcraft, from his Native American sources; so when certain of his patterned repetitions –

> Down the rivers, o'er the prairies,
> Came the warriors of the nations,
> Came the Delawares and Mohawks,
> Came ...[49]

– find an echo in 'The Explosion' –

> Down the lane came men in pitboots ...
> Came back with a nest of lark's eggs ...
> ... came a tremor ...

– the original Algonkian may be said to have left an impress, albeit faint, on Larkin's text. As already noted, the accented trochees of 'The Explosion' do not stem from Longfellow but were passed on by him from Schiefner's translation of the *Kalevala*: that is to say, the rhythm of Larkin's poem is more German than American. However, some features of 'The Explosion' may have been inherited *via* Longfellow and Schiefner from the Finnish poem itself. For example, there are several occasions when Larkin juxtaposes lines or phrases of almost identical meaning, giving the poem an uncharacteristically quaint and repetitious air. I am thinking of such a pairing as

> Shadows pointed towards the pithead:
> In the sun the slagheap slept.

or

> *The dead go on before us, they*
> *Are sitting in God's house in comfort ...*

or, again, the description of the sun as both 'Scarfed as in a heat-haze' and 'dimmed'. This sort of tautology (it goes without saying that if the sun is hidden behind a scarf it will be 'dimmed') is not only unusual for Larkin, it also goes against the larger tendency of twentieth-century verse to accord with Ruskin's dictum that poetry is the art of using one word to suppress many. Lonnrot by contrast, editing the *Kalevala* out of ancient folk material, thought always in paired lines of virtually synonymous meaning. The pattern is set from the very start:

> I have a good mind
> take into my head
> to start off singing
> begin reciting
> reeling off a tale of kin
> and singing a tale of kind.[50]

Through his studies in rural Roumania, a last European outpost of oral poetry, the early twentieth-century scholar Milman Parry demonstrated that ancient bards were only able to compose, memorize and recite works of epic length by constant resort to stock phrases (as in Homer, where daybreak is always 'rosy-fingered dawn'). These stock phrases not only act as aids to memory, mnemonic triggers, they also pad out the line to a known length. Even by these standards, however, the *Kalevala* is exceptional: in an epic of 22,795 lines there is only one line that is not coupled with a second of identical meaning – which is why the work totals an odd number of lines. In modern poetry, whose primary mode of composition and distribution is scripted rather than oral, these repetitive techniques inevitably acquire a comically anachronistic air. This fact is exploited by the American Postmodernist John Ashbery in his poem 'Finnish Rhapsody'. Here the coupling technique of the *Kalevala* (which is nodded to in Ashbery's title) is rendered parodic by its application to the contemporary world of shower baths and business regimes:

> He managed the shower, coped with the small spattering drops,
> Then he rubbed himself dry with a towel, wiped the living organism.
> Day extended its long promise, light swept through his refuge.
> But it was time for business, back to the old routine.[51]

A formal device originally devised as an *aide memoire* (Lonnrot's folk reciters were so copious in their repertoires that on one of his field trips he transcribed 13,000 lines of oral poetry in a fortnight), now becomes just another means of setting play in play. As we shall soon see, one of the problems with 'The Explosion' is that it does not accommodate what strikes the modern taste as the inherent comicality of its metrical models.

There is one further aspect of multiculturalism that might be considered before we move our discussion of 'The Explosion' towards a conclusion, and this time it concerns content as well as form. The poem recounts an explosion in a coal mine situated in an unspecified area of Protestant nonconformation. This is itself a blow against a monolithic Englishness, the Anglican Church, of which the Monarch is head, being much more closely identified with 'the establishment'. Moreover, the largest chapel-going mining community in the British Isles was in South Wales: it has been estimated that nonconformist groups built a chapel in Wales every eight days between 1800 and 1850, and by the start of the twentieth century there were over five hundred mines in the Welsh valleys.

Larkin had in his music collection two recordings by Louis Killen of 'The Trimden Grange Explosion', a disaster ballad commemorating a fatal explosion in the Durham coalfield in 1882.[52] Even if this Geordie ballad (with its hint of the *Hiawatha* metre) is the one that inspired 'The Explosion', it seems probable, as William Wootten notes, that this source was mediated by a 1930s coalfield song by Vernon Watkins, a Swansea poet much admired by Larkin:

> Reading Watkins's early poem 'The Collier', which depicts a pastoral scene of egg-stealing succeeded by an evocation of work as burial, and which transforms a pit disaster into a golden vision, makes the unreal qualities in Larkin's 'The Explosion' more explicable than any reference to Hardy or Lawrence.[53]

In short, this poem, which has repeatedly been cited as proof of Larkin's quintessential Englishness, may well be set in Wales. At the very least, its explicators might admit that 'The Explosion' is so worded as to permit Welsh readers, such as myself, the interpretative latitude to relate its narrative to our own country rather than to England.

Some of the evidence we have reviewed is circumstantial, some of it a matter of opinion rather than certitude. Nonetheless, even a preliminary drawing up of accounts will involve some such enumeration as the following of the different cultural strata shaping 'The Explosion': (i) that it is a late twentieth-century English poem (ii) with possible debts to the earlier

English author D.H. Lawrence (iii) set in an area, quite possibly Wales
combines the mining industry with chapel (rather than church)
(iv) the substance of the poem deriving in part from nineteenth-ce
English and Welsh disaster ballads (v) and modern derivatives su
Vernon Watkins's 'The Collier' (vi) the metre being imported from *Th*
of Hiawatha by the American poet Longfellow (vii) which exploited F
Rowe Schoolcraft's muddled Englishing (viii) of certain Algonkian n
(ix) which Longfellow set to the accented trochaic tetrameters A
Schiefner had employed in his German translation (x) of Elias Lon
Finnish epic the *Kalevala* (xi) which was compiled from Karelian
poetry (xii) that still carried traces of Baltic song, Russian storytelling
Viking influences. It is this extraordinary multicultural palimpsest
critic after critic has cited in confirmation of Larkin's Anglocent
Granted the international range of reference we have reviewed (and
are other sources that, for the sake of brevity, I have elided), it must s
be acknowledged that Larkin's cultural cosmopolitanism either vanqu
the poem's Englishness or else refigures Englishness itself as hybric
multicultural. Either way, it is a nice irony that those critics who t
Larkin for the Little Englandism of poems like 'The Explosion' are the
guilty of that sin, barbarously flattening into a cartoon Englishness a
that has implanted upon it the flags of Wales, the United States
Iroquois League, Germany and Finland!

We could leave the discussion there, the poem winning a hand
victory over its philistine interpretators; but 'The Explosion' is
problematic poem than we have thus far suggested – though in way
offer little comfort to the majority of its commentators. For in min
ing the influence of Longfellow (and omitting entirely the obl
influences of Schiefner and Lonnrot), the critics credit the poem wi
exaggerated degree of closure not only at the level of nationalism
also at the level of theology. Hence, for Draper 'the Easter symbolis
the eggs is a strong positive note at the end, heightened in effect b
printing of the line on its own as a final, one-line stanza; and it cr
a remarkably positive conclusion to the whole *High Windows* volv
He concludes that 'The Explosion' 'reminds us of the Larkin
though he could not himself subscribe to a religious faith, was well
to understand the very human need for religious communion, and
capable of giving deeply moving expression to that need'.[54]

Hollindale's reading accords with Draper, though, as before, his a
sis is superior in depth and subtlety: 'The need of religious consol
in the face of disaster is acknowledged and affirmed in the poem
the meeting of this need by a transcendent religious vision is recc

only provisionally, at arm's length so to speak, with a cautionary, non-committal imprecision'. Thus Hollindale correctly notes that the central statement of faith in 'The Explosion' –

> *The dead go on before us, they*
> *Are sitting in God's house in comfort,*
> *We shall see them face to face –*

– is italicized because it is quoted on behalf of others, 'those who could utter it with sufficient belief'. He also catches the manner in which the vision of the miners and the lark's eggs as having survived the disaster is rendered momentary, possibly suspect, by such characteristically nuanced phrases as 'it was said', 'for a second', 'somehow'. For Hollindale, then, '"The Explosion" retains the integrity of its scepticism. It is not a poem of faith, though it is a poem about the need for faith.'[55]

What even the admirable Hollindale is refusing to confront, however, is the damage done to Larkin's poem by the inherent risibility of the *Hiawatha* metre. Although Longfellow's poem was a popular success and a schoolroom classic from the moment of publication in the autumn of 1855, it just as quickly became the object of critical derision and poetic parody. Supernatural details, no doubt awesome in the Algonkian, but rendered laughable by Longfellow's jog-trot rhythms –

> He had mittens, Minjekahwun,
> Magic mittens made of deerskin;
> He could smite the rocks asunder,
> He could grind them into powder.[56]

– were seized upon by grateful parodists who instantly recognized how little adjustment was needed to make the epic ludicrous:

> Of the skin he made him mittens,
> Made them with the fur side inside
> Put the inside skinside outside.[57]

Indeed, within two years of the poem's publication Lewis Carroll wrote a parody, 'Hiawatha's Photography', that took Longfellow's ending –

> Thus departed Hiawatha,
> Hiawatha the Beloved,
> In the glory of the sunset,

> In the purple mists of evening,
> To the regions of the home-wind,
> Of the Northwest wind Keewaydin,
> To the Islands of the Blessed,
> To the kingdom of Ponemah,
> To the land of the Hereafter!

– the very section Hollindale proposes as a model for 'The Explos
with its gentle transition from life to death, and converted it into s
thing altogether more humdrum and bathetic:

> Hurriedly he packed his boxes:
> Hurriedly the porter trundled
> On a barrow all his boxes:
> Hurriedly he took his ticket:
> Hurriedly the train received him:
> Thus departed Hiawatha.[58]

'Immortality often attaches itself to the bad as firmly as to the g
said I.A. Richards, adding that 'few things are worse than *Hiawatha*
the present day, well over a thousand parodies of *Hiawatha* have
published, at least seven of them approximating the elephantine le
of Longfellow's original (what is an epic, after all, but a poem of
length that feels even longer). Whether or not this makes Longfell
poem immortal in its awfulness, Larkin's 'The Explosion' cannot inv
The Song of Hiawatha in a way that quarantines it from its parodies.
put it more bluntly, the metrics of 'The Explosion' are incongruo
comical.

The banality of the *Hiawatha* metre complements a process of s
tization and bowdlerization, for Longfellow exceeds Schoolcraf
expurgating the Algonkian tales of their Rabelaisianisms – no r
here for talking excrement or speaking sexual parts. Hiawatha him
entirely lacks the arrogance, titanism and sexual rapaciousness of n
myth heroes, and is specifically purged of the trickster qualities of c
ning, violence and deceit associated with Manabozho. Moreo
Longfellow offers as the culmination of Hiawatha's mission
instruction that his people should accept the advent of whites a
more particularly, of their religion. The later stages of the epic, w
the Black Robe chief, the Jesuit priest, arrives with his message of
vation through the Cross, would seem saccharine were it not for

knowledge that Longfellow is advocating the cultural assimilation (and, therefore, extinction) of the Native Americans.

This historical scheme in which Christianity suddenly arrives to take over the last act, like Fortinbras in *Hamlet* or the cavalry in a John Ford movie, is once again modelled on the *Kalevala*. Oral tradition projects a timeless present that simply accommodates the contradictions arising from the different, sometimes mutually hostile, cultural continuities of which it is constituted. Lonnrot faithfully documented such contradictions in every particular save one. Pagan and Christian beliefs had co-existed in Karelia for centuries, and this was reflected in the oral poems Lonnrot transcribed there. However, he filtered the Christianity out from the folk materials of his first forty-nine cantos and then brought it all together in the fiftieth and last canto, giving the *Kalevala* an implausibly pious conclusion. In this sense, both *The Song of Hiawatha* and the *Kalevala* fall victim to a form of Victorian sentimentality, betraying their rough-hewn autochthonous materials with a combination of religiosity and historical progressivism.

Critics have claimed that 'The Explosion' recognizes the human need for religious faith and offers a qualified affirmation of its nonconformist Protestant community. As we have seen, these same critics are at pains either to minimize or entirely suppress the influence of Longfellow and, in turn, the retinue of literary associations (from the *Kalevala* to Lewis Carroll) that follows in his wake. Restoring its literary lineage, its visible genetic inheritance, completely changes the emphases of 'The Explosion'. Using an author-centred terminology, one might assay that Larkin consciously intended to affirm the Christian conception of an afterlife but being a non-believer subconsciously reached for a poetic metre irrevocably identified with Victorian bowdlerization and sentimentality. Using a text-centred discourse, one might claim that 'The Explosion' relates a late nineteenth-century pit disaster to a theology then at its peak but establishes the supersession of that belief system by using a contemporaneous poetic measure that has dated particularly badly. Either way, a poem that purports to subscribe to Christian ideology exposes that religion's falsity by refusing to succeed, the rhetoric giving itself away, honestly ringing false.

VI   Bakhtin and Kristeva

In this chapter we have explored Larkin's half-admiring, half-contestatory relation to Modernism, Eliot in particular. Of all the lessons of Modernist poetry, intertextuality has been emphasized because it is central to the argument of this volume.[60] We have already seen how it bears upon the issue of narratology, every quotation being a boulder in the way of reductive conflations of author and narrator, and upon qualitative assessments, the success ('The Whitsun Weddings') and failure ('The Explosion') of Larkin's poems being partially determined by the skill with which the citations are orchestrated. In this coda a glance at the history of intertextuality as a concept will allow us to unveil one further aspect of Larkin's practice vital to our subsequent deliberations.

The term 'intertextuality' was coined by Julia Kristeva in the 1960s to describe the way in which every text is a permutation of prior texts and always, therefore, to some extent disconjoint, 'a polyvalency of non-unity'.[61] Kristeva and such of her successors as Riffaterre and Genette theorize the term in ways that emphasize its centrality to literary production. As we have seen, this emphasis beautifully elucidates the heterogeneity of the text and of the narrator constructed by that text. In Bakhtin, Barthes, Angenot and Bruce, the same literary theorization is more fully embedded in a theorization of language. Bakhtin was especially alert to the fact that because language develops in social interchange, rather than in the head of an isolated intelligence, all utterances involve the importing and naturalization of the speech of others, with elements of contestation and collaboration as well as passive inheritance. All words and phrases (other than neologisms) come to us second-hand and like hand-me-down clothes retain the scents of previous owners regardless of whether we know who they are. Consequently, for Bakhtin (as later for Barthes) intertextuality cannot be reduced to a problem of sources or influences, since what is entailed is the entire linguistic field of anonymous formulae, automatic phrasing, effaced classics (as when people use a Biblical or Shakespearian expressions without realizing it), regional or ethnic dialects, folk idioms, street slang and clichés.

As Mary Orr recently reminded us, it is possible to exaggerate the differences between Bakhtin and Kristeva: the essay in which Kristeva coined the term intertextuality was *about* Bakhtin.[62] Nonetheless, the distinction is useful, for if a Pound or Woolf might be said, like Kristeva, to detach Bakhtinian dialogism from its linguistic base to concentrate on the polyphony of high art, Larkin reattaches Bakhtin's 'heteroglossia' to the citationality of all language acts. How? By juxtaposing allusions to the canon of great literature with snatches of popular song, advertizing slogans, cinematic references, proverbs, invocations of children's novels, hand-me-down phrases, discarded buzz-words and common-stock profanities ('In a pig's arse, friend'! *CP*, 181).

Thus whole poems turn on the use of a cliché, as 'Next, Please', with its play upon the expression 'when my boat comes in'; 'I Remember, I Remember' with its reversal of 'sending to Coventry'; or 'Wires', with its salutary warning against platitudes regarding 'pastures new' and life always being greener on the other side. This practice is semaphored in many of the titles. 'Reasons for Attendance' is standard phraseology on official documents such as those issued by the medical profession. 'After-Dinner Remarks', 'Ultimatum' and 'Last Will and Testament' work in a similar way, referencing specific categories of routine usage. 'Nursery Tale' invokes a somewhat despised literary genre while 'Forget What Did' takes its title from Susan M. Coolidge's schoolgirl novel *What Katy Did* (Henry James' title, *What Maisie Knew*, was prompted by the same source). The cliché 'love at first sight' is abbreviated to 'First Sight' and 'a miss is as bad as a mile' to 'As Bad as a Mile'. 'Naturally the Foundation will Bear Your Expenses' is a standard formulation from the realm of arts fellowships and academic foundations. 'Take One Home for the Kiddies' is a shop-window slogan, 'Send No Money' a mail-order come-on, 'Sunny Prestatyn' a holi-day poster caption and 'The Life with a Hole in It' a rewrite of a famous advertising catch-phrase for Polo mints. 'Wild Oats' echoes the proverbial 'to sew one's wild oats'; 'Going, Going,' just stops short of the auctioneer's cry of 'Going, Going, Gone!'; while 'Love Again' tellingly recalls the Frederick Hollander-Sammy Lerner song 'Falling in Love Again', an ode to helpless promiscuity made famous by Marlene Dietrich in the movie *The Blue Angel* and subsequently recorded by Billie Holiday.

Intertextuality is to literature as memory is to consciousness. And just as lucid memories are shadowed by a mass of the half-remembered and repressed, so identifiable quotations are earnests of that vast hinterland of anonymous saws, platitudes and formulaic phrases. By incorporating both, free of a hierarchy of value, Larkin effects a democratization of Modernist allusion and shifts literary practice towards a Postmodernist poetics. Hence, the last line of 'An Arundel Tomb', 'What will survive of us is love', might be read as a rewrite of these lovely lines from Pound's 'Canto LXXXI':

> What thou lovest well remains,
>   the rest is dross
> What thou lov'st well shall not be reft from thee
> What thou lov'st well is thy true heritage[63]

Where the arch-Modernist Pound seeks to invest his lines with a suit-able *gravitas* by reverting to a neo-Biblical diction (lovest, thou, thee, thy),

Larkin translates the same sentiment, with no loss of profundity, into the language of popular song. One thinks of the Billy Wells album *Love Survives*; country singer Collin Raye's 'Love Remains'; the Randy Wood album *Our Love Will Never Die*; the 1960s hit 'Everlasting Love', variously recorded by Love Affair, Gloria Estefan and Jamie Cullum; Moby's 'My Love Will Never Die'; 'Our Love Will Survive' by Eddie Rabbitt; and the Donna Summer song 'True Love Survives' ('Only love will last forever, true love will survive'). By annexing the discourse of pop music, with its proximity to banality (countered in 'An Arundel Tomb' by a sceptical penultimate line), Larkin annexes a popular audience with its shared world of reference.

Something similar might be claimed for 'Born Yesterday', which abbreviates and colloquializes Yeats's magnificent 'A Prayer for my Daughter'. In *The Last of England?*, Randall Stevenson offers the poem's wish for Sally Amis, its dedicatee, 'may you be dull', as proof that Larkin wanted people to be 'numb, dumb or feelingless'. Stevenson fails to quote the immediately following lines:

> If that is what a skilled,
> Vigilant, flexible,
> Unemphasised, enthralled
> Catching of happiness is called.
>
> (*CP*, 84)

He also overlooks the poem's cinematic subtext. The title invokes a cliché of long-standing (as early as 1837, Frederick Marryat's *Snarleyvow* has 'I was not born yesterday, as the saying is'). However, three years before the Larkin, George Cukor's film *Born Yesterday* had made the curtailed title world famous. Judy Holliday won the 1951 Oscar and the Golden Globe award for best actress, beating such stiff competition as Gloria Swanson in *Sunset Boulevard* and Bette Davis in *All About Eve*, and the film picked up Academy Award nominations for best picture, best director and best screenplay. Holliday plays the vulgar mistress of shady businessman Broderick Crawford. When he hires William Holden to train her to act the cultured lady, the Pygmalion treatment succeeds too well: she successfully runs Crawford's business empire when he needs to lie low; Holden falls in love with her; and, her social and political consciousness newly awakened, she foils Crawford's attempt to buy influence on Capitol Hill. By deftly alluding to this story of a 'dumb blonde' outwitting manipulative men and captivating the cinema audience, Larkin underwrites his theme that those taken for 'dull' sometimes lead triumphant lives.

That this ability to maximize poetry's readership by alloying Kristevan and Bakhtinian citationaliy (*The Pisan Cantos* crossed with Donna Summer, Yeats with a Hollywood screwball comedy) has been of service to Postmodernism is suggested by *Jerry Springer – the Opera* (2002). A stage musical so scurrilous that BBC Television received 55,000 complaints *prior* to its screening, this Stewart Lee–Richard Thomas masterpiece, true to its title, alloys the most elevated of musical with the most debased of televisual genres (opera and the 'reality' chat show). Hilarious, surreal, blasphemous, beautiful and obscene (with a purported 3168 uses of the work 'fuck' and 297 of 'cunt'), this extraordinary show achieved cult status, attracting 'cross-over' audiences on a scale unimaginable for conventional opera. What an apt acknowledgement of Larkin's pivotal role in preparing the ground for a British Postmodernism that this pop-opera climaxes with a Jerry Springer speech whose last words are an intertextual reference: 'Hopefully, what will survive of us is love'.[64]

3
Larkin and Philosophy: Existentialism

I Writers take sides

The central contention of this volume is that Larkin responded to fifty years of unparalleled slaughter, much of it in the name of utopian certitudes, by creating at the mid-century a literature of radical scepsis. Not only do his novels and poems sabotage conventional pieties regarding church, state, nationality, marriage, gender, race and capital, but in the process they play a central role in the cultural transition to Postmodernist indeterminacy. That this formidable achievement should have passed largely unhonoured is the result of it having suffered an interpretative expurgation more disabling than Dr Bowdler's amputations. In particular, Larkin's attempt to maneuver incredulity into the inherited fields of certitude lends his work a philosophical dimension which has been entirely overlooked. This chapter will seek to counter the prevalent view that Larkin is a hopelessly naïve thinker best placed in an English empirical tradition suspicious of continental abstraction. Instead, it will propose that his 1950s poetry advances briskly from an apparent acceptance of Existentialism ('Next, Please'), via a deliberate embrace of the *mauvaise foi* demonized by Kierkegaard and Sartre ('Church Going'), to a penetrating critique of that philosophy ('Poetry of Departures'). In the subsequent chapter, it will be claimed that Larkin was constantly attracted to that which he rejected, so that across even his most ardently asserted opinions there regularly falls the brightening shadow of heresy. This focus upon *undecidability* is so drastic in its implications as to undermine the then nascent Structuralism and anticipate Deconstruction. As Larkin was doing this in complete ignorance of Structuralism and long before Deconstruction existed, he would undoubtedly have rubbished the very idea. However, that is to say no more than that his poems are more draconian than he realized.

By way of context, it is worth reminding ourselves that the rivalry between Communism and Fascism in the inter-war period, and between NATO and the Soviet bloc thereafter, meant that Larkin's career was conducted in an ideological climate dominated by a them or us, for or against, 'two camps' doctrine, with an intense psychological pressure to choose. As early as the International Writers Congress for the Defense of Culture, held in Paris in 1935, the Manichaean mentality manifested itself in the heckling to which anti-Fascists like E.M. Forster, who were not pro-Communist, were subjected by left-wing audiences avid for socialist demagoguery. As Valentine Cunningham remarked, the outbreak of the Spanish Civil War the following year initially produced in English poets a '"bliss was it in that dawn to be alive" kind of elan and exuberance'.[1] One product of this euphoria was a questionnaire that Nancy Cunard circulated to one hundred and fifty British writers in June 1937. The questionnaire is thought to have been devised by Auden and was signed by him and other leftist luminaries like Spender, Aragon and Neruda. It posed two scrupulously biased questions:

> *Are you for, or against, the legal Government and the people of Republican Spain?*
> *Are you for, or against, Franco and Fascism?*
> *For it is impossible any longer to take no side.*[2]

As the wording suggests, the primary purpose of the questionnaire was to mobilize opinion against Franco. In this it largely succeeded: of the replies, sixteen were neutral, five were against the Republican government and one hundred and twenty-seven were for the government. The responses were published by the *Left Review* in a six-penny pamphlet entitled *Authors Take Sides on the Spanish War*. In 1938 there was an American equivalent, *Writers Take Sides*.[3]

Ironically, the questions and titles devised by these well-meaning intellectuals echo the coercive wording of the most insidious 1914–18 recruiting poster, 'What did you do in the Great War, Daddy?', and anticipate the question with which Senator Joe McCarthy intimidated Cold War America: 'Are you now, or have you ever been, a member of the Communist Party?' At the dawn of the 1920s, F. Scott Fitzgerald ended his first novel, *This Side of Paradise*, 'Here was a new generation ... grown up to find all gods dead, all wars fought, and all faiths in man shaken'. As he put it in his classic essay 'Echoes of the Jazz Age', 'we are tired of Great Causes'.[4] Now here was the 1930s generation recreating the grandiose rhetoric, the war-mongering and the oppressive *either/or* mentality the 1920s generation had rebelled against.

'Poetry is a loyalty to language before it's a loyalty to anything else', Dennis O'Driscoll has excellently said.[5] By suffering themselves to be conscripted in the entirely admirable war against Fascism, the arts were subject to compromises, silencings and genuflections whose rhetoric bordered on the bogus. The linguistic collapse was apparent as early as Auden's 'Spain', which was sold as a shilling broadside in May 1937. The poem's reckless advocacy of 'the necessary murder' famously prompted George Orwell's admonition that such a phrase 'could only be written by a person to whom murder is at most a *word*'.[6] This sort of rhetorical fraudulence continues in the Newboltism of Cecil Day Lewis's 'The Nabarra' (1938) and Hemingway's Spanish Civil War novel *For Whom the Bell Tolls* (1940).

Although the youthful euphoria soon wore off, especially with the defeat of the Spanish Republicans, the *'it is impossible any longer to take no side'* ideology persisted. It is there, for instance, in the sub-Churchillian grandiloquence of Eliot's 'Defence of the Islands'. Written just after the evacuation from Dunkirk, its mood is sombre but resolute:

> ... say, to the past and the future generations
> of our kin and of our speech, that we took up
> our positions, in obedience to instructions.[7]

The poem was written to accompany an exhibition in New York of photographs illustrating the British war effort, subsequently published as *Britain at War* (1941). Eliot whose reply to the 1937 questionnaire was a model of procrastination had at last chosen sides.

If Eliot struggled to disconnect his Anglo-Catholicism from his anti-Semitism and arrive by the outbreak of war on the democratic side, Auden engaged in a series of tackings and traverses from Marxism and Freudianism towards Christian democracy. The left and right of British poetry met in the shadow of the cross: Christian rhetoric was almost compulsory as an aspect of national service. It is an index of this that a poem as portentous as Edith Sitwell's 'Still Falls the Rain' (1941) could be mistaken for major art. Moreover, this failure of literary decorum characterizing English poetry addressed to the horrors of our century, and feeling itself under moral pressure to make decisive choices, continued into the 1950s contaminating even supposedly sceptical Movement writers. Consider the case of John Wain.

In *Formula for Death: E = MC²* *(The Atom Bomb and After)*, French writer Fernand Gigon highlighted the case of Major Claude R. Eatherly, pilot of the aircraft that bombed Hiroshima and Nagasaki.[8] According to Gigon, when Eatherly realized the results of his mission he began to suffer 'brief moments of madness'. Military doctors diagnosed 'extreme nervous depression', and Eatherly was honourably discharged from the service with a pension of $237 per month. However, 'he seems to have regarded this pension as a premium for murder, as a payment for what he had done to the two Japanese cities, for he never touched the money'. Instead, he took to 'petty thievery', for which he was incarcerated in Fort Worth prison. Robert Jungk, respected author of those classics of Hiroshima Literature *Children of the Ashes* and *Brighter than a Thousand Suns*, added that Eatherly interpreted his mother's cancer as a sign that 'we shall all have to make atonement', tried to commit suicide when President Truman announced the manufacture of a Hydrogen Bomb, and engaged in robbery (some of the proceeds from which he paid into a fund for the children of Hiroshima) in order to suffer the punishment he felt to be his due. Seeking a divorce from her husband, Mrs Eatherly told the judge: 'he screams out in an inhuman voice that makes me feel ill: "Release it! Release it!" Then after a moment or two, during which my husband seems to be in hell, he shouts: "Not now, not now! Think of the children! The children are burning!"'

In the late 1950s Eatherly became a media icon, a secular saint whose private agony expiated public guilt. *Newsweek* described him as a 'Hero in Handcuffs'. Richard Avedon photographed him, hand to brow, as a tortured existentialist. He was praised by Bertrand Russell, the philosopher and anti-nuclear protestor. NBC Television devoted a programme to his case. A movie, *Medal in the Dust*, reached the scripting stage. And John Wain wrote 'A Song About Major Eatherly', which was broadcast on the BBC. This poem employs diverse styles (strict quatrains, irregular blank verse, *terza rima* and *vers libre*) to move its argument through successive stages: a précis of Eatherly's career; a moral disquisition on the price of murder; a philosophical meditation on our changing conceptions of hell (the proposition being that by ceasing to believe in the imaginary inferno of Christianity we have come to create real ones); finally, the suggestion that if Eatherly's passion cannot like Christ's redeem us, it *can* offer an image of atonement we might care to acknowledge, even emulate:

> But lay a folded paper by his head,
> nothing official or embossed, a page

torn from your notebook, and the words in pencil.
Say nothing of love, or thanks, or penitence:
say only 'Eatherly, we have your message'.[9]

Wain's poem not only set the seal on his peculiarly modern saint by dignifying his fall and rise with the permanency of art, but also set the seal on the poet's career by becoming a favourite anthology piece and school text. Larkin included it in *The Oxford Book of Twentieth-Century English Verse*. Thwaite praised it as one of Wain's 'most impressive poems' – 'certainly ambitious, but with an authoritative unifying strength'.[10] John Williams singled it out for respectful attention in *Twentieth Century British Poetry: A Critical Guide* (1987). Unfortunately, Wain's sonorous rhetoric, moral indignation and historicized eschatology are rendered meretricious by the poem's protagonist: far from being a hero, Eatherly went through the Second World War without seeing action; he neither commanded nor participated in the Hiroshima and Nagasaki raids; his penchant for petty crime was not prompted by the atomic explosions (he had earlier come near to dismissal from the service for cheating in exams); and at his divorce proceedings no mention was made of nightmare cries, Mrs Eatherly never having heard any. Eatherly was a con man, and in retrospect Wain's poem is mainly of interest for its part in the sanctification of a charlatan.

Of course, many great works of literature are based on false or partial knowledge – think of Shakespeare's *Richard III*, but the Eatherly *débâcle* makes unavoidably explicit the need for a mid-century rhetorical asepsis as drastic as that performed by the Imagists. Wain's language has not been chastened by the enormity of what it addresses, so that the Hiroshima atrocity becomes merely an excuse for specious sermonizing. One symptom of this is the high incidence of comatose adjectives (death is cold, blood is rank, hell is a furnace, saints are holy) whose sole purpose is to pad out the lines in an impeccable but deathly fulfilling of metrical norms. Far from being rendered speechless by the unspeakable, the poem becomes loquacious. This is not the undeluded lexis capable of analysing the evidence before it, interrogating received opinion or scenting the fruitily bogus. But such a deconstructive poetics is exactly what Larkin *did* provide.

II   Larkin and empiricism

Trying to take Larkin's measure in the context of the Movement is like trying to explain Elvis by concentrating on the Jordanaires. John Wain has some claims to be the original leader of the Movement: his 1953

First Reading series on BBC radio's third programme introduced poets like Larkin and Davie, while his novel *Hurry on Down* 'is usually taken to be the first example of the new fiction'.[11] I have singled him out to contrast with Larkin precisely because of this centrality.

The Movement writers are usually invested with a group identity on philosophical grounds. In *Harvest of the Sixties* (1995), Patricia Waugh offers a retrospective summary:

> Within literary cultures, one of the most influential and popular philosophy texts of the fifties had been A.J. Ayer's *Language, Truth and Logic*, first published in 1936 but reissued in 1950. Its anti-metaphysical, common-sense empiricism seemed appropriate to the sceptical and pragmatic mood of this decade and provided a perfect intellectual gloss on the temper of Movement writers such as Kingsley Amis, John Wain, Donald Davie, and Philip Larkin.[12]

This view was first propounded by Robert Conquest in his introduction to the *New Lines* (1956) anthology, which show-cased Movement poets, and was thereafter repeated like a recurring decimal, each time less valuably than before, by Press (1963), Thwaite (1969), Lodge (1977), Booth (1992) and Regan (1992) – the latter characteristically pretending to challenge this stale orthodoxy while actually endorsing it:

> While it would be unwise to regard Larkin's poetry as strictly 'empirical' (the term is problematical in *any* discussion of poetic technique), it would seem to be the case that Ayer's work (and the tradition of logical positivism from which it derived) gave to Larkin and his generation a welcome philosophical support for a literature that espoused the need for caution and scepticism.[13]

'A Song About Major Eatherly' is *not* cautious and sceptical, it is strident and pompous.

The aforementioned may be counted among Larkin's supporters; his detractors repeat their arguments, but in a tone of utter contempt. Appleyard regards 'Larkin's aversion to intellect' as the very embodiment of the Movement's 'tub-thumping literary empiricism'; Nuttall sees him as 'a veritable apostle of modesty, much of whose poetry not only discards the free imagination, but along with Professors Ayer and Eysenck, doubts its very existence'; Eagleton asserts that in Larkin's poetry 'a modest disillusioned pragmatism suspicious of all dogma turns into a kind of absolute dogma in itself'; and Duncan derides 'his emotional deadness to ideas'.[14] That the commentaries of these pundits are

littered with howlers – two or three a page in Appleyard's case – seems
an expression of scorn, as though Larkin's intellect was too limited to
reward careful attention.[15]

While Larkin's defenders see it as positive and his detractors as negative, they agree that he is an empiricist – though Graham Holderness,
alone of their number, endeavours to explain what that means. Larkin's
is a 'mimetic, representational poetry' that deals with concepts in 'specific situations' rather than in the abstract as 'developed through argument or exposition'. This accords well with philosophical empiricism,
which is 'the basing of thought and action on observation and experiment, rather than theory or idea'.[16] Larkin's 'use of common speech' is
appropriate for 'a poetry of common life and common experience' and
has the advantage of a 'quality of accessibility uncommon in twentieth-
century' verse.[17] For all its 'subtlety, wit, irony' and 'intelligence', however, this poetry pays a high price for being so closely tied to the
experiential:

> he is content to accept and imitate the surface of life, unwilling to
> drive deeper into systematic thought or into new structures of lan-
> guage; unwilling to explore the depths and complexities of experi-
> ence or of words.[18]

For Holderness, then, Larkin's triumph is compromised and inhibited
by the pragmatic constraints of the very philosophy that furnishes its
finest moments.

This is a sophisticated but not, finally, a persuasive argument. Like the
other critics named above, Holderness tends to present empiricism as
cosily commensical: *Language, Truth and Logic*, written when Ayer was
twenty-five, may not have worn well, but its lucid exposure of the
meaninglessness of metaphysical, religious and moral discourses retains
its capacity to disconcert – more so in an age of rising fundamentalisms.
Besides, Larkin's assault upon essentialist thinking, largely conducted by
turning a deconstructive approach to language upon the predicates of
dominant ideologies, goes beyond empiricism or logical positivism in
its critique of foundationalism.

III Larkin and Existentialism

The period when Larkin was developing his mature style was one when
Existentialism was hegemonic in philosophy and literary Modernism.
While he was writing *The Less Deceived* and *The Whitsun Weddings*, older

authors associated with Existentialism were being crowned with laurels; Eliot winning the Nobel Prize in 1948, Hemingway in 1954, Camus in 1957 and Sartre declining it in 1964. This was also the period when younger dramatists were reinventing literary Existentialism in the form of the Theatre of the Absurd.

To claim that his achievement goes beyond all this may seem implausible, not because he is an empiricist but because, if we fillet his *oeuvre* in the appropriate manner, we can construct a Larkin as systematically existential as Kafka, Sartre or Camus. As early as 1951, in 'Next, Please', he was analysing one facet of Sartre's m*auvaise foi* ('bad faith' or 'self-deception'). This is the proposition that we lead sham, inauthentic lives by endlessly deferring real decision-taking of the kind that would bring us face to face with the insoluble enigma of ourselves. Instead, we seek consolation in fantasy projections of what we will do *one day*, when the circumstances are propitious (when we meet Mr or Mrs Right, when the kids are grown up, when we win the lottery – or, to adapt the prevailing metaphor of the poem, when our boat comes in):

> Something is always approaching; every day
> *Till then*, we say,
>
> Watching from a bluff the tiny, clear,
> Sparkling armada of promises draw near
> (CP, 52)

The poem also endorses the existentialist view that this squandering of life's limited but real possibilities is the result of our forgetting that time is scant and death final: 'Only one ship is seeking us, a black– / Sailed unfamiliar, towing at her back / A huge and birdless silence'. In this sense, there is already implicit in 'Next, Please', as there is explicit in late poems like 'Vers de Société' ('The time is shorter now for company', *CP*, 182) and 'The Mower' ('we should be kind / While there is still time', *CP*, 214), a Heideggerian orienting of the self to the poignant, delible fact of now and here and this (what 'The Old Fools' calls 'the million-petalled flower / Of being here', *CP*, 196).

At the same time, Larkin remains finely aware, not only that the omnipresence of death belittles and equalizes whatever choices we might make in life (in the words of Sartre's *Being and Nothingness*, 'it's all the same whether one becomes a solitary drunk or a leader of the people'), but also that each of our choices is accompanied by existential *angst* at the array of alternative options thereby annulled.[19] 'To My Wife' puts it thus:

> Choice of you shuts up that peacock-fan
> The future was, in which temptingly spread
> All that elaborative nature can.
> Matchless potential! but unlimited
> Only so long as I elected nothing;
> Simply to choose stopped all ways up but one
>
> (*CP*, 54)

This is the pathos of action; decision is never simply self-fulfillment but is always, simultaneously, self-renunciation. (Larkin did not publish this poem, perhaps because it does not grasp the full complexity of the situation it describes: choosing a wife does replace optionality with commitment, as the poem claims; however, *not* choosing a wife also robs one of choice, since one's marital options remain open only so long as one enjoys none of them!)

The philosopher who most sustainedly explored the anxiety of choice was Kierkegaard, as the titles of some of his major works attest: *Either/Or*, *Fear and Trembling* and *The Concept of Dread*. In the first of these Kierkegaard investigated the nature of decision with reference to what he regarded as binding commitments. Two such undertakings, which for him, as for Larkin, can seem to be in contention, were marriage and vocation. His own inability to go through with his marriage to Regina Olsen is an earnest of the seriousness of these decisions, Kierkegaard breaking his engagement to more comprehensively pursue his destiny as a philosopher. To take a decision of this order is to pledge one's future, and as the future cannot be foretold such an engagement is always freighted with risk and attended by panic. Alan Bennett has already remarked Larkin's similarity to Kafka in his marital ditherings, but thus far no one has noted that the ontological terrain mapped in *Either/Or* is almost identical with that of Larkin's marriage poems.[20]

Yet for existentialists this *angst is* simultaneously a sort of vertigo on the precipice of choice, what Kierkegaard calls 'the dizziness of freedom'.[21] For a self is not given ready-made. What is given is a limited plurality of options, and as one projects oneself into this possibility rather than the others one begins to determine who one shall be. If the first thing to do is to choose choice, in the long run what is chosen is oneself. In Sartre's words: 'Man is nothing else but that which he makes of himself. This is the first principle of Existentialism.'[22] For the existentialist, choice, however curtailed by chance, is the essence of the human condition, constitutive (rather than merely expressive) of identity.

Larkin shared this view of the power of choosing as the core of our identity. Thus the disintegration of self in 'The Old Fools' is marked by 'the power / Of choosing gone' (*CP*, 196), and the hospital patients in 'The Building' are characterized by the loss of optionality:

> some are young,
> Some old, but most at that vague age that claims
> The end of choice, the last of hope ...
> (*CP*, 191)

It is also worth remarking that the interrogative mood is ubiquitous in Larkin's work, whole poems turning on a single question (sometimes posed in the opening lines, as at the head of an exam answer):

> What are days for?
> (*CP*, 67)

> Why should I let the toad *work*
> Squat on my life?
> (*CP*, 89)

> Why be out here?
> But then, why be in there?
> (*CP*, 80)

> ... what
> Is sex?
> (*CP*, 80)

> Where do these
> Innate assumptions come from?
> (*CP*, 153)

> Where has it gone, the lifetime?
> (*CP*, 195)

> What do they think has happened, the old fools,
> To make them like this?
> (*CP*, 196)

> ... but why put it into words?
> (*CP*, 215)

Every one of the 'great themes' addressed by Larkin (love, sex, ␣
time, death, belief) becomes a site of catechism and choice in a ma␣
apparently congruent with the Existentialism of the day. In Heideg␣
words: 'it is questioning that is the piety of thought'.[23]

The difference is that by turning onto the issue of selfhood the ␣
tioning that Existentialism claims to favour, Larkin deconstructs c␣
nal aspects of this late Modernist ideology. For existential thoug␣
characteristically driven by the need to attain, and positively dis␣
everything and everyone that stands in the way of a totalized, ho␣
selfhood that finally answers all questions. Kierkegaard, the fath␣
Existentialism, sets the pattern with his vision of the 'crowd' a␣
enemy of true being: 'A crowd in its very concept is the untruth, by␣
son of the fact that it renders the individual completely impeniten␣
irresponsible.' Nietzsche favoured the still less complimentary term␣
herd' which, in turn, becomes Heidegger's faceless, anonymous '␣
('*das Man*'), Sartre's *les autres* and Jaspers' 'mass'.[24] In all these case␣
proposition is that the self is lost in the 'they' – as Heidegger h␣
'everyone is the other, and no-one is himself' – and that it is onl␣
overthrowing this 'they-self' that one can achieve authentic b␣
Thus, not only do most existentialists see the necessity to reject␣
ventional morality, they often seem to be saying that conformi␣
rules is *ipso facto* inauthentic and the civic virtue of law-abiding cit␣
no more than unthinking habit. Conversely, the tendency to ␣
authentic existence dependent upon the rule-breaking intensity ␣
'own-liness' of choice inevitably tempts some existentialists to deif␣
rebel, the traveller, the thief, the murderer or the pervert, becau␣
going against the grain they have confronted the radical optativene␣
the human condition and chosen to become what they are. H␣
Sartre's *Saint Genet*, which sanctifies Jean Genet as liar, thief, hom␣
ual prostitute and consort of murderers, as well as distinguished w␣

It is this crass either/or with its reductive opposing of 'authentic'␣
'inauthentic', that in 1954 Larkin wittily but devastatingly criticiz␣
'Poetry of Departures'. For nearly three-quarters of its duration the␣
rative admiringly recounts hearsay about someone who has overthr␣
quotidian norms and made the breakthrough into authentic existe␣
'*He walked out on the whole crowd*' – the audacity of the act underl␣
by the use of Kierkegaard's word 'crowd'. Those who live inauth␣
lives fully recognize the ontological significance of what they des␣
as 'This audacious, purifying, / Elemental move'. Moreover, our n␣
tor, who initially differentiates himself from these folks, concu␣
their assessment, moving in the process from a Heideggerian 'the␣

a communal 'we': 'We all hate home ...'. When he subsequently reverts
to the first person singular it is as a spokesman for the inauthentic 'they'
whose compromised, riskless habits he shares:

> I detest my room,
> Its specially-chosen junk,
> The good books, the good bed,
> And my life, in perfect order

The degree of alienation here is profound, the narrator listing 'my life'
as one of the things he 'detests', and implicating in this self-hatred
many aspects of the dominant culture (as in that veiled allusion to the
Bible, 'the good books'). Hence, the almost sexual *frisson*, half-admiring,
half-envious, at news of someone having escaped the prison-house of
norms.

But now, towards the close of the third of the four stanzas, our narrator flushed and stirred with vicarious arousal, the poem springs its trap,
arguing that it is precisely this identification with the rebel ('Surely
I can, if he did?') that helps us stay sober and industrious. In this sense,
the rebel creates the conformity he affects to despise. He (and in existentialist literature it always is a *he*) needs a dominant value system to
define himself against, thereby validating his authenticity, quite as
much as the conforming majority needs its rebels (how we cherish the
tale of Gauguin's escape to the South Sea Isles and cling to that old half-
truth about Rimbaud becoming an Abyssinian gun-runner) in order to
ventilate a suffocating here with the exotic breezes of elsewhere. The
authentic and inauthentic have thus been equalized, like the chequered
pattern on a chessboard; far from being the *Either/Or* of Kierkegaard's
title, they are relational terms that need each other in order to signify
at all.

No sooner has this blow landed than our narrator delivers another
that hits Existentialism where it really hurts (*'Take that you bastard!'*). For
in the last stanza he claims that the only reason he does not join the
Kerouac generation *On the Road* (that novel was published the year after
this poem, Larkin having demolished in advance its key premise) is that
it would be programmatic, a reprehensibly perfect contrivance. By applying to existential rebellion that word 'perfect', used earlier of the narrator's synthetic existence ('my life in perfect order'), 'Poetry of Departures'
proposes that the authentic life is as 'artificial' as the inauthentic one. By
turning spontaneity into a programme and making a rule of breaking
rules, Existentialism ends up as prescriptive as the petite bourgeois

conformity it derides. 'Everyone is the other, and no-one is him
laments Heidegger, in a last-ditch attempt to meet the crisis of m
nity with a naked, vulnerable but ultimately unified and resolute
hood. By contrast, Larkin's narrator is multiple, constituted of bot
'I' and the 'thou', at once conformist and nonconformist, siding wit
'Sober and industrious' while simultaneously quickening to the ant
the drop-out adventurer. This seemingly innocuous poem th
explodes Existentialism on three grounds: its authoritarian totaliz
of the self, its fetishizing of 'authenticity' and its patronizing attitu
the 'inauthentic' they. In the process, it proclaims Larkin's sece
from that culture of coercion associated with the *Writers Take Sides* r
set. Confronted with Kierkegaard's *either/or*, Larkin perceives, i
choice to be made, but a paradox to be confronted.

IV   Larkin and *'mauvaise foi'*

In *Fear and Trembling* (1843), Kierkegaard uses the Biblical sto
Abraham and Isaac to demonstrate that at the heart of Christi
there lies a terror and irrationality so profound that theology
neither 'absorb' it nor explain it away.[25] God's demand that Abra
sacrifice his beloved only son, and Abraham's readiness to compl
outrages to conventional reason and morality – more so when G
perceived as the essence of everything ethical. The act itself is a
since no one stands to gain by it – not God, not Abraham, certainl
Isaac. Nor can the fact that the commandment was a test of fai
used in moral justification as Abraham would fail the test if he prep
to kill Isaac in *the expectation* that God will relent at the last minute.
relents precisely because Abraham has no such expectations. This i
existential 'leap' into the moral abyss that for Kierkegaard is the es
of faith. Kierkegaard's use of this Old Testament story has ca
controversy for committing him to the view that barbaric acts ca
sanctioned by an appeal to faith. Kierkegaard's point is that th
precisely the view propounded by the Bible but that polite so
cannot stomach the existential terror at the core of its own syste
values. Every Sunday Abraham is praised as the 'father of faith' by
meaning clergymen who would call the police or the lunatic asyl
they met a real child-murderer who justified his actions with
blasphemous claim that God put him up to it. In his later v
Kierkegaard applied similar arguments to the New Testament. *Tra
in Christianity* (1850) takes it as axiomatic that Christ's majesty i
cause of his crucifixion and that the mark of the true believer

position so far outside conventional ethics as to incur hostility and persecution. The mere sight of Jesus, a carpenter's son with a retinue of fishermen, prostitutes, vagrants and lepers, would have scandalized nineteenth-century 'Christendom' which for Kierkegaard was little more than a repository of bourgeois smugness. From this fierce either/or, Kierkegaard's last pamphlets and articles proceed to a vitriolic critique of the institution of the church. The clergy is vilified for hypocritically prospering in the praise of Christ's sufferings. Church rites and rituals are 'a fake, a forgery': infant baptism is dismissed as an absurdity since spiritual rebirth demands decision, dedication and suffering, and cannot simply be conferred at birth; Confirmation likewise functions 'as a false guarantee' of acceptance into the faith; the marriage ceremony is a 'Christian comedy'; and the confining of religious observances to weekends and public holidays is denounced as the 'Christianity of the Christmas pudding'.[26] In his ferocious drive to sift the wheat of Christian truth from the chaff of Christendom's institutional life, Kierkegaard concluded that even the buildings and their fitments stood in the way of spiritual illumination. 'We have what might be termed a complete inventory of churches, bells, organs, basins, collecting boxes, altarpieces, hearses, and so forth' but 'the air confined in this lumberroom has developed poison'. The answer is simple: 'Let it collapse, this lumberroom ... And let us again serve God in simplicity, instead of treating him as a fool in magnificent buildings'.[27] This is the position Kierkegaard had reached in July 1855, four months before his death at the age of forty-two, and this is the position that ninety-nine years later, to the month, Larkin systematically reversed in the poem 'Church Going'.

The most striking feature of 'Church Going' is its use of Yeats's big verse paragraph and capacious length (seven stanzas of nine lines apiece) to foreground, not so much the narrator's stream of conscious-ness, with its random flux of sensation, as his ratiocinative process. This *rendering thought visible* tips the poem towards reason rather than belief, philosophy rather than theology. It is noticeable, for example, that the word 'wonder' in such expressions as 'Wondering what to look for; wondering too ...' or 'I wonder who / Will be the last ...' is rather a syn-onym for 'ponder' than a cognate of wondrous, wonderful or wonder-ment, with their Biblical associations.

Nonetheless, the fact that the narrator's tone modulates across the poem's trajectory from flippancy to sonority, from apparent contempt ('the place was not worth stopping for') to apparent acceptance ('It pleases me to stand in silence here'), deceives some into reading the

poem against itself, recuperating it for Christianity. Watson clai
identify 'deeply felt longings for sacred time and sacred s
Parkinson feels that 'The whole tone of the poem expresses d
about the validity of atheism'; Whalen detects 'an oddly religious
in the narrator's 'agnostic humanism'; while Garland struggles ag
the knowledge that these views are false:

> And yet, at the risk of appearing sentimental about the poet w
> I knew to be a non-believer (because he told me so, and he wa
> a man who lied) I cannot help but feel – from myself – not in I
> a few shreds of ambiguity. ... [A] form of surreptitious belief.[28]

As we shall see, 'Church Going' is resolutely secular, setting cogi
Yeats against transcendental Yeats.

As the title punningly declares, the narrator's going to church
firms that the church is going. This is, so to speak, a funeral servic
just *in* but *for* the church. The theme of termination is reinforced i
first line ('there is nothing going on'), continues in a tracery of
and rhymes on the word 'end' ('the holy end', 'Here endeth', 'a
end', 'tending'), and is supplemented by a deal of terminal di
(stopping – stop – loss – gone – last – last – Dispersed – dead).

Nor is there anything mistily ineffable about the enumerative
with which the narrator poses and then gives four-part answers to
damental questions. Pondering the future use of churches, the pos
ities considered are (i) that a few cathedrals be kept on show whi
rest are abandoned to sheep pens or the like; (ii) that they be avoid
unlucky places; (iii) conversely, that they attract the superstitious
come to touch particular stones for luck, to gather herbal cures (
ples') or to spot ghosts; and (iv) that nature be allowed to reclaim t
These four options may be read as alternatives or as evolutionary s
in the church's demise. As for the question of who will be 'the very
visitor to the site, the narrator's speculations are (i) the church-g
equivalent of the 'scholars *manqués*' in 'For Sidney Bechet', writter
lier in the same year; (ii) the collector with an eye for valuable anti
(iii) the 'Christmas addict' in love with church ceremonial; and (iv
representative, // Bored, uninformed' yet ready to acknowledge 'A
ous house on serious earth it is'. Once again, the narrator's tho
process is lucid and systematic.

This is not to deny that the narrator's argument contains contradic
and *aporias*. He regularly protests his ignorance of church rituals
fitments ('some brass and stuff / Up at the holy end', 'Someone w

know: I don't', 'much at a loss', 'wondering what to look for', 'uninformed', 'I've no idea') but knows what the abstruse term 'pyx' refers to
(the receptacle in which is kept the consecrated bread for communion).
Again, he speaks sneeringly of 'the crew' who know about 'rood-lofts', but
his very use of that expression places him among their number. The last
third of the poem begins with the query 'who / Will be the last, the very
last, to seek / This place for what it was'; but not one of the four types he
enumerates, including his own representative, can be said to do that since
none of them visits the church to worship God. If they are not to be read
as weaknesses in Larkin's construction of character, these wobblings may
be taken as evidence of the narrator 'thinking on his feet'. This serves to
soften the relentlessness of the reasoning, making it the product of internal debate and reconsideration. Yet despite these hesitations, enumera-
tions and interrogatives (seven of the poem's eighteen sentences take the
form of questions), the stark truth is that God is entirely absent from the
poem, his death or abscondence so complete as not to merit comment.
The word 'God' only crops up once, in a throwaway colloquialism ('God
knows how long'). The clause 'When churches fall completely out of use'
is 'disarmingly matter of fact' in its acceptance that Christianity is
defunct.[29] The line 'But superstition, like belief, must die' is equally categorical that the miasma of the cultish that lingers round the sites of dead
religions will evaporate in its turn. Whitehead could scarcely be more
wrong in his claim that 'What the speaker senses in the place is the power,
a word often used by St Paul of the Holy Spirit, which cannot die'.[30]

At which juncture the reader may well ask, what is there left for 'awkward reverence'? The poem's closing movement meditates on four overlapping answers, each as comfortless as the next for quasi-Christian
commentators. The first possible object of veneration is the building
itself. Having reflected that 'the place was not worth stopping for', the
narrator honestly admits 'Yet stop I did: in fact I often do'. The irony is
that it is God's absence ('Once I am sure there's nothing going on / I step
inside') that creates the 'unignorable silence' which it pleases the narrator 'to stand in' and which creates the echo-chamber for his mock sermon. What he finds this special silence fit for is thought, not prayer.

A second related answer is the very cruciform plot on which the church
stands, as suggested in the lines 'tending to this cross of ground' and
'gravitating ... to this ground'. However, the narrator's projection of the
church's future to the point where nature reclaims its dilapidated edifice
('Grass, weedy pavement, brambles, buttress, sky, // A shape less recog-
nizable each week') gives a decidedly terminal aspect to these lines. The
church that was raised to the heavens may soon be razed to the ground.

The third answer is more cheering because it is more secular: t
gious belief enabled the church to unite 'what since is found /
separation', the essential phases of the human life cycle. In in
Larkin glossed this crucial passage as follows:

> Of course the poem is about going to church, not religion – I
> suggest this by the title – and the union of the important s
> human life – birth, marriage and death – that going to church
> sents; and my own feeling that when they are dispersed into
> istry office and the crematorium chapel life will become thi
> consequence.

The seventh stanza goes further, suggesting that the church n
unified our lives but granted them a teleology:

> A serious house on serious earth it is,
> In whose blent air all our compulsions meet,
> Are recognized, and robed as destinies.
> And that much never can be obsolete ...
>
> (*CP*, 98)

Resounding lines, but irreligious: for what 'never can be obsolet
human aspiration to have our lives make sense; and in ackno
ing that Christianity furnished such a coherency, the poem ad
archaic language – blent (from Yeats's 'Among School Children'),
connoting that this doctrine's explanatory power is a thing of th

The closing lines of the poem emphasize this interpretation b
ping birth and marriage from the three life stages 'blent' und
roof, the emphasis falling entirely upon death. The fourth rea
reverence is that the church we once attended to be reassured
immortality confronts us with our mortality, not least becaus
mortality. The 'many dead' who 'lie round' give the 'lie' to the a
the concept of rebirth is beyond resurrection; eternity has no futu
'ground' is 'proper to grow wise in' ('in' as in burial) because it co
us with our own imminent annulment. Rather than the metap
absolute of Kierkegaard, then, Larkin presents God as an historic
cept. Kierkegaard castigates the church as an obstruction to the
apprehension of God: for Larkin, the death of God removes an o
tion to proper appreciation of the church's civic virtue. Kierl
attacks the birth, marriage and death services as social rituals

of spiritual significance: Larkin praises them on identical premises, for providing a kind of social cement. Larkin does acknowledge a loss, of course, but not the one Watson identifies ('deeply felt longings for sacred time and sacred space'): for the poem only mourns God's death (and then only by implication) to the extent that He was the church's rationale for bringing baptism, marriage and funeral services into a single frame of meaning.

'Church Going' thus takes its place alongside 'To the Sea' and 'Show Saturday' as a poem that embraces *mauvaise foi*: that is to say, all three celebrate social customs in direct ratio to their metaphysical meaning-lessness, their *inauthenticity*. It might be rejoined that while Kierkegaard's work influenced a succession of Christian existentialists like Jaspers, Barth and Tillich, there is an alternative tradition of atheistical existen-tialists numbering such influential figures as Nietzsche, Sartre and Camus; and that therefore 'Church Going' does not so much reject Existentialism as its theological branch. This is incorrect. Kierkegaard invented most of the key concepts and terms of Existentialism in both its theistical and atheistical guises: existence, freedom, choice, responsibility, authentic-ity, anguish, absurdity; and the pressure to choose whether or not to believe in God is as intense from each side of the existential either/or. It follows that Larkin's liminal position – that God's importance is secular but can only be facilitated through false belief – constitutes an affront to both.

Larkin's rejection of Existentialism's tendency to make choice compul-sory (where is the freedom in that?) led him to meditate on the antino-mial structure of ideology and the coerciveness implicit in all binary thinking. In the process, he moves beyond Existentialism into the philo-sophical territory associated with Structuralism and Poststructuralism, and something will need to be said about both if we are to calibrate the depth of Larkin's thought.

4
Larkin and Philosophy: Poststructuralism

I Larkin and Poststructuralism

Structuralism became highly fashionable in the 1960s and 197C
means of analysing cultural phenomena in accord with the lin
theories Ferdinand de Saussure formulated before the First Worl
In other words, Structuralism may be regarded as a Modernist m
ology dislodged from its proper moment in history. It emphasiz
systemic relationships within a cultural discourse, the abstract
and conventions that governed the production of me;
Structuralist criticism was therefore less interested in interpretin
cultural artefacts mean than in explaining *how* they can mean
they mean. Each signifying element in the discourse was seen as
ing its meaning not from its reference to the world outside but
its relationships of contrast with other elements within the syste
particular, binary opposites (mind/body, good/evil, man/wo
presence/absence, nature/culture, left/right, up/down, on/off, etc.
perceived as fundamental to the way cultural discourses generate
ing. Saussure himself built his argument concerning language a
the distinctions between *langue* and *parole*, signifier and sig
diachronic and synchronic. Another linguist, Roman Jakc
extended this vocabulary to encompass the oppositions betwe
metonymic and metaphoric, or the syntagmatic and paradigmatic
of language. In the realm of narratology, A.J. Greimas proposed th
binary opposites subject/object, sender/receiver and helper/opp
are common to all stories. And in anthropology, Claude Levi-S
sought to analyse different societies through the grid of such
pairs as sacred/profane, myth/history, nature/culture, wild/
raw/cooked and inedible/edible.

Perhaps most spendthrift with binaries, certainly most scintillating, Roland Barthes often piled them up as variant ways of saying the same thing. When springing to the defense of such contemporary French experimentalists as the novelist Alain Robbe-Grillet, he employed the distinction between the avant-garde and the classic Realist text. In *Essais Critiques* he distinguishes between the *écrivain* who is engaged in an exploration of language and the *écrivant* who uses it to write up or write out his or her message. In *S/Z* the contrast is between the *scriptible* (or writerly) and the *lisible* (or readerly) text. The latter term is applied to texts, usually in the Realist tradition, that involve no true participation from the reader other than the consumption of a fixed meaning. A readerly text can be readily understood in terms of already familiar conventions and expectations and is thus reassuringly 'closed'. The writerly text, by contrast, does not have a single 'closed' meaning; instead, it obliges each reader to produce his or her own meanings from its fragmentary or contradictory hints. Ideally, and the concept is very much a theoretical ideal rather than a description, the writerly text is challengingly 'open', giving the reader an active role as co-writer, rather than as passive consumer. The nearest actual equivalents of this ideal would seem to be the more difficult works of Modernism and Postmodernism. Finally, we might remark that in his scattered writings on theatre, Barthes repeatedly makes use of fundamental contrasts: surface versus depth, outside versus inside, lightness versus heaviness, critical distance versus sympathetic identification, mask versus character, sign versus reality, discontinuity versus continuity, emptiness or ambiguity versus fullness of meaning and artificiality versus naturalness.

In *Barthes par Barthes* he looks back on some of the binary oppositions that play such a crucial role in his writing, describing them as 'figures of production'. In a section entitled 'La Machine de l' écriture' ('The Writing Machine'), he speaks of his enthusiasm for these conceptual oppositions: 'like a magician's wand, the concept, especially if it is coupled, *raises* a possibility of writing'. And in a paragraph entitled 'Forgeries' he says 'the opposition is *struck* (like a coin)'.[1] In other words, Barthes find binaries intellectually productive in a way that makes them vital to his writing, and is fully conscious that the antitheses are relational (like the two sides of a coin) and need each other in order to signify. The trouble is that he is always so passionately in favour of one half of the equation and against the other that he often seems to be trying to create a single-sided coin like the one in the Borges short story. Hence, in every one of the twelve binary pairs enumerated in the previous paragraph Barthes sides with the first term against the second – that is, he privileges the avant-garde over

the Realist, the *écrivain* over the *écrivant*, the *scriptible* over the *lisible*
face over depth, mask over character, and so on. It is precisely this o
sion with binary opposites and their hierarchical organization, the
term being regarded as higher or better than the second, that Jac
Derrida sees as characterizing not only Structuralism, but Western
losophy as a whole. His desire to problematize such pairings, with
reductive either/ors, leads him on to that type of Poststructuralist pra
sometimes known as Deconstructionism.

In 1967 Derrida published three major books devoted to the que
of writing: *Of Grammatology*, *Writing and Difference* and *Speech*
Phenomena. In these volumes Derrida gives rigorous attention tc
paradox that the 'Great Books' of the Western tradition are filled
writings that privilege *speech*. By closely analysing these writings De
attempts to uncover the ways in which the Great Books rebel ag
their own stated intention to demonstrate that the spoken is superi
the written. Thus, when Socrates tells Phaedrus that proper teac
must take place orally rather than in writing, he nevertheless en
claiming that the truths of oral communication are '*inscribed in* the
(just as Saussure, making the same point, would describe language
'dictionary in the head').[2] When Plato decides to preserve Socrates'
teachings in written form, he can only maintain his master's disdai
writing by producing a text that denies its own textuality, a pie
philosophical literature that wants its literarity to be overlooked. A
Rousseau, he built an entire Romantic ideology out of the view th
was the intervention of writing that led to the fall of humankin
wrenching us out of myth into history, out of nature into culture
of communal immediacy into an alienated individualism. Yet ever
to Derrida's delight and in direct contravention of his own philoso
cannot resist blurting out his personal preference for the role of au
for making his confessions in print rather than in the confessie
'I would love society like others, if I were not sure of showing mysel
only at a disadvantage, but as completely different from what I am.
part that I have taken of writing and hiding myself is precisely the
that suits me. If I were present, one would never know what I
worth.'[3] In other words, it is the very act of writing that makes
Rousseau, even though he writes against writing!

At one level Derrida is unravelling this contradiction in the Wes
intellectual tradition so as to counter its relentless *logocentrism*
assert that it is through writing that knowledge is transmitted
achieves whatever it can by way of objectivity and truth. Howeve
project is not a question of simply *inverting* the received ord

priorities, so that henceforth writing will somehow take precedence over speech and its associated values. More than this, it involves the dismantling of all those binary distinctions that organize philosophical texts, to the point where opposition itself – the very ground of dialectical reason – gives way to a process where opposites merge in a constant *undecidable* exchange of attributes. Indeed, Derrida has preferred to use the word 'writing' to mean any linguistic act, scripted or oral, that strives to mean what it says while honestly admitting the inherent undecidability of language. That is, 'writing' is language (spoken or written, for the eye or for the ear) with its undecidability exposed. Writing *is* undecidability.

To take one example: in Plato's *Phaedrus*, Socrates approvingly recounts the myth of Thoth offering the invention of writing to the God Ammon as 'a *pharmakon* for meaning and wisdom'.[4] The Greek word *pharmakon*, rather like the English word drug, may be translated as 'poison' or 'remedy', 'toxin' or 'medicine'. In rejecting the invention of writing on the grounds that it will do harm rather than good, Ammon takes this ambiguous, undecidable word and returns it decided: *writing is a poison*. Derrida's point is that every time Plato uses the word *pharmakon* the meaning he wishes to repress returns to haunt his argument opening it up to a diametrically opposed reading. Down the centuries, translators and tidy-minded commentators have felt it necessary to follow Plato, Socrates and Ammon in suppressing one of the two principal meanings of *pharmakon* in order to give speech an easy victory over the poison of writing. Instead of countering Plato's argument, for instance by simply reversing the hierarchy of its binary opposition, Derrida insists on its instabilities, showing how it is inhabited at every turn by an undecidability that it cannot fully master, that every time it denounces writing as a poison it simultaneously (though unintentionally) praises it as a cure. This undecidability is a threat to the traditional foundations of philosophy, robbing us of the comforting sense that we occupy a world governed by decidable categories, by clearly demarcated either/ors, by privileged foundational terms against which subordinated second terms can be measured and found wanting. Derrida's work has been to intensify the disruptive play of the undecidables embedded in language, not out of a desire to create havoc, but out of a horror of dogmatics, totalities, teleologies, immediatist doctrines and absolute truth claims. And in this, I am suggesting, he has affinities with Larkin.

That Larkin is fully alive to the role of binaries in the production of meaning is apparent even from the titles of his poems. A minority

consist of direct or indirect antitheses, as in 'Arrivals, Departures'
'Love Songs in Age' respectively. More commonly, a poem with
egorical title will be matched elsewhere in the *oeuvre* by another
the equally adamantine but opposed meaning, as in the follo
pairings:

Coming	Going
Arrival	Poetry of Departures
Spring	Autumn
Success Story	To Failure
Here	The Importance of Elsewher
First Sight	Long Sight in Age
Dublinesque	Poem about Oxford
The horns of the morning	When the night ...
Aubade	Afternoons
Modesties	Wants
No Road	Bridge for the Living
Morning at Last	How to sleep
Summer Nocturne	Winter Nocturne
I Remember, I Remember	Forget What Did
Days	Night-Music
Mother, Summer, I	Winter
Self's the Man	The Whitsun Weddings
The Winter Palace	Thaw
Nursery Tale	The Old Fools
Continuing to Live	Disintegration
Solar	The moon is full tonight
Born Yesterday	Last Will and Testament
Essential Beauty	Ugly Sister
Strangers	Letter to a Friend ...
The Dance	Sad Steps
Waiting for Breakfast ...	After-Dinner Remarks
I have started to say	Nothing To Be Said
This is the first thing	Compline
Sinking like sediment through the day	Lift through the breaking day
Reference Back	Posterity
At Grass	Cut Grass

Some of these poems were written years apart, others consecutively ('Dublinesque' and 'Poem about Oxford', for instance, or 'The Whitsun Weddings' and 'Self's the Man'). Either way, their titular susceptibility to being double-columned telegraphs a profound engagement with antinomies.

Born in 1922, getting properly underway as a writer in the late 1940s, finding his mature style in the early 1950s, Larkin begins in the knowledge that all Modernist utopias have been implemented and found to be disastrous. Instead of lining themselves up with one side of a binary opposition – utopian versus dystopian, Communist versus Fascist, Christian versus Jew, Victorian terrace versus Modernist towerblock – Larkin's sceptical, undeluded poems are hungry for duality, doubt, paradox and contradiction; in short, for a type of dialectic between the *either* and the *or* that renders them both/and. As the oddly overlooked poem (much nearer to being a credo than has been acknowledged) 'Ignorance' makes clear, for Larkin it is doubt that makes the world go round:

> Strange to know nothing, never to be sure
> Of what is true or right or real,
> But forced to qualify *or so I feel*,
> Or *Well, it does seem so*:
> *Someone must know.*
>
> (*CP*, 107)

The poem confesses the narrator's bewilderment and sense of inadequacy; yet in a century of organized zealotries, frequently murderous, the unassertive assertion of the right to doubt establishes as a principle of human freedom that one should not be convicted for lacking conviction.[5]

As the double-columned titles indicate, at its starkest this living in contradiction involves poems confidently asserting an opinion that is just as confidently reversed in a subsequent work. (Though, indeed, when one looks more closely, the element of reversal is often written – in invisible ink, as it were – between the lines of the original declaration.) If 'Reasons for Attendance' boldly declares a preference for the loneliness of the artistic vocation over the conviviality of social life, 'Vers de Société' comes to the diametrically opposed conclusion. If 'Wants' seems to endorse the Freudian concept of the death wish ('Beneath it all, desire of oblivion runs', *CP*, 42), 'Aubade' begs to differ:

> ... this is what we fear – no sight, no sound,
> No touch or taste or smell, nothing to think with,

> Nothing to love or link with,
> The anaesthetic from which none come round.
>
> (*CP*, 208)

'Places, Loved Ones', categorically announces:

> No, I have never found
> The place where I could say
> *This is my proper ground,*
> *Here I shall stay.*
>
> (*CP*, 99)

But 'Here' contradicts this, the very title alluding to the lines qu
above in order to counter them. And if poems like 'To My V
'Counting', 'Dockery and Son' and 'This Be The Verse' establish L.
as the most committed bachelor in modern letters, the one most
cally opposed to marriage and parenthood, then 'Wedding Wind'
Arundel Tomb' and 'The Whitsun Weddings' make him the
famous celebrant of matrimony in contemporary British poetry.
and again, that which has been decided is reopened by a subseq
poem that decides the issue, just as decisively, on the opposite side

As we shall see, other poems incorporate this dialectic, this ra
alterity, into a single narrative, thereby fracturing the perceiving su
and rendering suspect the concept of a unified consciousness as des
ated by Existentialism. Before moving to an analysis of Larkin's de
structive techniques, however, I want to establish that this susta
undermining of binary oppositions is deliberate and not the produ
procrastination or confusion. The simplest way to do this is to d
ment that the deconstruction of antinomies is not just a part of Lar
literary practice, it is a conscious theme throughout the *oeuvre*.

As early as *Jill* (begun in 1943), the business of unsinewing dualiti
important enough to provide the novel with its climax. In the
pages, the protagonist John Kemp lies in an Oxford University sicl
with bronchial pneumonia. Throughout the story John's working-
inferiority complex and sexual diffidence have been played off aga
the insouciance and bravado afforded his student room-n
Christopher Warner by superior social status. In his delirium, John
templates the failure of his relationship with Jill:

> the fact that in life he had been cheated of her was not the w
> truth. Somewhere, in dreams, perhaps, on some other level, they
> interlocked and he had had his own way as completely as in life

had been denied it. And this dream showed that love died, whether fulfilled or unfulfilled. He grew confused whether she had accepted him or not, since the result was the same: and as this confusion increased, it spread to fulfilment or unfulfilment, which merged and became inseparable. The difference between them vanished. ...

Then if there was no difference between love fulfilled and love unfulfilled, how could there be any difference between any other pair of opposites? Was he not freed, for the rest of his life, from choice?

(J, 242–3)

The power of John's vision is challenged on the last page of the novel by a description of Christopher leaving Oxford for London where his girlfriend Elizabeth will 'become his mistress' (*J*, 247): Kemp's ineffectuality is compensated for by his deconstruction of either/or choices; but it is the blinkered, selfish Warner who gets the girl. The visionary passage nonetheless demonstrates that at the height of the war the twenty-one year old author was resistant to the bullying *Writers Take Sides* mentality and establishes in his first published volume a major preoccupation of all his writings.

Thus, by 1946 the problematizing of dualistic thinking had become the subject of numerous poems. 'Many Famous Feet Have Trod' carries traces of Eliot, Yeats and Auden, but momentarily clarifies into something arresting and unique:

> A silver piece:
> That's life; and, dealing in dichotomies,
> This old discoloured copper coin is death.
> Turn it about: it is impenetrable.
> Reverse and obverse, neither bear
> A sign or word remotely legible:
> But spin the silver to a sphere,
>
> Look in, and testify. Our mortal state
> In turn is twisted in a double warp
>
> (CP, 15–16)

This was written seven years before Crick and Watson presented their model for the DNA molecule comprising two complementary helically coiled chains linked by hydrogen bonds – the famous 'double helix'. Though the poem addresses the human condition ('Our mortal state') rather than, specifically, the genetic code, its claim that life is a 'silver piece' whose 'Reverse and Obverse' faces are completely illegible meaning inhering in the 'double warp' of the spinning coin, antici the formulation of the scientists.

In 1949, this same problematizing of antithetical thinking is in the 'devaluing dichotomies' of the poem 'On Being Twenty a year later in the poem 'If, My Darling's admission that it is 'do yolked with meaning and meaning's rebuttal'; and, a further yea in 'Maturity's pained awareness of 'This pantomime/Of compensa act and counter-act' (*CP*, 62). How to elude the coercive either/c binary opposites is the shared question. It has already been rema that 'To My Wife' considers what might be gained for freedom delaying the moment of choice and commitment. We have observed how other poems explore liminal spaces, as when 'Ch Going' slips between the Scylla and Charybdis of Christianity atheism to propose that religion's secular truth is the paradoxical of its theological falsity. Still other poems examine the extent to wi the act of choice is the possession of the chooser (as with the 'Yc mothers' in 'Afternoons', of whom it is said 'Something is pusl them / To the side of their own lives'). However, to properly pu Larkin's address to this issue we must move from the themes of poems to their mechanics.

II Deconstructive techniques: The four-act structure

In a 1964 interview with Larkin, Ian Hamilton observed that man his poems close with a 'kind of built-in or tagged-on comment on th selves' so that 'the whole poem doubles back on itself' at the minute. 'I hadn't realized I did that sort of thing', Larkin replied, tho he was impressed enough to repeat Hamilton's *aperçu* in a subsequ interview with Neil Powell. (*FR*, 23, 31). What Hamilton had inc pletely grasped, though he came nearer than anyone else, was Lark preference for a four-act structure with closing reversal.

This model was perfected over many years with much trial and er A comparatively early success, 'If, My Darling', uses a stark but effec two-part argument: the first three verses list the conventional trappi of bachelor existence that cry out for wifely intervention (undi plined servants, for instance) and the next five itemize the unwhe some contents of the male mind that, were they to become kno would swiftly deter any such feminine ministrations. 'The March P: 'Places, Loved Ones', 'Reference Back', 'Send No Money' and 'H Windows' adopt a more complex tripartite structure. 'Places, Lo

Ones' provides a particularly clear illustration as each stage in the argument has a single stanza allocated to it: *verse one*, I have never found either the place which or the person who commanded my devotion; *verse two*, but wishing to be swept off one's feet may be a way of absolving oneself of responsibility when things go wrong (I was powerless to resist ...); *verse three*, on the other hand, to have missed out on such an overwhelming experience carries its own potential for self-delusion, the temptation being to hide a sense of failure by pretending to have willed what one merely settled for.

The ruminative richness of this poet so often arraigned for intellectual depthlessness should already be apparent; however, matters reached a new level of complexity in a succession of masterpieces that includes 'Reasons for Attendance', 'Poetry of Departures', Toads', 'Self's the Man', 'Toads Revisited', 'Dockery and Son' and 'Vers de Société'. All of these use a four-act structure with closing reversal in a manner that anticipates by up to fifteen years a central mechanism of Derridean deconstruction (see Figures 4.1, 4.2 and 4.3). Such a practice begins by isolating a particular binary; next establishes that the terms are placed in a violent hierarchy, one being privileged over the other (good over bad, man over woman, white over black, etc.); follows this by reversing the classical opposition; and finally displaces the second term from its new position of superiority, resisting the replacement of one hierarchy with another and effecting a more general displacement of the system. Derrida accepts that binaries are too deeply embedded in the operations of language and mind to be extinguished; instead, he works within the terms of the system so as to breach it. As does Larkin.

Consider 'Self's the Man' (*CP*, 117–18). This takes the husband/bachelor dichotomy and quickly sketches in the socially approved view that wedlock brings maturity: 'Oh, no one can deny / That Arnold is less selfish than I. / He married a woman ...'. The name Arnold invokes everyman: it is, for instance, an anagram of Ronald and near anagram of Donald, and incorporates further names like Dan, Ron, Rod, Aron and Roald (as in Roald Dahl), together with masculinist terms like lad and lord. It may also invoke the Matthew Arnold of that favourite anthology piece 'Dover Beach', a poem which presents monogamous love as the only answer to life's terrors.

The first five stanzas carry on in this vein, presenting Arnold as more responsible than our unmarried protagonist. Already, however, the conventional hierarchy is being undone by the narrator's sneering tone: 'He married a woman to stop her getting away / Now she's there all day'.

LARKIN'S FOUR-ACT STRUCTURE
BINARY OPPOSITION: THE SOCIAL LIFE v. THE ARTISTIC VOCA'

Reasons for Attendance

ACT ONE: THE CONVENTIONAL HIERARCHY	The trumpet's voice, loud and authoritative Draws me a moment to the lighted glass To watch the dancers – all under twenty-fiv Shifting intently, face to flushed face, Solemnly on the beat of happiness.
The narrator envies the conviviality of the group.	– Or so I fancy, sensing the smoke and swea The wonderful feel of girls. Why be out her
ACT TWO: THE REVERSAL OF THE CONVENTIONAL HIERARCHY	But then, why be in there? Sex, yes, but wh Is sex? Surely, to think the lion's share Of happiness is found by couples – sheer
The narrator asserts the values of the individual against those of the group.	Inaccuracy, as far as I'm concerned. What calls me is that lifted, rough-tongued (Art, if you like) whose individual sound Insists I too am individual. It speaks; I hear; others may hear as well,
ACT THREE: EQUILIBRIUM BETWEEN BINARY OPPOSITES	But not for me, nor I for them; and so With happiness. Therefore I stay outside, Believing this; and they maul to and fro, Believing that; and both are satisfied,
The values of individual and group are equal relative to the point of view.	
ACT FOUR: DEFLATION OF BINARY OPPOSITES	If no one has misjudged himself. Or lied.
But they are also equal in their potential for deceit and self-deceit.	

Figure 4.1

LARKIN'S FOUR-ACT STRUCTURE
BINARY OPPOSITION: BACHELOR v. HUSBAND

Self's the Man

ACT ONE: THE CONVENTIONAL HIERARCHY Arnold is less selfish than I and is therefore my moral superior.	Oh, no one can deny That Arnold is less selfish than I. He married a woman to stop her getting away Now she's there all day, And the money he gets for wasting his life on work She takes as her perk To pay for the kiddies' clobber and the drier And the electric fire, And when he finishes supper Planning to have a read at the evening paper It's *Put a screw in this wall* – He has no time at all, With the nippers to wheel round the houses And the hall to paint in his old trousers And that letter to her mother Saying *Won't you come for the summer.* To compare his life and mine Makes me feel a swine: Oh, no one can deny That Arnold is less selfish than I.
ACT TWO: EQUILIBRIUM BETWEEN BINARY OPPOSITES We are equally selfish and therefore moral equals.	But wait, not so fast: Is there such a contrast? He was out for his own ends Not just pleasing his friends; And if it was such a mistake He still did it for his own sake, Playing his own game. So he and I are the same,
ACT THREE: REVERSAL OF THE CONVENTIONAL HIERARCHY I am more self-aware and therefore his moral superior.	Only I'm a better hand At knowing what I can stand Without them sending a van –
ACT FOUR: DEFLATION OF THE BINARY OPPOSITION Or perhaps I am just better at deceiving myself.	Or I suppose I can.

Figure 4.2

LARKIN'S FOUR-ACT STRUCTURE
BINARY OPPOSITION: EMPLOYMENT v. UNEMPLOYMENT

Toads

ACT ONE:
Why cant I give up
the 'toad' work?
	Why should I let the toad *work*
	  Squat on my life?
	Can't I use my wit as a pitchfork
	And drive the brute off?
	
	Six days of the week it soils
	  With its sickening poison –
	Just for paying a few bills!
	  That's out of proportion.

ACT TWO:
Lots of people do.
	Lots of folk live on their wits:
	  Lecturers, lispers,
	Losels, loblolly-men, louts –
	  They don't end as paupers;
	
	Lots of folk live up lanes
	  With fires in a bucket,
	Eat windfalls and tinned sardines –
	  They seem to like it.
	
	Their nippers have got bare feet,
	  Their unspeakable wives
	Are skinny as whippets - and yet
	  No one actually *starves*.

ACT THREE:
But I am too
toad-like to
risk it.
	Ah, were I courageous enough
	  To shout *Stuff your pension!*
	But I know, all too well, that's the st
	  That dreams are made on:
	
	For something sufficiently toad-like
	  Squats in me, too;
	Its hunkers are heavy as hard luck,
	  And cold as snow,
	
	And will never allow me to blarney
	  My way to getting
	The fame and the girl and the money
	  All at one sitting.

ACT FOUR:
Employment and
unemployment have
their attractions. Perhaps
doing one while
fantasizing about the
other is a way of having
both.
	I don't say, one bodies the other
	  One's spiritual truth;
	But I do say it's hard to lose either,
	  When you have both.

Figure 4.3

This prepares the ground for the challenge mounted in stanzas six and seven which propose that, although Arnold and the narrator chose differently, each chose what he wanted and so are equally selfish. From this position of equality the narrator, in stage three of the deconstructive process, reverses the classical hierarchy by explicitly asserting the superiority of his own position ('I'm a better hand / At knowing what I can stand'). Just when victory seems assured, with the complete reversal of the original proposition (married men are morally superior to unmarried), the poem delivers its punch line:

> Only I'm a better hand
> At knowing what I can stand
> Without them sending a van –
> Or I suppose I can.

In a last-minute twist of the sort Hamilton was first to identify, the narrator admits that his superiority may be utterly self-deluding. The reversed hierarchy is itself undone and the reader invited to contemplate the violence of all such either/or choices.

As Alan Bennett spotted, the plot of 'Self's the Man' is not dissimilar to that of the highly successful sitcom, *The Likely Lads*, which appeared eight years after the poem was written.[6] Set in Newcastle, the television show revolved around the contrast between the free-spirited Terry (played by James Bolam) and the domesticated, hen-pecked Bob (Rodney Bewes). Terry would present his bachelor existence as promiscuous and adventurous while Bob would counter that his pal was a stalled adolescent. As in the poem, the viewer was left to surmise that the pair were equally unsatisfied sexually: Terry because his notion of freedom ultimately entails eluding rather than embracing female blandishments; Bob because his aspiring wife Thelma is the sort to measure out sexual favours on a reward and punishment basis.

'Self's the Man' uses innuendo to establish this same theme of sexual frustration. The line 'He was out for his own ends' hints that Arnold got married for sex, as in the slang expression 'to get one's end away'. The presence of 'nippers' confirms that intercourse took place at least on a few occasions; but now his wife would sooner he practices DIY than love-making – It's *Put a screw in this wall'*, rather than 'screw' her. The nippers add to the problem, of course, the 'pram in the hall' marking not just the end of art, as Larkin's idol Cyril Connolly proclaimed, but also the end of sex (children as nature's contraceptive!).[7]

But the hints of masturbation in the hand/erection motif of the last stanza suggest that the narrator's sex life is no more enviable. The true purport of the poem, as of *The Likely Lads*, is the difficulty of sustaining sexual gratification in a libidinal economy structured around the husband/bachelor binary. The effect in both cases is to intensify audience consciousness of the need for subject positions outside this constrictive binary.

III   Deconstructive techniques: The interpellation of the other

In his groundbreaking study *The Movement* (1980), Blake Morrison acknowledges the skill with which Larkin included hesitations, reversals and qualifications as a means to dramatize the narrator's 'puzzling process'.[8] Although the other Movement poets employed the same devices, none could match the Larkin of, say, 'Dockery and Son' –

> Dockery, now:
> Only nineteen, he must have taken stock
> Of what he wanted, and been capable
> Of ... No, that's not the difference, rather, how ...
> (*CP*, 152–3)

or 'Vers de Société':

> Are, then, these routines
>
> Playing at goodness, like going to church?
> Something that bores us, something we don't do well
> (Asking that ass about his fool research)
> But try to feel, because, however crudely,
> It shows us what should be?
> Too subtle, that. Too decent, too. Oh, hell ...
> (*CP*, 181)

Despite the generosity and inclusiveness of this stream of ratiocination, underlined by Larkin's characteristic slippage between first person singular and first person plural cases, Morrison feels that the technique can be excluding:

Larkin's poetry minimizes the interpretative process by including it within the text: what is inferred by the reader is limited by what has already been inferred by the speaker, whose own struggle to 'discover meaning' is what the poem dramatizes. The reader is 'helped' (he cannot be confused as to what the poem means), but he is also restricted (the only meaning he takes away from the poem is the one found for him by the speaker).[9]

Eight years later reviewing the *Collected Poems*, Greer complained that 'despite Larkin's virtuoso manipulation of tone and colloquial ellipsis, the reader is seldom allowed any role other than complicity in what is being confided'.[10] This may also be what Bennett means when he complains that Larkin can be 'bullying'.[11]

My own view is that even Larkin's most assertive narrators generate alterity rather than consensus. One way they do this, unremarked by Morrison, Greer or Bennett, is by summoning up 'the antiphonal voice of the heckler' (in Geoffrey Hill's marvellous phrase). That is to say, Larkin's penchant for writing poems in opposed pairs, in a kind of dissensual call and response, also makes itself felt in single works through an interpellation of the 'other' into the narrator's shoes. One index of this is the way Larkin's poems have been 'answered' in poems by other hands. In his contribution to *Larkin at Sixty*, Robert Conquest claims to have entertained his pal across the years with a succession of verse *ripostes*:

> He has long since become used to condensations of or commentaries on his poems in limerick form. I can't remember the one on 'Dockery and Son' – I'm not even sure it was in limerick form – but at any rate it was a four- or five-line verse giving Dockery's reply, to the effect that he had no intention of being 'added to', but was merely the victim of a faulty contraceptive.[12]

However facetious, Conquest's limericks acknowledge the way Larkin's poems invite as part of their purport the opposing of the narrator's viewpoint. At a higher level of intensity, so do those poems of Maurice Rutherford that stand in a one-to-one correspondence with Larkin pieces. 'Mr Larkin' ('This was Mr Larkin's bike') subjects our poet to the Bleaney treatment. Similarly, 'This Be The Curse' reverses the relational logic of 'This Be The Verse':

> I fucked them up, my Mum and Dad;
> I didn't mean to, but I did
> by cropping up late, when they'd had
> their seventh and, they'd thought, last kid.[13]

This is not just good poetry, it is good criticism – the best there is re
ing Larkin's narrative antiphonics. One could well imagine Ruthe
rewriting 'Self's the Man' from Arnold's point of view, thereby con
ing the poem's deconstructive project.

But there is more. For when Greer accuses Larkin of sexis
Rossen observes, in the middle of her analysis of 'Self's the Man',
'women tend to play a role in his writing which finds him no
from misogyny', they are overlooking the fact that by the end o
poem's four acts both binary positions (bachelor/husband) have
undermined and a space created for female responses.[14] Indeed
exaggerated Music Hall tones of the poem summon a distaff rejoi
perhaps along the following lines:

> Oh, no-one can deny
> That Vera is less selfish than I.
> She married a man to stop him getting away
> Now he's there all day,
>
> And while she wheels the kids round the houses
> He blows his screw on the horses,
> Consoling himself down the pub
> While she serves the nippers grub ...

What we have, then, is a poem that not only includes binary pola
but is shadowed by their gender opposites (single man: married
single woman: married woman). Nor is the poem heterosexist in it
sumptions, for it is possible (though not obligatory) to read the r
tor's distaste for marriage and parenthood as informed by homos
feeling (and, therefore, the shadow text as informed by a lesbian
spective). Far from being exclusive, the poem is remarkably inclu
occupying and abnegating a multiplicity of subject positions in a
ner that suggests equivocity rather than hierarchy. What other poe
match Larkin's silent summoning of the narrator's ideological c
nents into the centre of the narrative? Eliot's Jew (in early collect
'jew'), Lorca's *Guardia Civil* and Plath's Daddy receive no such invit
to descant on the narrator's prejudices.[15]

In *S/Z* (1970), Barthes proposed that the 'I' which reads is 'al
itself a plurality of other texts' and is allowed by *avant-garde* liter
(less so classic Realism) the maximum liberty to produce meanin
putting what is read in touch with this plurality.[16] This is what L
was doing by the 1950s. The multiplicity of roles subsumed in 'Self

Man' may be regarded as mutually exclusive (bachelor or husband, homosexual or heterosexual, spinster or wife, etc.) and as offering different points of entry to the poem for readers of these separate modalities. However, if it is permissible to suggest that Arnold is not a different person from the narrator but his alter ego, that part of himself tempted by the marriage option, then all those subsidiary subject positions incorporated in the poem are facets of the one identity. Granted this, it follows that the narrator's multi-facetedness speaks to the multiplicity within every reader, liberating each one of us from the oppressive fiction that subjectivity is a coherent definitional field rather than a site of overlapping, contradictory and conflicting forces. Even such an apparently lightweight poem offers a profound ontological challenge to dominant labelling philosophies. By its close, it is possible to argue that 'Self's the Man' might more appropriately be titled 'Self's the Men' or, better still, 'Selves are the Man'.

IV   Deconstructive techniques: Ellipsis

In *Lives of the Poets*, Michael Schmidt pays Patricia Beer an exquisite compliment: 'What she doesn't say and how she doesn't say it are a vivid lesson in an age when from so many sleeves hung psychotic hearts'.[17] No modern British writer, not even Beer, surpasses Larkin's skill at omission. Literary ellipsis can be permanent or temporary: in many detective novels the plot relies on marked gaps (*whodunnit?*) being sustained for the duration of the story only to be filled in at the *denouement*. In a different sense, the reception theorists Ingarden and Iser have drawn attention to those indeterminacies of the literary text which it is the job of the reader to flesh out in order that the narrative be fully concretized. Larkin's ellipses resist concretization, the poem's purport relying upon such omissions and therefore being thwarted by forced readings. While Larkin's gaps encourage free play, generating a limited plurality of interpretative options, they do not validate a critical practice which fills them in and denies their existence. Yet this has been the defining methodology of the late millennial bowdlerism blighting Larkin studies.

The poem 'Counting' is a mere eleven lines long, thirty-seven of its forty-seven words being monosyllabic, the diction and grammar such as a primary school child might comprehend. But not the G.M. Lecturer in English at Hertford College, Oxford. Faced with this –

> Thinking in terms of one
> Is easily done –

> One room, one bed, one chair,
> One person there ...
>
> But counting up to two
> Is harder to do
>
> (*CP*, 108)

– Tom Paulin declares: 'One is ace and masculine, two is trouble and female'; adding, for good measure, Larkin's 'poems are often sceptical assertions of male autonomy' and 'one of his deepest prejudices was against women'.[18] As a glance at his own poems will verify, words are not Paulin's strong suit; but there is a serious cognitive problem here, a real misunderstanding of the English language. When he scans the lines above, what he reads is

> Thinking in terms of one
> Is easily done –
> One room, one bed, one chair,
> One *man* there ...
>
> But adding a *woman* too
> Is harder to do

In order to accuse the poem of sexism, Paulin has first had to sex it; the piece itself, like the majority of Larkin's poems, is resolutely non-gender-specific, as applicable to women as to men.[19]

As already remarked with regard to 'The Whitsun Weddings', Larkin's attitude to social class is subjected to a similar critical violence. Consider for a moment a squib Larkin included in private correspondence but never bothered to finish, let alone publish:

> I want to see them starving,
>   The so-called working class,
> Their wages weekly halving,
>   Their women stewing grass,
>
> When I drive out each morning
>   In one of my new suits
> I want to find them fawning
>   To clean my car and boots.
>
> (*SL*, 541–2)

The spirit in which the piece was written might be guessed by the fact
that the letter to Conquest (then resident in the United States) of which
it was a part signs off, 'I'll let you know when to start sending food
parcels'. Nonetheless, the normally judicious Bennett claims 'Larkin was
sincere; he was being really himself'. He concludes, 'The man who
penned that might have been pleased to come up with the slogan of
the 1968 Smethwick by-election: "If you want a nigger neighbour, Vote
Labour"'.[20] Elsewhere Carey tuts, 'Those stanzas do not appear in the
Collected Poems, and most of Larkin's admirers would be glad to forget
them'.[21] What Bennett and Carey are effacing is the effect of the poem's
most glaring ellipse: the title. Both unconsciously plug the gap with
some such interpolation as 'The Political Testimony of Philip Larkin' –
though even then the idea that Larkin, so readily moved to tears by any
form of cruelty, genuinely wanted to see the working class starving is an
absurdity. But look what happens if we substitute a different heading:
'The Ballad of the Fascist Bastard', perhaps, or 'Colonel Blimp's Epitaph';
the poem instantly switches political allegiance, becoming a prime candidate for an anthology of socialist satires.[22] Even this supposedly
deplorable right-wing doggerel is, on closer inspection, 'double-yolked
with meaning and meaning's rebuttal'; unriddling, rather than endorsing, the Left–Right political dichotomy.

The foregoing examples demonstrate that Larkin's bowdlers convert
him from a poet of doubt to a poet of certitude, even to the point of bigotry, not by censoring his words but deleting his deletions. The same
applies to questions of geographical location and identity, as we shall
see in the next chapter where Larkin's putative English nationalism will
be found a comparable critical contrivance. For the moment, it is sufficient to observe that Larkin's drafting process typically entailed deleting
site-specific references from his poems in the interests of widening reader
identification: the word 'England' was erased from 'Church Going' and
'The Whitsun Weddings' at manuscript stage, and the phrase 'this north-
eastern port' written out of 'Letter to a Friend about Girls'. 'Livings' I renders such deletions visible in the following manner –

> Every third month I book myself in at
> The——Hotel in——ton for three days.
> The boots carries my lean old leather case
> Up to a single, where I hang my hat.
> One beer, and then 'the dinner', at which I read
> The——*shire Times* from soup to stewed pears.
>
> (*CP*, 186)

– Larkin sounding the erasures when he recorded the poem by fill
the blanks with 'blank' (intoning 'The Blank Hotel in Blankton', e

Larkin distinguished his verse practice from that of Robert C
with the remark 'his poem couldn't possibly refer to anyone but
whereas the point of mine is that it applies to everyone' (*SL*,
Deleting local names and map references was one means for eff
this universalization. That ellipsis had for Larkin a related bu
founder, almost eschatological, significance may be suggested by a
consideration of 'The Building'. The opening lines depict with grea
cision Hull's multi-storey hospital:

> Higher than the handsomest hotel
> The lucent comb shows up for miles, but see,
> All round it close-ribbed streets rise and fall
> Like a great sigh out of the last century.
> The porters are scruffy; what keep drawing up
> At the entrance are not taxis; and in the hall
> As well as creepers hangs a frightening smell.
>
> (*CP*, 191)

Hull is not named, nor the Royal Infirmary, nor its position at the
junction of Derringham Street and Anlaby Road, nor even the
hospital – and this despite the sixty-four lines detailing the ir
tion's activities. This series of erasures or voidances enacts the p
true subject, that great unspeakable annulment hospitals ex
defer:

> All know they are going to die.
> Not yet, perhaps not here, but in the end,
> And somewhere like this. That is what it means,
> This clean-sliced cliff; a struggle to transcend
> The thought of dying ...
>
> (*CP*, 192–3)

What began as a description of one hospital becomes a disquisitio
the symbolic meaning of all hospitals, for Larkin less a scene o
and recuperation than the anteroom to the charnel house. Close o
vation of Hull Royal Infirmary provides the necessary detail, bu
erasure of the name and place universalizes the building so that
it signifies is evident to readers everywhere. More chillingly, the
tions holing the text bespeak what 'Ambulances' calls 'the so

emptiness / That lies just under all we do' (*CP*, 132). This is ellipsis as an irruption of oblivion's soonness into the nowness of life.

V Deconstructive techniques: The disaggregation of regular forms

The theme of 'Self's the Man' is enacted in its structure. This is somewhat unconventional in its combination of rhyming couplets and the quatrain stanza (aabb // ccdd // eeff) rather than either the two-line unit (aa // bb // cc // dd) or the alternately rhymed quatrain (abab // cdcd // efef). Much more disruptive is the application of couplets to lines of highly variable lengths so that rhymes arrive unexpectedly, throwing the rhythm off balance. The poem consists of five lines of five syllables apiece, six lines of six syllables, eight lines of seven syllables, four lines of eight syllables, three lines of nine syllables, two lines of ten syllables, no eleven-syllable lines, one line of twelve syllables and three thirteen-syllable lines. Of the sixteen couplets making up the poem, only three involve equalized lines, the overwhelming majority yoking unlikes together in unions that are full of strain. Indeed, in the second couplet of stanza one and the first of stanza two, the shortest line length (five syllables) is paired with the longest (thirteen), one partner being nearly three times the size of its mate. If in a poem about marriage the couplet symbolizes coupledom, the predominance of irregular pairings suggests endless variation within the marital union with 'normal' couples in the minority. This is not an untypical example of the external architecture of a Larkin poem expressing its internal truth, in this case that one of the ways in which the married/not married binary is false is that marriage is not a unitary condition but a single word applied to a multiplicity of modalities.

Even poems that at first glance appear highly regular are found on closer inspection to be anything but. 'Here' consists of four big verse paragraphs in the style of Yeats. However, less than half of the poem's thirty-two lines are pentametric, the majority veering irregularly between nine and twelve syllables; and the eight-line stanzas alternate in a species of structural schizophrenia between two different rhyme schemes, verses one and three adhering to an ababcddc pattern whereas stanzas two and four are rhymed abbacdcd.

A more frequent disaggregative procedure in Larkin's *corpus* is that considered in Chapter One in relation to 'For Sidney Bechet': namely, the adoption of a rhyme scheme disproportionate to the stanza length, so that the last verse fails to complete the rhyming pattern and has therefore to

be supplemented with a one or two line coda. This model will be exp
at greater length in Chapter Five with particular reference to 'I Remen
I Remember'. For the present it is sufficient to record that while L
uses poetry as a discourse for deconstructing all other discourses, he
so in a manner that subjects it to the same destabilizing strategie:
Larkin, form is content and the disaggregation of form a deconstru
practice.

VI Deconstructive techniques: The split simile

One of Larkin's favourite devices for heightening the reader's awar
of the fact that words are what we see, as well as what we see thrc
was what I shall call the split simile. The word simile is Latin for l
Literary tradition holds that an effective simile involves a compa
that is surprising, so that the original subject is defamiliarized b
connection; but a comparison that, however unlikely, *is* finally 'lik
Dr Johnson's pithy formulation: 'A simile may be compared to
converging at a point, and is more excellent as the lines approach
a greater distance.'[25]

Larkin experimented throughout his career with similes that a
similitude so that the trope deconstructs, its hidden wiring exp
to view. In the 1940s he tried the technological metaphors o:
pylon poets, imaging 'flowers like periscopes' (*CP*, 260) and rela
how an 'evening like a derelict lorry is alone and mute' (*CP*, :
After escaping the MacSpaunday influence he continued to use
to conjoin elements so disjunct that the word calls attention t
own failure, separating more than it binds. The poem 'None o
Books Have Time' follows its ungrammatical title with the equally
concerting assertion: 'Selflessness is like waiting in a hospital /
badly-fitting suit on a cold wet morning' (*CP*, 124). But is it? The
ile at the end of 'The Whitsun Weddings' has elicited a bewilde
array of mutually exclusive interpretations, including the specula
that it invokes Weetabix crammed in a carton: 'I thought of Lor
spread out in the sun, / Its postal districts packed like square
wheat' (*CP*, 116).[26]

Carol Ann Duffy's favourite Larkin poem, 'Money', ends with this
lucinatory verse:[27]

> I listen to money singing. It's like looking down
>   From long french windows at a provincial town,

> The slums, the canal, the churches ornate and mad
> In the evening sun. It is intensely sad.
>
> > (*CP*, 198)

To claim to be able to *hear* money is peculiar enough; to add that the category of noise it emits is that of song is stranger still; to equate this sound with sight adds a touch of synaesthesia to the confusion; while the comparison of the presumably joyous or seductive music with so dismally surreal an urban view is utterly perplexing. Though not quite as estranged as the simile in the third line of 'The Love Song of J. Alfred Prufrock' –

> Let us go then, you and I,
> When the evening is spread out against the sky
> Like a patient etherized upon a table[28]

– this is a trope worthy of early Eliot or his master, Laforgue.

VII Deconstructive techniques: The oxymoron

The writer Adeline Yen Mah, who knew Larkin in the 1960s, has remarked his fascination with the ubiquity of antonymic pairings in the Chinese language. This has arisen because although Chinese has a comparatively limited vocabulary (approximately 50,000 characters as against the 600,000 words in English), the pronunciational base is disproportionately small. As a result, characters with entirely different orthographies and meanings have similar or identical pronunciations. To avoid confusion, 'Chinese has evolved into a bisyllabic language' with 'over 80 per cent of the terms in everyday speech' consisting of 'two or more characters. Bisyllabism has been achieved by adding a second word to clarify or classify the first word'.[29] Whereas 'two words with opposite meanings are seldom placed together side by side in English', Yen Mah writes, 'we Chinese frequently use antonyms to represent a concept'. Hence, the compound *advance/retreat* means movement; *success/failure* means outcome; *big/small* means size; *buy/sell* means business; and *black/white* means morality. She concludes:

> We Chinese do not think of antonyms as irreconcilable contradictions but as interdependent complementary forces or two faces of the same coin: Placing them next to each other enables us to view a particular phenomenon from opposite standpoints while contemplating the entire concept.[30]

Larkin was no doubt compelled by Yen Mah's account of this ling
figure because it bore some relation to his use of the neglected
of *oxymoron*. Deriving from the Greek *oxy* (sharp) and *moros* (
oxymoron (literally, pointedly foolish) is a figure of speech conta
a direct contradiction in terms, a compressed paradox, as in the
'bittersweet' or the phrase 'living death'. In everyday utterance
figures are usually accidental and treated as solecisms. However, |
licence permits its use for special effects. It was particularly po
in the sixteenth and seventeenth centuries with Wyatt, Shakes
('O heavy lightness'), Milton ('darkness visible'), Donne ('O beg
riches!') and Crashaw using it extensively. There are some fai
nineteenth-century examples, as in Tennyson's 'And faith unfai
kept him falsely true', but for the most part oxymoron has slipped
the modern poet's armoury. Its most visible presence today is in i
form, satirical websites listing the supposed oxymorons of institut
bodies – 'government helpline', 'tax concessions', etc.

The nearest equivalents in English literature to the verb/
noun/noun, adjective/adjective pairings enumerated by Yen Mah are
ants on standard adjective/noun and adverb/verb grammatical i
though whereas such pairs are usually based on complementarity
poetic device of oxymoron twists them towards the antonymic pole. S
of Larkin's duos are so skewed to non-complementarity that they moi
tarily defy understanding: 'restless silence', 'peopled air', 'squealing |
'musical brocade', 'untidy air', 'Reprehensibly perfect', 'Unresting de
'Stationary voyage', 'Extinction's alp' and, more convolutedly, 'inno(
guilty-innocent'. Sometimes these violent antinomies suffuse surroun
passages with a spirit of contrariety: the startling 'happy funeral' of
Whitsun Weddings' leads on to a 'religious wounding' and the remark
swell/fall conjunction of the poem's close ('there swelled / A sens
falling') with all its implications of life and death, tumescence
detumescence (*CP*, 116). What distinguishes Larkin's use of oxymora f
that of his illustrious predecessors is this sense that for him they are I
device of embellishment than the expression of an entire deconstruc
sensibility.

VIII   Deconstructive techniques: Negative qualifiers

For half a century critics have recycled, like the uncollected bag;
on an airport carousel, the stereotype of Larkin as the High Pries
Miserabilism. Detractors like Scupham (for whom Larkin is

melancholic mouse-trap maker of Hull'),[31] Newton, Rosenthal, Appleyard, Eagleton, Stevenson and Duncan are able to claim that any positives in Larkin's verse are drained of life by a swarm of qualifiers: but, yet, if, as if, but if, only, whether, unless, although, almost, just, rather, hardly and perhaps. Equally numerous, they may add, are negative prefixes and suffixes: *dis-* (disbelief, disapproved, disused, dismantled, displaced, disappointing); *in-* (incomplete, inexplicable); *im-* (imprecise, imperfect); and *-less* (scentless, weightless, natureless, birdless). What subtler minds like Ricks, Thwaite, Longley and Watt have remarked is that the combination of a positive with a negative qualifier is not the same as an unqualified negative and actually serves to collapse the false extremes of nihilism and idealization, allowing Larkin to explore in almost Jamesian detail infinitely subtle gradations of meaning and emotion.[32]

Limiting ourselves for the sake of brevity to vocables prefixed with *un-*, we can quickly discover examples that are indisputably negative in meaning: unworkable, unswept, unanswerable, uniformed, unsatisfactory, unrecommended, untruthful and untruth. However, just as numerous are cases of *what might have been* in which the negativity may be attributed to free will rather than to deterministic forces and may therefore have been otherwise: 'my childhood was unspent': 'Unchilded and unwifed'; 'the unraised hand calm, / The apple unbitten in the palm'; 'love unused, in unsaid words'; 'unshared friends and unwalked ways'. Other such usages shade towards the positive end of the emotional spectrum, describing conditions of tranquillity: undisturbed, undriven, unhurried, unforced, untried, untroubled, untalkative, unriven, 'the soul unjostled, / The pocket unpicked'. Yet more positive are those words that express energy (unresting) or freedom (unbarred, unfenced, unhindered) or opportunity (potential is 'unlimited'). Outright positives include: unfakable, unlosable, unspoilt, undiminished, unfingermarked, unmolesting; expressions such as 'set unchangeably in order', 'blindingly undiminished' and 'unvariably lovely there' increasing their powers of affirmation by incorporating (so as to negate) a hint of the negative. When one remembers that R.J.C. Watt's invaluable *Concordance to the Poetry of Philip Larkin* lists approximately one hundred and fifty different *un-* words (and nearly fifty with the suffix *-less*), this taxonomy can be seen to be crude – though its very roughness may serve to counter the preposterous view of Larkin's diction as unvaryingly desolated and desolating. He gets a broader emotional range out of negatively prefixed words than do most poets from the open dictionary.

IX   Deconstructive techniques: Paronomasia

Larkin's puns have attracted occasional comment without anyone remarking that they are systemic in his practice because intrinsic to his view of language. Moreover, his word play is rarely euphemistic: the notorious opening of 'This Be the Verse' ('They fuck you up, your mum and dad') has a double meaning, that parents psychologically damage their offspring and that they copulate their children into existence, both of which are totally explicit. These are not puns as instances of *innuendo* or *double entendre*, expressions whose dual interpretations are hierarchically arranged, the primary polite meaning masking a secondary indecent one which is thereby reduced to a hint. These are puns as verbal nitroglycerine, unstable compounds so packed with contradiction that they might explode at a moment's notice exposing the binary structure of language.

This point can be secured by examining a representative example. It has already been remarked that Larkin is at once the most committed bachelor in modern letters and the most famous celebrant of marriage. Selecting and sequencing his poems in an appropriate manner we can construct a narrative that choreographs all the principal stations in the marriage progress: sexual attraction ('Lines on a Young Lady's Photograph Album'), marriage ('Maiden Name'), the young family ('Afternoons'), a long-established relationship ('Talking in Bed'), the death of one of the partners ('Love Songs in Age') and the burial of both ('An Arundel Tomb'). Like the individual novels of Galsworthy's *Forsyte Saga*, these poems can be read as encapsulating in the family unit the cycle of human life, one generation replacing another, all passing through the same stages – youthful optimism, middle-aged compromise and the prospect of death.

Thus, the 'Young mothers' of 'Afternoons' combine an image of maternal fulfillment with the disquieting sense that already

> Their beauty has thickened.
> Something is pushing them
> To the side of their own lives.
>
> (*CP*, 121)

There may be some small consolation in knowing that a new generation of courting couples arises ('the lovers are all in school') and that, younger still, the toddlers they set 'free' in 'The new recreation ground' are hunting for 'acorns' (symbolizing that their turn will come to grow into oak trees). We might also concur with Lolette Kuby that Larkin 'at once side-steps special pleading and endows the plight of the women with more rather than less poignancy by showing it to be an intensification of the plight of everyone'.[33]

Yet at the poem's heart (literally, its middle lines) there is a terrifying pun that rips across the generalized sense of pathos making it seem complacent:

> ... the albums, lettered
> *Our Wedding*, lying
> Near the television

The wedding albums that emblematize all that these young women have to set against 'the wind' that 'Is ruining their courting-places' are a deceit. How can this be, when 'Lines on a Young Lady's Photograph Album' seems to believe that the camera does not lie, that what it depicts is 'In every sense empirically true'? The answer comes in another of Larkin's poems about photography, 'Whatever Happened?'

> 'Perspective brings significance', we say,
> Unhooding our photometers, and, snap!
> What can't be printed can be thrown away
>   (*CP*, 74)

The individual image may not falsify, but the process of picture selection does. How many family albums impartially document rows, sexual frustration, despair, divorce? Those are the photographs we do not take or else suppress so as to compile the consoling pictorial fiction that the wedding ceremony we put our trust in has yielded the promised happy ever after.

The full force of Larkin's problematizing of this Romantic ideology is only felt when we add that the other five 'love' poems enumerated above employ the same devastating pun.[34] In 'Lines on a Young Lady's Photograph Album' the female addressee is told that by rendering permanent her youthful beauty her picture collection deceives:

> ... you lie
> Unvariably lovely there,
> Smaller and clearer as the years go by.
>   (*CP*, 72)

In 'Maiden Name' the bride's replacement of her father's surname
that of her husband is presented as a species of mendacity:

> you cannot be
> Semantically the same as that young beauty:
> It was of her that these two words were used.
>
> Now it's a phrase applicable to no one,
> Lying just where you left it
>
> (*CP*, 101)

'Talking in Bed' is even more shocking in that the pun in the se
line, though reversed in the third, traces the theme of deception t
site of conjugal relations: 'Talking in bed ought to be easiest, /]
together there goes back so far' (*CP*, 129).

In 'Love Songs in Age' a widow shedding possessions on movin;
smaller residence decides to keep the love songs of her youth ('they
so little space'). The poem's message, that the romantic love peddl
the songs, which promised to bring so much happiness, 'had not
so then, and could not now', is foreshadowed at the start: 'The c
pleased her: / One bleached from lying in a sunny place' (*CP*,
Finally, 'An Arundel Tomb' posits that the handholding of the ear
countess sculpted in effigy was simply

> A sculptor's sweet commissioned grace
> Thrown off in helping to prolong
> The Latin names around the base.
>
> (*CP*, 110)

Twentieth-century eyes, unable to read the Latin and blind to the
ues of that armorial age, misread the gesture as expressive of a cor
of love that is a modern invention. It is in this sense that 'Tim
transfigured them into / Untruth' (*CP*, 111), the innocuous state
that 'The earl and countess lie in stone' (repeated as 'They would
think to lie so long') simultaneously conveying a drastically opp
meaning.

This single pun, successively applied to courtship, wedlock, wi
hood and burial, allows Larkin to combine in the same breath an
mation of marital love with the accusation that it is a mons
confidence trick. These meanings being irreconcilable, the pun';
guistic instability exposes the rhetorical violence of society's attem

reduce desire to an either/or choice – to wed or not to wed – with the usual coercive privileging of the first term in the binary. Larkin's puns, like his split similes, oxymora and negative qualifiers are not symptoms of authorial malaise, they are literary embodiments of a profoundly anti-foundational practice.

X Conclusion

We began Chapter Three with the critical consensus that Larkin was an empiricist, which at best means a philosopher without a philosophy and at worst a person incapable of sustained intellection. This was a view in which Larkin sometimes conspired, as in a letter to Vernon Watkins: 'I admire profoundly the incredible gloss you put on life, but I couldn't do it, I just don't think that way – in fact, I don't think any way' (*SL*, 392). If this remark was taken at face value and set beside Coleridge's dictum that 'no man was ever yet a great poet, without being at the same time a profound philosopher', then we would have to conclude (as so many commentators have) that Larkin is a minor poet.[35]

We end this chapter with the contrary view that Larkin is a master of the excluded middle. The law of the excluded middle states that by using separate words to distinguish two extremes showing continuous variation between them, we make a sharp distinction appear where there is none in fact. This law applies not only to moral (good/bad), legal (sane/insane) and class distinctions (bourgeois/proletarian); it also applies to physiological matters of the kind that might be thought to be 'natural' and, therefore, anterior to relativistic value structures – the sexing and racing of human bodies, for instance. Biological sex involves so many variables (external genitalia, gonadal sex, chromosomal sex, hormonal sex, etc.) that the human body evidences an endless sequence of permutations. Hence, biological sex exists on a sliding scale with 'male' at one end of the spectrum and 'female' at the other, almost everyone occupying a space somewhere in between. Much the same holds true with regard to race: no one is black, as coal is black, as African-American performers like Billie Holiday and Sammy Davis Junior found to their chagrin when white employers required them to emphasize their 'otherness' by wearing blackface; and no one is white, as snow is white – except, of course, Michael Jackson. The absurdity of trying to compartmentalize bodies in this way is encapsulated in the following summary of racial reclassifications by the Home Affairs Minister in *apartheid* South Africa: 'nine whites became colored, 506 coloreds became white, two whites became Malay, 14 Malay became white ... 40 coloreds became black, 616 blacks became colored, 87 coloreds became Indian, 61 Indians became Malay ...'.[36] Larkin's desire to elude binaries in the interest of restoring the excluded middle was not a case of occupying a liberal centre-ground, it was an attempt to articulate expanses of experience that remain largely undefined. The characteristic note is struck in *A Girl in Winter*:

> 'No you don't understand', said Jane in an irritated voice ... 'I might get married, I might start shorthand-typing again, I might even go in a factory or be a waitress, I might even stay on here. Don't you see? Just because I don't see any point in doing anything, it doesn't mean I see any point in doing nothing.'
>
> (*GW*, 153)

Thirteen years later, the same vexed attempt to think in the gap between contraries gives 'Talking in Bed' its disconcerting climax:

> It becomes still more difficult to find
> Words at once true and kind,
> Or not untrue and not unkind.
>
> (*CP*, 129)

As with black/white or male/female, the true/untrue and kind/unkind polarities obscure myriad other possibilities: by invoking a condition that is *not untrue* without being *true*, the poem raises to consciousness that continuous variation which runs through absolute truth, relative truth, partial truth, unintended truth, unintended lies, lies of omission, lies of commission and absolute falsehoods. The same applies to the sliding scale of kindness.

For Larkin, this compromised liminal terrain between the *either* and the *or* is the ideological habitat of humankind under the conditions of modernity. In the chapters that follow we shall witness the application of his home-grown deconstructionism to the subjects of nationality, gender, politics and subjectivity. The effect in every case is such as to de-naturalize, de-essentialize and de-stabilize the discourses of power. Not the least impressive aspect of his endeavour was Larkin's steely resistance to the 'Those Who Are Not For Us Are Against Us' mentality of contending Fascists, Communists, McCarthyites, Existentialists and Christian Revivalists in the period during which he was writing.

It should be stressed, by way of clarification, that I am not offering a deconstructionist reading of Larkin but a reading of Larkin as a deconstructionist *avant la lettre*. Nor am I saying that Larkin was cognizant of developments in Poststructuralism: I am saying that Larkin is philosophical in somewhat the same sense as Derrida; for while I find the poet the more enjoyable of the two, they alike invite us to warm our hands, not at the Bonfire of the Vanities, but at the Bonfire of the Binaries.[37]

5
Larkin and Englishness

I A rootedly English poet

'We recognize in Larkin's poems the seasons of present-day England, but we recognize also the seasons of an English soul – the moods he expresses are our moods too ... the England in his poems is the England we have inhabited.' So said Donald Davie in *Thomas Hardy and British Poetry* (1973), adding that Larkin was 'the effective unofficial laureate of post-1945 England'.[1] Shortly thereafter a special 'Philip Larkin Issue' of Harry Chambers's magazine *Phoenix* appeared with a cover photograph of the poet seated beside a large sign, surmounted by an heraldic shield of the Cross of St George, reading ENGLAND. These are two examples of the way in which, by the early 1970s, Larkin was being imaged as a quintessentially English poet. Would things have been any different had critics known then what Motion's biography has subsequently revealed, that immediately before posing for this emblematic and much reproduced photograph Larkin urinated copiously behind the word ENGLAND?[2] Alas not, for even those who rushed to vilify Larkin after the disclosures of the biography and the *Selected Letters* still saw him as epitomizing Englishness, though of a kind that was outmoded and morally reprehensible.

So it is that over the past forty years the pro and anti camps have concurred in the view that Larkin's national identity is fixed, defining and mono-cultural. Among his critical champions, Heaney describes him as 'a poet ... of composed and tempered English nationalism'; Grubb claims that 'Larkin offers the patriotism of the rooted'; Alan Gardiner declares that Philip Larkin strikes a chord of sympathetic response in every English reader'; while for Whitehead 'his poems may be compared to a picture gallery illustrating the social history of England in the latter part of the twentieth century'.[3] From the opposing viewpoint, Corcoran still sees Larkin's poems as expressing 'the social religion ... of an enduring Englishness'; Alvarez finds in Larkin's narrators 'the image of the post-war Welfare State Englishman'; Nigel Alderman believes that 'Larkin's position as a belated national poet ... corresponds to England's problematic status as a belated nation'; while Paulin more intemperately declares that 'Larkin's snarl, his populism and his calculated philistinism all speak for Tebbit's England'.[4]

Not only is there, in Steve Clark's words, 'a striking convergence between the apparently antithetical viewpoints of those who think Larkin should be banned ... and those who concede the defects in the life, but separate the achievements of the poems from it';[5] there is also a striking convergence as to which poems shall be called upon to validate this universal belief in Larkin's Anglocentrism, the clear favourites being 'Church Going', 'Show Saturday', 'To the Sea' and 'The Explosion'. Just as striking is the perversity of this undertaking since even these carefully selected poems refuse to conform to the one-dimensionality attributed to them.

We have already remarked that 'The Explosion' combines polyglot citationality with a coal-and-chapel culture that may be identified with the Welsh valleys. Much the same applies to the other poems on the list. Appleyard claims that 'even the idea of wandering into parish churches has a Little England quality about it' and that this 'made it an exemplary activity to inspire' Larkin's 'Church Going'.[6] However, the poem was written in Belfast and according to Larkin 'came from the first time I saw a ruined church in Northern Ireland' (*FR*, 56, 83). 'Show Saturday' was prompted by visits to the Bellingham Show in the historically disputed borderlands between England and Scotland. As for 'To the Sea', that combines reminiscences of family holidays in both England and Wales. If Larkin really was trying to offer the unalloyed Englishness attributed to him by his explicators, one would have to declare him wilfully incompetent; but not only was he happy to draw inspiration from all over the British Isles, he characteristically deleted the site-specific references so as to widen still further the franchise of identification.

A specimen case is provided by 'Livings' III which, in Everett's words, is almost 'invariably referred to as a poem "about Oxford"', presumably because Larkin had been a student there.[7] Thus, Timms declares that 'It is spoken by a young Oxford don – a reference to "the wood from Snape" indicates that the setting is Oxford rather than Cambridge'.[8] This deduction might seem to be confirmed by a letter Larkin wrote a few months before penning the poem: 'I journeyed down to All Souls recently to attend a sumptuous dinner party. ... I sat drunk in the smoking room at one a.m. and dreamed of a former existence' (*SL*, 445). However, there are two Snapes, one in Suffolk and the other in North Yorkshire, neither of them anywhere near Oxford. Similarly, the 'sizar' of the third verse is a form of bursaried scholar – students paid reduced fees in return for undertaking menial tasks – formerly found in Cambridge University and Trinity College, Dublin, but never in Oxford. How typical of Larkin's bowdlers that they should insist on tying the poem to an originatory landscape and rule out of account the locales actually in contention – in this case, Dublin, York and Cambridge.

The full absurdity of this position becomes apparent if we return for a moment to the poems Larkin wrote between 1950 and 1955 when he was living in Belfast. Some of these poems, including 'Church Going', appeared in English periodicals and anthologies before being gathered in Larkin's first great book, *The Less Deceived* (1955), and the English editors who gave these works their first airings perceived them as having been penned by an Irishman. The reputable poet and critic G.S. Fraser included Larkin in the 1953 anthology *Springtime*, describing him as a 'Northern Ireland regional poet'. He went on to say that 'Irish poets, like Mr Larkin, though writing in standard English, reflect another regional value, that of rootedness'.[9] Not only were the very same poems that in the 1950s constituted proof that Larkin was rootedly Irish redeployed in the following decades as proof that he was rootedly English, but sometimes it was the same critics making the opposing claims. In 1955 the 'Notes on Contributors' section of Alan Brownjohn's magazine *Departure* stated categorically that Larkin 'was born in Northern Ireland'. Writing a 1986 obituary article in the *Listener*, however, Brownjohn unblushingly commented that 'Larkin's poetry shows all the reticence and reserve of his quintessential Englishness'.[10]

It might, of course, be countered that the early commentators were simply being misled by Larkin's Irish surname and Belfast address. The fact remains that readers as sensitive as Fraser and Brownjohn found nothing so incontrovertibly English in the poems as to queer their assumption that he was Irish. The conclusion is inescapable that the poems are radically unhoused and that it is the critics who assign them a national identity – now this side of the Irish Sea, now that – in accord with what they know, *or think they know*, about the author. To put it another way, Larkin's admirers and his detractors have latterly agreed that he is a thoroughly Anglocentric poet in complete obliviousness to the fact that they are not so much discovering Englishness as constructing it.

II   'I Remember, I Remember'

The reductionism of these anglicizing critics might be calibrated by contemplating 'I Remember, I Remember' (*CP*, 81–2), the only Larkin poem
to mention England in its very first line, the only poem which discusses
by name his birthplace of Coventry, a poem which expressly addresses
the issue of roots – and a poem which these commentators studiously
avoid. The reason for this is swiftly apparent, for from the start the
poem is skewed against expectation in a manner that is alienated, bewildering and mildly surreal.

Hence, the use of the word 'England' in the opening line, far from conveying a sense of belonging, momentarily holds out the prospect that the
narrator is foreign – just as if we read a poem beginning 'When I was trav-
elling through France ...', we might infer that the speaker is not French.
The explanation comes in the sequent words, 'by a different line / For
once', which disclose that the narrator is not viewing England with the
eyes of a foreigner but from the estranging perspective of an unfamiliar
train route. However, this explanation, far from orientating the reader for
the duration of the poem, is immediately followed by the surreal image of
'men with number-plates/Sprint[ing] down the platform'. What Orwellian
England is this in which not only are speeding cars obliged to carry regis-
tration plates, but so are speeding men? Once again, a moment of disori-
entation is followed by a stabilizing gesture, and one that this time
promises major anchorage: '"Why Coventry!" I exclaimed, "I was born
here"'. Coventry was the centre of the automobile industry, England's
answer to Detroit (though not, alas, Tamla Motown), and the men sprint-
ing down the platform are returning from having delivered cars. This is a
scene that could only be witnesses in this place. It is site-specific.

Coventry is in the Midlands – a little too westerly to be the middle of
the Midlands, but nonetheless a close contender for the title of ompha-
los of England. To claim to be born there is not just to establish a geographical point of origin but an umbilical relation to Englishness. Yet
no sooner has one parsed this resounding conclusion to the first stanza
than the poem starts unsinewing the national identity that has just
been established. The second stanza begins with the narrator anxious to
repossess his home town and, thereby, his sense of belonging:

> I leant far out, and squinnied for a sign
> That this was still the town that had been 'mine'
> So long, but found I wasn't even clear
> Which side was which.

The fact that the narrator had not only been born in Coventry bu
resided there for many years is repeated in the reference to 'all t
annual 'family hols', but this is insufficient to invest him wit
autochthonous identity:

> 'Was that', my friend smiled, 'where you "have your roots"?'
> No, only where my childhood was unspent,
> I wanted to retort, just where I started …

If the first third of the poem tantalizingly proffers a succession c
words betokening safe berth (England – here – mine – roots)
above lines are the pivot where the argument elbow-crooks i
relentlessly negative and eviscerating grammar and diction (I wa
No – unspent – I didn't – wasn't – I never – I never – was not – nor –
Nothing). What is being negated is the conventional paradig
Englishness. The inventory systematically covers, only to nu
many of the tropes and emblems of national identity: the English ga
the English love of eccentricity (the 'old hat'); family unity a
antidote to depression; an uncomplicated model of English m
ness ('the boys all bicep'); an 'English rose' ideal of unspoilt, sh
womanhood ('the girls all chest'); the farm as version of En
pastoral; the wider community as an extended family ('the d
guished cousin of the mayor'); this benign social machinery f
tating the individual's accession to subjecthood ('I could be / "R
myself"'), sexual maturity and creativity (the poems 'set up in l
ten-point').

This sequence of negations culminates in the punch line, t
graphically isolated for effect, 'Nothing, like something, happens
where'. At one level, this might be taken to mean that Coventry i
sort of place where nothing happens – as opposed to London, sa
which it is commonly said that something is always happening t
However, a more accurate reading would be that any place, Lond
much as Coventry, can as readily be a site of emptiness as pleni
The fact remains that growing up in the navel of England our n
tor claims to have encountered none of the formative experienc
the national character and in that sense to have avoided conscri
into the collective being. He has come up England by a diff
genetic or *cultural* line. To this day, he remains an internal exile
cannot even recognize the town where he was born and raise
looks into the heart of Englishness and descries a minus sign, an abs
a round zero.

III The English pastoral tradition

But there is more. For 'I Remember, I Remember' is opulently ballasted with a cargo of the already said and the purport of this citationality is to debunk an English literary tradition that Larkin's conservative commentators see him as embodying. In this sense, the poem comes up England by a different *poetic* line.

The allusions begin as early as the title, which invokes two famous anthology pieces. The first is Thomas Hood's 'I remember, I remember', whose closing stanza reads:

> I remember, I remember
> The fir trees dark and high;
> I used to think their slender tops
> Were close against the sky:
> It was a childish ignorance,
> But now 'tis little joy
> To know I'm farther off from heav'n
> Than when I was a boy.[11]

The second is Winthrop Mackworth Praed's 'I Remember, I Remember', which includes the lines:

> I remember – I remember
>   How my childhood fleeted by, –
> The mirth of its December,
>   And the warmth of its July;
> On my brow, love, on my brow, love,
>   There are no signs of care,
> But my pleasures are not now, love,
>   What Childhood's pleasures were.[12]

Both poems drag a tail of further allusions in their wake. For instance, Hood's poem appears to be indebted to 'Stanzas on Revisiting Shrewsbury' by John Hamilton Reynolds, beginning 'I remember well the time, – the sweet school-boy time'. In a more general sense, Hood and Praed carry into the Victorian era a Romantic ideology such as one finds in Blake, Coleridge, Lamb, Shelley and, as here, Wordsworth:

> My heart leaps up when I behold
>   A rainbow in the sky:

> So was it when my life began;
> So is it now I am a man;
> So be it when I shall grow old,
>   Or let me die!
> The Child is father to the Man;
> And I could wish my days to be
> Bound each to each by natural piety.[13]

The particular target of Larkin's satire is a Romantic sentimentaliz
of infancy comprised of two strands: that childhood innocen
preferable to adult experience; and that nature is superior to culture
country to the town. However, the tessellation of quotes and echo
which the poem is constituted carries the argument forward intc
modern period in order to demonstrate how this Romantic idea
came to suffuse the literary construction of Englishness.

In terms of poetry, the *locus classicus* here is 'Adlestrop' by Edw
Thomas. Forty years before Larkin, Thomas provided the template
poem that moves from an opening echo of the Hood–Praed title tc
description of an unexpected stop on a railway journey:

> Yes. I remember Adlestrop –
> The name, because one afternoon
> Of heat the express-train drew up there
> Unwontedly.[14]

As with Larkin and Coventry, this poem presents Adlestrop as a p
where nothing happens:

> The steam hissed. Someone cleared his throat.
> No one left and no one came
> On the bare platform.

In this case, though, the nothing is profound, replete, an eternal
apprehension of Englishness rather than the vacuity Larkin's narr
perceives at the heart of the national identity. The form it takes is
of a timeless English landscape (stocked with willow herb, grass
meadowsweet) and a pregnant silence against which birdsong rip
out from Adlestrop to the adjacent counties.

> And for that minute a blackbird sang
> Close by, and round him, mistier,
> Farther and farther, all the birds
> Of Oxfordshire and Gloucestershire.

Adlestrop, with its Saxon name, is at the heart of the Cotswolds, England's largest area of outstanding natural beauty. Though geographically quite close, it is also a world away from the industrialized and war-damaged city of Coventry. Thomas's lines encapsulate that moment known to every railway passenger from the days of steam: the sudden silence that descended when a train made an unscheduled stop and the countryside that had hitherto been no more than a passing kaleidoscope was revealed in all its beauty. Despite the advent of the locomotive, the poem seems to say, the England of Wordsworth, Hood, Praed or Hardy is all still going on just over the horizon if only the hurrying commuter will stop long enough to pay heed. Where Larkin's version is dominated by the word 'No' and its derivatives, culminating in 'Nothing', Thomas's resoundingly begins with the one-word sentence 'Yes'. Where the Larkin is all absence and nullity, the Thomas is all presence and affirmation. Yet the difference between them must not be attributed to the differing personalities of the authors; if anything, Thomas was the more melancholic of the two. Rather, it should be remarked that Thomas conceived his poem in June 1914, the very month that ended with the assassination of Archduke Franz Ferdinand of Austria. Unwittingly, the already poignant lines of 'Adlestrop' captured the last exhalation of an English pastoralism that, like Thomas himself, was soon to be consumed in the First World War.

Of course, not all the texts in the tradition Larkin is debunking are in verse. In an interview with Neil Powell he claimed:

> Really that poem started off as a satire on novels like *Sons and Lovers* – the kind of wonderful childhoods that people do seem to have. I was thinking how very peculiar it was that I myself never experienced these things, and I thought one could write a funny poem about it. So I did. It wasn't denying that other people did have these experiences, though they did tend to sound rather clichés: the first fuck, the first poem, the first this that and the other that turn up with such wearisome regularity.

> (*FR*, 31–2)

Comparing the novel with the poem confirms Lawrence's early masterpiece as a specific butt of the humour. The non-existent farm where our narrator could be himself parodies Paul Morel's experience of Willey Farm outside the Nottinghamshire mining village of Eastwood. The busty girls the Larkin protagonist did not meet there – forerunners of

the equally unattainable 'bosomy English rose' of 'Wild Oats' – re
us of the Miriam Leivers ('at twenty she was full-breasted and l
ously formed') and Clara Dawes ('he noticed her breasts swelled i
her blouse') that Paul did.[15] The bracken and burning imagery c
fantasy sex scene lampoon a typically over-wrought passa
Lawrence (additional satirical spin being provided by the fact tha
became a burning mist' was a comedy catchphrase from the 1950s
programme *Bedtime With Braden*):[16]

> Just as he was, so it seemed the vigorous, wintry stars were stron
> with life. He and they struck with the same pulse of fire, an
> same joy of strength which held the bracken-frond stiff near hi
> held his own body firm. It was as if he, and the stars, and the
> herbage, and Clara were licked up in an immense tongue of f
> which tore onwards and upwards.[17]

The imaginary episode concerning the narrator's poetry and 'a d
guished cousin of the mayor' reminds us of those scenes in *Sons and*
where Paul Morel is thrice awarded first prize for paintings exhibit
Nottingham Castle, one of them being purchased for 20 guineas by
Moreton. Among other things, then, 'I Remember, I Remember' is La
declaration of independence from the Lawrentianism that had imp
his development in the 1940s.

There are many other writers not directly alluded to in the poem
partake of the ideological formation Larkin is condemning. Son
them – A.E. Housman, Mary Webb, H.E. Bates, Laurie Lee – come
into the modern period. As late as 1960, reviewing C. Day Lewis's
biography *The Buried Day*, Larkin mordantly observed: 'This i
Forrest-Reid-Walter-de-la-Mare view of life: nothing quite equals be
kid' (*FR*, 229). Shortly before his death, he reiterated the point i
interview with Haffenden: 'some writers seem to stop at twenty
rather than start there: Betjeman, Day Lewis'. As for himself, he cla
to take the diametrically opposed view: 'Whenever I read an auto
raphy, or even a biography, I tend to start half way through, wher
chap's grown-up and it becomes interesting' (*FR*, 47).

Something of this is encapsulated in that striking archaism 'uns
(Coventry is 'where my childhood was unspent'). Its initial neg
sense, that the narrator did not spend the happy childhood enjoy
others, may be used to explain the feelings of grievance he apparentl
harbours towards Coventry ('You look as if you wished the place in

However, this is partially offset by the counter-meaning: that because he did not spend it *then*, the narrator has saved up his childhood, like money, and can spend it *now* with the greater wisdom of adulthood. In this perspective, the narrator is an example of Freudian deferred gratification and the alternative styles of 'spent' childhood caricatured in the verses that follow appear suspiciously precocious, possibly bogus. This is underlined two stanzas later in the syntactical parallelism of 'I *never* ran to' and 'I *never* trembling sat' (my italics) which tacitly suggests that the Wordsworthian–Lawrentian picture of childhood is a *never-never* land. In effect, Larkin is accusing of infantilism the entire literary tradition with which he is most closely identified by Anglocentric commentators.

IV   The literature of deracination

It is already apparent from the foregoing that Larkin's poem is as freighted with intertextual references as the works of Pound, Joyce or Eliot, and we shall shortly explore other affinities with the very exilic Modernists he is usually thought to abominate. Before we do, it might be appropriate to pull into the same frame of argument that minority of critics, like Adam Piette and James Fenton, who interpret 'I Remember, I Remember' as Larkin's attempt to vanquish a Coventry childhood tainted by his father's Fascist sympathies.

Contemplating the second stanza of the poem, Piette, the more sophisticated of the two, opines:

> Buried deep in the squint syntax of the lines (in the knowledge we now have about Coventry and the part Larkin's father, as a treasurer, played in making it Larkin's home town) is the question 'Whose side were you on in the war that made Coventry unrecognizable!' 'I wasn't even clear / Which side was which'. These lines retain the trace of the uncensored memory of his father's treacherous allegiance ('which side was he on?'), as well as containing a concentrated reference to the consequence of that censorship, the devaluing of dichotomies the wartime Larkin suffered as a result of the war's annulment of his childhood.[18]

One of the attractions of this approach is that it offers a much more problematized view of Larkin's relation to Englishness than that of the Anglocentric majority. On the other hand, it shares with the latter

a tendency to equate the narrators of the poems with the p
what is essentially a biographical reading strategy. That thi
reductive methodology that does violence to the poems may b
gested by mention of two other pieces Piette discusses in thi
text. He describes 'On Being Twenty-six' as a '1940s poem exp
about the Coventry raid' – a very strange use of the word 'expl
when Coventry is neither named nor described in unequivocal
In the case of 'Coming', the narrator is directly linked to Lark
the erasure of childhood ('And I, whose childhood / Is a forg
boredom') and the poem then given an emphatically Freudian
pretation:

> He comes, in the sexual sense, on witnessing the orgasmic
> ('unusual laughter') accompanying the sexual congress ('adult
> ciling') of his parents, the primal 'scene'.

However, the poem itself does not disclose that the narrator is ma
alone that the male in question is Larkin, nor that the 'adults' ar
parents. Indeed, it is not vouchsafed that there are only two grow
nor that they are of opposite sexes. In every one of these cases, wh
critic knows of the author's life is being used to close the poems
into a monologically biographical meaning that entails ident
unspecified geographical locations, gendering non-gender-specifi
tagonists, and investing the narrator of 'I Remember, I Remember'
a Fascist father despite the fact that the poem tells us nothing w
ever about either parent!

One of the weaknesses the Piette–Fenton position shares with t
the anglicizing critics is a denial of Larkin's intertextuality and,
fore, of the constructedness, the literariness, of any given narrator.
case of 'I Remember, I Remember', I shall mention four ur-text
mediate the narrative tone and structure. The poem's master st
reversing the Hood–Praed conventions of nostalgic remembra
comes from a favourite Larkin novel, *Those Barren Leaves* (192
Aldous Huxley. In an extended passage that begins – '"I reme
I remember ...". It is a pointless and futile occupation, difficult no
less not to indulge in' – the character Francis Chelifer rehearses jus
a list of denials as constitute Larkin's poem, including a negati
home ('I am glad the place is sold') and kin ('The child, I thought,
up to forget that he is of the same flesh with his parents; but th
not forget.')[19] The obliteration of the past that Piette and Fenton
ute to Larkin's ambivalence about the bombing of Coventry

already be found fifteen years before the blitz in a work of fiction an entirely different author wrote and set in Italy.

A second prototype from outside the English pastoral tradition provides the poem with its chilly scepticism regarding nativity; for, as one or two critics have already noted, Larkin's opening *distich* – 'Coming up England by a different line / For once, early in the cold new year' invokes the opening of T.S. Eliot's 'Journey of the Magi': 'A cold coming we had of it, / Just the worst time of the year / For a journey ...'.[20] There is the shared emphasis on the words 'cold', 'coming' and 'year'; on the motif of travel through unfamiliar landscapes; and on the wintry setting. The poems also have in common a complex and unsettling sense of alienation: Eliot's narrator arrives at the birth of Christ and is strangely underwhelmed – 'it was (you may say) satisfactory'; Larkin's narrator arrives at the site of his own nativity and is similarly unimpressed ('I suppose it's not the place's fault'). It is also worth remarking that the expatriate American Eliot, like the *deraciné* Huxley, invokes the Hood–Praed–Thomas continuity in order to negate it: 'All this was a long time ago, *I remember*' (my italics).[21] What we have then is a double inversion of the consensual stereotype of Larkin: he not only satirizes the English poetic tradition he is commonly identified with, but he does so by employing the tactics of the exilic cosmopolites he is usually placed in opposition to.

A third model that may have contributed to the construction of our narrator is possibly even more unexpected. In the autumn of 1940, at the very height of his Lawrentian fever, Larkin went to hear Stella Gibbons speak to the English Club at Oxford University. Gibbons's 1932 novel, *Cold Comfort Farm*, played havoc with the literary cliché of pastoral England as a setting for unbridled sexual passion –

> All the trees and hedges came into full leaf overnight; and from behind the latter, in the evenings, cries could be heard of: 'Nay, doan't 'ee, Jem', and 'Nay, niver do that, soul', from the village maidens who were being seduced.[22]

and Lawrence is identified as the culprit: 'by God, D.H. Lawrence was right when he had said there must be a dumb, dark, dull, bitter belly-tension between a man and a woman'.[23] Here, then, was a precursor for the scepticism regarding Lawrence that prevails in the second half of Larkin's poem and for the hilarity of its articulation.

Critics of a biographical persuasion are plausibly able to claim that the narrators of those poems that diminish childhood – 'Coming',

'I Remember, I Remember', 'Forget What Did' – not only resembl⟨
other but also are of a piece with the Larkin of the interviews:

> No doubt when I get to my dotage all those dusty motor-car
> days in Coventry will seem vivid and delightful, but just now t⟨
> far away. My childhood wasn't unhappy, just boring. ... ⟨
> school, I was an unsuccessful schoolboy. You must remembe⟨
> I was very short-sighted and nobody realized it, and also that I
> mered, so that really classes were just me sitting with bated b⟨
> dreading lest I should be called on to say something.
>
> (F⟨

However, the conflation of poet and persona should be resiste⟨
because they do not sometimes strike identical attitudes but be⟨
that is precisely what they do – self-consciously attitudinize. The⟨
arity of the performance may be suggested by comparison wit⟨
fourth intertext, the author's preface to *The Thurber Carnival*, whic⟨
published in both Britain and the United States in 1945.

> James Thurber was born ... at 147 Parsons Avenue, Colu⟨
> Ohio. The house, which is still standing, bears no tablet or pla⟨
> any description, and is never pointed out to visitors ...
> Thurber's boyhood (1900–1913) was pretty well devoid of si⟨
> cance. I see no reason why it should take up much of our time.
> is no clearly traceable figure or pattern in this phase of his life. ⟨
> gold-rimmed glasses forever needed straightening, which gav⟨
> the appearance of a person who hears somebody calling but
> make out where the sound is coming from ...
> Thurber's life baffles and irritates the biographer because of it⟨
> of design ...
> Thurber's very first bit of writing was a so-called poem. ... I⟨
> no value or importance ...[24]

Larkin was only twenty-seven when he wrote 'Coming' and in his⟨
thirties when he wrote 'I Remember, I Remember'; yet both deplo⟨
rhetorical properties of the fifty-year old Thurber: the eeyore-ish ton⟨
reversal of the Romantic view of childhood, the absence of any earl⟨
interest, the lack of physical prowess epitomized by the need for s⟨
cles, the lack of a precocious poetic talent, the lack of identification⟨
one's roots such as might later be memorialized by a plaque (we will
back to that shortly), and, above all, the lugubrious, deflating hu⟨

I am not suggesting that Thurber directly influenced Larkin, though he may have, but simply that their narrative stance is almost identical and that, therefore, one did not have to have a Fascist father and a blitzed home in order to adopt it. Indeed, one did not even have to be English.

One urbane, melancholic New Yorker (Thurber); one expatriate English intellectual, later a promoter of hallucinogenic drugs (Huxley); one expatriate American Modernist (Eliot); and one satirical proto-feminist (Gibbons) – not the literary company Larkin is normally thought to have kept, and assuredly not the company of the misogynistic blimp concocted by his commentators.

V   The travel and transport motif

The internationalism of this literary compound has its complement in the physical mobility of the narrator, the travel and transport motif enacting the theme of geographical unfixity. In spirit, the narrator's perspective is not dissimilar to that of Stephen Dedalus who in *A Portrait of the Artist as a Young Man* declares:

> When the soul of a man is born in this country there are nets flung at it to hold it back from flight. You talk to me of nationality, language, religion. I shall try to fly by those nets.[25]

Or again –

> I will not serve that in which I no longer believe, whether it call itself my home, my fatherland, or my church: and I will try to express myself in some mode of life or art as freely as I can and as wholly as I can, using for my defence the only arms I allow myself to use – silence, exile, and cunning.[26]

The difference is that at the end of the novel Stephen prepares to quit Dublin for an unnamed destination abroad (in the earlier version, *Stephen Hero*, Paris is specified), whereas Larkin's narrator quits Coventry for an unnamed destination that is presumably located somewhere on the British Rail network. He is an internal rather than an external exile.

In this, 'I Remember, I Remember' is representative rather than atypical of Larkin's *oeuvre*. The whole spectrum of rail travel is discontinuously mapped across the *Collected Poems*: pre-Beeching branch services ('The local snivels through the fields'); main line journeys south ('The Whitsun Weddings') and north ('Dockery and Son'); railway hotels ('Friday Night

in the Royal Station Hotel'); platform posters ('Sunny Prestatyn'); th
rors of British Rail food (the 'awful pie' of 'Dockery and Son') and s
And the dozen or so poems recounting train journeys are supplem
by another two that refer to cycling, five that allude to bus travel, e
describing car journeys and four concerned with aeroplane flights. In
if Larkin's narrators can sometimes seem unduly disdainful of the pu
who succumb to post-war consumer capitalism – I am thinking of p
like 'Take One Home for the Kiddies', 'Going, Going' or the referer
the 'cut price crowd' in 'Here' – then it should be added that just as e
if less conspicuously, they are imbricated in this Postmodern affluenc
commodification. Hence the chronological and material progression
the bicycle of 'Church Going' (*The Less Deceived*) via the train journe
'Dockery and Son' (*The Whitsun Weddings*) to the automotive wo
'Going, Going' (*High Windows*). When it comes to travel and tran
Larkin's narrators have steadily gone up in the world.

What makes 'I Remember, I Remember' iconic is the way it inc
rates so many different forms of motion: running (the men who 's
down the platform', 'that splendid family / I never ran to'), cy
('those cycle-crates'), automobiles (the 'men with number-plates
'comic Ford'), as well as rail ('Coming up England by a different
There is also a good deal of physical activity on the part of our nar
actual ('I leant far out', 'I sat back') or implied (the fact that he v
boots rather than shoes may hint that he is a practised walker).
poet who is often thought of as sedentary – the desk-bound libr
who hated foreign travel – this poem is remarkably restless.

It is symptomatic of this excitability that the very first thing our
rator thinks of when trying to repossess Coventry is the quitting
('From where those cycle-crates / Were standing, had we anr
departed // For all those family hols?'). This memory of annual d
tures from Coventry leads immediately to the current departure, the
next words being 'A whistle went: / Things moved'. Ironically, this
tinuing sequence of uprootings provides the context for that discu
of roots that is the principal item on the poem's agenda. Hence this
tling juxtaposition: '"Was that," my friend smiled, "where you;
your roots'?" / No ...'. A poem about roots which ought, if Larkin'
ics are correct, to be an affirmation of autochthony is instead a pae
praise for itinerancy. And, as so often in Larkin, whose love of pai
masia is rarely acknowledged, this ideological purport is encapsulat
a complex pun: for in place of *roots* we are offered *routes*; or, this
Coventry, perhaps one should say *Rootes* – the local car giant w
insignia, the old Coventry Cathedral, was emblazoned in the cent

the steering wheel. It is precisely our narrator's mobility that permits him an undeceived perspective ('By now I've got the whole place clearly charted') on origins: vagrancy affords panoramic vistas closed off by the low horizons of one's local habitation. In essence, Larkin employs the travel and transport motif to unhouse narrative from the false givens of regional and national identity.

Something of the same effect is apparent in 'Here' (*CP*, 136–7) which is often, wrongly, said to be set in Hull. The poem is punctuated by five uses of the word 'Here': once in the title, once at the start of a line and three times at the beginning of a sentence, so that all begin with a capital letter. These five resounding 'Heres' prick out different stages in a progress. The title ushers in a first verse that describes a journey north-eastwards towards Hull, probably by train (the reference to the occasional 'harsh-named halt' suggests rail rather than road travel). The next two verses describe the city itself ('Here domes and statues, spires and cranes cluster'), unnamed but unmistakable because at that time Hull possessed Britain's only 'slave museum'. Then the narrative moves 'out beyond its mortgaged half-built edges' to the 'Isolate villages' of the Plain of Holderness, before sweeping onwards through a succession of 'Heres' ('Here silence stands … . Here leaves unnoticed thicken') to the coast ('Here is unfenced existence').

At first glance, 'Here' provides the antidote to an earlier work, 'Places, Loved Ones', which begins:

> No, I have never found
> The place where I could say
> *This is my proper ground*
> *Here I shall stay* …
> (*CP*, 99)

The very title seems to echo this last line with a view to contradicting it: after all, as biographical critics might aver, Larkin did 'stay' in Hull for the second half of his life. Some might claim that the title simultaneously nullifies the words 'Why, Coventry! … I was born *here*' (my italics) from 'I Remember, I Remember', Larkin privileging his adoptive over his home city. But as we have seen 'Here' actually swings towards, through and then out the other side of Kingston upon Hull in a continuous cinematic panning action (more than three-quarters of the poem are comprised of a single sweeping sentence) that moves ceaselessly forward until the land and the words give out. The poem pauses in Hull, where Larkin died,

scarcely longer than 'I Remember, I Remember' pauses in Cov
where he was born. Like so many of Larkin's verse travelogues,
poems accept deracination as a predicate of the human condition i
era of modernity. This is what is signified by the repetitious syn
'Here', which might more fittingly (if less euphoniously) be retitled
and now Here and now Here and now Here and now Here'.

Shortly after the composition of 'I Remember, I Remember'
recruited Larkin to 'The Movement', whose membership was alread
to include Kingsley Amis, Robert Conquest, Donald Davie, D.J. En
Thom Gunn, Iris Murdoch and John Wain. More recent commen
have tended to see Amis as Larkin's only true elective affinity withi
grouping. However, while it is hard to imagine the Larkin in leather
goggles astride a Harley-Davidson, 'I Remember, I Remember' is
than might be expected to the Thom Gunn of the Californian bik
poems. It might even be claimed that the purport of the Larkin is ide
with that of Gunn's 'On the Move', whose resonant last line de
'One is always nearer by not keeping still'.[27] The difference is that G
narrator is stationary, watching from a fixed point as the leather
roar towards him –

> On motorcycles, up the road, they come:
> Small, black, as flies hanging in heat, the Boys,
> Until the distance throws them forth

– and recede as rapidly away:

> A minute holds them, who have come to go:
> The self-defined, astride the created will
> They burst away

Larkin's strategy is the more radical, rendering mobile narration i
Indeed, it might be claimed, only half-jokingly, that because he se
narrators in motion, viewing reality's supposedly fixed terms
vehicular vantage points that are unfixed and unfixing, Philip Lar
the *movement* poet *par excellence*.

VI Form as content

As so often with Larkin, the theme of the poem is enacted in the s
ture, which is comprised of seven stanzas of five lines apiece, an
abccbaabc rhyme scheme. This is an extraordinarily asymmetrical pa

The nine-line rhyme scheme is most uncommon. Draping it over a five-line stanza compounds the complexity. Refusing to run the poem to forty-five lines (5 × 9), or some multiple thereof, entails a calculated rejection of that formal closure in which verse and rhyme patterns achieve congruence. That is to say, there is no point, not even the conclusion of the poem, at which the end of a rhyme unit and the end of a stanza coincide. Given the choice between completing the last stanza with the rhyme scheme incomplete or completing the rhyme scheme with the last stanza incomplete, Larkin opts for the latter and tacks a one-line coda on the end of the poem. This is a strategy he will repeat throughout his career: where this poem has seven verses of five lines plus a one-line coda, 'For Sidney Bechet' has five verses of three lines plus a two-line coda, 'The Explosion' has eight verses of three lines plus a one-line coda, and 'The Building' has nine verses of seven lines each plus a dangling last line. 'The Card-Players' is equally but differently fractured, being a traditionally rhymed fourteen-line sonnet (abbacdd-cefeggf) divided not into the conventional octave and sestet (eight and six lines, respectively), but into a first verse of thirteen lines followed by a second verse consisting of a single line.

In the case of 'I Remember, I Remember', this transcribes as follows: abccb // aabcd // effed // defgh // iihgg // hijkl // lkjjk // 1. As this quaint algebra demonstrates, fracturing the nine-line rhyme scheme over a five-line stanza makes even the recurrence of the rhymes highly irregular: stanza five contains two couplets; stanzas one, three and seven contain a couplet each plus another pair of lines rhymed non-adjacently; stanza two contains a single couplet; while stanzas four and six contain no rhymed lines at all. By contrast, 'Adlestrop's four quatrains, conventionally rhymed on the second and fourth lines (like nursery rhymes, schoolroom poems, marching songs and hymns), bespeak simplicity, regularity and tradition.

When one adds that the line lengths of 'I Remember, I Remember' vary between nine and twelve syllables, only one of the seven stanzas maintaining the pentameter throughout, it can truly be claimed that critics who blithely refer to Larkin's use of traditional forms and regular metres are wilfully misreading their man. This mismatch between stanza length and rhyme scheme embodies the theme of dislocation, of old established institutions and meanings falling asunder. The thematic refusal to endorse comforting English stereotypes is matched by the formal refusal of the consolations of satisfied metrical norms. In his own less attention-seeking way, Larkin is adhering to the Modernist principle that the way a work is written is internal to what it teaches.

The same holds true for imagery and narrative closure, though few Larkin critics have discovered as much. Larkin's reputation is for conversational tone, purity of diction, transparency of figuration and perfect *denouements*. Hence, Timms finds 'the last line' of 'I Remember, I Remember' 'immensely powerful, partly owing to its felicitous phrasing, but more to its honesty'. He adds:

> ... it is astonishing that Larkin has been able to make the tone of the poem so straightforwardly conversational, and even more so that he can report convincing dialogue. In his preface to *Lyrical Ballads*, Wordsworth argued for a poetic diction that should be drawn from the spoken language of the day. His practice did not fully follow his theory; but here, Larkin perfectly achieves an idiom that is living and contemporary. And he does this without lapsing into flatness, as that marvellous last line proves.[28]

We have already remarked that 'I Remember, I Remember' has a punch line ending, typographically isolated for effect; but if we use this emphatic last line as a litmus test we quickly find that Larkin's tropes are more opaque than transparent, his endings less determinate than question-begging.

First we have a simile that flouts its own writs of convention: 'Nothing, like something ...'. The word *simile* is Latin for *like*. But 'nothing' and 'something' are antonyms. The simile short circuits; the likeness is not like. The confusion caused by the split simile (how can binary opposites be like?) is compounded by the next word: 'Nothing, like something, *happens* ...'. Nothing is unlike something precisely because the former betokens absence and the latter presence; which in turn makes the expression 'Nothing happens' a solecism since there is, literally, *no thing* extant as a precondition of happening. Is the poem gesturing towards a third modality, somewhere between nothing and something; a liminal state in which nothing has moved from non-existence, and thus become something – an absent presence, perhaps?

Inching painfully to the last word in the hope of bringing the sentence (never mind the poem) to a resolution, we find our troubles multiplied: 'Nothing, like something, happens anywhere'. The completed sentence amalgamates two separate propositions: nothing happens anywhere; and something happens anywhere. The ambush lies in the replacement of the expected 'everywhere' with 'anywhere'. To say 'lightning strikes anywhere' implies a certain randomness and infrequency (even a capriciousness) of occurrence; 'lightning strikes everywhere' is much more comprehensive. But how can both 'Nothing' and 'something' exhibit randomness and infrequency of occurrence? To put it another way, what *is* when (presumably most of the time) nothing and something are *not* happening? The point of asking these questions is not to answer them but to demonstrate that they have not already been answered.

We have now seen that every step of this five-word construction is a hermeneutical booby-trap; what looked to Timms like a resounding punch line is so perforated with interpretative *aporia* as to constitute a succession of bafflements. On this evidence, Larkin's justly celebrated skill at exiting from a poem should not be mistaken for closure.

VII   The mid-century institutionalization of Modernism

Thus far we seem to be recruiting Larkin to the Modernist camp, as though he identified himself with the international avant-garde against the native English Realists in a stark antithetical relation. This is a simplification that fails to register the complexity of the ideological formation he was seeking alternatives to. Born of the Second World War, the ideology in question was a compact of English nationalism, Anglicanism, Monarchism and welfare-statism. Combining as it did late imperial pride and Churchillian indomitability with the levelling camaraderie of compulsory national service and universal food rationing, this post-war consensus over-arched party affiliations and changes of government. Both Labour and Conservative administrations adopted a version of the Keynesian mixed economy in which the state accepted responsibility for the level of output and employment, capital accepted a significant degree of public ownership and a division of the social product more favourable to the proletariat than ever before, and the unions accepted a predominantly privately owned economy. However, what is repeatedly lost sight of is that this mid-century concord took as its expressive means the Modernist idioms that a quarter of a century earlier were perceived as dissident and transgressive. By the time Larkin was in his teens and twenties the revolutionary Modernism of his year of birth had been mainstreamed and museumified; yesterday's revolution was today's counter-revolution. Modernism was subsumed in Butskellism.[29]

Church, State and Crown all played a part in this process of cultural assimilation, even if this was less a matter of institutional policy than individual initiative. In the case of the Anglican Church, for instance, Bishop Bell of Chichester played a part in commissioning Eliot to write choruses for a religious pageant called *The Rock* (1933) and invited him to write *Murder in the Cathedral* for the 1935 Canterbury Festival. I 1940s the Reverend Walter Hussey of St Matthew's Ch Northampton, commissioned Henry Moore to sculpt a *Madonn Child*, Graham Sutherland to paint a *Crucifixion* and Benjamin Britt compose the cantata *Rejoice in the Lamb*. Subsequently, as De Chichester, Hussey invited Chagall, John Piper and Ceri Richar design stained-glass windows and commissioned music from Ber Bernstein, Rubbra, Tippett and Walton.[30]

Shortly after the outbreak of hostilities, the government was recruiting young Modernists to the patriotic cause, as when Pipe Sutherland were commissioned as official war artists by the dir of the National Gallery, Kenneth Clark. Sometimes the state-spon war art overlapped with the Church's agenda: in addition to pai *The House of Commons after Bombing* and *The Ruined House of Com* (both 1941), Piper executed a whole series of bombed church pic including *Coventry Cathedral*; *St Mary le Port, Bristol*; *Christ Cl Newgate Street, after its Destruction in 1940* and *All Saints Chapel*, Hiring avant-garde artists (Piper's 1938 showing at the Lo Gallery was uncompromisingly abstract) to record the devast inflicted upon parliament and church effectively presented the as anti-Modernist, anti-democratic and anti-Christian. The Cr too, was central to the formation of this ideological consens when Queen Elizabeth, the future Queen Mother, commissi Piper to execute two series of watercolours of Windsor Cast wartime.

When in the later 1940s and the 1950s the spirit of post-war reg ation was epitomized in major patriotic pageants and reconstru projects it was invariably the language of Modernism that employed. Even so radical a composer by British standards as B was continually in demand on such occasions, composing *Peter G* for the reopening of Sadlers Wells Theatre in 1945, *Billy Budd* fo Festival of Britain 1951, *Gloriana* for the coronation of Queen Elizab in 1953 and the *War Requiem* for the consecration of Cov Cathedral in 1962. This same conjunction of Church, State, Crow Modernist aesthetics was apparent at the Festival of Britain, perhap event that determined the shape of British architecture for the thirty years. Opened by King George VI, it was intended to marl centenary of the Great Exhibition of 1851, itself a testament to i trial power and imperial values. The festival site was designed b Modernist architect Hugh Casson, its most famous temporary stru being the abstract Skylon and its most notable permanent one the I

Festival Hall. In essence, this union of tradition and modernity was intended to symbolize an historic culture reinventing itself at the dawn of a new age.

VIII   Coventry Cathedral

The relevance of this is that the rebuilding of Coventry Cathedral, the single most publicized (and subsidized) symbol of English post-war renewal, was taking place at the very moment Larkin penned 'I Remember, I Remember'. Whether or not he intended it as such, the poem can be read as an act of secession from that ideological consensus that had conscripted Modernism and rendered it part of the status quo.

We have already remarked that a minority of critics has interpreted 'I Remember, I Remember' as an 'act of concealment' designed to obscure the fact that Larkin's father was a Nazi sympathiser who 'in a manner of speaking' called 'down a curse on the city': James Fenton suggests that the poem 'might as well have been entitled "I Suppress, I Suppress"'.[31] For such commentators it was Larkin's shame or embarrassment at his father's Fascism that led him to insist that his 'opaque childhood' ('Forget What Did') was 'a forgotten boredom' ('Coming') and, in that sense, to add his own obliteration of Coventry to that of the Luftwaffe. However valid as a psycho-biography of the author, this approach not only does great violence to particular poems, as we have seen, but also fails to register the twin triumphs of Larkin's critical distance from the patriotic myth of the city's crucifixion and resurrection.

Contemporary accounts of the Coventry blitz stressed the Nazi terror, the blanket bombing of a defenceless city, the sacrilegious destruction of the fourteenth-century cathedral, and the plucky resourcefulness of the survivors. The *Birmingham Gazette* for 16 November 1940, two days after the raid, carried the headline 'Coventry – our Guernica', thereby comparing the city's destruction by Hitler to Franco's destruction of the non-strategic Basque centre famously memorialized by Picasso. *The Times* went further in presenting the city as the blameless victim of barbarian blood lust, describing the 'butchery at Coventry' as 'the wanton slaughter by a people pretending to be civilized who, it would seem, kill mostly for the joy of destroying'.[32]

This sort of myth-making involved the suppression of inconvenient truths. The Guernica analogy is decidedly strained: the Basque town was not a military target, Coventry was; Guernica was utterly destroyed, Coventry was not; and despite being one thirtieth the size of Coventry, Guernica suffered three times the number of fatalities. The fact that

Coventry was an important manufacturer of aircraft and armamen
played down since it made the city (unlike Guernica) a legitimate
and one the British government might be blamed for not anticip
would come under attack. Again, the evidence of fights and lootin
suppressed in order to exaggerate the stoicism of the citizens: in fac
home secretary when he visited the scene was struck by Coventry's
sive 'air of defeatism' and threatened to put the city under martial l

The scale of the atrocity was also swiftly mythologized, and in
that continues to obfuscate. Much is made of the fact that 500 to
explosive were dropped on Coventry on 14 November; but whil
undoubtedly represented a shocking escalation in bombing dens
is put in perspective by the knowledge that the British would
average 1600 tons per night in their equivalent raids on Germany
also indisputable that the centre of Coventry was devastated i
attack. However, when the current guide to Coventry Cathedral
that this was 'so significant ... that the Luftwaffe coined a new
to describe the wholesale destruction of cities, *zu Coventrieren*
coventrate"', it needs to be remembered that (in the words of A.J.P. Ta
'even in ravaged Coventry the factories were back to full produ
five days after the raid'.[34] The death toll is also instructive, not
because the commentators are categorical in giving a figure bu
agree as to what it is. The newspapers at the time unanimously of
the conveniently round figure of 1000 dead. Piette follows the I
rian Norman Longmate in citing 663 fatalities. Louise Campbell,
ing twenty years later than Longmate, gives 568 as the defin
statistic. In *Philip Larkin: A Writer's Life*, Motion equally unhesitat
puts the number at 554. Coming into the present century, M
Gilbert's *Churchill at War* gives the figure as 507 – a fifty per cent re
tion on the original speculative statistic. By contrast, the *Encyclop*
Britannica's statement that 'at least 35,000 people and pe
135,000' were killed at Dresden not only acknowledges the \
greater horror of the Allied atrocity but honestly admits the diffi
of arriving at accurate statistics.[35]

Larkin visited the scene of devastation the same day as the *Birmin*
Gazette headline, desperately trying to find out if his parents were
bered among the victims. Two years later, still only twenty-one ye
age, he fictionalized the incident in his novel *Jill*, in which Coven
pseudonymized as Huddlesford. Though he subsequently describe
as 'juvenilia', the bombing of Huddlesford is described with a chast
and gravity quite at odds with the mythologizing of Coventry preva

in the larger culture (*J*, 19). Hence, of the newspaper accounts of the raid on Huddlesford we are told:

> The raid had been too large to ignore and the morning papers had gone to the other extreme, extracting every ounce of horror and pathos they could. … The dominating picture showed an old man gazing fiercely up at the sky: it was captioned THEY'LL GET IT BACK!
>
> (*J*, 211)

The press stories are so hyperbolic that our protagonist John Kemp imagines 'the whole town was a heap of wreckage', but when he gets there he finds the damage much less uniform – 'dozens of places he knew well had been wrecked' but other areas, including his home patch, are intact ('He could see his house, number forty-eight, standing in line with the rest, just as it had always done') (*J*, 214–15). Again, the media heroics (THEY'LL GET IT BACK!) are deflated by the prevailing pessimism John registers in a desultory conversation in a pub: '"I reckon they'll do this everywhere," said the young man, looking up again. "Everywhere. There won't be a town left standing"' (*J*, 218). It is worth reminding ourselves that Larkin Junior wrote this remarkably accurate and dispassionate account without benefit of hindsight while the war still raged. Perhaps one incidental benefit of having a father with Larkin Senior's unlovely political commitments was a heightened awareness of the propaganda emanating from *both* sides in the conflict.

If Larkin's writings refuse to partake of the myth of Coventry as innocent victim, they also reject the myth of Coventry as phoenix. The intention to rebuild Coventry Cathedral was announced the day after the raid.[36] Two years later Sir Giles Gilbert Scott, designer of the red telephone kiosk, was commissioned to undertake the task. When his detailed proposals were published in 1944, however, the stolidly traditional design met with a hostile reception. Scott tendered his resignation and the Harlech Commission recommended an open architectural competition to find a replacement. In October 1950 the competition conditions were published and 219 designs submitted from architectural practices around the world. The following year all 219 were exhibited at Larkin's old school, King Henry VIII, Coventry, and Basil Spence was declared the winner. Coming after the Scott *débâcle*, many linked Spence's victory with the Festival of Britain, which opened three months earlier and for which he had designed the Sea and Ships Pavilion, as proof that the Modernists had captured the architectural mainstream.

In the run-up to the composition of 'I Remember, I Remember'
development followed hard upon another, every step accompanie
radio, press and television attention. In 1952, Spence's model fo
new cathedral was exhibited at the Royal Academy Summer Exhibi
Sutherland was commissioned to design the seventy by forty-four
tapestry, the largest in the world; and Piper was invited to desigr
stained-glass baptistery windows. On 31 July 1953 the Cove
Cathedral Act received the royal assent. In 1954, the year of Lar
poem, a licence for the building work to commence was issued; v
on clearing the site began; and Jacob Epstein accepted the invita
for a sculpture of St Michael and the Devil to be positioned on the e
rior of the east wall of the cathedral. In March 1955, a few mo
before 'I Remember, I Remember' was published, work on the fou
tions got underway. A year later the Queen presided at the official
emony of the laying of the foundation stone. In 1958, the year La
recorded *The Less Deceived* – including 'I Remember, I Remember' –
the Marvell Press, the weaving of the tapestry commenced and
Chapel of the Cross was dedicated. In 1959, the year the L.P. of *The*
Deceived was released, the nave walls were completed, Epstein's sc
ture was cast, Piper was hired to design the vestments and John Hu
began engraving the panels of the west window. Finally, on 25
1962, the consecration ceremony took place in the presence of
Queen, the Archbishops of Canterbury and York, and a host of di
taries from around the world.

In the weeks that followed a festival was held in the cathedral fea
ing the first performances of specially commissioned compositions s
as Britten's *War Requiem* and Tippett's opera *King Priam*. Spence's be
Phoenix at Coventry, published to coincide with the consecration,
serialized in *The Sunday Times* and became an international best-se
Virtually every one of the Modernist practitioners involved in the ca
dral project already possessed or shortly acquired the highest hono
Epstein, Spence, Sutherland, Piper, Tippett and Peter Pears v
knighted; Britten declined a knighthood but was made a life peer ur
the title Lord Britten; while Elizabeth Frink became a Dame of the O
of the British Empire.

This, then was the 'Nothing' that was happening in Coventry at
time of the composition and publication of 'I Remember, I Rememb
While it is hard to imagine that Larkin was oblivious to events in
home town that were so uniquely in the public eye, the poem ma
no mention of them. Yet that very silence is an earnest of the po

critical distance from the mid-century cultural hegemony. Just when the Modernists of the first and second generations were making their peace with the old avant-garde shibboleths of Queen, country, church, title and capital, Larkin's steely poem goes resolutely about its undeceived business. It is ironical indeed that he whose Little Englandism is routinely compared unfavourably with the radical alienation of the Modernists is actually the one who maintains that God is dead, that routes are preferable to roots, that a ruined church in Ireland is more inspirational than a bombed and rebuilt cathedral in England ('Church Going' was written a few months on from 'I Remember, I Remember'), and that the post-war cultural consensus epitomized by Coventry must be renounced. If Larkin explicitly negates the clichés of the English pastoral tradition, he implicitly negates the assimilated Modernism of the day, groping towards a Postmodern 'third way' that will be both and neither.

That he was right so to do is suggested by the mediocrity of so much of the art in question. For a brief honeymoon period the Coventry synthesis carried critical and public opinion before it. Architectural gurus like Henry Russell Hitchcock, Nicholas Pevsner and Lewis Mumford praised the building. In the 1964 revised edition of his *Contemporary British Art*, Herbert Read compared with Picasso's *Guernica* Sutherland's struggle in the Northampton and Coventry religious images to render Modernism fit for public themes.[37] Read saw the Coventry tapestry, *Christ in Majesty*, as a pinnacle of Sutherland's career rather than the proof that his real but minor talent had overreached itself. Gradually, however, the conviction hardened that the cathedral lacked sanctity: whatever the actual beliefs of those involved, it came to be perceived as the sort of banal Christian monument that might be raised by a committee of agnostics. Fifteen years later, the heroine of Penelope Lively's novel *The Road to Lichfield* contrasts her present response to the cathedral with her enthusiastic reactions soon after the consecration:

> The cathedral is as it was in nineteen sixty-three but I am not ... somewhere along the way I appear to have lost my taste for it. I can't think how I ever approved of the tapestry, it seems hideous now, and the furnishings have dated so. Very Festival of Britain.[38]

Larkin's poem, by contrast, has retained both its humour and its toxicity – as the following epilogue demonstrates.

IX   Epilogue: A tale of two plaques

On 29 January 1998, the president of the Larkin Society, Ant
Thwaite, unveiled on the city's railway station a Coventry He
Plaque commemorating 'PHILIP LARKIN: POET AND CONVENT
(1922–1986)'. Larkin actually died in 1985, but never mind. The
mony excited considerable interest in the local and national medi
general line being that public opinion in Coventry resented
monopoly on the poet's memory and wished to reclaim him for th
of his birth. The plaque was erected by Coventry and Warwick
Promotions with the enthusiastic support of Virgin Rail. Of c
there were plenty of precedents for such a venture: in Adlestro
Edward Thomas poem of the same name is displayed in its entiret
once, but twice – once in the bus shelter above the old railway
plate (the station itself disappeared in the Beeching cuts of 1966
again on a wall of the village church. But what to quote or
plaque when the only Larkin poem that so much as men
Coventry is 'I Remember, I Remember'. With a critical acumen d
many of Larkin's commentators, those responsible chose the follo

> Coming up England by a different line
> For once, early in the cold new year,
> We stopped, and, watching men with number-plates
> Sprint down the platform to familiar gates,
> 'Why, Coventry!' I exclaimed. 'I was born here'.

That's it! A thirty-six-line poem is truncated to the first five lin
make the poet appear what he is not, a celebrant of rooted English
Of course, the censoring of six-sevenths of the text involves a
acknowledgement that only drastic surgery could amputate Larkin
the desired semblance of a 'COVENTRIAN'. Yet the truth is that, h
started as a centre for the manufacture of bicycles and then becom
United Kingdom's principal site of automobile production, mc
Coventry was always a vehicular city, an emblem of movement r
than stasis. It might reasonably claim to be the place most respor
for setting the nation's populous in motion.[39] This being so, wou
not have been a more fitting as well as a grander thing for Covent
applaud the fact that one of its sons, quite contrary to the reputatio
rooted Anglocentrism foisted on him by his critics, had in 'I Remer
I Remember' produced something truly unique: namely, the gre
anti-roots poem in contemporary English letters?

6
Larkin and Gender

I The mid-century reinscription of patriarchal values

The period 1940–60 witnessed the deepest entrenchment of patriarchal values since the Victorian era, often with specific reference to parliamentary acts of the 1840s and 1850s. In Chapter Three we remarked the intense ideological pressure to take sides that was exerted upon writers and artists during the Spanish Civil War and the Second World War. Evidence for this military conscription of literature reinscribing heterosexual norms is afforded by the career of Noël Coward, a remarkable case of a once-dissident author assuming the lineaments of a wartime national monument. In the 1914–18 conflict, Coward spent nine months in the army, much of it cleaning latrines, desperately pulling strings so as to avoid active service. After a breakdown, probably simulated, he was discharged with a six-month pension. For nearly twenty years thereafter Coward wrote and starred in plays which – in addition to his camp Postmodern masterpieces *Hay Fever*, *Private Lives* and *Present Laughter* – consistently addressed such taboo topics as drug addiction (*The Vortex*), extra-marital sex (*Fallen Angels*), homosexuality (*Semi-Monde*), troilism (*Design For Living*), and the culpability of church and state for the slaughter of the Great War and the betrayal of post-war promises (*Post-Mortem*). Many of these plays were censored or banned.

By the late 1930s, Coward was putting his queer shoulder to the wheel. (It is instructive how bellicose non-combatants can become when they have passed the age of conscription.) His 1939 play *This Happy Breed* tracked a lower middle-class family through the twenty years between the Armistice and the Munich crisis, offering in microcosm a picture of English patriotism, decency and duty in the face of the coming storm. In 1941 he wrote the screenplay for *In Which We Serve*,

starring in the film version he co-directed with David Lean. Base
real episode in Lord Mountbatten's life, the film offered the cre
Royal Navy ship as the epitome of the transcendence of class co
in a national crisis. The Admiralty loaned 250 sailors to act as extra
Royal family visited the set during filming; and while Coward
direct references to Mountbatten, in some sequences he wore the l.
naval cap as a visual clue to the *cognoscenti*.

At the manifest level the film espouses, indeed helps to create
mid-century ideological formation we dissected in the previous ch
At the latent or sub-textual level it undergrids this ideology with a
patriarchal assumptions that have to be kept subliminal in orde
their inherent contradictions be overlooked. Hence, the image o
unity is essentially propaganda: the incidence of industrial strike
markedly during the war years as compared with the 1930s.
Coward's English nationalism frustrates his desire to present the
crew as a microcosm of the United Kingdom, reducing the Scot
Welsh to supporting roles while Paddy, as usual, is conspicuous t
absence. Most pertinently for present purposes, the crew of H.M.S.
is male. The film takes it as paradigmatic that the women will s
home with the children, thereby constituting that feminized basti
decency, that motherland or Britannia, in defence of which the men
and die. Coward de-problematizes the way in which the war was
dered, presenting as natural and immutable the following patri
principles: that men shall rule over women and children; that olde
shall rule over younger; that upper class shall rule over lower; that E
shall rule over non-English; and that white shall rule over non-wh

This ideology, variously adapted and reformulated, is evident thr
out the mid-century decades in the countless films in which
Hawkins, John Mills and Richard Todd refought and rewon the S
World War (with foreign actors such as Victor Beaumont, Anton Dif
Carl Duering, Walter Gotell and George Mikell – many of them ref
from Fascism – endlessly condemned to play Nazis, like that bask
team that toured the world losing to the Harlem Globe-trotters).
there, too, in the best-selling war novels of Alistair Maclean and Nic
Montsarrat in which heterosexual and military prowess are equate
Montsarrat's *The Cruel Sea* (1951), for instance, masculinity is put t
test by women at home and the U-boats at sea; only those who are s
fast, loyal and proficient in both spheres survive.

This libidinal economy was enforced by a punitive use of Vict
obscenity laws that intensified in the post-war period. For mo
Larkin's life the official list of banned books included works by Rab

Defoe, Balzac, Flaubert (*Madame Bovary*), Maupassant, Céline, Upton Sinclair and Sartre. Pepys's *Diaries* and Sterne's *Tristram Shandy* were only available in expurgated editions. The peak year for the destruction of obscene publications was 1954, 'when an astonishing 167,000 volumes were sent to the guillotine or used to stoke the furnaces of Scotland Yard'.[1] Even seaside postcards came under attack, one hundred and sixty-five designs being condemned, thirty by the master of the genre Donald McGill. (McGill pleaded guilty to obscene libel to avoid being imprisoned. He was seventy-nine years old.)

The significance of this for a writer of Larkin's generation may be gauged if we remember that the year of his birth saw the publication *and the suppression* of Joyce's *Ulysses*. Sir Archibald Bodkin, the director of Public Prosecutions, enforced the ban after reading only forty-two of the novel's seven hundred and thirty-two pages, and did so without reference to court or jury.[2] Six years later, Radclyffe Hall's *The Well of Loneliness* was banned as 'an offence against public decency', its lesbian love story affronting heterosexual norms.[3] Most persecuted was D.H. Lawrence, for young Larkin 'the greatest writer of this century, and in many things the greatest writer of all time'. (*SL*, 101) The unexpurgated *Lady Chatterley's Lover* was not prosecuted on one occasion, but repeatedly: between 1950 and 1960 alone, nineteen different printings were referred to the director of Public Prosecutions; Customs routinely seized copies sent from abroad to private individuals; and in 1955, the year of *The Less Deceived*, a Soho bookseller was imprisoned for selling the novel.[4] In this context, modelling the twenty-four hour structure of *A Girl in Winter* on that of *Ulysses* may be read as a small act of solidarity and the lesbian writings of Brunette Coleman take on a subversive aspect.

That this repression impeded the development of Larkin's idiomatic means can be verified with reference to the *Lady Chatterley* trial, which receives a mention in 'Annus Mirabilis':

> Sexual intercourse began
> In nineteen sixty-three
> (Which was rather late for me) –
> Between the end of the *Chatterley* ban
> And the Beatles' first LP.
>
> (*CP*, 167)

What began in 1963 was not the sex act itself, of course, but its uncensored artistic representation (hence the references to Lawrence and the

Beatles). The relevance of this to Larkin's practice is that when Per
was put on trial in October 1960 for publishing *Lady Chatterley* unb
lerized, prosecuting counsel based the case for censorship on th
quency with which the words 'fuck', 'cunt', 'balls', 'shit', 'arse', '
and 'piss' were employed.[5] In the same period the Lord Chambe
empowered by the Theatres Act of 1843, was deleting 'poof', 'rog
and 'balls' from Osborne's *The Entertainer* (1957); 'titties' from O
Entertaining Mr Sloane (1964); and 'fuck all' and 'bugger' from Pi
Landscape (1967).[6]

It was in 1962, precisely 'Between the end of the *Chatterley* ban' (
and 'the Beatles' first LP' (1963), that Larkin wrote 'Sunny Prestatyn'
its lexicon of 'tits', 'crotch', 'cock', and 'balls' (*CP*, 149). Shortly there
'The Dance' added 'shit' (*CP*, 156); 'High Windows', 'fucking and bl
(*CP*, 165); 'Sad Steps', 'piss' (*CP*, 169); 'Posterity', 'fart' and 'ba
(*CP*, 170); 'The Card-Players', punningly, 'turd' and 'prick' (*CP*,
'Poem about Oxford', 'arselicker' (*CP*, 179); 'This Be the Verse', '
'fucked' (*CP*, 180); 'Vers de Société', 'craps', 'arse','bitch' (*CP*, 181–2);
Life with a Hole in It', 'sod' (*CP*, 202); and in 1979, with his last si
cant poem 'Love Again', 'wanking' and 'cunt' (*CP*, 215).

Like the return of a repressed memory, there surface in Larkin's
poems pre-Victorian registers of profanity that had been purged
English literature by the 1857 Obscene Publications Act. Think of E
coy resort to French in 'Gerontion' ('Rocks, moss, stonecrop,
merds') or Hemingway's mealy mouthed expletives in *For Whom th
Tolls* ('you lazy drunken obscene unsayable son of an unnam
unmarried gypsy obscenity').[7] Norman Mailer's use of the euphe
'fugging' in *The Naked and the Dead* prompted the actress Ta
Bankhead, when they were introduced, to enquire if he was the y
man who did not know how to spell. In this perspective, Larkin's c
diction might be regarded as a half-way house between the censo
of the Modernist era and the brilliant incontinent obscenit
Tarantino's Postmodernist cinema (think of the pre-credit convers
in *Reservoir Dogs*: 'Let me tell ya what "Like a Virgin"s about. It's a
some cooze who's a regular fuck machine. I mean all the time, mor
day, night, afternoon, dick, dick, dick, dick, dick, dick, dick, dick,
dick, dick') or of *Jerry Springer – the Opera* (in which the expletives
up like incoming planes above Heathrow).[8]

Too physically inept for school sports; cursed with a stammer tha
vented him from publicly exploiting his command of language;
ciently vexed by an authoritarian father to side with his dithering mc
rejected for military service on the grounds of poor sight; correspor

from home with conscripted buddies, Jim Sutton and Kingsley Amis, like the wife or girlfriend left behind in wartime flicks: Larkin was thoroughly at odds with the mid-century libidinal economy. This alienation is conspicuous in his writings which from the late 1930s onwards experiment with ways of exposing the arbitrariness of the connections between sex (the biological given), gender (the socially constructed) and desire (or sexual orientation). These deconstructive experiments might be divided into three overlapping phases, the second of which has been seriously misread by his critics while the third and most important has been completely overlooked. The first phase (1939–49) looks like a case of 'slashing about in a bewilderment' (in Henry James's phrase) as Larkin frenziedly moved through anti-war, homosexual, masturbatory, lesbian and heterosexual woman-centred narratives. In the second phase, beginning in 1950 with 'If, My Darling', he adopted the strategy of expressing the poem through a coarse male narrator who by performing masculinity to excess exposes its structural inadequacies. The final phase, initiated in 1948 with 'An April Sunday Brings the Snow', is the dominant mode of Larkin's mature verse and entails the erasure of all indicators of the gender of the narrator and addressee so that the binary certitudes on which patriarchy is predicated (male/female, masculine/feminine, heterosexual/homosexual) are compromised and subverted.

II   Queering the wartime libidinal economy

Larkin was seventeen when the Second World War commenced. His destabilization of gender norms begins with the anti-heroism of poems like 'Conscript', 'Observation' and 'After-Dinner Remarks' with their awkward, diffident yet oddly tenacious resistance to wartime constructions of masculinity. As its title suggests, the 1941 poem 'Conscript' presents war as something one has to be press-ganged into, the very opposite of 'The Volunteer' by C. Day Lewis. 'After-Dinner Remarks' goes further, defining male non-combatants as 'neuter' in that they do not fit the prescribed gender binary of women who stay at home and men who go off to fight. The term 'neuter' carries pejorative associations (the *Oxford English Dictionary* gives eunuch as a synonym), as though their liminal position is downright unmanly. However, the thrust of the poem's argument is that these castrati who 'remain' at home survive, whereas 'real men' die horribly:

> Choose what you can: I do remain
>   As neuter: and meanwhile

> Exploding shrapnel bursts the men
> Who thought perhaps they would disdain
> The world
>
> > (*CP*, 241)

Approaching the age of conscription, Larkin is proposing that the vailing patriarchal values are captive and deathly.

'I see a girl dragged by the wrists' (1944) offers a more radical q ing of wartime machismo. The male narrator, observing first dragged playfully through snow and then two old men shovellin snow onto a cart, surmises that he will only achieve the spontane the former via the laboriousness of the latter: 'Each dull day and despairing act // Builds up the crags from which the spirit leaps' (*CP*, What compels the attention is the way this tripartite structure (t antithesis, synthesis) is unable to contain, and therefore seems a ra alization of, seething polymorphous perversity. The initial surprise adult male identifying with a girl is compounded by his insistence he would like to be her:

> Perhaps what I desired
> – That long and sickly hope, someday to be
> As she is –
>
> > (*CP*, 278)

> To be that girl! – but that's impossible
> > (*CP*, 279)

This is more strange in that the girl is the submissive partner. More it is not disclosed who is doing the dragging, so although the sce playfully erotic the reader cannot be sure that the dominant part a man. To imagine the girl's captor to be female is to face the diz prospect of a work of wartime literature in which a man of militar craves the role of subordinate partner in a lesbian relationship.[9]

Similar complexities arise at the poem's close with an allusion t unicorn, in Christian iconography a symbol of innocence – though the effect is far from innocent:

> If I can keep against all argument
> Such image of a snow-white unicorn,
> Then as I pray it may for sanctuary
> Descend at last to me,
> And put into my hand its golden horn.

Although snow-white, Larkin's unicorn retains something of its archaic pagan mystery. The word 'horn' is slang for the male sex organ in a state of arousal: Partridge's *Dictionary of Historical Slang* delightfully cites *old horny*, the male member; *hornification*, a priapism; *Miss Horner*, the female pudenda; and *cure the horn*, to have sexual intercourse. The hand/horn conjunction of the last line therefore has masturbatory connotations. At one level of meaning, a poem that begins with a man envying a captive lesbian ends with him fantasizing giving a 'hand-job' to a mythical beast. Written as the allies prepared for the Normandy landings, 'I see a girl' projects an image of manhood in which the martial values have been supplanted by hints of bondage, sapphism, homosexuality, submissiveness and bestiality.

Young Larkin wreaked comparable havoc with the woman-centred works of his first phase, not least those attributed to Brunette Coleman. The name is less 'the female pseudonym' described by Booth than a heteronym, designating an imaginary author of real works.[10] The name itself puns on that of Blanche Coleman, the leader of a contemporary all-female jazz band: what the real Blanche did for music, her fictional 'sister' Brunette would do for literature. The works attributed to Brunette are the novels *Trouble at Willow Gables* and *Michaelmas Term at St Bride's*; the seven-poem sequence, *Sugar and Spice*; the essay 'What Are We Writing for?' and a fragment of autobiography, 'Ante Meridian'. Most of these works consciously explore the connections between gender and genre by focusing upon the 'little Copernican universe' (*TWG*, 269) of the girl's school. Brunette acknowledges that schoolgirl literature is characteristically nostalgic but defends the *Sugar and Spice* poems with the claim that such escapism can be humane and consolatory in a wartime context:

> These poems were all written in the August and September of this year [1943], and I make no apology for presenting a collection of what may seem 'trivia' in these disturbed times. I feel that now more than ever a firm grasp of the essentials of life is needed.
>
> (*TWG*, 243)

This last is at once a camp pose, wonderfully arch and facetious, and a sturdy defense of the sanity of schoolgirl fiction when compared with the insanity of the actual world of men. One is reminded, however distantly, that Cézanne met the accusing question 'What did you do in the Franco-Prussian War?' with the unflinching rejoinder, 'I strengthened my sense of the motif'.

Most of the works in the Brunette canon honour the conventions of their genre while heightening the lesbian subtext that is present but denied in the originals. The poem 'Femmes Damnées' is the most accomplished of Brunette's creations and the one that most productively problematizes her existence by abandoning the boarding school setting. 'Femmes Damnées' is an abbreviated translation of one of two poems of that name Baudelaire wrote on the subject of lesbianism.[11] The choice sits ill with the conceit of Brunette's own sapphism, whether 'closet' or 'out', as the French original is condemnatory – much more so than the second 'Femmes damnées' which immediately follows it in *Les Fleurs du Mal*. It also strains the heteronymic identity that, in Englishing Baudelaire, Brunette substitutes for his critique of the lesbian lovers a new and to modern eyes more telling moral condemnation.

The most visible sign that Brunette is rewriting Baudelaire for a later century is that of length: her poem is less than a quarter the size of his (twenty-four lines against one hundred and four). In the process, she relocates the action from France to England, from urban to suburban, from past to present. It is symptomatic of these changes that the prosaic and contemporary Rachel and Rosemary replace the Second Empire names of Baudelaire's lovers, Delphine and Hippolyte. Thematically, the most extreme amputations are Hippolyte's four-stanza speech combining a statement of love for Delphine with apprehension that lesbianism is a mortal sin, and the narrator's closing five-stanza denunciation –

> – Descendez, descendez, lamentables victimes,
> Descendez le chemin de l'enfer éternel ![12]

– whose fire and brimstone tones confirm Hippolyte's worst fears.

The stripping away of Victorian rhetoric releases the poem from didacticism as though Brunette's project was to present a more up to date, less judgemental view of the lesbian lovers. This is not what happens. Baudelaire's Delphine is strong and ardent, like a big cat; but if there is something predatory in her approach to Hippolyte it is with a view to winning her lover's adulation. Brunette's equivalent is predacious in a more critical, destructive sense:

> Stretched out before her, Rachel curls and curves,
> Eyelids and lips apart, her glances filled
> With satisfied ferocity; she smiles,
> As beasts smile on the prey they have just killed.
>
> (*CP*, 270)

Half way through the poem we are told: 'Rosemary sits. Her hands are clasped. She weeps.' Nor has her anguish diminished by the last line: 'The only sound heard is the sound of tears.' Rosemary's grief is neither prompted by Hippolyte's fear of eternal damnation nor mollified by Hippolyte's feelings of love and gratified desire. She is the more distraught of the two.

In depicting Rachel's triumph as murderous and Rosemary as inconsolable, Brunette has exchanged the easy moralizing of the Baudelaire (lesbianism is infernal) with a point of Jamesian conviction: the charge against Rachel is not homosexuality but violation. Larkin exposes Coleman's limits by discovering a theme that is beyond her expressive range but central to his own, the theme of real or symbolic rape. 'Femmes Damnées' is the lesbian precursor of such heterosexual violations as John Kemp's drunken assault upon Gillian (*Jill*), Robin Fennel's attempt to bully Katherine Lind into having sex (*A Girl in Winter*), the Victorian rape in 'Deceptions', or Titch Thomas's graphic penetration of the poster girl in 'Sunny Prestatyn'. In this purview, sexual coercion is wrong whether perpetrated by a man or a woman.

Finally, it is worth remarking that 'Femmes Damnées' confirms Barbara Everett's perception that Eliot was Larkin's role model when importing French Symbolism. The morning sun throwing 'patterns on the curtains' echoes the 'magic lantern' that 'threw the nerves in patterns on a screen' in 'Prufrock'. There are affinities between the description of the desolate Rosemary sitting with her hands clasped and the woman in 'Preludes' 'Sitting along the bed's edge' with her feet 'clasped' in 'soiled hands'. The account of the photos and books in the living room mirrors Pipit's view at the start of 'A Cooking Egg'. Rachel's name and feline ferocity invoke the 'Rachel née Rabinovitch' who 'Tears at the grapes with murderous paws' in 'Sweeney Among the Nightingales'. The way she smiles, 'As beasts smile on the prey they have just killed' also brings to mind the voluptuous Grishkin of 'Whispers of Immortality' who devours men as South American cats devour tropical monkeys.[13] By translating Baudelaire through Eliot, Larkin not only queers national boundaries – English, French and American registers thickening the palimpsest – he further queers the gender boundaries. For now we can say that Rachel Wilson preys upon Rosemary, as Robin Fennel preys upon Katherine, and Grishkin and Rachel née Rabinovitch prey upon men. In every case it is neither the gender nor the sexual orientation that is being condemned but the abuse of sexual power. More than any other poem in the collection, 'Femmes Damnées' explodes the Brunette Coleman heteronym by invalidating the kindergarten binary of her title *Sugar and Spice*.

III Performing masculinity to excess

In the second great phase of Larkin's assault upon patriarchal values he hit upon one of the two narrative strategies that would dominate his major poems, that of performing masculinity to excess the better to expose its present malformation. These are the notorious bachelor poems in which ungendered narrators seem to side with sexist men ('Deceptions', Sunny Prestatyn', 'The Card-Players') or coarse male narrators take centre stage and spout their unlovely views direct ('If, My Darling', 'Self's the Man', 'High Windows', 'The Life with a Hole in It', 'Love Again'), the two modes being united in their apparent misogyny and increasing resort to obscenities. In both cases the ugly convictions on display are undermined by puns, citations and rhetorical excess, the poems challenging the male stance and inviting us to consider alternatives. In seeming to tell one story (the misogynistic one) while actually telling another (the anti-patriarchal one), Larkin typically requires the reader to keep the words on the page under reassessment; but by conflating author and narrator, biographical critics fail in this duty and bowdlerize the most significant areas of meaning.

One way we can explore this is by considering the manner in which three eminent Larkin scholars – Rossen, Tolley, Booth – have established a consensual reading of one of the more 'sexist' poems, 'Letter to a Friend about Girls'. Despite occasional disclaimers, all three critics tend to assume that most of Larkin's poems are narrated by the same person; that the person in question is Larkin himself, so that the poems are essentially autobiographical and suffer little literary or fictive mediation; and that, therefore, other types of material, Larkin's private correspondence for example, can be placed on the same interpretative or diagnostic plane as the poems.

Rossen is at once the most expansive and reductive of the three, beginning her discussion of the poem with a catchpenny psychoanalysis of the author: 'Larkin's fury against women is not so much a declared state of siege against them personally as it is an internal battle raging within himself'.[14] Then she proceeds to conflate the author with the narrators of his poems:

> Women tend to play a role in his writing which finds him not far from misogyny; at the least he capitalises on the energy which derives from seeing sexual politics solely from the man's point of view, and from projecting much of his frustration onto women, thus locating the source of his anger there.

Having adopted an elevated, politically correct viewing position from which to look down on the poet's sexual politics, she identifies a reprehensible dichotomy in his representations of women:

> Larkin's ... bachelor characters usually assume that beautiful women will pay absolutely no attention to them. Should one be so fortunate as to meet a 'bosomy English rose', as does the speaker in 'Wild Oats', one may be certain that the beauty will be 'trying' for her part, 'not to laugh'. Moreover the only available women are either ugly (and therefore undesirable) or, ironically, devalued by their accessibility.

She then declares that 'this division between different types of women appears most notably in "Letter to a Friend about Girls", where the poet' – the poet, note, no longer 'the speaker' or narrator – 'regrets his comparatively unsuccessful attempt to seduce attractive women, concluding "all the while / I've met a different gauge of girls from yours"'.[15]

Tolley's altogether briefer treatment of the poem accepts most of Rossen's premises, such as the division of the women into two kinds, but in shuttling between the poet and his narrator endeavours to be more understanding of Larkin's presumed viewpoint: 'One suspects that the girls the speaker of the poem met better represented the type of girl that Larkin found congenial than did the girls the speaker wished he could meet'.[16] Decent though it is of Tolley to strive to avoid Rossen's condescension to a major author, it is nonetheless disturbing that his interpretation of this literary text is made to rest upon an unverified speculation about the type of girl its author found congenial. Would he, one wonders, appreciate readers of his critical books attributing the evaluations expressed therein to guesses about his own sexual preferences?

Even Booth, an altogether subtler analyst, begins his discussion of the poem by relating it to a past crisis in Larkin's personal life and then goes on to posit Kingsley Amis as the recipient of the 'letter':

> As time passed, Larkin developed beyond the immediate pain of the crisis of 1950, though it still re-emerges here and there in wry retrospective formulations. 'Letter to a Friend about Girls', completed in 1959, for example, shows a relaxed attempt to ironise the pattern of his own personal sexual history in terms of the comic categories of Amis's fiction. At last, Larkin confides, he has realised his friend's secret. They are, and always have been, on different planes of existence.[17]

At a stroke, a floating text, unanchored from certitude, rife for interpretative play, which mentions neither Larkin nor Amis, has been closed down into a letter from the one to the other. Booth's one hermeneutical flourish, which at least has the virtue of being provocative, not to say perverse, is to claim that the ugly, morally repressed and sexually unwilling women the narrator complains of are actually preferable to, or at least more worthy than, the beautiful concupiscent ones his pal enjoys sex romps with. Recognition of this in turn makes our narrator the moral superior of his addressee because, Booth claims, his attitude to women is less exploitative:

> Beneath the droll contrast between this friend's facile conquests and his own comic failures with women, the poet seems almost to be identifying himself with his particular 'gauge' of women, sympathising with them, and defending them from his friend's disregard. A faint note of moral earnestness even creeps in. … Both he and the women are in the same unhappy boat. Clearly this poet will never be able to see his women as birds to be bagged. That is the mere stuff of fantasy. His view of womankind is exasperatedly sympathetic rather than predatory.[18]

Once again one notices the insistence with which Booth, entirely without evidence, conflates Larkin with the narrator by describing the latter as a poet: 'the poet seems almost to be … . Clearly this poet … .' Once again (to paraphrase Barthes) the 'author' is being inscribed in the text so as to impose a limit upon it, to furnish it with a final signified, to terminate the writing. All three critics, then, agree on the fundamentals: the narrator is Larkin; he and the addressee have widely discrepant levels of success in their sex lives; and Larkin puts this down to the fact that he meets less beautiful and less compliant 'girls' than does his pal.

In seeking to demonstrate that the poem is open to two diametrically opposed readings, one of which our commentators are blind to, I want first to discredit their biographical approach since this minimizes the textuality of a text which is at considerable pains to have its literarity acknowledged. The very title draws attention to this, not just because it underlines its own scriptedness (poems are sometimes oral, but letters are invariably written), but also because it invokes three entire literary genres – namely, the genre of letters, the genre of the epistolary novel and the genre of the verse epistle. Clearly the most pertinent of these is the category of the verse epistle, since that is the one to which our poem belongs, but the other two genres also provide a plethora of meaningful parallels with our text. To take one possibly fortuitous but nevertheless striking example from the genre of letters: the title of our poem is remarkably close to the title of a book by Winifred Holtby, an earlier author with strong Hull connections (her most celebrated novel, *South Riding*, is set in the city), of whose works Larkin was aware. Holtby's *Letters to a Friend* (1937) gathers her correspondence with a woman companion who went to live in South Africa, the latter always being addressed as Rosalind and Holtby always signing herself as Celia in an allusion to the female friends in *As You Like It*. We therefore have two Hull authors writing letters to friends of the same sex through the voices of characters drawn from Shakespeare plays – for, as we shall shortly see, the Larkin poem appears to be narrated by Horatio to Prince Hamlet.

Whether or not they were authorially intended, more such fruitful parallels abound within the genre of the verse epistle, the letter written in verse. This genre originates with Horace's *Epistles* and Ovid's *Heroides*, with most European languages contributing to the tradition. Famous examples in English literature include Ben Jonson's *The Forest*, Pope's *Epistle to Dr Arbuthnot*, Byron's *Epistle to a Friend*, Auden's *New Year Letter* and the Auden–MacNeice collaboration, *Letters from Iceland*. Byron was no particular favourite of Larkin's, yet one cannot help noticing that the title of Larkin's poem is identical with *Epistle to a Friend* except that the latter uses the older word for a letter; moreover, the Byron prototype similarly involves a male narrator explaining that it is his unhappy love life that prevents him from partaking of his male addressee's cheeriness. In the case of the Auden–MacNeice volume, we know that Larkin admired it since within four years of its publication he and fellow schoolboy Noel Hughes had modelled upon one of its contents their own identically titled 'Last Will and Testament'. As it happens, Auden and MacNeice derived this title from 'The Last Will and Testament' of the splendidly scurrilous French poet Jacques Villon, some of whose verses Larkin later went on to translate. However one approaches it, then, the title is so gravid with intertextuality as to forewarn us against reading the ensuing poem as unmediated autobiographical self-disclosure.

Suitably alerted to this multi-layering by the title, the attentive reader will catch the Biblical echo in the words 'where to want / Is straightway to be wanted, seek to find' from stanza two of the poem proper (*St Matthew*, chapter 7, verse 7: 'Ask, and it shall be given you; seek and ye shall find'). Some readers may think they descry in the opening line of stanza three, 'And beauty is accepted slang for yes', itself reminiscent of the 'enormous yes' of Larkin's 'For Sidney Bechet', a distant echo of the celebrated ending of Joyce's *Ulysses*. Is our narrator complaining that he

never gets the unfaithful wives, the promiscuous Molly Bloom
friend has such success with? Harder to miss – though our critics
age it – is the literary allusion in the *saeva indignatio* of stanza four,
Latin words being excerpted from Jonathan Swift's epitaph *ubi
indignatio ulterius cor lacerare nequint* (he has gone where savage
nation can tear his heart no more). Famous as a satirist (another
that we should not take our narrator at face value), Swift published
one inconsiderable pamphlet under his own name. His preferred
was to mediate texts through complex heteronyms – the Dublin d
of *The Drapier's Letters*, for instance, or Lemuel Gulliver who is pres
as not just the narrator but the author of *Gulliver's Travels* (or,
complicated still, as the author of papers his friend Richard Sym
has edited for the public). Italicized for emphasis, this two-word c
tion is a red light against biographicalism. In addition to these li
references, the poem is replete with clichés, platitudes and form
turns of phrase at the deployment of which Larkin was a dab
phrases like 'we play in separate leagues. ... I couldn't credit. ...
have their world. ... But there, don't mind ... I'm happier now I'v
things clear. ... Must finish now'. There is a sense in which such
neyed expressions are themselves quotations, but ones that have los
quote marks.

Using citations like these as stepping stones, some rock-solid, c
more speculative, the reader traverses the text from a title tha
freighted with allusions to this ending, which is almost as de
textured:

> Must finish now. One day perhaps I'll know
> What makes you so lucky in your ratio
>
> – One of those 'more things', could it be? *Horatio.*

The epistolary theme of the title is echoed at the close by the
'Must finish now', permitting one to read the italicized name at the
Horatio, as the signatory of the letter. But which Horatio? Is the na
punning reference to Horace as a founding father of the verse ep
Could it refer to the most famous Horatio in English history, Adm
Lord Nelson – not that he was notably unsuccessful with the 'girls'! O
haps to his namesake, Horatio Hornblower, the hero of C.S. Fore
maritime novels? And what about the murdered son in Kyd'
Spanish Tragedy? The answer is provided by the phrase 'more thin
direct quotation from Hamlet's words to Horatio at the end of th

Act of Shakespeare's play: 'There are more things in heaven and earth, Horatio, / Than are dreamt of in your philosophy' (Act I, Scene V, lines 166–7).[19]

It is bewildering that three commentators writing from English departments in three countries so pursue their biographical interpretation that they suppress this extensive evidence of literary mediation, neglecting even to mention the Horatio who narrates the poem – and this despite the fact that he is a character drawn from the most canonical text in English literature. (To be totally accurate, Rossen does make one fleeting acknowledgement of our narrator, though as she refers to him as 'the *successful* figure of Horatio' [my italics], it might be kinder to overlook the fact.)[20] But the situation is yet more absurd, for the very commentators who muddle the poet with his narrators, often using his personal life and private correspondence to buttress their case, unanimously come up with a reading the exact opposite of that which Larkin favoured. In a real letter to a real friend, fellow poet Anthony Thwaite, Larkin said of this piece:

> ... what it was *meant* to do was to postulate a situation where, in the eyes of the author, his friend got all the straightforward easy girls and he got all the neurotic difficult ones, leaving the reader to see that in fact the girls were all the same and simply responded to the way they were treated. In other words, the difference was in the friends and not in the girls.
>
> (*SL*, 428–9)

Paradoxically, the critics who commit the Intentionalist Fallacy (ignoring Lawrence's admonition 'Never trust the artist. Trust the tale.') not only get the author's view completely wrong but in the process opt for the more reactionary reading.[21] They see Larkin employing a reliable narrator, whereas Larkin himself thinks the meaning of the poem depends upon our realization that the narrator is unreliable. Where Larkin's interpretation implies a critique of the male narrator's attitude to women, the critics see him as sharing the narrator's views. Whether overtly judgemental (Rossen), evasive (Tolley) or ingeniously defensive (Booth), all three critics accept a division of the women into two kinds, whereas Larkin himself sees no such distinction but rather two different kinds of male attitude. I am not quoting Larkin's private view of the poem as though it carried particular weight, since that would be to embrace the very Intentionalist Fallacy I am accusing our critics of adopting. Instead,

I am using the evidence of the Thwaite letter to demonstrate just ⬛
disastrous it is to confuse Larkin with his narrator and thereby as⬛
that one knows the poet's mind. Furthermore, I am claiming that ⬛
valid support as can be found for the Larkin interpretation lies not i⬛
letter to Thwaite but in the very literary mediations that debar one ⬛
reading the poem as versified autobiography.

This point can be secured if we return for a moment to Horatio⬛
signatory of our verse epistle, and consider the way in which his ⬛
brings into play yet another literary text that shadows Larkin's ⬛
throughout. For it would be ridiculous to pretend that 'Letter to a F⬛
about Girls' so works through Horatio's character that his narr⬛
could be mistaken for an excerpt from Shakespeare's *Hamlet*, the p⬛
detailing being resolutely twentieth century with its references to ⬛
versity tutorials, telephone booths, away football matches and sala⬛
Sunday newspapers. We therefore deduce that a modern letter-wri⬛
using Horatio's name in much the same manner that Winifred H⬛
signed herself Celia and addressed her correspondent as Rosalinc⬛
have thus identified three main levels of narration: Larkin is the *a*⬛
of the poem; our modern *narrator* is the author of the letter; and Ho⬛
is a *persona* adopted by that narrator. What concerns us here is th⬛
adopting the *persona* of Horatio writing to Prince Hamlet, our mo⬛
narrator has given metaphorical expression to his slightly Poot⬛
sense of unimportance, of not being one of life's heroes, of being ⬛
player, part of the retinue of his more dashing pen pal. And this in⬛
brings to mind such lines as the following from 'The Love Sor⬛
J. Alfred Prufrock':

> No! I am not Prince Hamlet, nor was meant to be;
> Am an attendant Lord, one that will do
> To swell a progress, start a scene or two,
> Advise the prince; no doubt, an easy tool,
> Deferential, glad to be of use,
> Politic, cautious and meticulous;
> Full of high sentence, but a bit obtuse;
> At times, indeed, almost ridiculous –
> Almost, at times, the Fool.[22]

In the passage quoted above, the literary references (such as the all⬛
to the 'high sentence' of the Clerk of Oxenford in Chaucer's *Cante*⬛
Tales) adds to the prevailing impression that the speaker is too pom⬛

dufferish and middle-aged to be Horatio, bearing perhaps a closer resemblance to Polonius. Nonetheless, the parallels are suggestive: there is, for example, the same tripartite division in the narratology, with Eliot as author, Prufrock as narrator and Polonius as a Shakespearian persona of that narrator.

If such resemblances can be used to license further comparisons, then it might be hazarded that Larkin's narrator, like Prufrock, is singing a 'Love Song' that has no love object – that, indeed, both men's inability to find a suitable recipient for their songs exposes the stark fact that neither of them is capable of love. Prufrock makes no sexual approach to the female object of his musings, partly for fear that his advances would not be welcomed –

> Would it have been worth while
> If one, settling a pillow or throwing off a shawl,
> And turning toward the window, should say:
> > 'That is not it at all,
> > That is not what I meant, at all.'[23]

– and partly because he seems to doubt his own ability to complete the sexual act: 'Should I, after tea and cakes and ices, / Have the strength to force the moment to its crisis?' This dread of impotence is given a castrational aspect by his comparing himself with St John the Baptist beheaded at the behest of the sexually predatory Salome, a comparison so worded as to simultaneously invoke the Samson neutered, blinded and shorn by Delilah ('I have seen my head [grown slightly bald] brought upon a platter'). Larkin's protagonist is less sexually timid:

> you mine away
> For months, both of you, till the collapse comes
> Into remorse, tears and wondering why
> You ever start such boring, barren games

The language is saturated with *double entendres*, with all those metaphors of mining and boring, but the fact that these attempts at consummation are 'barren' implies that he is no more successful than is Prufrock. Both men have the air of being foxed by the trigonometry of love, unsure of how to relate to women and inclined to retreat from the fray, baffled and self-pitying. Prufrock's escapist tendency to idealize

women ('I have heard the mermaids singing') and our letter-writ●
belittle them –

> They have their world, not much compared with yours,
> But where they work, and age, and put off men
> By being unattractive, or too shy,
> Or having morals

– may be regarded as two extremes of the same masculinist impu●
justify romantic failure by pretending that women exist on a pla●
far above or so far below that of men as to thwart love's alchemy. ●
reading is a tenable one – and after all, our protagonist's inability t●
suade these women into bed with him is hardly surprising when ●
clearly despises their values and deplores their looks – then the ●
pretation offered by Larkin in his letter to Thwaite is validated. ●
alert to Larkin's love of paronomasia may feel that this readi●
clinched in the one-word closing sentence with its gross but de●
pun: Horatio/whore ratio. A man who thinks of women in this ●
authors his own amorous failure.

This is not to say that the Rossen–Tolley–Booth interpretati●
thereby annulled, even if its conclusions were arrived at by reduc●
biographical means. Theirs is the most obvious reading of the poen●
one the narrator himself advances, the one Larkin wanted us to see b●
we go on to see through it. And however much the literary parall●
endorse the interpretation Larkin provided in the Thwaite letter, ●
important not to exaggerate their significance for the *differences* bet●
our text and the works invoked are just as expressive as the resembla●
In the 'Love Song of J. Alfred Prufrock', for example, Eliot gives the r●
a far clearer moral perspective on the first person narration than ●
Larkin in 'Letter to a Friend'. The title of the Eliot poem is immedi●
followed by a six-line epigraph from Dante's *Inferno*, which prolept●
implies that Prufrock's alienated condition constitutes a modern ty●
Hell. These sorts of framing devices are precisely what Larkin withh●
making it much less easy to assess his narrator. Indeed, Larkin's let●
Thwaite indicates that his doubts about the poem's merit stem fron●
fact that it was more undecidable than he intended:

> Dear Anthony,
>   Can I enlist your aid as a literary critic? I have had the enclosed p●
> knocking around for ten years now, and every so often I take it out, ●
> it slightly, and try to bring myself to send it off somewhere, but ●

always held back by the oppressive thought that it really isn't any good. Can you decide for me – or, at any rate, let me have your opinion?

I suppose the very fact of my indecision means it is no good really: what it was *meant* to do was postulate a situation where, in the eyes of the author, his friend got all the straightforward easy girls and he got all the neurotic difficult ones, leaving the reader to see that in fact the girls were all the same and simply responded to the way they were treated. In other words, the difference was in the friends and not in the girls. The last line originally ran '– One of those "more things", could it be, Horatio?', making it a letter from Hamlet to Horatio: to make it a letter from Horatio to Hamlet may make better or worse sense, according to whether you think Horatio was a nicer chap than Hamlet or not. Certainly (presumably) Hamlet was a more neurotic chap than Horatio.

If anything, this prose letter is even more riddled with uncertainty than the verse letter on which it seeks adjudication: uncertainty as to Larkin's own judgement ('Can you decide for me'); uncertainty as to the poem's worth ('I have had the enclosed poem knocking around for ten years now …'); uncertainty as to whether or not it fulfills the author's intentions ('what it was *meant* to do …'); and uncertainty as to whether Horatio should address Hamlet or *vice versa* – all of these wobblings hilariously encapsulated in the 'Certainly (presumably)' of that last sentence. And these wobblings are amply justified, for Larkin does *not fulfill* his stated intention – at least, not decisively enough to rout the Rossen-Tolley-Booth-narrator position once and for all. Yet in this failure lies the poem's success, for Larkin has produced against his will an entire text that is as undecidable as Derrida's *pharmakon*; a text that will sustain, stanza by stanza, two diametrically opposed expositions; a text which therefore unmoors meaning from certitude and narrative from closure. The notion that women are divisible into two types, the uninhibited and the repressed, confronts the notion that on the contrary it is men who are divisible into those two categories. These opposed views endlessly interrogate and destabilize each other, thereby making a mockery of our overly assured and prescriptive gender binaries. For this poem is at once sexist and a critique of sexism, an example and an *exposé* of misogyny; a celebration of and a satire upon male camaraderie and its attendant phallocentrism; a study of the unfair way the world distributes life's pleasures and of the type of loser who creates the destiny he complains of; a poem which says precisely what its critics claim and which says the exact opposite.

This extraordinary, if unintended, feat is one for which it is difficult to find literary equivalents. In the category of verse one might refer the peculiar exegetical status of Larkin's text to the genre of the palinode, a poem or song retracting some earlier statement by the poet. A notable example in English is Chaucer's *The Legend of Good Women*, written to recant his earlier defamation of women in *Troilus and Criseyde*. The difference is that Larkin has combined the ode and its answering palinode in a single text, which allows one to take either of the two principal interpretations as original declaration and either as subsequent retraction. The poem is completely reversible. In the words of 'If, My Darling', it is 'double-yolked with meaning and meaning's rebuttal'.

IV   Gender ellipsis and essentialist criticism

Tolley, Rossen and Booth are Larkin admirers whose biographicalist methodology obscures the alluvial richness of poems of masculine excess like 'Letter to a Friend', thereby making it easier for a Paulin or Greer to pillory the poet for sexism. Neither camp appreciates that those Larkin novels and poems that entrench gender binaries can on closer inspection be found to have scripted reversal into their narratives so that what was once certain is overturned and society's writs of convention held up for interrogation. The same holds true with those poems – the overwhelming majority – whose radical ellipsis divests narrative of gender inflections in a determined attempt to sabotage category restrictions. Paradoxically, the less Larkin discloses about the sex of narrator and addressee, the more flagrant the biological essentialism of his exegetes. A case in point is John Carey's influential essay 'The Two Philip Larkins'.[24]

With the usual late millennial bowdler's disregard for the distinction between speech and text, Carey identifies two 'voices' in Larkin's verse, one of which he genders as male and the other female. There are whole poems in the male voice ('I Want to See Them Starving') or the female voice ('Deep Analysis', 'The Explosion'), though Carey's principal point is that most of the poems, especially the great ones, are alloys of the two: 'What I want to argue is that both voices, and the frequent alternation between them, are essential for Larkin's distinctive poetic voice'.[25] It is a commonplace of Larkin criticism that part of his greatness is attributable to the speed and deftness with which his poems modulate between different language registers – from the sacred to the profane, from the demotic to the arcane. In many ways, Carey's is a subtle and persuasive contribution to this well-established line of investigation, offering illuminating and close-grained readings of half-a-dozen poems.

The problem is that as the argument proceeds Carey seeks to validate his gendered distinction between the two voices by heaping up synonyms, adjectives and analogues. The upshot is that in the very act of demonstrating that Larkin's poems *combine* male and female, he *separates* the sexes so diametrically as to seem beyond all conjoining. Far from unmooring gender from certitude and robbing us of the comforting but lazy sense that we occupy a world governed by decidable categories – which is what Larkin does – Carey is able to ascribe every known value and characteristic, without hesitation, to one sex or the other. Hence, the male voice is said to be –

> single, agnostic, sceptical, scoffing, resentful, pessimistic, regretful, sardonic, misanthropic, negative, abrasive, crude, insensitive, blunt, inhibited, sneering, vulgar, stridently masculine, obscene, stridently obscene, offensive, aggressive, swaggering and coarse

– whereas the female voice is:

> oracular, measured, wistful, bardic, sensitive, educated, idealistic, tender, worshipful, nervous, positive, fruitful, rejoicing, celebratory, joyful, full of glad acceptance, procreative, concerned with human love, for sexual union and fertility and the continuity of life, reconciling, religious, tending (in the spiritual sense) towards remoteness and transcendence, nurturing, feeding, (possessed of) an acute discriminating perception of the natural world, positive, trusting, full of lyrical and oceanic yearning ...

Carey sums up the differences between the two by saying of the female side: 'This voice feels where the first voice thinks, it transcends the reality that the first voice analyzes, it inclines more to religion and the supernatural'.[26]

At one point Carey disarmingly acknowledges 'If we designate, as I'm suggesting we should, the two voices or two personae in Larkin as male and female, we do, I admit, run the risk of gender stereotyping'.[27] However, this fleeting apologia, no sooner granted than forgotten, seems comically inadequate alongside these monstrous sexual stereotypes. There can surely be no good reason for claiming that religious

belief is female (was Simone de Beauvoir not a woman?) and ag⌐
cism male (was Jesus an agnostic?), or that the use of swear word⌐
masculine prerogative (if he lived in Hull, as I do, and as Larkin⌐
instead of Oxford, Professor Carey would soon be disabused of that⌐
sion), or for describing the 'discriminating perception of the na⌐
world' as a female aptitude rather than a human one (was Wordsw⌐
a woman?).

Instead of acknowledging the factitious and arbitrary nature of ⌐
sexual differences, Carey seeks to entrench them at the biograp⌐
level: 'If we regard Larkin', he writes 'as divided between the male⌐
the female, then it might lead us to speculate about his mother's an⌐
father's role in forming his personality'.[28] Pursuing the paternal⌐
Carey remarks 'the older Larkin's intolerance, his admiration for Hi⌐
Germany' and 'his contempt for women'. However 'if we look a⌐
poem that Larkin wrote about his father's death, we find, surprisi⌐
that it is slanted towards femaleness'. Quoting 'An April Sunday B⌐
the Snow', Carey comments:

> The father here is cast, as it were, in the mother's role. It is the fa⌐
> who nurtures, feeds, provides sustenance for the family. The p⌐
> too, has the sensitivity of perception I have been associating with
> female Larkin. The observation that plum blossom looks white, ⌐
> you see snow against it, when it looks green, speaks for an acute,
> criminating perception of the natural world.

For Carey, the feminine tenderness in the depiction of the dead fa⌐
is dispelled by the poem's bleak resurrectionless close: 'It is a femi⌐
poem with a masculine ending'.[29]

This might seem like a perfect illustration of the gender ambig⌐
I am claiming for Larkin's poetry. So what is the problem? Well, to b⌐
with, the poem makes no mention of either Sydney or Philip Lar⌐
Nor does it refer to an unnamed father and son, asking us to dec⌐
who they are. It mentions no men at all. Nor does it mention ⌐
women. It is completely non-gender-specific. It does not even spe⌐
that the deceased is parent to the narrator nor that he or she is the o⌐
of the two. The poem Carey discusses is one (like Sylvia Plath's) enti⌐
'Daddy', or which situates a father figure in a real topography after ⌐
manner of Robert Lowell's 'Terminal Days at Beverly Farms', or wh⌐
carries the epigraph *i.m., Sydney Larkin*. In other words, it is the p⌐
Larkin chose not to write. By not specifying the relationship invol⌐
'An April Sunday' posits that all forms of love – parental, filial, sibl⌐

romantic, erotic, companionate, heterosexual, homosexual – are rendered equivalent by the physics of grief and loss. To put it another way, by employing ungendered narrators and addressees, Larkin undermined patriarchy's overly insistent demarcation between masculine and feminine, gay and straight, death recognizing no such distinctions.

But there is more! For to adopt a biographical approach that constructs the narrator in the image of the author is not only to insist that the protagonists of 'An April Sunday' are male but also that they are white. By saying nothing about the ethnicity or skin colour of narrator and addressee – we do not even know if they share the same race – the poem is inclusive, allowing equal entry to readers of every creed and colour. Carey has sexed and raced a poem that resolutely does neither. Consequently he does not perceive that the equality of sorrow among the bereaved across all racial and sexual categories makes 'An April Sunday' a testament to our common humanity.

The foregoing argument is not intended to deny biographical evidence that the poem's composition was prompted by Sydney Larkin's premature death from cancer. However, it would be a barbarous critical methodology that sought to tie the meanings of an artwork to the incident that triggered its creation: one might as well confine one's account of a butterfly to a description of the chrysalis from whence it emerged. Carey not only 'fills in' Larkin's radical ellipses, substituting a purely subjective poem for the universal one before him, he also overlooks the dissensual invocation of Vernon Watkins. The observation in the first stanza of the Larkin that plum blossom looks white until seen against snow, when it looks green, comes from Watkins's 'Music of Colours: White Blossom':

> White blossom ...
>
> The spray looked white until this snowfall.
> Now the foam is grey, the wave is dull.
> Call nothing white again
>
> Buds in April ...
> They will not break, not break, until you say
> White is not white again, nor may may.
> White will not be, apart, though the trees try
> Spirals of blossom, their green conspiracy.[30]

The observation Carey attributes to 'the female Larkin' in fact derives from a Welshman.

Larkin made no secret of his admiration for Watkins, though les
poet than as a role model in the combining of paid employment with
dedication to an unremunerative art (*RW*, 29–30; *FR*, 212–3). 'Mu
Colours: White Blossom' transcends his usual arid perfectionism an
added to over the years to make a discontinuous long poem that has
claims to be his greatest achievement. What concerns us here i:
Larkin quotes his friend and mentor's finest poem with a view to neg
its central message. For 'Music of Colours' asserts that the relational r
of the colour spectrum – the way plum blossom changes hue depei
upon what it is seen against – and, indeed, the cultural relativism d
modern condition, is corrected by the absolute truth of Christi
Christ's dazzling purity is such that by comparison nothing earthly c
called white at all. As the poem concludes: 'I know you, black swan'
  This is the religious faith that Larkin negates at the close of 'An
Sunday' by presenting the death of the addressee with such finality
whole point of the poem is that the only afterlife granted t<
deceased is the posthumous survival, itself sufficient for only one sun
of the plum jam. By showing Watkins's resurrectional hopes to d
for less than a harvest of fruit, the twenty-five-year-old Larkin was
ing a drastic gesture towards a new cultural formation, the or
would help to bring about, the one that did not believe in God r
the self-evidence of Carey-style sexual differentiation.
  While the assurance with which Carey sexes poems, even pa
poems ('It is a feminine poem with a masculine ending'), like a z
gist scrutinizing the genitalia of laboratory rats, is of unriv
bizarrerie, his tendency to slip from biographicalism into biolc
essentialism is far from unique. It was observed in the introduction
an international tribunal of critics (Timms, Tolley, Hope, Mori
Longley, Booth) has established 'Reference Back' as Larkin's mum p
as 'An April Sunday' is his dad poem. Andrew Swarbrick declares:

> The poet is on a visit home. Bored and dissatisfied, he pl.
> favourite jazz-record as a temporary distraction, only to hea
> mother's inappropriate and banal comment at the end of it:
> *was a pretty one*'. ... Henceforth, the poet's favourite blues recorc
> always recall to him this moment when the rift between mothe
> son became apparent.[31]

This is decidedly odd as it is not vouchsafed that the narrator is I
and the addressee Eva Larkin; nor that the relationship is that bet

mother and son; nor between male and female; nor that the narrator is
a poet; nor that the narrator is the visitant (the words 'wasting my time
at home, that you / Looked so much forward to' may signify that the
addressee is a guest who relishes periodic visits to the narrator's home);
nor even that the narrator likes jazz, since the lines

> I
> Played record after record, idly,
> Wasting my time
>
> (*CP*, 106)

may as readily be taken to mean that listening to such records is a waste
of time. It *is* verifiable that the narrator, like Larkin, was born in 1922,
'the year after' King Oliver recorded 'Riverside Blues'; however, there is
no evidence in the poem that the track was the narrator's favourite blues
number, nor is there testimony in his copious jazz criticism that it was
Larkin's. The consensus on 'Reference Back' involves commentators substituting their gendered certitudes for Larkin's radical ellipses and indeterminacies.

   The same applies to those poems thought to have been inspired by
Larkin's girlfriends. Motion, Dawson, Booth and Swarbrick agree (in
the latter's words) that the poem 'No Road' is 'directly related to the
Ruth Bowman relationship'.[32] Very *indirectly*, I would say, since nothing specific about that pairing, not even the sexes of the protagonists,
survives in the text. Similarly these critics tie 'Latest Face', 'He Hears
That His Beloved Has Become Engaged', 'Maiden Name' and 'Long
roots moor summer' to Larkin's infatuation with Winifred Arnott.
Hence, Booth:

> 'Long roots moor summer to our side of earth', dated June 1954 ...
> shows the other, selfless Larkin. It concerns a very specific absence –
> from Winifred Arnott's wedding. Here, his own refusal to participate
> in marriage is not selfishly defended. Instead, the poet celebrates the
> wedding ...[33]

Once again, the poem does not specify that the narrator is Larkin or a
poet or male; nor that the addressee is Winifred or a woman; nor on
what day, month or year the action takes place.

   This perpetual reinscription of girlfriends Larkin has banished from
his texts assumes farcical proportions in those cases where the identity

of the originatory 'muse' is a matter of dispute. The following di
charts how biographical critics have claimed either Maeve Brenr
Betty Mackereth to be the addressee of three late poems:[34]

POEM	ADDRESSEE	CRITIC
'Love Again'	Betty	Booth (1992)
	Maeve	Booth (2005)
	Maeve	Motion
	Maeve	Brennan
	Maeve	Bradford
'Morning at Last'	Maeve	Dawson
	Betty	Booth (1992)
	Betty	Booth (2005)
	Maeve or Betty	Motion
	Maeve	Brennan
	Maeve	Bradford
'When First We Faced'	Maeve	Dawson
	Betty	Booth (1992)
	Betty	Booth (2005)
	Maeve	Motion
	Maeve or Betty	Brennan
	Betty	Mackereth
	Maeve and Betty	Bradford

In much the same way that critics assigned the identical poe
Ireland or England depending upon what they knew, or though
knew, about the poet, so do they assign lovers. The result is as edify
the sight of Booth and Day arm-wrestling over the precise location
high windows in the poem of that name (Booth says Larkin's top-flo
at 32 Pearson Park while Day opts for Larkin's office in the Brynmor
Library).[35] A dispassionate observer would swiftly deduce that poems
to such variant readings must be radically unhoused from biogra
certitudes. Yet Larkin scholarship largely neglects the implications of
aporias in the endless, eyeless pursuit of the missing referent.

This argument can be secured with a brief but summative treat
of 'Talking in Bed', which Hope, Dawson, Booth and Motion co
'one of the few poems he wrote about himself and Monica'.[3]
Monica in question is Monica Jones, dedicatee of *The Less Dec*
Larkin's long-term, long distance companion with whom he s
house in the last years of his life. As before, the hermeneutical que
textual meaning is replaced by a biographical quest for an origin
'muse'; a poem which is entirely non-gender-specific is discuss

though narrator and addressee were named and sexed; and the subjective dimension is allowed to obliterate larger, more inclusive areas of meaning.

In practice, the poem's complete gender ellipsis permits the following narrative permutations: man addressing woman (heterosexual); woman addressing man (heterosexual); woman addressing woman (lesbian); and man addressing man (homosexual). As the poem's argument remains the same whichever of these permutations is assayed, it refuses to privilege one type of relationship over another. For instance, it entirely eschews the view, so widespread at the time, that gay relationships are inherently unstable compared to heterosexual ones. Conversely, it dismisses in advance that master narrative of the 1970s feminist novel in which a depressed housewife discovers the meaning of life by eloping with a girl-friend ('heterosexuality is the problem, lesbianism is the solution'). Whatever their sexual orientation, the poem asserts, human beings find it profoundly difficult to remain honest and kind over a long-term relationship.[37]

Larkin's role model in this complete gender ellipsis was Auden. Homosexual acts were imprisonable crimes until 1967 (with the supreme logic of the British law the punishment for loving other men was to be incarcerated in a world devoid of women). As a student at Oxford, Auden had been blackmailed by a man who found him in bed with John Betjeman.[38] At the other end of his life, *Time* magazine dropped a 1963 cover story on Auden because the managing editor objected to honouring a homosexual. Auden's answer was to write poems whose narrators and addressees were neither sexed nor gendered, smuggling his homoeroticism past the censor by rendering it subtextual. As Michael Schmidt says:

> Many of the poems answer to a gay reading, indeed seem to answer *only* to a gay reading, yet their desire, their occasion, is densely encoded in them. In each case a reader is free to say, 'but *perhaps* he meant', and this is the freedom he wanted us to have.[39]

Larkin recognized the inclusivity of this stratagem, its potential to universalize and equalize. 'Talking in Bed' was written in 1960, seven years before the Sexual Offences Act decriminalized homosexuality. No doubt prompted by Larkin's relationship with Monica Jones, as biographical-ists insist, its adoption of the Auden model makes the poem itself heterosexual or homosexual depending upon the reader's sexing of the characters. In direct contravention of British law, the rewards and pains of the two modes of love are equal in the eyes of the poem.

The complexity of Larkin's sexual politics is matched at the e▮
level, for 'Talking in Bed', like 'An April Sunday', is unraced as w▮
unsexed. The heterosexual, lesbian and gay permutations enume▮
above intersect with same-race and cross-racial pairings to yie▮
abundance of narratological reading positions: not just, say, black
to black woman (heterosexual) or black woman to black woman ▮
bian), but black man to white, brown, yellow or red woman, and s▮
As before, the differently raced interpretations are treated equally,
being as precious and as precarious in every case.

The overwhelming majority of the poems work in this way, ▮
gender and racial ellipsis to bespeak our common humanity. La▮
then, is the very opposite of the misogynist and racist depicte▮
detractors like Greer, Paulin, Jardine and Newsinger. Indeed, the▮
the more guilty of those sins since before they can mount these ac▮
tions they must first sex and race poems that he did not. Unanch▮
from biological essentialisms, his poems invite readers to experi▮
with a variety of narratological interpretations, some of which will ▮
better than others in particular cases, but no one of which can be ▮
to squeeze out all its rivals and effect biological closure. A respon▮
criticism – responsible to Larkin's anti-essentialism and to the mult▮
tural democracy in which we live – must be sensitive to such ideo▮
cal complexity. The critics reviewed in this chapter belong to ▮
pro-Larkin camp but their author-centred methodology unwitti▮
endorses the view that the works speak only for white middle ▮
Englishmen. However charitably we word this, it is not a tolerable ▮
ical incompetence that plays into the hands of the zealots who s▮
trialed Larkin's works for moral misdemeanors of which they ▮
entirely innocent. It is a scandal.

7
Larkin and Politics

I   J'Accuse

The most virulent critics of Larkin have been Marxists, New Historicists and self-appointed guardians of political morality like Terry Eagleton, Stan Smith, Tom Paulin, Lisa Jardine, Neil Corcoran, Germaine Greer, Antony Easthope and John Newsinger. The key points in the shared argument are that Larkin lived and wrote in a period of de-colonization; that instead of welcoming this, his poems are nostalgic for a lost golden age associated with the British Empire when every class, race and sex knew its place in the social hierarchy; that he therefore views history as a record of decline and sets his back against any form of change; and that the core of this ideology is a vision of England which, in Seamus Heaney's words, 'could be called Elysian'.[1] However, Heaney comes to praise Larkin. The spirit in which these critics approach the subject is better represented by another Ulster poet, the Belfast ranter James Simmons. He summarizes Larkin's position thus: 'This is a seedy time, I am a seedy man, but there was a time when real things happened (real religion, real jazz) and some of us remember'. Like other left-wing commentators, Simmons bemoans Larkin's lack of extremism: 'He isn't a fierce conservative, no Roy Campbell, but a seedy one'.[2] The South African poet Roy Campbell was a supporter of General Franco.

I have already proposed that Larkin's novels and poems are anti-patriarchy, anti-heterosexism, anti-homophobia, anti-biological essentialism (racial or sexual), anti-the marital monopoly and atheistical. We have also glimpsed his anti-capitalism, of which more anon. This radical political agenda is totally ignored by the aforementioned critics who nominate as Larkin's only political poems a handful of minor pieces in which they claim to descry his uglier allegiances. It is symptomatic that

Paulin's brutal essay, 'In Times When Nothing Stood: Philip Lark
titled after a three and a half line squib Larkin virtually disow
'please don't print it', he urged Charles Monteith (*SL*, 581) – rather
any of the poems upon which his reputation rests. Other favourit
gets are 'The March Past', 'MCMXIV', 'Homage to a Governm
'Naturally the Foundation will Bear Your Expenses', 'Going, Going
'The Winter Palace'.

Granted their political affiliations, it is surprising how often
left-wing critics are lured into error by utter disdain for a working
city like Hull. This is Terry Eagleton, erstwhile Thomas Warton Pro
of English at Oxford University: 'The Hull setting was symbolicall
for Larkin: as the twentieth century unfolded its wars and revolu
he cowered behind the book stacks in this remote provincial outp
The most blitzed city in the United Kingdom proportionate to size,
was not a place to hide from the horrors of war. As the third larges
in the country (not quite the backwoods stockade of Eagleton's fa
the city suffered eighty-six major Luftwaffe raids: eighty-five per c
its housing was damaged or destroyed, as was half its shopping c
two million square feet of factory space and substantial parts o
docks.[4] Larkin came to Hull from Belfast, which was also blitzed
grew up in Coventry, the first city to face such devastation. It be
belief that Larkin, whose life was almost entirely lived in cities sco
by the holocaust, should 'be hawked upon from the height of a d
ing spire'.[5] Is this what Regan meant when he claimed that 'for
thirty years Eagleton has been steadfast in his commitment t
socialist transformation of class society'?[6]

It was also Eagleton who fronted the Larkin *J'Accuse* in which sa
pillars of the English academic establishment collected a cheque fr
television company for blackguarding a poet who, safely dead, o
not answer for himself. Eagleton later explained his motivation:

> That I find things in Larkin to admire should come as a surprise
> to those who can't speak French. For the TV programme in wh
> pilloried him was of course entitled *J'Accuse* (a celebrated enoug
> erary cry), and to those who wrote angrily to me in defense of L
> (and there were a lot of them), protesting that I was being prejud
> one-sided, unbalanced, I could only reply with the query: 'l
> your French?' For the whole point of the TV series was of course
> avowedly to throw the usual 'balance' to the winds and go for the
> lar; one doesn't expect the prosecuting counsel to hand the ac
> an alibi.[7]

'J'Accuse' were the first words of an open letter the novelist Emile Zola wrote in 1898 attacking the French establishment – the President, the army, the judiciary, the government, the press – for imprisoning one Captain Dreyfus as a German spy. The victim of anti-Semitism, Dreyfus was entirely innocent of the charge but was given a life sentence on the notorious Devil's Island. Zola was found guilty of libel, fled to England and in 1902 died in a bizarre accident that some consider state-sponsored murder. In 1906 Dreyfus was exonerated. As the original 'J'Accuse' involved a lone writer taking on the establishment (possibly at the expense of his life) and the second involved the establishment rubbishing a lone writer, one must either return Eagleton's query 'how's your French?' or else attribute to shamefaced cant this flagrant abuse of Zola's title.

Not the least alarming aspect of the critique mounted by these historicists is its carelessness with historical evidence. This is from Research Professor John Lucas's contribution to the television programme *J'Accuse*:

> For example in that poem 'Going, Going' OK, good glum poem, in its way, about what's wrong with England, the concrete and tyres that are all that's left. But who put the concrete and tyres there? Why doesn't he talk, if he's going to write about going, going, about the England that is responsible for the concrete and tyres. Why? Because he can't talk about Mrs Thatcher whom he adores.[8]

As the poem was written and published in 1972, a more likely explanation for its not discussing Mrs Thatcher is that she did not assume high office for a further seven years.

A second related exhibit concerns the question posed at the end of the Larkin chapter in Neil Corcoran's *English Poetry since 1940*:

> Is the English pastoral of 'The Explosion' not implicated in a very specific English politics too? Is it conceivable that 'The Explosion', for all its brittle beauty of image and cadence, represents English miners in a way not entirely dissimilar to the way the *kitsch* porcelain statue which Margaret Thatcher was seen admiring on British television screens after the Falklands war represents British soldiers?[9]

The poem was written in January 1970, under the Labour government of Harold Wilson (not the Heath government, as Corcoran supposes). Mrs Thatcher came to power nearly a decade later and not before the elapse of a further three administrations. In a decade of such drastic changes of government and policy it is hard to comprehend which 'very specific English politics' are being invoked. Besides, Corcoran's insistence upon the 'English politics' of 'English miners' in an 'English pastoral' ignores the possibility, aired in Chapter Two, that 'The Explosion' might more plausibly be situated in South Wales.

What on earth is going on? The answer is that Larkin's quasi-Marxist detractors are using his extra-curricular remarks as a guide to the poems – the sort of vulgar fallacy that students of literature used to be taught to avoid in their first year. The urtext jinxing the interpretations of Lucas, Corcoran, Eagleton and Paulin is Larkin's interview with the *Observer*. 'I've always been right-wing', the poet declared. 'It's difficult to say why, but not being a political thinker I suppose I identify the right with certain virtues and the left with certain vices. All very unfair, no doubt' (*RW*, 52). When asked *which* virtues and vices, he replied: 'Well, thrift, hard work, reverence, desire to preserve – those are the virtues, in case you wondered: and on the other hand, idleness, greed and treason'. A categorical either/or, then, reverence versus treason, with Larkin emphatically coming down on one side and against the other (as who would not if that really were the choice?). However, this moment of decisiveness is swiftly followed by Larkin's most notorious political statement which, quite contrary to what commentators like the hapless Lucas claim, renders his position decidedly undecidable:

> *What do you think about Mrs Thatcher?*
> Oh, I adore Mrs Thatcher. At last politics makes sense to me, which it hasn't done since Stafford Cripps (I was very fond of him too).

The archness of the verb 'adore' hints at satire, inviting an exaggeratedly camp intonation. Duly alerted, the reader notes that not only has Larkin disassociated himself from all those Tory Prime Ministers who intervened between the eras of Cripps and Thatcher – Churchill, Eden, Macmillan, Douglas-Home, Heath (quite a *salon de refusés* for one who claims to be an instinctive Conservative) – but, of course, Stafford Cripps was Chancellor of the Exchequer in the post-war *Labour* government, arguably the most left-wing administration in British history.[10] Suddenly, the monological is rendered dialogical, the either/or becomes both/and, Right and Left become opposites that attract, and all that is categorical becomes provisional, contradictory, undecidable. This, as we shall see, is very much the territory explored in Larkin's so-called political poems.

II Larkin's 9/11 view of history

In Chapter Four it was observed that critics who emphasize Larkin's Englishness see his poetry as upholding the immutability of the national character and the stability of the social order. We have now added that Marxist critics represent Larkin as deeply resistant to historical change. Both are wrong. Larkin's writings characteristically meditate on moments of historical dislocation or revolution: the end of the aristocracy in 'An Arundel Tomb'; the death of God in 'Church Going'; the destruction of the old imperial order during the First World War ('MCMXIV); the Wall Street crash and ensuing Great Depression ('Livings', I); the blitz on Coventry during the second World War (*Jill*); the sixties sexual revolution in 'Annus Mirabilis': or, at a more local level, the destruction of a mining community when the menfolk are killed in a pit disaster ('The Explosion'). Far from a conservative commitment to stasis, Larkin articulates a 9/11 view of history; and while some of these epochal shifts are presented as regrettable – world wars, economic depressions and mining accidents *are* regrettable – the poems often side with the forces of novelty (no modern poet has more strenuously resisted the temptation to backslide from atheism into a pre-Nietzschean religiosity).[11] Sometimes, in classic deconstructive style, the two perspectives are brought together in a single frame of reference, the pessimism of an ageing narrator being played off against the more welcoming, optimistic outlook of a younger generation ('Annus Mirabilis', 'High Windows', 'Sad Steps') – whatever this perspectivism offers, with its suggestion that the optimism with which historical change is viewed is relative to the age of the observer, it is not the conservative consolation of historical fixity.

As 'Triple Time' amply demonstrates, even Larkin's analysis of nowness is in contradiction of the stasis attributed to him by detractors (*CP*, 73). The poem is comprised of three stanzas, each focussed on a different facet of time – present, future and past, respectively. What makes the poem interesting is the way in which it tracks the movement of a single moment along the temporal axis, so that what we get is not three different nows but three different views of the same droplet of time. The true subject of the poem, then, is the impurity, the relativity of the moment, each successive now taking on different colorations relative to the temporal location of the viewer. The argument might be summarized as follows: *stanza 1*, what is now the present (which is dull); *stanza 2*, was once the future (which was promising); *stanza 3*, and will soon be the past (a retrospective panorama of missed opportunities).

Our Marxist chums might counter that this seeming relativity is in practice undermined by the downhill gradient upon which these different temporal locations are graphed, so that history is once again perceived as a record of decline. There are two answers to this. First, because the passage of time described in the poem simultaneously marks an increase in the age of the narrator, the decline is not in history but in the life prospects of the observer. Larkin was ever mindful that the fundamental difference between youth and age is that the former has in prospect life, the latter death. This reading of 'Triple Time' would set it alongside 'Annus Mirabilis', 'High Windows' or 'Sad Steps' in the manner outlined above. The second answer is predicated on the fact that the types of temporal instability discussed in the poem are far too complex to be dismissed as knee-jerk pessimism. Since what was the future, in becoming present, failed to live up to past expectations, the past itself might be reassessed for false optimism. Indeed, if we could give up the bad habit of *expectancy* (as the poem 'Next, Please' urges) with its rose-tinted view of the future, we might stop experiencing the present as anti-climactic. This is a positive message to take away from an apparently negative poem and once again foregrounds Larkin's gift for uncovering trove buried between binaries (in this case, optimism and pessimism).

A similar temporal complexity arises at the macro-historical level. Corcoran regards 'The Explosion', 'Going, Going' and 'MCMXIV' as testaments to Larkin's commitment to 'the religion of an enduring Englishness' characterized by 'continuity and persistence' and set in 'a pastoral no-time' that is static and eternal. The very diction, grammar and typography of the poems are designed to suspend this vision of England outside real historical time with its constant change and turmoil. Hence, '"MCMXIV", whose title freezes the date of the beginning of the First World War also freezes the organic ideal into a participial stasis'. This same poem's 'notation of the way the English fields of 1914 "shadow ... Domesday lines"' makes '1914 transparent to a lengthy national history', while the closing refrain of 'Never such innocence again' begs vital questions about the massive inequalities characterizing that defunct society. The poem's pathos is the product of mere 'nostalgia' and 'therefore seems remarkably unearned'.[12]

The first thing to register is the illogicality of selecting poems specifically addressed to moments of cataclysmic and irrevocable change as proof of Larkin's commitment to an eternalized, immutable Albion. In the case of 'MCMXIV' (*CP*, 127–8), Larkin saturates his description of the naïve young volunteers with allusions to the First World War literature that catalogued the horrors they would go on to face. In this way, he combines in a complex simultaneity two different views of the scene, theirs and ours. Corcoran catches none of the citations and so misses this temporal doubling, accusing Larkin of a one-dimensionality that is all his own.

So it is that the placing of the titular date in Roman numerals, 'MCMXIV' for 1914, which Corcoran offers as proof of Larkin's desire to freeze history at that point, can be taken to signify impending social disaster: the use of a 'dead' language not only means that few today can unhesitatingly translate the title's meaning, as though we were looking across an unbridgeable cultural divide, but the lettering proleptically gestures towards the gravestones soon to stand over the young men depicted. Similarly, 'Domesday' does not just point back at the Norman conquest, as though invoking a millennium of social continuity, but forwards to Wilfred Owen's 'Anthem for Doomed Youth' – or, more apocalyptically, to the Biblical Day of Judgement when the world will end. The opening reference to 'Those long uneven lines', echoed later in the 'Domesday lines', invokes the Sassoon of 'The General' –

> 'Good morning; good morning!' the General said
> When we met him last week on our way to the line.
> Now the soldiers he smiled at are most of 'em dead ...

or 'Base Details':

> if I were fierce and bald, and short of breath,
> I'd live with scarlet Majors at the Base,
> And speed glum heroes up the line to death.[13]

The description of the queue of volunteers 'stretched outside' carries further morbid resonances, as though anticipating their being stretched out like the corpses in Rosenberg's 'Dead Man's Dump' ('They left this dead with the older dead, / Stretched at the cross roads') or carried on stretchers like the mortally wounded in Sassoon's 'Aftermath' ('Do you remember the stretcher-cases lurching back/With dying eyes and lolling heads ...?').[14]

This hint of the funereal is picked up in the 'dark-clothed children' of the second verse, forerunners of the 'Death-suited' narrator of 'Dockery and Son' (*CP*, 152). The third stanza takes this further, the names 'hazed over / With flowering grasses' and the 'Domesday lines / Under wheat's restless silence' carrying connotations of burial – reminiscent, perhaps, of the young men 'gone under earth's lid' in Ezra Pound's 'Hugh Selwyn Mauberley'.[15] Even the poem's poignant close, with its account of

> the men
> Leaving the garden's tidy,
> The thousands of marriages
> Lasting a little while longer

echoes Edward Thomas's 'In Memoriam (Easter, 1915)' and, more faintly, 'The River-Merchant's Wife: A letter' from Pound's *Cathay* (1915), one of 'the most durable of all poetic responses to World War I' as Kenner memorably called it.[16] In all these cases, what ensued after 1914 is brought to bear upon our assessment of that year through an extensive filigree of quotes and invocations. Corcoran inflates the poem's nostalgia by severing its elements of retrospection – the backward glance to 1066 – from these plethoric gestures forward, thereby stripping the poem of its nearness to catastrophe.

It is also misleading of Corcoran to simplify into a golden age the picture of English society contained in 'MCMXIV'. 'Archaic' is a devastating adjective to apply to the youthful volunteers of just eight years before Larkin's birth, as though they belonged to an earlier phase of evolution. The 'established' names on the sunblinds of the shops are 'bleached', as if about to fade, fitting emblems of a mastodonic society tottering towards extinction. 'The farthings and sovereigns' refer to a now defunct coinage, the pun on the latter word suggesting that the monarchy too is a thing of the past. And Corcoran's claim that the poem favours 'a traditional English class hierarchy' is surely undone by the scrupulously worded account of 'servants/With tiny rooms in huge houses'. If we substitute 'compact' for 'tiny', the servants' quarters might sound modern, even desirable. If the houses were 'grand' rather than huge, the ruling classes might be exonerated. As it is, the violent juxtaposition in a single line of two such discrepant adjectives implies an unsustainable gap between social classes, less employer and employee than exploiter and exploited.

The incremental effect of these puns and citations is to counterpoise the poem's nostalgia (if such it is) with the discomforting conviction that the old order had been in place so long that only a calamity could dislodge it. In this sense, the poem presents the Great War as the product of that society's refusal to evolve and the young men as implicated in their own destruction by their very innocence. That the closing message does not support the sentimental vision of

the past identified by Corcoran is italicized in the 'Never before'
formula –

> Never such innocence,
> Never before or since ...
> Never such innocence again.

– which Larkin adopted from Pound's trenchantly anti-imperialist
poem, 'Mauberley':

> Daring as never before, wastage as never before.
> Young blood and high blood,
> fair cheeks, and fine bodies;
>
> fortitude as never before
>
> frankness as never before,
> disillusions as never told in the old days,
> hysterias, trench confessions,
> laughter out of dead bellies.[17]

By using the Pound citation to foreshadow the ghastly consequences of
the young men's innocence, Larkin characteristically ends the poem on
a pun which Corcoran characteristically misses. The *Oxford English
Dictionary* defines innocence as 'Freedom from cunning or artifice;
guilelessness, artlessness, simplicity; hence, want of knowledge or sense,
ignorance, silliness'. Roget's *Thesaurus* gives as cognate terms simple-
mindedness, naivete and ignorance. Sir Walter Scott's *Waverley* is even
more forthright: 'in Scotland ... a natural fool' is called 'an innocent'.
This double meaning is a commonplace of our culture, as in the axiom
that being innocent (i.e., ignorant) *of* the law does not make one innocent (i.e., not guilty) *before* the law: thus, the burglar cannot hope for
acquittal on the grounds that he did not know theft was a crime. The same
innocence/ignorance pun has been a staple of English literature from at
least the time of Shakespeare (who makes great use of it in the first and
last Acts of *A Winter's Tale*, for example).

Summoning this double meaning into play at the poem's close,
Larkin censures as well as respects the values of the day, the innocence
of the volunteers being the precondition for their slaughter, their ignorance of what they were committing themselves to making them complicitous in their own genocide. Corcoran grasps the poem's elegiac

regret that a simpler age has disappeared forever, but not this shadow theme of innocence's historical guilt. Preferring the way of the less deceived, Larkin gives his homage to the purity of motive of the volunteers a darker inflection: Never such innocence again, *please God!*[18]

III   Deconstructing the right/left binary

In 1988 Germaine Greer described Larkin as 'anti-intellectual, racist, sexist, and rotten with class-consciousness'.[19] Five years later John Newsinger dubbed him 'a reactionary bigot; racist, sexist and gripped by class hatred'.[20] (In an undergraduate essay such closeness to Greer would be marked down as plagiarism.) I offer these as evidence that the inability of Larkin's ideological opponents to parse his puns, citations, ellipses and dualities mars interpretation of his address to contemporary politics as disastrously as it does his treatment of earlier periods of history. The irony is that today's critical consensus that he is ineluctably right-wing was yesterday's equally adamantine view that he was a leftist. Alvarez's polemical introduction to *The New Poetry* (1963) described the protagonist of 'Church Going' – or 'Church-going', as he carelessly puts it – as 'the post-war Welfare State Englishman' and identified Larkin with 'the predominantly lower-middle class, or Labour, ideal of the Movement'.[21] Donald Davie saw Larkin as offering a 'Little Englandism of the Left', corresponding, he supposed, to Betjeman's 'Little Englandism of the Right'.[22] As late as 1973, Frederick Grubb was proclaiming 'The Building' the 'most socialist thing the *Statesman* [has] printed in years'.[23] As with those poems that were assigned to first Ireland and then England; now Maeve, now Betty; 32 Pearson Park or the Brynmor Jones library – the alert reader deduces that Larkin is unriddling the very left/right binary with which his commentators try to snare him.

At the age of fourteen or fifteen, Larkin wrote a spoof play called 'Merry Christmas' in the second scene of which a Socialist and a Fascist stand on adjacent soapboxes haranguing the electorate.[24] Larkin arranged the speeches in two columns, ensuring that each occupies exactly the same number of lines in his typescript. In performance, of course, the speeches would be delivered simultaneously, the right/left binary being rendered ridiculous by the fact that each obscured the audibility of the other. Even on the page, the reader is invited to see past the antithetical ideologies to the shared elements of demagoguery, verbal abuse of the opposition and closeness to violence. When the curtain descends, conflict has broken out, the Socialists armed with broken bottles and the Fascists with razors and coshes. Written in 1936 or 1937, when Europe's intelligentsia was split between those who pimped for Hitler and those for Stalin (*for it is impossible any longer to take no side*), the playlet anticipates by nearly forty years the format of Derrida's *Glas* (1974). This theoretical text is divided throughout into two columns, the left-hand one quoting and discussing the nineteenth-century German philosopher Hegel, the right-hand one doing the same for the twentieth-century French novelist and playwright Jean Genet. Philosophy and literature confront, contaminate and destabilize each other in an unwinnable contest that calls into question but does not evaporate the distinction between the two. The sophistication of Larkin's mature political poems lies in their ability to maintain this deconstructive approach while merging the opposed ideological narratives into a single column of verse.

Consider the case of 'Going, Going' (*CP*, 189–90), the most notorious of all his poems addressed to contemporary British politics. We have already quoted Lucas's anachronistic accusation that Larkin's adoration of Mrs Thatcher inhibited the dishing out to the Tories of their share of the blame for the parlous state of the nation recorded in the poem. Smith finds in the piece an unlovely mix of nostalgia for 'the traditional England of pastoral', with its 'charming yokels', and middle-class 'disdain sharpening to odium' for the 'lower orders' newly enfranchised by the Welfare State and jostling for their share of the consumer boom.[25] Regan concurs, detecting a 'right-wing hostility', an 'exacerbated mood' that 'spills over into a dismal and intolerant attitude to the crowd in the M1 café, whose "kids are screaming for more"'.[26]

Perhaps the most developed criticism of this kind is that provided by the poet Sean O'Brien in his book *The Deregulated Muse* (1998). Quoting these lines from 'Going, Going' –

> And that will be England gone,
> The shadows, the meadows, the lanes,
> The guildhalls, the carved choirs.

– O'Brien comments:

> Purveyors of Heritage would have been quick to enlist Larkin: the invertebrate narcosis of these lines seems like an invitation. We are not all that far from the 'English lane' down which, according to Dame Vera Lynn, we shall walk together when we meet again. In his fine book *Literary Englands*, during a discussion of Orwell's *The Lion and the Unicorn*, David Gervais notes Orwell's insistence that

'Nothing ever stands still' and comments 'standing still is, more often than not, what most imaginary Englands are designed to do'. Certainly, Larkin's desired England lacks flexibility in the face of change. ... Larkin's historical sense, you might say, leaves the history out in favour of religiose pageantry.[27]

There is a level of generalization at which this is persuasive; and I have already acknowledged that poems like 'Going, Going', 'MCMXIV' and 'The Winter Palace' are minor (which begs the question of why Larkin's left-wing critics routinely avoid his best works). Nonetheless, this much-derided poem is altogether more combustible than is recognized and in ways that explode the arguments of a Smith or O'Brien.

Since O'Brien mentions him, we might begin with the fact that Orwell's essay 'England your England' is one of a number of texts that shadow 'Going, Going' (another is Betjeman's poem 'The Town Clerk's Views'). Larkin's landscape of 'cars', 'more parking allowed' and 'tyres' is anticipated by 'the to-and from of the lorries on the Great North Road' described by Orwell. Larkin's England of 'The shadows, the meadows, the lanes' echoes Orwell's of 'winding roads, green fields and red pillar-boxes'. Larkin's 'bleak high-risers' mirror Orwell's 'vast new wildernesses of glass and brick'. However, Larkin parallels Orwell in order to disagree with his conclusion that England is essentially immutable:

> The Stock Exchange will be pulled down, the horse plough will give way to the tractor, the country houses will be turned into children's holiday camps, the Eton and Harrow match will be forgotten but England will still be England.[28]

Larkin, by contrast, argues that change can sometimes be so rapid and so irrevocable that an entire cultural disposition is lost:

> It seems, just now,
> To be happening so very fast;
> Despite all the land left free
> For the first time I feel somehow
> That it isn't going to last

Their respective positions, then, are almost the opposite of what O'Brien claims: it is precisely because he sees history as convulsive that Larkin treasures its brief interludes of peace and stability; whereas

Orwell's more complacent position accords well with Dame Vera Lynn's patriotic hit 'There'll always be an England'.

As for the right-wing (Regan), proto-Thatcherite (Lucas) temper of the poem, it is worth reminding ourselves that 'Going, Going' was commissioned by the Tory party but proved so little to their liking that they censored it before publication. The commission came from Robert Jackson, a Fellow of All Souls and subsequently a Conservative M.P., on behalf of an environmental working party convened under the Countess of Dartmouth. At the behest of the Secretary of State for the environment in Edward Heath's Tory government, the working party published in 1972 an H.M.S.O. Document entitled *How Do You Want To Live? A Report on the Human Habitat.* Larkin's poem was printed as a preface – hence its original title, 'Prologue' – above a photograph of industrial Teesside. However, the published piece was different from the poem Larkin wrote in two particulars. In the first stanza the word 'sports' was silently substituted for 'louts':

> beyond the town,
> There would always be fields and farms,
> Where the village louts could climb
> Such trees as were not cut down

Motion describes 'the countryside' in 'Going, Going' as 'the landscape of a nebulous golden age' which Smith imaginatively peoples with 'the charming yokels of an earlier pastoral'.[29] Larkin's Tory paymasters, by contrast, felt that 'louts' insufficiently conveys the charm of the indigenous rustics. Even less to their liking was the poem's suggestion that big business rapacity and government folly were combining to despoil the countryside, so they excised the following passage:

> On the Business Page, a score
>
> Of spectacled grins approve
> Some takeover bid that entails
> Five per cent profit (and ten
> Per cent more in the estuaries): move
> Your works to the unspoilt dales
> (Grey area grants)!

Although he regarded the poem as 'thin ranting conventional gruel' (*SL*, 452), Larkin wrote to friends objecting to this official censorship

('It makes my flesh creep': *SL*, 459) and the offending passages were defiantly restored when two years later he included the poem in *High Windows*. His new title, with its echo of the auctioneer's cry (Going, Going, Gone!) seems calculated to rub salt in the wound.

It should be obvious to anyone presuming to explicate the politics of 'Going, Going' that even those parts that escaped bowdlerism were deeply critical of successive Conservative administrations, the Tories having been in power for all but six of the previous twenty-one years. The object of Larkin's ire is not consumerism itself but the way in which failing governments pacify the electorate with material rewards while refusing to address the pressing needs of the nation, in this case impending ecological disaster. This is the point of these admittedly ill-judged lines –

>   The crowd
>   Is young in the MI café';
>   Their kids are screaming for more –
>   More houses, more parking allowed,
>   More caravan sites, more pay.

– underwritten as they are by Blake's 'More! More! Is the cry of a mistaken soul'. What concerns us here is that 'Going, Going' presents this as a post-Cripps phenomenon, inaugurated by Harold Macmillan and trumpeted in his 'most of our people have never had it so good' speech of 1957.

Anyone familiar with the period will catch in the 'more houses' tag a reference to the fact that Macmillan achieved prominence as Minister of Housing (1951–4) when he exceeded the Tories' promise to build 300,000 new houses per year (and unwittingly brought about a period of high inflation). The poem's vehicular leitmotif (the car – the MI café – more parking – concrete and tyres) invokes the road-building programme of Macmillan's administration: Britain's first stretch of motorway, the Preston bypass, was opened in 1958, and in November 1959 the first section of the MI was opened to considerable fanfare. As for the 'cast of crooks and tarts', the Macmillan–Heath years were plagued with criminal and sexual scandals. 1963 was the year of both the Great Train Robbery and of the Profumo affair (the War Minister, John Profumo, resigning over a sex and espionage scandal involving call girls Christine Keeler and Mandy Rice-Davies). Within months of the poem's completion, the Conservative Home Secretary, Reginald Maudling, had to resign over the Poulson corruption scandal, and the following year Lord

Lambton, Under-Secretary of State for Defence for the Royal Air Force, and Earl Jellicoe, Lord Privy Seal and Conservative Leader of the House of Lords, both resigned over sex scandals. Through it all Lord Boothby survived, Tory grandee, long-term cuckolder of Prime Minister Macmillan, and reputed friend of the murderous Krays and frequentor of East End rent boys.[30]

The 'First slum of Europe' phrase is also pertinent: just three days before the poem was written, Edward Heath signed the Treaty of Accession in the Palais d' Egremont in Brussels, taking the United Kingdom into the European Economic Community. The poem does not expressly state that this is a bad thing but it does imply, by juxtaposing them in a single sentence, that the 'cast of crooks and tarts' who have made Britain a 'slum' have also taken it into Europe. Once again, the Tories are the target. It is true that 'Grey area grants' were introduced on a small scale by Wilson's Labour government following the 1969 report by Sir Joseph Hunt. However, Wilson left office in 1970 and it was not until 1972, the year of 'Going, Going', that the Conservative government of Edward Heath implemented the Hunt recommendations on the large scale. This involved extending 'assisted area' status to the whole of North West England, Humberside and Yorkshire, including the Yorkshire Dales: hence 'move / Your works to the unspoilt dales / (Grey area grants)!'[31]

The poem that Lucas accuses of shying away from apportioning blame to Larkin's beloved Tories is little short of an inventory of their governmental embarrassments and disasters.[32] The wonder is that so much of it survived the blue pencil. O'Brien is correct to spot a weakness in Larkin's invocation of the England that is being despoiled ('The shadows, the meadows, the lanes, / The guildhalls, the carved choirs'). Motion puts this beautifully: 'as the poem performs its polemical function it becomes stereotypical: a little smaller than life where it means to grow larger'.[33] The shrillness is reminiscent of the Lawrence of *Kangaroo*: 'It is the end of England. It is the end of the old England. It is finished. England will never be England any more'.[34] Nonetheless, this is a far more nimble and astute piece of work than it has been given credit for. Far from being bleakly pessimistic and politically inert, the poem is an alarm call, an eleventh-hour cry for environmental action before 'Going, Going' is followed by 'Gone' and the fall of the auctioneer's hammer. Typically, the poem ends in a pun: if enough readers respond to the gloomy 'I just think it *will* happen, soon', they can alter its inflection to 'I just *think* it will happen soon'.

Besides, any work that offends the Tory government sufficiently for them to expurgate it while simultaneously sending professional lefties like Smith, Lucas and O'Brien barking madly up the wrong tree is worthy of serious respect. And there is something delicious about Larkin's habit of placing poems in institutional corridors where they will go off like a malign firework: not just 'Going, Going' in *A Report on the Human Habitat* but 'Continuing to Live' as *A Keepsake for the New Library* and 'The Life with a Hole in It' as a contribution to a *Poetry Book Society Christmas Supplement* (what an antidote to Yule Tide saccharine to read of 'the shit in the shuttered château'!).

A similar destabilizing of the left/right binary is effected by 'Naturally the Foundation will Bear Your Expenses' (*CP*, 134), of which Derek Walcott has said 'There is not a more acid portrait of English academic hypocrisy'. Like Larkin's poems of masculine excess, 'Naturally the Foundation' is narrated by the butt of its satire, his pompous self-regarding views ironized by the deflationary nursery-rhyme structure. By allowing him to boast and sneer, the first-person narration exposes his opportunism (he is recycling the same lecture for two universities, BBC radio and a publishing house), his elitism (he disdains the ordinary 'Crowds, colourless and careworn'), his pretentiousness (he uses the word 'Auster' to mean 'south') and his name-dropping (he refers familiarly to E.M. Forster as 'Morgan').

What concerns us here is that this odious academic careerist is usually regarded as left-wing. He has a republican contempt for the Queen. Anti-imperial sentiment may inform his dismissal as 'Wreath-rubbish' of the Remembrance Day service at the cenotaph in Whitehall. He relishes even a second-hand acquaintance with Forster, the distinguished novelist and leading spokesperson for the left-leaning intelligentsia, 'who in conservative demonology corrupted the Cambridge traitors'.[35] Forster famously declared that loyalty to friends ranked above loyalty to country, and whether our protagonist's intercontinental networking and expense-account junketings enact or debase that proposition he is presently engaged in his own little passage to India. Some commentators see in 'Professor Lal' a reference to an actual linguist 'whose attempts to promote the use of "Indian English" were often treated with derision by conservative intellectuals'.[36] John Wain summed up: 'What comes through is a deep antipathy to the *New Statesman* intellectual with his automatic contempt for ... the English popular mind, his opportunism which proceeds by "contacts", and his glossy internationalism'.[37]

However, 'Naturally the Foundation' is less clear-cut than this consensus would suggest, tempting a minority of commentators into a confused but revealing response. According to Larkin, 'one editor refused it on the grounds, and I quote, that it was "rather hard on the Queen": [and] several people have asked what it was like in Bombay!' (*FR*, 25) The poet and critic Colin Falck enquired, 'should we really, in this post-Nazi age, be dismissing "solemn-sinister, Wreath rubbish" in a piece of light verse?'[38] In *Larkin at Sixty*, Robert Conquest waspishly recounts a further case:

> ... anything approaching irony always runs into this trouble. Larkin has had an ... absurd example of it in connection with 'Naturally the Foundation will Bear your Expenses'. The late Tom Driberg wrote a letter to the *New Statesman* heartily agreeing with Larkin about his supposed attack on ceremonies for the war dead and saying how he sympathized with the sneer at 'wreath-rubbish in Whitehall'. Of course the poem is in fact a very hostile caricature of this smug anti-patriotism. How could even Driberg imagine otherwise? He seems to have been blinkered by the assumptions of the lumpenintelligentsia that all above a minimal level of education, sensitivity, creativity and so on must be lowest-common-factor lefties. At any rate, Larkin's political views (though one should stress that this applies in matters far beyond the purely political) are on the traditional far right.[39]

By the time he wrote the above, Conquest was enjoying a distinguished American career as the coldest of Cold Warriors. One senses the right-wing glee with which he puts the boot into Driberg, Labour M.P. and promiscuous homosexual. And indeed, Driberg, Falck and Larkin's unnamed editor are all guilty of that conflation of author and narrator that I am decrying. Yet Conquest's reading is as one-dimensional as theirs and as reliant upon suspect appeals to authorial intentionality ('Larkin's political views ...'). Observing how *Paradise Lost* quickened at Satan's appearance and sagged in the presence of Christ, William Blake declared that Milton was secretly of the Devil's party. The first stanza and last five lines of 'Naturally the Foundation' are rather cryptic, whereas the middle passage in which the narrator gives unbuttoned expression to his prejudices achieves high communicability. Hence the repeated resort by critics of all persuasions to the 'Wreath-rubbish' quotation. Perhaps Driberg was not entirely wrong and Larkin's poem thrills to the heresy it purports to satirize.

But there is more. For in a poem whose packed details have attracted a wealth of annotation, no one has bothered to elucidate the significance of the name 'Comet' in the very first line. After all, 'Naturally the

Foundation' might as easily have begun without specifying a name ('Hurrying to catch my jet plane ...') or by choosing a different one:

> Hurrying to catch my Boeing
> One dark November day,
> Which soon would have me glowing
> In the sunshine of Bombay

The answer is that the Comet was the world's first jet-propelled airliner, that it was a British project designed to compete with the Americans in the market for civil aircraft, and that for a decade prior to the poem's composition it had a world-wide reputation for disaster.[40] Its first commercial flight took place in May 1952. Less than a year later a Comet crashed on take-off from Karachi killing everyone on board. The plane's wings were modified but the following month another Comet crashed at Calcutta airport, again with no survivors. The following January a third Comet plunged into the sea off Elba with the loss of all aboard. Comets were grounded for two months to permit investigations but within a fortnight of flights being resumed another crashed at Rome airport. And so on.

This wretched story allows us to glimpse the sting in the poem's tail: our conceited protagonist sets off in a Comet apparently unaware that the plane's disastrous history was particularly associated with flights to the subcontinent of India – first Karachi, then Calcutta, Bombay next? Nor is this a simple case of a pinko intellectual getting his come-uppance, for although the Labour government of 1945–51 supported the project, development of the Comet was particularly associated with the Tories. The original idea was conceived during Churchill's wartime coalition and its subsequent realization was closely identified with his son-in-law Duncan Sandys. As Minister of Supply in the 1950s, Sandys persuaded the Economic Policy Committee to not only finance development of the Comet but also cover the commercial risk by placing government orders for the plane.

The nursery rhyme metrics required to expose the narrator of 'Naturally the Foundation' as meretricious have the unfortunate effect of depriving the poem of the expansiveness of Larkin's major works. For all its satirical wit, it is somewhat cryptic and crabbed. Yet who can gainsay a poem that manages to bring down with one hand of gravel two such ripe fowl as Driberg and Conquest, with their competing either/or reductionisms. Far from the political one-dimensionality of either of their interpretations, this is a cautionary tale in which left-wing arrogance meets Tory incompetence and the reader is released from both.

IV Larkin and consumer capitalism

'MCMXIV', 'Going, Going' and 'Naturally the Foundation' are among the specimen cases hostile critics use as evidence of Larkin's crypto-Fascist tendencies. In every case, no matter how slight, we have found the poems to be possessed of a deftness, gravitas and mobility that eludes his traducers. The ground on which this hermeneutical battle has been fought is theirs, the poems of their choosing, theirs the terms of engagement; but in the present section of this chapter I want to move onto the attack – or, to extend the military metaphor, to open a new front.

One place we might begin is with Regan's view that 'in Larkin's poetry, there is a sedulous avoidance of any direct treatment of recent history'.[41] Stevenson makes the point more emphatically, presenting Larkin as the avatar of 'an English tradition last truly evident in Victorian or Edwardian writing', his fondness for Hardy confirmation that he was 'backward-looking in theme as well as style'.[42] Contrast these opinions with the words of the Scottish poet Douglas Dunn, who if he were not so much his own man might be described as Larkin's protégé:

> What influenced me heavily was the up-to-dateness of observation in Larkin's verse. Rather like the sensation contemporary readers testify to have felt when faced with Auden's poetry of the 1930s. Larkin's poems of the 1950s and 1960s often feel as if they're addressing themselves to the moment, to the clock itself.[43]

Dunn is not talking about cashing in on the topical in an unofficial equivalent to the Poet Laureate's verses on the latest royal birth, wedding or death. He is gesturing towards something much more profound, the way Larkin's poems vibrate to cultural transformation, registering innovations in fashion, consumer durables, popular song, advertisements, contemporary clichés, changing sexual mores and value structures.

This may sound more superficial than profound but the change from Modernist to Postmodernist culture is usually associated with a dramatic shift in the economy of the West from industrial to consumer capitalism. That is, from an economy based on heavy industry – coal, iron, steel – to one based on commodification (fashion, cosmetics, television, packaging, tourism, pornography, catering, computer software, public relations, information processing, etc.). If the necessary prop of industrial capitalism, and in that sense its purest creation, is the proletarian, the factory worker, the necessary and defining invention of the later mode of production is the consumer. This consumer is perceived as a *tabula rasa*, an endless Third World to be repeatedly colonized with needs it never knew it had and which capitalism can maintain itself by fulfilling. For economic historians this replacement of industrialism by consumerism, rather than by the communism predicted by Marx, is the signal event of the century, facilitating other social revolutions such as those associated with second-wave feminism, de-colonialization and the collapse of the Soviet Bloc. No British poet calibrated this economic revolution more comprehensively than Larkin.

For an author commonly perceived as fuddy-duddy, Larkin was quick to embrace the diction of consumer novelty: Odeon cinemas, Mecca dance halls, high-risers, split-level shopping, deodorants, the Pill, Bri-Nylon, Baby-Doll nighties, the Comet, the MI café, transistors, the Beatles' first LP, microfilm, air-conditioning. He also catches the idiomatic speech generated by this affluence, with its trans-Atlantic inflections and its slangy scorn for traditional values: crummy, the wife in pod, cut-price, clobber, jive, wanking, paperbacks, jeans, booze and birds, sneakers, get stuffed.

This new vocabulary heralds a new materialism. The descriptions in 'The Large Cool Store' and 'Here' of the supermarkets catering to this new age of consumption are as replete with catalogues and inventories as the stores are with goods, the poems resembling customers' shopping-lists:

> (Knitwear, Summer Casuals, Hose,
> In browns and greys, maroon and navy) ...
>
> Lemon, sapphire, moss-green, rose
> Bri-Nylon Baby-Dolls and Shorties
> (*CP*, 135)

> Cheap suits, red kitchen-ware, sharp shoes, iced lollies,
> Electric mixers, toasters, washers, driers –
> (*CP*, 136)

It was observed in Chapter Five that if Larkin's narrators sometimes seem disdainful of the punters who succumb to consumer capitalism, they are just as often imbricated in this post-war affluence and commodification. We cited the example of the chronological and material progression from the bicycle of 'Church Going' (*The Less Deceived*) via the train journeys of 'Dockery and Son' (*The Whitsun Weddings*) to the automotive world of 'Going, Going' (*High Windows*). Much the same might be said regarding recorded music: from the vinyl jazz singles of 'Reference Back' (1955) to the long-playing pop albums of 'Annus Mirabilis' (1967); and from the domestic radio with 'glowing wave-bands' in 'Broadcast' (1961) to the compact portable 'transistors' of 'To the Sea' (1969). The expansion from audio to audio-visual media is also documented: 'The jabbering set' of 'Mr Bleaney' (*CP*, 102) might yet be a radio rather than a TV; but three years later the lower-income families of 'Afternoons' place their wedding albums 'Near the television' (*CP*, 121). Larkin even dates the consumer boom for us in his references to 'a *Which*-fed argument' (*CP*, 157) and 'some bitch / Who's read nothing but *Which*' (*CP*, 181). The Consumer Association was founded in 1957, the year Macmillan became Prime Minister. The Association's magazine, *Which?*, ranks products by price and performance as a guide to the best purchase.

Some of the poems analyse the discourse of modern advertizing more penetratingly than do the paintings of pop artists like Andy Warhol, Roy Lichtenstein and James Rosenquist, often taken to be the epitome of Postmodernist art. 'Essential Beauty' (*CP*, 144–5) not only captures the way billboards dwarf their surroundings, literally hiding unpalatable realities behind their giant surfaces –

> In frames as large as rooms that face all ways
> And block the ends of streets with giant loaves,
> Screen graves with custard ...

– but also registers their seizure of the laboratory of platonic essences:

>   ... they rise
> Serenely to proclaim pure crust, pure foam,
> Pure coldness to our live imperfect eyes
> That stare beyond this world, where nothing's made
> As new or washed quite clean, seeking the home
> All such inhabit.

For Larkin, the products of consumer capitalism are not manufactured to satisfy needs but to create them. The advertisement's imagery of an ideal world free from the ravages of decay and death is a technology of desire; craving its eternalized perfection, its promise of fulfillment, deepens dissatisfaction with our actual lives. Hence the enchantment of 'Money' (*CP*, 198) with its siren song that there are no woes so intrinsic to the human condition that they cannot be salved by retail therapy: 'I am all you never had of goods and sex. / You could get them still by writing a few cheques'. Just one more indispensable change of car, house, cosmetic or spouse and there we will be – there we will be, in the Golden Future!

'Sunny Prestatyn' (*CP*, 149) pursues the idea of advertisements as engines of desire by focussing upon that favourite trope in the commodifier's lexicon, the selling power of sex. The product in this instance is the resort of Prestatyn on the North Wales coast abutting the chilly Irish Sea. The poster 'rebrands' the resort as a Mediterranean confection of sun, sand and sex, replete with palm trees and gorgeous girls. In one of the finest essays ever written on Larkin, Steve Clark has stripped the first verse of its localizing references to expose the sexual 'come-on' encoded in the poster's iconography:

> the girl
> Kneeling up
> In tautened white satin
> Behind her, a hunk ...
>   palms
>   expand from her thighs and
> Spread breast-lifting arms[44]

Many commentators claim that the falsity of the poster's erotic enticement merits the contempt of its defacers. Within 'A couple of weeks'

> the space
> Between her legs held scrawls
> That set her fairly astride
> A tuberous cock and balls

In this perspective the graffiti represents a healthy Lawrentian rejection of commodified sex. However, this interpretation underplays the violence of the reaction, the observation that 'Someone had used a knife ... to stab right through / The moustached lips of her smile' punning viciously on vaginal violation. The autograph *Titch Thomas* may hold clues: 'Titch' means small, 'Thomas' (as in John Thomas) is slang for penis; is the vandalizer compensating for his sexual inadequacies? Or is he simply indignant that no beach babe urged 'Sonny, press that in' when he went to 'Sunny Prestatyn'? Either way, the graffiti is not the mark of indifference but suggests advertisements' power to incite strong feeling.

The same is true of fashion. Larkin was finely aware in advance of Postmodernist and Cultural Studies theorizing, that the products of consumer capitalism are not mere accessories to subjectivity, but are constitutive of identity, assigning the purchaser a subject position that mediates selfhood. The descriptions of the women's fashions in 'The Whitsun Weddings' present them as the means by which contemporary society constructs femininity:

> and then the perms,
> The nylon gloves and jewellery-substitutes,
> The lemons, mauves, and olive-ochres that
>
> Marked off the girls unreally from the rest.
>
> (*CP*, 115)

'The Large Cool Store' (*CP*, 135) locates this cultural formation in a pre-cise historical moment. The store sells 'cheap clothes' to people who work in 'factory, yard and site'. Beyond the garments for 'the weekday world' there 'Spread the Stands of Modes for Night'. These are 'machine-embroidered' rather than hand-stitched and they are made from syn-thetic fabrics like 'Bri-Nylon' rather than expensive silks and satins. In other words, they have been produced by just such 'factory' workers as they are being marketed to. The historical moment is that in which con-sumer capitalism woke up to lower-income groups as an untapped mar-ket for erotic lingerie. It is the moment when the female factory worker was reconfigured as a Postmodernist consumer. As for the date: nylon became commercially available in the later 1930s; the term 'shortie' was coined in 1949; the term 'Baby-Doll' was popularized by the 1956 movie of the same name, scripted by Tennessee Williams; Bri-Nylon was a Courtaulds trade brand of the 1950s and 1960s; and the poem was writ-ten in 1961. This is what Dunn meant about Larkin's poems being pressed up against their historical moment.

At first our narrator seems taken aback to think 'their sort', working-class women, 'share that world' of eroticization; but upon reflection accepts that what 'women are' or 'what they do' under this new cultural dispensation is enact the 'unreal wishes' of men, effecting orgasmic 'ecstasies' by means which are 'synthetic, new / And natureless'. Although the gender of the narrator is not directly specified, the use of the word 'our' in the last stanza situates the narrative in the male domain whose sexual fantasies this lingerie caters to. In other words, the sexuality under discussion is not natural, unacculturated; it is a precipitate of the economic logic of consumer capitalism. Larkin postulates that in reinventing itself capitalism reinvented the sexuality of working women – what was once repressed for purposes of social control is now granted a commodified de-inhibition – while leaving the same patriarchal business interests in charge. This is, in any meaningful sense, a profoundly political poem.

V Larkin and Thatcherism

Although Larkin's writing career was over before Margaret Thatcher assumed high office, his most virulent critics repeatedly arraigned him for 'Thatcherism'. I want to end this chapter by exploring two aspects of his analysis of the post-industrial society that unsettle this gross simplification. The first concerns the way in which the rise of consumer capitalism was synonymous with the Americanization of Western Culture.[45] Like every British Prime Minister since the Suez *débâcle*, Mrs Thatcher made it a mark of policy to adopt a kneeling posture when speaking of the United States: 'They are our greatest allies, the lynchpin of freedom and Nato'. Of President Reagan she said: 'The West could have no better or braver champion'; 'I am his greatest fan'.[46] She was equally whole-hearted in her welcome of the Disneyfication of culture associated with the new consumerism: 'a lot more of our jobs will come from the service industries – from the McDonalds and the Wimpys, which employ a lot of people, from the kind of Disney Land they are starting in Corby'.[47] A defunct Northamptonshire steel town, Corby was to be reinvented as Wonderworld ('For everyone, everything wonderful in a world of its own'), a ninety-acre, £500 million theme park or 'leisure city'. By 1983, when Mrs Thatcher made this speech, a massive area of land had been ploughed and prepared for development. A quarter of a century later, that abandoned site, reclaimed by nature, is all that remains of Wonderworld.

By contrast, Larkin combined responsiveness to the extraordinary fertility of consumer culture with scepticism regarding the workings of capital and a dislike of American imperiousness. As early as 1960, in 'Faith Healing' (*CP*, 126), he was satirizing American evangelism of the sort Billy Graham had introduced to Britain just six years earlier. 'Stewards' chivvy the supplicants towards the 'loving care' of the Minister where they are allotted a mere 'twenty seconds' each, 'the deep American voice… / Directing God' to heal 'this eye, that knee'. The sense of Britain's gently shambolic religious habits being invaded by Yankee zealotry is compounded by the almost Fordist processing of the petitioners and the feeling that God is there to do the evangelist's bidding rather than vice versa.

If 'Faith Healing' shows American cultural imperialism working through the commodification of religion, 'Posterity' shows it working through the commodification of knowledge. The American academic Jake Balokowsky is deeply out of sympathy with his latest biographical subject, who he variously describes as an 'old fart' and a 'bastard' (*CP*, 170), but he pursues the project for career gain. Robert Giroux at the New York publishing house of Farrar, Strauss and Giroux tried to suppress 'Posterity' from American editions of *High Windows* on the grounds that the references to 'Tel Aviv', 'Myra's folks' and making 'the money sign' were anti-Semitic.[48] If we accept Giroux's assumption that Jake is Jewish-American, however, it is the American side of that hyphen that is under attack. Jake's wanting 'to teach school in Tel Aviv' seems altruistic rather than venal; it is his American commitments that trap him in the New World culture of microfilm, air-conditioning, jeans, sneakers and coke dispensers. The dark side of American materialism shadows a line like 'His air-conditioned cell at Kennedy' with its invocation of Henry Miller's dystopia *The Air-Conditioned Nightmare* (1945), the pun on prison-cell and the reminder of a presidential assassination. On 24 December 1963, Idlewild Airport was renamed Kennedy International to honour the memory of John F. Kennedy who was murdered the previous month. 'Posterity' was written on 17 June 1968, which not only means that it is set *at most* four and a half years earlier, but also that the airport name change had just twelve days earlier acquired extra poignancy with the assassination in Los Angeles of Senator Robert Kennedy.

Marooned by the rising tide of affluence and effluence, Jake becomes an object of sympathy as much as satire. Larkin put it this way in a letter to the poet Richard Murphy:

> I'm sorry if Jake Balokowsky seemed an unfair portrait. As you see, the idea of the poem was imagining the ironical situation in which one's posthumous reputation was entrusted to somebody as utterly unlike oneself as could be. It was only after the poem had been published that I saw that Jake, wanting to do one thing but having to do something else, was really not so unlike me, and indeed had probably unconsciously been drawn to my work for this reason, which explains his bitter resentment of it.[49]

There is surely something touching about his plan to 'get a couple of semesters leave // To work on Protest Theatre', as though his rebellious inclination to drop out and teach in Israel has been displaced into nostalgia for America's dissident drama of the Depression era. The fact that he can get paid leave to research socialist art is another acute Larkin perception, consumer capitalism being willing to commodify anything that will sell, including its own opposition, secure in the knowledge that there is no better way to nullify dissent than to canonize and market it.

A second aspect of Larkin's ideology that conflicts with Thatcherism concerns capitalism's equation of economic and biological reproduction. 'Every man a capitalist, and every man a man of property', said Mrs Thatcher in justification of the Conservative policy of selling off council homes. 'Housing is the start'.[50] The Prime Minister elaborated:

> In about twenty-five years' time there will be quite a lot of people, who will be inheriting something, because for the first time we will have a whole generation of people who own their own homes and will be leaving them, so that they topple like a cascade down the line of the family, leaving to others not only their houses but some of their shares, some of their building-society investments, some of their national-savings certificates. ... That is popular capitalism.[51]

In this scenario, the old principle of the captains of industry that the building of a business empire required the fathering of sons to inherit and develop it is, in the era of consumer capitalism, broadened to include other kinds of inheritance and to be less exclusively patrilineal. Nevertheless, heterosexuality still supports bourgeois ideologies to the extent that procreation mirrors production.

Larkin's sexual ideology is fundamentally opposed to this patriarchal algorithm in which recreation is confused with procreation and procreation with property. For Larkin, the sexual life is primarily concerned with obtaining pleasure from the body; in Thatcher's neo-bourgeois perspective, this is desire deprived of its goal – the very negation of productive work. Think of those novels and poems reviewed in the previous chapter that sympathetically explored masturbation, homosexuality, lesbianism, unattached heterosexual women and bachelorhood – every one a slap in the face for Thatcherite standards of propagation. There is also a discontinuous, mainly subtextual address to prostitution that surfaces most conspicuously in the consistently bowdlerized 'Dublinesque'.

Larkin told Maeve Brennan that 'Dublinesque' was 'a dream – I just woke up and described it'.[52] Commentators have contentedly followed this lead, presenting the poem as an innocent and beguiling dreamscape.

Much is made of its deft invocation of Dublin in the Victorian and Edwardian era – the women's 'wide flowered hats, / Leg-of-mutton sleeves, / And ankle-length dresses' date it to before the First World War. Booth, Whalen, Tolley, Motion and Regan all remark such evocative details as the 'pewter' light, the 'stucco' housing, the easy conjunction of gambling and religion in 'race-guides and rosaries', and the mixed sadness and joy of the 'wake'. This historically distanced setting, with its Celtic Twilight charm, lures Whitehead into the unsubstantiated speculation that the poem is based on a painting by Jack B Yeats.[53] Even less convincingly, Booth offers as a literary source 'Down by the Salley Gardens' by Jack's brother, the poet W.B. Yeats.[54] The Nighttown sequence of Joyce's scurrilous *Ulysses* seems more the kind of thing (the novel's temporal location, 16 June 1904, also accords with the poem's period details). For not one of these critics observes – perhaps they are too abashed to admit – that as the only mourners are 'A troop of street-walkers', the likelihood is that the deceased was a prostitute or procuress, possibly the 'Kitty, or Katy' of the closing lament. (As the sex of the deceased is not specified, it could be a man – a generous client, perhaps, or protective pimp. However, this makes the last stanza tangential, if not redundant, in a way that is not so if the departed is a woman.) Regan's attempt to hitch the funeral to a socialist agenda seems particularly ill-judged, his description of the scene as an 'enlarging, ennobling' image of 'working-class solidarity' ludicrously ignoring the fact that the procession consists entirely of harlots, the rest of society – even Kitty's former punters – apparently ostracizing the occasion.[55] Clearly, Larkin is doing something more interesting than endorsing a platitude about proletarian camaraderie.

But what, precisely? Overturning the stereotype of a whore, for a start. The descriptive language ('great friendliness', 'honouring', 'fond of', 'great sadness', 'All love, all beauty') shows the dead harlot to be as capable of inspiring deep feeling as the surviving ones are of experiencing it. There is a daintiness, a delicacy of expression – 'Some caper a few steps, skirts held skilfully' – quite at odds with the presumed sordidness of their profession. But if the poem celebrates a prostitute's life in a manner that is non-judgemental, it still makes a point of naming her profession as though it wants that absence of condemnation to be noticed. This might appear to invite the riposte that 'Dublinesque' sentimentalizes a grubby profession in which women are debased for the delectation of men. There is some truth in this. However, it is possible that the core values celebrated in the work – poetry, song, dance, sex, love, beauty and the Irish wake (as opposed to

English funerals) – would survive translation into today's world of male escorts, ladettes and toy boys. Larkin knew in 1970 what many of today's career women proclaim, that of the two types of sex, paid (prostitution) and free (marital), free sex is much the more expensive. In a very real sense, this is a poem in praise of a sexuality that is detached from the normal social concomitants of family, marriage, parenthood, property and capital accumulation.

If 'Dublinesque' counters the Thatcherite mantra of private property by honouring a tart, someone who was herself public property, the bachelor poems approximate the same position from the opposite direction. Hence, 'Dockery and Son' challenges the Law of the Father by employing a narrator who has refused to become one. The poem underlines this theme by running a continuous parallel with the Dickens novel, *Dealings with the Firm of Dombey and Son*. Even the title of this novel makes explicit the capitalist equation between business and physical reproduction, though neither actually proves 'firm': Dombey loses his son and heir, Paul, at the same time that his business starts to unravel with the loss of one of his ships, the *Son and Heir*.

'Dockery and Son', like 'Self's the Man', is a poem in which a confirmed bachelor compares his life with that of an acquaintance (Dockery and Arnold, respectively) who has married and fathered children. In both instances the narrator's position shifts or evolves across the poem's trajectory. Initially he asserts the superiority of his unmarried status; then he moves to a more relativistic stance in which it is admitted that each has chosen right according to his point of view; finally this compromise position is undercut when the narrator expresses a momentary doubt about his chosen path; 'For Dockery a son, for me nothing, / Nothing with all a son's harsh patronage'. In a very real sense, then, both poems articulate the inwardness of the other (to use the language of the Postmodern philosopher Emmanuel Levinas). The implications of this for Larkin's concept of selfhood will be pursued in the next chapter. What concerns us here is that the values Dockery personifies are those which capitalism normalizes; whereas the narrator, whatever his doubts, queries this normalization and invites a consideration of the alternatives. This exploration of alterity is conducted in the honest understanding that life is short, that 'Whether or not we use it, it goes', and that death is final.

The narrative is set in motion when our forty-year old protagonist, revisiting his old college, is informed by the Dean that although 'Dockery was junior to you … His son's here now'. The narrator muses that Dockery must have become a father 'At nineteen, twenty?', whereas he at twice that age is still (as 'The View' puts it) 'Unchilded and unwifed' (*CP*, 195). The phrasing and diction of these deliberations has a Dickensian sensitivity to the capital implications of these familial decisions. When the narrator admits that for him 'To have no son, no wife, / No house or land still seemed quite natural', the reader notes how swiftly mention of a son leads on to what might be his patrimony (the house and land). When he speculates of Dockery, 'Only nineteen, he must have taken stock / Of what he wanted', our attention is drawn to the pun on 'stock' as in family or breed (livestock) and in either of its business senses, whether as the raw material of manufacture (such as one might stockpile in a stockyard) or as capital investment (stocks and shares).[56] When the narrator asks 'Why did he think adding meant increase?', the numerical trope suggests a computing of profit and loss as much as biological reproduction. Set this stream of introspection against 'the fumes / And furnace-glares of Sheffield', the 'joining and parting' railway lines of the industrial north, and it is difficult not to read the narrator's resistance to patriarchy as simultaneously an alienation from the capitalist mode of production. Thatcher's production/reproduction pairing is doubly disavowed.

I began this chapter with the claim that Larkin's poems and novels are sustainedly anti-patriarchy, anti-heterosexism, anti-nuclear family, anti-homophobia, anti-nationalism, anti-theism, anti-biological essentialism and anti-capitalism. Stating his position in this way is unfair to the extent that it endorses the stereotype of Larkin as miserabilist, helplessly negative about everything. In practice, as we have seen, he is anti-heterosexism but not anti-heterosexual; an atheist who acknowledges religion's civic virtues; a celebrant of consumer culture who opposes capitalism's reduction of all value to the pecuniary – 'Our children. ... / All we can hope to leave them now is money' (*CP*, 171). Moreover, his nullifications are reserved for the hegemonic – God, the church, the family, the nation, American imperialism, corporate capitalism, compulsory heterosexuality – and are therefore strategic rather than fundamentalist. He negates the mandatory in the name of freedom; not so as to replace it with an equally monolithic alternative, but so as to create a space within which binaries are unfixed, either/ors confounded, and anti-foundational thinking can begin. That this radical political agenda has been entirely overlooked by the pink professorate is the measure of their fecklessness: the poet arraigned for holding the wrong convictions was wrongfully convicted.

8
Larkin and Identity

According to Antony Easthope 'the empiricist tradition affirms (1) that the subject is coherent and autonomous, (2) that discourse is in principle transparent and (3) that the real can be experienced directly'. Explicating the first of these points in relation to English culture, he added:

> As always in an epistemological scenario, subject and object are joined reciprocally, so that the English subject and the English real correspond to each other. In that the English real is simply autonomous, given, the English subject is similarly not constructed but always already merely *there* as the subject of or for knowledge/experience.[1]

For Easthope, Larkin is a stylistic 'reactionary' whose Movement empiricism entails a 'gesture beyond language to a real which is directly experienced and by the same token to an autonomous self capable of that experience'.[2]

In Chapter Four it was remarked that Larkin's concept of selfhood is more choral than singular, his narratology being defined by dissensual interpellations of the 'other'. In Chapters Two and Four it was proposed that Larkin's language, far from being 'transparent', is characterized by citationality, paronomasia and ellipsis. As for his supposed equating of a unified self with an unproblematized concept of Englishness, we have repeatedly observed that many of the poems used to support this view were originally perceived as Irish. Despite these glaring flaws in the argument, there has emerged a younger generation of critics who are still peddling the view that Larkin espouses an empirical philosophy predicated upon holistic notions of selfhood.

Thus Ian Gregson, in *Contemporary Poetry and Postmodernism*: *Dialogue and Estrangement* (1996):

> Larkin ... repeatedly starts his poems by painstakingly notating self-consciously mundane parts of the 'real' world in a way which not only establishes a stable, apparently objective setting, but implicitly constructs a speaker who observes and responds in a reliable way. The result is that a firm but unspoken sense of self is established – an essentially realist self whose coherence is unquestioned.[3]

That last half-sentence concisely summarizes just what I do not believe about Larkin's poetry. What follows is a tripartite challenge to the Easthope–Gregson position: the first part argues that questioning the coherence of the self is an overriding preoccupation of Larkin's verse; the second proposes that when this assault upon identitarianism is combined with Larkin's profound sense of deracination, the poetry accords with diasporic rather than indigenous models of selfhood; the third part proposes that Larkin's perpetual awareness of the inescapability and finality of death means that even at its most replete subjectivity is provisional and temporary.

I   Larkin's critique of identitarianism

Larkin's work is often read as a desperate rearguard defense of masculine identitarianism, poems like 'Love' and 'Counting' shoring a fragile male ego against inner and outer agents of erosion. For Paulin, 'Larkin's poems are often sceptical assertions of male autonomy' and his 'favourite romantic value, "solitude", designates the consciousness of the autonomous English male professional'.[4] Fudging the line between the private life and the public art, Longley concurs: 'His poems and letters reiterate the fear of being invaded, diluted, controlled or possessed by another. Spending the self is equated with spending money – you don't get it back.'[5] The admirable Clark sounds the same note in his account of the 'self-conserving detachment' of 'the Larkin persona' but quickly goes on to point out that 'the actual practice of interpretation reveals a precarious, intermittent and paradoxical authority in these texts, at least as much concerned to disown and disavow as to impose and dominate'.[6]

Clark is surely correct, for Larkin trenchantly deconstructs the metanarratives of nationality, sex, race, class and political affiliation commonly used to undergird holistic notions of selfhood. In their very minimalism, even Larkin's most starkly monological poems contribute to his tireless campaign to prove that there is no such condition as the first person singular. When the narrator of 'Love' says 'My life is for me' (*CP*, 150), he unwittingly acknowledges a Descartian split between the self which possesses and the self possessed. 'Counting' is usually kenned as an egotist's diatribe against intimacy:

> Thinking in terms of one
> Is easily done –
> One room, one bed, one chair,
> One person there,
> Makes perfect sense; one set
> Of wishes can be met,
> One coffin filled.
>
> But counting up to two
> Is harder to do;
> For one must be denied
> Before it's tried
> (CP, 108)

However, that assertive opening contains its own undoing: 'thinking in terms of one' brings two selves into play, the one who thinks and the one thought of; thus, while such thinking 'Is easily done' and appears to make 'perfect sense', it is inherently false. It is because selfhood is never fully present to itself, 'I' as subject never identical with 'I' as object, that 'counting up to two/Is harder to do'. How can I satisfy myself when there are two of me and only 'one set/Of wishes can be met'?

The argument is elaborated in more canonical poems like 'Home Is So Sad' and 'Poetry of Departures' in which first person narrators no sooner obtain the singular requirements of 'Counting' – 'One room, one bed, one chair' – than they discover in themselves an *alter ego* who is far from satisfied:

> I detest my room,
> Its specially-chosen junk,
> The good books, the good bed,
> And my life, in perfect order
> (CP, 85)

For Larkin, to be alone is to reanimate the formulaic phrase 'alone *with* oneself', as distinct from 'alone *as* oneself'. I is plural.

Some poems greatly complicate this model by presenting subjectivity as not just doubled but populous, a possible reminder of Larkin's love of the American poet Walt Whitman. Whitman's representative narrator is at once singular and democratically inclusive: 'One's self I sing – a simple, separate Person; / Yet utter the word Democratic, the word *En masse*'.[7] In a manner analogous to Larkin's 'Self's the Man', as discussed in Chapter Four, Whitman's most famous poem 'Song of Myself' might more appropriately be titled 'Song of My Selves':

> Do I contradict myself?
> Very well, then, I contradict myself:
> (I am large – I contain multitudes.)[8]

Indeed, in his own less expansive, less aggrandizing way, Larkin makes the same connection between multiple selfhood and democratic process:

> Since the majority of me
> Rejects the majority of you,
> Debating ends forthwith, and we
> Divide.
>
> > > (*CP*, 50)

Entirely eschewing the first person singular, the narrator presents a self that is an assembly of contending voices: hence the conceit on parliamentary terms like 'majority', 'debating', 'minorities', 'unopposed' and 'Divide' (as in a division, or vote, by members of the House of Commons). The characteristic pun on 'and we / Divide' (the line break underlining the point with a typographical division) means both that the narrator and addressee agree to terminate their relationship, to separate; and, since 'the majority of me' rejects your company but the minority does not, we (the two voting blocs in my head) *divide* over the issue, the majority prevailing. The paronomasia implies that acknowledgement of our multiple selfhood is intrinsic to democracy, entailing as it does the overthrowing of the inner autocrat.

This line of thought is polysemically pursued in the eye/I pun in poems like 'Long Sight in Age' and 'Latest Face':

> Latest face, so effortless
> Your great arrival at my eyes
>
> > (*CP*, 53)

The primary meaning is obvious; but as the poem goes on to explore the different responses the narrator might make to this new love object – as it were, the different selves the beloved might summon into being (ardent pursuer, cool assessor, love denier) – there is a secondary sense of 'Your great arrival at my I's'. If these contending selves must resolve their differences and arrive at a considered response to the beloved, presumably through such an internal *division* as that described above, then a further pun is entailed on the 'ayes' of a House of Commons vote.[9] Far from upholding 'the sovereignty of the ego', as Easthope and Gregson aver, these poems dramatize the difficulty of extracting either an executive decision or a sense of collective responsibility from the debating chamber in one's head.

As if this were not enough, Larkin's writings simultaneously engage in a quest for ontological origins whose fruitlessness becomes an evisceration of origins and even of the concept of origination. Typically, an ontological question is posed, the answer to which opens a subsequent question in a potentially endless interrogation. What determines the life we lead? If character does, as Novalis and Hardy claim, then what determines our character? If our parents do, then does their influence work through nature or nurture? If nature, how far back along the genetic chain must we track to find the root of our personality? If nurture, do our parents influence us more through the lives they lead or the ones they fail to lead? And so on. The heroism of this endeavour lies in Larkin's pursuit of this catechism to the point where every false concept of selfhood is unsinewed and we are brought face to face with the insoluble enigma of the ultimate binaries: life and death, presence and absence, language and silence. The irony is that *the very poems critics try to unriddle by referring them back to biographical origins are poems that systematically invalidate the theory of origination.*

It would be wrong to present this inquisition as a successful quest for the meaning of life; like Chekov, Larkin seems to believe that the writer's business is not to arrive at conclusions but to present the human condition so truthfully that the reader cannot evade it. This is not a consolatory art in the usual senses, though it is peculiarly exhilarating in its throwing over of the zimmer-frames of dogma and credulity. In a typical Larkin paradox, an anti-foundationalism which clarifies why identity is contingent and relativistic has a liberating effect upon the reader. It is freeing to be told the truth about the extent of our unfreedom.

The first point to be observed is that however different they may otherwise be, Larkin's narrators have a shared apprehension that 'Something is pushing them / To the side of their own lives' (*CP*, 121). This perception is endlessly reformulated, as in 'Dockery and Son' –

> Life is first boredom, then fear.
> Whether or not we use it, it goes,
> And leaves what something hidden from us chose
>
> (*CP*, 153)

or 'The Life with a Hole in It':

> Life is an immobile, locked,
> Three-handed struggle between
> Your wants, the world's for you, and (worse)
> The unbeatable slow machine
> That brings you what you'll get.
>
> (*CP*, 202)

That these quotations both begin 'Life is ...' suggests a worrying away at the identical issue across the twelve-year interval separating the poems. At the same time, the mechanical image of 'The unbeatable slow machine' extinguishes all possibility of an anthropomorphic deity behind the coercive verbs of pushing, choosing and bringing. The forces at work are clearly too impersonal for comparison with Hamlet's 'There's a divinity that shapes our ends, / Rough-hew them how we will' (V.ii.36–7). What these deterministic forces are is systematically investigated in the poems but, as a glance at 'High Windows' will demonstrate, Larkin's lucidities have been obscured by the biographicalists.

Virtually all commentators on the poem conflate the author and narrator in the manner exemplified by Booth: 'The poet's exasperation at growing older and his envy of youth leads him into a sulky admission that quite probably forty years back his pious elders similarly envied his own freedom from religious guilt'. This conflation allows him to 'fill in' the ellipse regarding the poem's title and last stanza: 'The "windows" here are those of Larkin's top-floor flat in Pearson Park, Hull.'[10] Needless to say, the poem makes no mention of Larkin, a poet, a flat, a park or Hull. Besides, 'High Windows' was written in February 1967 and Larkin was born in August 1922. Booth is in the farcical position of claiming that 'forty years back', *when he was four years old*, Larkin had already formulated atheistical beliefs sophisticated enough to compel the envy of 'his pious elders'. Basic chronology dictates that the narrator of 'High Windows' cannot be Philip Larkin.

It is true that the narrator begins the poem bitterly jealous of the sexual liberation of the young and then wonders if 'forty years back', when he was their age, he had been the object of comparable envy because of his generation's religious freedom. If we hazard that the sexually active 'kids' are approximately twenty years old, then add the forty years since the narrator was that age, he must have been born in 1906 or 1907. As if to underline the point, he swiftly moves from the first person singular to a representative stance, presenting himself as spokesman for an entire age range: 'I know this is paradise // Everyone old has dreamed of all their lives'. Larkin was forty-four at the time and can scarcely be accounted 'old'. The narrator, by contrast, is approximately as old as the century and can provide an overview of its generational upheavals – this is, to an extent, the poem's subject. Hence, the combine harvester (verse two) dates from 1926; the contraceptive pill became commercially available in 1960 but was widely used by the young only after October 1966 when the Family Planning Association started advising the unmarried on its benefits: the 'kids' enter their twenties in the decade of 'the pill' as the narrator entered his twenties in the decade of combine harvester. The latter was a factory product, symbolizing the extension of industrialization to the farm, whereas the oral contraceptive was a, possibly *the* representative product of the new consumerism. The social supersession under discussion is not just personal, it is structural; not just religious and sexual, but economic: the generation gap between the narrator and the kids is that between industrial and consumer capitalism.

Larkin said of 'High Windows', 'it shows humanity as a series of oppressions, and one wants to be somewhere where there's neither oppressed nor oppressor, just freedom' (*FR*, 59). Most commentators follow this scenario, dividing the poem into three: verses 1–2, the struggle for sexual liberation; verses 3–4, the struggle for religious liberation; verse 5, a transcendental image of release from struggle. My own view is that the poem's argument approximates to Larkin's classic four-act structure, the overall effect being to challenge the sovereignty of history only to affirm it (see Figure 8.1). Contemplating the record of struggle in which each generation's liberation promised but failed to deliver the 'paradise' of unconditional freedom, the narrator imagines a spatially and temporally unbounded condition released from contingency. However, the unwritten question that follows any enjambement, invisibly inscribed in the right-hand margin, must in the case of the

**LARKIN'S FOUR-ACT STRUCTURE
BINARY OPPOSITION:
THE DREAM OF FREEDOM v. HISTORICAL CONTINGENCY**

High Windows

ACT ONE: I envy the young their sexual freedom	When I see a couple of kids And guess he's fucking her and she's Taking pills or wearing a diaphragm, I know this is paradise
	Everyone old has dreamed of all their lives - Bonds and gestures pushed to one side Like an outdated combine harvester, And everyone young going down the long slide
ACT TWO: Perhaps when young I was envied my religious freedom	To happiness, endlessly. ⌐I wonder if Anyone looked at me, forty years back, And thought, *That'll be the life*; *No God any more, or sweating in the dark*
	About hell and that; or having to hide *What you think of the priest. He* *And his lot will all go down the long slide*
ACT THREE: An image of transcendent release from historically contingent freedoms	*Like free bloody birds.*⌐ And immediately Rather than words comes the thought of high windows: The sun-comprehending glass, And beyond it, the deep blue air, that shows
ACT FOUR: But that image is itself historically contingent in its bleak post-Nietzscheanism.	Nothing, and is nowhere, and is endless.

Figure 8.1

penultimate line of 'High Windows' lead to a profound feeling of defla-
tion at what follows:

> Rather than words comes the thought of high windows:
> The sun-comprehending glass,
> And beyond it, the deep blue air, that shows [shows *what?*]
> Nothing ...
>
> (*CP*, 165)

Indeed, the crushing sequence of 'Nothing ... nowhere ... endless'
brings the poem's ending near to that 'total emptiness forever' (*CP*, 208)
that is the central dread of 'Aubade'. As Everett says, this is a vision of
transcendence in a world without transcendentals: the visionary
moment is undercut by the last line reversal.[11]

'High Windows' proposes that while the hunger for liberty will always
impel humanity to rebel against social constraints, the larger aspiration
to pure freedom is illusory, even the way we picture it being historically
determined and culturally specific. Hence, the narrator's vision of eternity is not itself eternal; it is eternity after Darwin, Marx and Nietzsche –
abstract, minimalist, godless. A poem commonly taken to express, if not
'a sedulous avoidance ... of recent history', then a desire to escape it,
actually posits that not only are our earthly paradises historically
located and defined, but so are our other-worldly ones.

Confirmation that for Larkin all human aptitudes and desires, no matter how instinctive, are historically contingent comes in 'Annus Mirabilis'
which situates a narrator at a moment of transition between two libidinal
economies. The poem combines a joke at the self-aggrandizement of the
1960s for imagining it had invented sex ('Sexual intercourse began/In
nineteen sixty-three') with an acknowledgement that the decade witnessed an unmooring of sexuality from marriage that released it from the
repression and self-disgust of the preceding period:

> Up till then there'd only been
> A sort of bargaining,
> A wrangle for a ring,
> A shame that started at sixteen
> And spread to everything.
>
> (*CP*, 167)

The narrator's complaint that this epochal shift came 'just too late for
me' lugubriously admits that a selfhood constructed in one episteme

cannot easily adjust to a new regime even when the change is welcome – subjectivity is not that free of its socio-cultural context. As with the protagonists of Larkin's other 9/11 poems, our narrator's identity is doubled against itself, riven between old and new dispensations.

Larkin's view of the family's role in identity formation also tends to the historically specific. Several late poems hint darkly at 'violence / A long way back' (*CP*, 215) warping a narrator's personality in ways that are hard to correct: 'An only life can take so long to climb / Clear of its wrong beginnings, and may never' (*CP*, 208). However, even those poems that notoriously lay the blame at the parental door – 'They fuck you up, your mum and dad' – characteristically open upon a potentially infinite ancestral recession: 'But they were fucked up in their turn'. In what is a recurrent trope of Larkin's thinking on the subject, repetition replaces origination at the source of identity construction. And how is this familial pattern replicated, nature or nurture? 'This be the Verse' suggests nurture:

> But they were fucked up in their turn
> By fools in old-style hats and coats,
> Who half the time were soppy-stern
> And half at one another's throats.
> (*CP*, 180)

The emphasis is on cultural and behavioural codes – clothing, inconsistent conduct, emotional repression – rather than genetics, DNA or biological determinism.

The same is true with 'Mother, Summer, I' in which a son ruefully admits that although he was 'summer-born / And summer loving' he has internalized his mother's timidities regarding hot weather. The diction deployed to delineate the mother's attitude is far from admiring ('hates', 'shakes', 'suspiciously', 'swarms', 'lurking', 'worried') and the son acknowledges her influence as a baleful one:

> Too often summer days appear
> Emblems of perfect happiness
> I can't confront: I must await
> A time less bold, less rich, less clear:
> An autumn more appropriate.
> (*CP*, 68)

In effect, the narrator claims to have learned from his mother how not to fully live – as she, no doubt, learned in her turn from the grandparental generation. Identity, then, is neither holistic (the narrator is torn between following and resenting the mother's example) nor foundational (the personality type is replicated down the generations rather than being *sui generis*).

These propositions receive support elsewhere in the *Collected Poems*. 'Dockery and Son' speculates that selfhood may come down to something as gratuitous as introjected habit:

> Where do these
> Innate assumptions come from? Not from what
> We think truest, or most want to do:
> Those warp tight-shut, like doors. They're more a style
> Our lives bring with them: habit for a while,
> Suddenly they harden into all we've got
>
> (*CP*, 153)

One poem goes so far as to begin, 'Continuing to live - that is, repeat / A habit' (*CP*, 94). The corollary, that identity is acquired rather than given, performative rather than essentialist, is supported by 'When first we faced, and touching showed' which presents love as a learned experience and, therefore, a non-originatory one (though no less felt for that):

> When first we faced, and touching showed
> How well we knew the early moves,
> Behind the moonlight and the frost,
> The excitement and the gratitude,
> There stood how much our meeting owed
> To other meetings, other loves.
>
> (*CP*, 205)

For Larkin, at the point of origin there is always already repetition; or, to put it another way, there is no moment of inauguration that will allow us to arrive where we started and discover who we are.

Granted his admiration for Lawrence, it might have been anticipated that Larkin's quest for origins would privilege the somatic. However, the poems accept subjectivity's embodiment while honestly admitting that the consciousness which is already doubled against itself (and, more often than not, doubled again) is rarely at one with its physical habitation. The sexuality that is affirmed in 'Wedding Wind', 'The Whitsun Weddings' and 'Dublinesque' is also a 'time-honoured irritant' (*CP*, 36). The corporeality of 'The Card-Players' is at least as repulsive as it is relishable. The occasional sense, even in rude health, that our bodies are monstrously other, is exacerbated whenever infirmity strikes. Larkin is merciless in his rendition of age and decrepitude –

> Do they somehow suppose
> It's more grown-up when your mouth hangs open and drools,
> And you keep on pissing yourself, and can't remember
> Who called this morning?
>
> (*CP*, 196)

and presents physical decay as proof of a mind/body split:

> our flesh
> Surrounds us with its own decisions ...
> That when we start to die
> Have no idea why.
>
> (*CP*, 107)

One of the things this perspective highlights is the instability of the body as a site for unified selfhood. Those who live in a world governed by clear demarcations find definition gravitating towards edges: as the nation state's integrity depends upon the maintenance of its frontiers, so is the body defined by its epidermal contours any breaching of which threatens its survival. But as the narrator of 'Skin' wittily acknowledges, the looking-glass experience is that of being daily affronted by the way in which, as it grows, ages and withers, the body's contours morph:[12]

> You must learn your lines –
> Anger, amusement, sleep:
> Those few forbidding signs
>
> Of the continuous coarse
> Sand-laden wind, time;
> You must thicken, work loose
> Into an old bag
> Carrying a soiled name.
> Parch then, be roughened, sag ...
>
> (*CP*, 92)

The narrator's skin is addressed as an inconstant 'you' within the larger 'me'. Thus, while the body is a major determinant of a sense of ourselves, it cannot be used to bring physical closure to the identitarian debate since what it does is add one more participant in the experiencing of ourselves as multiple.

Is there, then, no site of pure bodily sensation unmediated by culture? For Larkin, the only animal states outside or anterior to language are, precisely, those of animals; and the tenderness of his regard for beasts stems in part from his admiration for their physical immediacy. 'At Grass' (*CP*, 29–30) describes retired race horses who once were acculturated to a world 'Of Cups and Stakes and Handicaps':

> Summer by summer all stole away,
> The starting-gates, the crowds and cries –
> All but the unmolesting meadows.
> Almanacked, their names live; they
>
> Have slipped their names, and stand at ease,
> Or gallop for what must be joy

Returned to a primal state that precedes competition, the social spectacle and even their names, the horses gallop for no other reason than the 'joy' of doing so. This is a condition humans may observe but not emulate for we are the language animal, our brains hardwired for signs. Hence, in 'Maiden Name' the bride does not 'slip her name' for an extra-linguistic realm of unmediated physicality, she exchanges one signifier freighted with social meaning for another:

> Marrying left your maiden name disused.
> Its five light sounds no longer mean your face,
> Your voice, and all your variants of grace;
> For since you were so thankfully confused
> By law with someone else, you cannot be
> Semantically the same as that young beauty:
> It was of her that these two words were used.
> (*CP*, 101)

Though Larkin would never have theorized it in this way, his poems ask us to think of identity as a production which is always multiple, always in process and always constituted within, not outside, representation.[13]

II Diasporic identities[14]

Tom Paulin has said of the poems, 'Larkin's snarl, his populism and his calculated philistinism all speak for Tebbit's England'. Paulin supports this equation with the following excerpt from a Norman Tebbit speech:

> Nor as a small densely populated island with a closely integrated population living cheek by jowl sharing common ethics, ambitions and standards – and prejudices too – can we afford to import large numbers of immigrants who neither share nor care for those ethics, ambitions and standards – and with prejudices of their own – nor can we allow them to set up foreign enclaves in our country.[15]

For Tebbit, 'Multiculturalism is a divisive force. One cannot uphold two sets of ethics or be loyal to two nations, any more than a man can have two masters'.[16] In perhaps his most notorious encapsulation of this argument, Tebbit reduced the problems of identity under the conditions of modernity to a sporting metaphor: the incomplete assimilability of some immigrant communities was proven by the fact that they supported their countries of origin in cricket matches against England.

Tebbit usually denied the racial dimension of these arguments: 'nationality is in the long-term more about culture than ethnics'. However, the race/culture distinction was one he sometimes blurred: 'most people in Britain did not want to live in a multicultural, multiracial society, but it has been foisted on them'.[17] Besides, such speeches were made in a context established by the inflammatory rhetoric of Enoch Powell. Ever since his notorious 'rivers of blood' speech of 20 April 1968, Powell had been fulminating against 'those who not only visibly do not share ... a common identity' with the English but who are being 'encouraged to maintain and intensify their differences'.[18] According to Powell, the only solution was to combine immigration control with repatriation of immigrants already settled in the United Kingdom. Powell's campaign won astonishing public support, a gallop poll of June 1968 recording that seventy-four per cent of Britons supported his stance on immigration. In his private correspondence, Larkin sometimes placed himself among that number.

The difficulty facing critics like Paulin, Greer, Newsinger and Jardine is that the critique of identitarianism that we have discovered in the poems commits them to an anti-racist, anti-nationalist ideology diametrically opposed to the crasser letters. Paul Gilroy has usefully reminded us that

> The essential trademark of cultural insiderism which also supplies the key to its popularity is an absolute sense of ethnic difference. This is maximized so that it distinguishes people from one another and at the same time acquires an incontestable priority over all other dimensions of their social and historical experience, cultures and identities. Characteristically, these claims are associated with the idea of national belonging ...[19]

The problem is compounded by the fact that because 'black history and culture are perceived, like black settlers themselves, as an illegitimate intrusion into a vision of authentic British national life that, prior to their arrival, was as stable and as peaceful as it was ethnically undifferentiated', the black community adopts an answering essentialization of its own. Hence, Gilroy adds, 'the ethnic absolutism that currently dominates black political culture'. This same tendency has long been apparent in Irish, Scottish and Welsh cultures, which repeatedly appeal to racialized models of the Celt versus the Anglo-Saxon when reviewing their troubled relationships with England. We are presently in danger of recreating the problem with regard to British Muslims. Realities that are complex, transactional and hybrid come to be perceived as 'a collision between fully formed and mutually exclusive cultural communities'.[20] Roots are privileged over routes.

'I suppose 99% of people would say I'm very establishment & conventional', Larkin wrote as late as 1972, 'To me I seem very much an outsider' (*SL*, 460). A sense of incomplete belonging was to Larkin what captivity was to the Jews, exile to the Irish and enforced diaspora to Western blacks: deracination underwrites them all – as, it might be claimed, it underwrites modernity. Indeed, emigration is a critically neglected master trope of Larkin's novels and poems: the very titles attest as much – 'Going', 'Coming', 'Arrival', 'Poetry of Departures', 'Strangers', 'Autobiography at an Air-Station', 'Arrivals, Departures', 'Home Is So Sad' and 'The Importance of Elsewhere'. However discontinuously, such works between them mount a sustained, even systematic, analysis of deracinated identities. Larkin's characteristic unhousing of narrative from racial positioning combines with his belief in multiple selfhood to challenge the imperial and national binary, so strictly demarcated, between civilized and primitive, centre and margin, white and black, indigenous and immigrant.

One cluster of poems describes in affirmative tones those who are quitting these shores for other lands. Examples include Larkin's very first published poem, 'Ultimatum', which proclaims 'the need for emigration' (*CP*, 243); and, at the other end of his career, 'How Distant', in which 'the departure of young men' for a new world is used to encapsulate all that is hopeful about the 'Assumption' of a new 'century' (presumably the twentieth) (*CP*, 162). A second cluster is equally warm in welcoming immigrants to these shores. An early poem 'Like the Train's Beat', contrasts a 'Polish airgirl' with the 'English oaks' that flash past a train window highlighting 'her foreign talk'. Yet far from isolating her as an undesirable alien, her unEnglish vivacity is presented as an enrichment of an exhausted culture, 'a voice/Watering a stony place' (*CP*, 288). Much the same obtains with the Katherine Lind of Larkin's greatest novel, *A Girl in Winter*, another welcome refugee from the Nazis.[21]

Some poems even narrate the immigrant experience in the first person singular: 'Arrival', for instance, which begins in a 'new city', the narrator declaring 'I land here to stay' – the verb 'to land' suggesting disembarkation from aeroplane or ship (*CP*, 51). Again, the heraldically titled 'Strangers' begins describing outsiders in 'our' midst, remarking how they neither give nor receive a welcome. At the start of the third verse there is a dramatic shift of focus as the narrator speculates what it means 'to live there, among strangers'; now they apparently constitute the majority and we are guests on their turf rather than hosts on our own. No sooner have we reconfigured the narrative from one in which immigrants are coolly viewed through English eyes to one in which an English immigrant warily scans an adoptive country than we are ambushed again:

> And to live there, among strangers,
> Calls for teashop behaviours:
> Setting down the cup,
> Leaving the right tip
>
> (*CP*, 40)

The institution of the teashop (so unlike the European café-bar or the American diner), the petite-bourgeois etiquette of the prevailing 'teashop behaviours', the obsession with 'leaving the right tip' – these might all be thought to typify the England of the early 1950s, when the poem was written. In which case, we are no longer looking at strangers, whether at home or abroad, through English eyes; we are looking at the

English *as strangers* through the anthropological gaze of an outsider or immigrant.

The switch of narrative viewpoint in 'Strangers' suggests an equivalency of status for the exilic subject whether emigrating from or migrating to England, neither race nor nationality being used to privilege one condition over the other. Moreover, the way the poem explores the tonic effect of experiencing oneself as foreign necessarily entails a doubling of consciousness, a sense of the self as transacted through the tension between two or more cultures. *The bifocalism of bilocalism is privileged over the monocularity of cultural embeddedness.*

This case is put with great subtlety in 'The Importance of Elsewhere' (*CP*, 104), in which an English narrator states that he felt more at home in Ireland than in England, but that it was his very foreignness that generated the sense of belonging. That is, his not being at home in Ireland made him feel that he belonged; his being at home in England made him feel that he did not. Hence, elsewhere is not an alternative to here, another either/or, it is that aspect of the here that makes it bearable. Once again Larkin has avoided converting the other into the same, in this case Irishness into Englishness, but instead allows the self to be constructed by the transactions between the two in a gesture that is implicitly hybrid, pluralistic and multicultural. Indeed, if we assume that this introjection of Irishness as constitutive of English selfhood is a model for the definition of Englishness in its relations with the other countries of the world, then this is a truly postcolonial construction of subjectivity. Certainly, the declaration in the last line of the poem that he is less happy in England because 'Here no elsewhere underwrites my existence' places the narrator at the opposite pole from Tebbitry.[22]

According to Eagleton, 'Larkin's art ... falls ... in that dip in the mid-century in which the energising impulses of modernism have now faded, but the equally inspiring currents of what I suppose we must call post-colonialism are yet to be born'.[23] In truth, Larkin's preoccupation with doubled selfhood, especially when related to geographical unfixity, is remarkably consonant with, and sometimes anticipates by two or three decades, the very postcolonialism Eagleton would use to belittle him. In *The Black Atlantic*, for instance, the admirable Paul Gilroy traces the notion of bifarious identity through the works of a succession of crucial non-white theoreticians: W.E.B Dubois (and his concept of 'double-consciousness'), James Weldon Johnson ('dual personality'), Richard Wright ('double vision'), Frantz Fanon ('self-division'), Homi Bhabha ('the mimic man'), Edward Said and Gayatri Chakravorty Spivak ('the post-colonial subject'), and Gilroy himself (the diasporic self).[24]

The dualities encompass innumerable interconnected shades of meaning: the sensation of being held in a tension between a loved place lost and a new found land; the displacements and enrichments of enforced bilingualism; the self-consciousness of minorities forever obliged to measure who they are against how they are perceived by the host society; the conviction that in this world of travel, transport and translation, the representative human condition is hybridity; and the suspicion that under the aegis of modernity what belonging amounts to is the endeavour 'to make the condition of chronic rootlessness habitable'.[25] Despite what Gilroy acknowledges as 'the special stress that grows with the effort involved in trying to face (at least) two ways at once', profound ontological gains accompany this release from the tyranny of the local and the production of a selfhood capable of generating alternatives to itself.[26]

Not only is this general ontology congruent in all essentials with such pieces as 'How Distant', 'Strangers' and 'The Importance of Elsewhere', but specific poems may be placed in a proleptic relation to particular contributions to postcolonial theory. 'Breadfruit', for example, anticipates by seventeen years Edward Said's *Orientalism* (1978). In this contentious classic, Said uses the term Orientalism to identify the West's projection onto the Orient of an identity that is assumed to be timeless, degenerate and exotic. For instance, the Oriental female familiar from a thousand depictions of Salome, the Harem, the Turkish bath and the belly dance, is presented as concupiscent, alluring and predatory – the temperamental opposite of chaste Victorian womanhood. This eroticizing of race, in which non-white pigmentation becomes the mark of the licentious other, is also central to the animalizing of the peoples of the African diaspora. The very physicality that credits the black man with an enviable uninhibitedness in the realm of sexuality ('he's an animal in bed') testifies to his evolutionary regressiveness.

In 'Breadfruit' (*CP*, 141), an Orientalist fantasy of 'native girls' carrying 'breadfruit' and promising 'to teach them how to execute / Sixteen sexual positions on the sand' lures English 'boys' into a pursuit of paradisal sex that ends in marital hell. Where Gauguin abandoned his bourgeois marriage to pursue Tahitian girls, these lads (so to say) allow a dream of Tahiti to trap them in Surbiton. As 'old men' they still daydream of native girls, now pictured 'naked', but more as an expression of sexual malaise than Eastern promise. The Orientalist fantasy is not only false in itself – by the end of the poem the repeated 'Whatever they are' applies as much to the native girls as the breadfruit – but by holding out unreal objectives blinds the boys to the realities of that which they do embrace.

They 'Jive' (dance) at 'the Mecca' (local dance hall) instead of jiving (having sex) at Mecca (not the holy site of Islam but the Orientalist den of unspeakable eroticism). The breadfruit have become a reverse Edenic apple: not so much the fruit of the Tree of Knowledge, leading to the Fall into sexuality, as the fruit of the Tree of Ignorance, leading to frustration. It may also be relevant to the poem's satire on lubricious misconceptions that breadfruits are not the succulent kin of the melon or mango, but are fibrous, starchy and inedible raw.

It is par for the course that such Larkin detractors as Paulin, Eagleton and Jardine forbear to mention 'Breadfruit' and, equally lamentable, that those Larkin supporters who do (Whalen, Tolley, Clark) contrive to overlook the racing of the poem. Small chance, then, that either party will pause long enough to register that Larkin's thematic preoccupation with multiple selfhood and deterritorialization, combined with his preferred techniques of ellipsis and citation, open the majority of his poems to white and non-white readings. A consideration of 'The Dance' and 'Sympathy in White Major' will supplement what was said in Chapter Two regarding the racing of 'The Whitsun Weddings'.

Motion, Brennan, Bradford, Longley and Booth concur in reading 'The Dance' as a transcript of reality:

> The long unfinished poem 'The Dance' (*CP*, 154–58), on which he worked between June 1963 and May 1964, shows him embarking on a new romance with all the tongue-tied embarrassment of youth. His relationship with the woman referred to in this poem, Maeve Brennan, a colleague in the University Library, had become established in 1961 when he was 38, and it is Maeve's hands which are heard clapping at the end of the exquisite 'Broadcast', written in this year (*CP*, 140).[27]

In practice, most of this autobiographical detail is stripped from the poem: there is certainly nothing to support Booth's claim that the narrator is a 'poet', or 'a forty-one year-old', or that the beloved is a Roman Catholic of Irish extraction (like Maeve Brennan), or that the action takes place at the University of Hull in 1962.[28] However, it is the case that the narrator's unease at a University party is underlined by invocations of the poems T.S. Eliot wrote as a young man in the United States, especially 'The Love Song of J. Alfred Prufrock'. The protagonist's humiliating glimpse of himself in a mirror before setting off for the dinner-dance –

> But contemptuous speech
> Fades at my equally-contemptuous glance,

> That in the darkening mirror sees
> The shame of evening trousers, evening tie.

is matched by comparable passages in 'Prufrock' –

> My morning coat, my collar mounting firmly to the chin,
> My necktie rich and modest, but asserted by a simple pin[29]

and a 'Portrait of a Lady':

> I feel like one who smiles, and turning shall remark
> Suddenly, his expression in a glass.
> My self-possession gutters; we are really in the dark.[30]

There are similarities in the fleeting descriptions of the siren women: 'And your arms are bare' ('The Dance'); 'Arms that are braceleted and white and bare' ('Prufrock'). Similarities, also, in the excruciating self-consciousness of narrators almost anticipating failure: 'And I wish desperately for qualities // Moments like this demand, and which I lack' ('The Dance');

> And indeed there will be time
> To wonder 'Do I dare?' and 'Do I dare?'
> Time to turn back and descend the stair
> With a bald spot in the middle of my hair
> ('Prufrock')

The protagonists are also united in the dread that they have left it too late for love:

> How useless to invite
> The sickened breathlessness of being young
>
> Into my life again!
> ('The Dance')

> I grow old ... I grow old ...
> ('Prufrock')

Any form of citation draws attention to the constructedness of the narrator at the expense of expressivist or confessional poetics. Moreover, Prufrock is an American whose shadow presence in 'The Dance' must at some level serve to unhouse the narrative from authorial belonging: he uses terms like 'snicker' rather than 'snigger', 'butt-ends' for 'fag ends';

even the configuration of his name bespeaks his citizenship of the United States (compare J. Edgar Hoover, F. Scott Fitzgerald). The Eliotic allusions are supplemented by further trans-Atlantic echoes. There may be a glancing invocation of the 1956 Lerner and Loewe musical *My Fair Lady* ('And oh, the towering feeling / Just to know somehow you are near!') when the narrator of 'The Dance' sets out ('All this, simply to be where you are'). The phrasing 'So you looked at me, / As if about to whistle' brings to mind the words Marie 'Slim' Browning (Lauren Bacall) addresses to Harry 'Steve' Morgan (Humphrey Bogart) in the 1944 movie of Hemingway's *To Have and Have Not*: 'You know how to whistle, don't you, Steve? You just put your lips together and ... blow.' Above all, the frequent mentions of jazz bring in to play meanings that are not just trans-Atlantic but also cross-racial.

These enrichments begin with the opening words: 'Drink, sex, and jazz – all sweet things, brother'. The no-nonsense tone of this twentieth-century rewrite of the old refrain 'Wine, women and song' is deepened by the hint that the idiomatic phrasing is American, perhaps African-American. Both the *New Dictionary of American Slang* and *Juba to Jive: A Dictionary of African-American slang* give 'brother' as a mode of address between blacks ('All you brothers here, and you white people too ...'). Moreover, the narrator's scorn at the 'muddled middle-class pretence' at jazz that invariably accompanies 'a dance' of the sort he is to attend is continued in subsequent stanzas: *verse 2*, 'Some band we have been "fortunate to secure"'; *verse 4*, 'the deafening band'; *verse 5*, 'the mock jazz'. It is perfectly permissible, though not obligatory, to read these remarks as signifiers of race and the narrator as a black jazz *aficionado* contemptuous of (in all senses) pale British imitations. Any suggestion that such a reading strategy essentializes blackness as indicative of 'authenticity', with whiteness as the binary marker of inauthenticity, is nicely off-set by the fact that our narrator is not good at dancing ('I face you on the floor, clumsily') – so much for the stereotype that everyone of African descent 'has rhythm'![31]

Such speculations, all plausible, none verifiable, do resonate with parts of the poem. For instance, the moment in verse four when the narrator notes

> I stalk your chair
> Beside the deafening band, where raised faces
> Sag into silence at my standing there

can easily be read as the uncomfortable lapse into silence of a white group when a single black person enters 'their' space. Approaching the venue in verse two, the narrator thinks '*Alien territory*', and the motif of outsiderdom is repeated in verses nine –

> How right
> I should have been to keep away, and let
> You have your innocent-guilty-innocent night
> Of switching partners in your own sad set.

– and eleven: 'I see your lot are waving'. What does the beloved share with her 'lot', her 'own sad set', that excludes him? Why, granted that he is employed at the same institution, does he seem so ill attuned to their conversational repertoire?

> Professional colleagues do
> Assemble socially, are entertained
>
> By sitting dressed like this, in rooms like these,
> Saying I can't guess what

Is it possible when a 'shoptalking shit' and 'his bearded wife' lead the reluctant narrator 'To supper' where he observes how 'they in tempo scoff // Small things I couldn't look at', that what is being referred to is a difference of ethnic cuisines? Certainly, the vexed love relation takes on extra poignancy in a raced context:

> In the slug
> And snarl of music, under cover of
> A few permitted movements, you suggest
> A whole consenting language, that my chest
> Quickens and tightens at, descrying love –
> Something acutely local, me
> As I am now, and you as you are now

Hypothesizing the narrators of 'The Dance' and 'The Whitsun Weddings' as non-white offers a fascinating rationale for their feelings of social exclusion from rituals of love and marriage they quicken to.

To those who protest against the racing of these poems one can only rejoin that they must themselves have already raced them white. By conflating author and narrator, the biographicalists who dominate Larkin scholarship have certainly done so, they just do not feel the need to render the process conscious. Their racing of the poems as exclusively Anglo-Saxon not only entails suppressing cosmopolitan citations, jazz echoes and African-Americanisms, it also involves substituting critical certitude for textual ambiguity. Larkin's characteristic ellipsis in this regard conjures a silence readers are invited to (but cannot conclusively) fill. After all, it is not the case that the narrator has no race but that, not knowing what it is, we find ourselves trying out different ethnicities for their explanatory value. Reading the narrator as now white, now black, brings out – excuse the pun – different shades of meaning, all of which are part of a poem's purport. It is noticeable that Larkin does not summon white and non-white narratives asymmetrically, playing off the insiderdom of the one against the outsiderdom of the other, but summons them both on the basis of alienation. At the same time, he resists a glib interchangeability of black and white, since that shared alienation may well have different causes (such as race and class, respectively). This is a sophisticated contribution to the discussion of deracinated identities.[32]

Our last exhibit, 'Sympathy in White Major', reverberates differently to Larkin's skill at unhousing narrative from geography and race. In Chapter Two we honoured Barbara Everett for excavating the poem's French substrate: like the Americanisms in 'The Dance', the echoes of Gautier, Mallarmé and Baudelaire serve to disconcert accusations of Little Englandism. The diasporic implications of this international citationality can be teased out with the help of George Hartley's account of the poem's narratology:

> The speaker in 'Sympathy in White Major' starts by mixing a large gin and tonic to drink a 'private pledge' to a man who *'devoted his life to others'*. It soon becomes clear he is drinking an ironic toast to himself: 'While other people wore like clothes / The human beings in their days / I set myself to bring to those / Who thought I could the lost displays'. These 'other people' are the ones who selfishly 'use' 'human beings' in love and marriage, discarding them like clothes when they are worn out or out of fashion. The speaker has made the choice of the solitary life devoted to preserving the high points in life of those more actively involved in it.[33]

However, Hartley goes on, the narrator acknowledges his sense of failure in the 'dated eulogisms' of the last stanza. The closing line of the poem underscores this by taking a term of approbation from 'the days of the British Raj' that had already been 'guyed in Edwardian Music Hall' and using it sarcastically. 'Whiteness, or moral worthiness, is also the whiteness of the man untainted by experience, but finally it denotes cowardice: the white feather sent to the Major who wouldn't volunteer for active service, the musical-military pun in the title.'

Hartley's account is convincing and may be mapped onto the template of Larkin's favourite four–act structure as illustrated in Figure 8.2. This model is not only typical of the doubling of identity we have traced through Larkin's poetry, it also accords well with Jacques Lacan's Poststructuralist concept of the split subject – which has in turn been crucial to Homi Bhabha's postcolonial theories of ambivalence. Lacan argues that at the moment of enunciation the subject is split between enunciator and enunciated, the speaking subject (I) and the spoken subject ('I'). The subject is therefore never fully present in speech, never self-identical, but split between signifier and signified. 'It is this rupture that allows for the logic of a statement such as "I am lying", where the speaking subject tells the truth and the spoken subject is lying.'[34]

Thus far we have been elaborating upon Hartley's division of the narrative into the speaking and the spoken subject, a distinction applicable to a single narrator. Once this distinction is acknowledged, however, it is possible to claim that the poem works as well if the division pertains to two different narrators on the following model: *Act One*, first narrator toasting the second; *Act Two*, second narrator speaking of himself; *Act Three*, first narrator speaking ironically of the second; *Act Four*, with a sarcastic aside at the end. It might be countered that the words 'private pledge' indicate the privacy of a narrator talking to himself; but Google lists over eighteen million uses of this phrase and every one of the several hundred I randomly sampled entailed an addressee other than the speaker ('US officials said Libya was following through on a *private pledge* to Washington to discontinue such dealings'). Besides, the word 'private' may be read as a punning antithesis to the eponymous 'Major', implying a difference of social rank between the two narrators. This separation might account for their marked differences of style, the first narrator's staccato, enumerative idiom contrasting with the fluent, minimally punctuated stanza of the second narrator.

If there is just one narrator commenting on his own life, then it is a very bitter poem indeed, the testament of a man who belatedly realizes that by devoting his life to others he has squandered it. His reward, being praised by his admirers as *'the whitest man I know'*, is scant compensation for the sense of waste and invites the acid reply of the last

LARKIN'S FOUR-ACT STRUCTURE

Sympathy in White Major

ACT ONE: Hartley's speaking subject (I)	When I drop four cubes of ice Chimingly in a glass, and add Three goes of gin, a lemon slice, And let a ten-ounce tonic void In foaming gulps until it smothers Everything else up to the edge, I lift the lot in private pledge: *He devoted his life to others.*
ACT TWO: Hartley's spoken subject ('I')	While other people wore like clothes The human beings in their days I set myself to bring to those Who thought I could the lost displays; It didn't work for them or me, But all concerned were nearer thus (Or so we thought) to all the fuss Than if we'd missed it separately.
ACT THREE: I in mock praise of 'I' ...	*A decent chap, a real good sort,* *Straight as a die, one of the best,* *A brick, a trump, a proper sport,* *Head and shoulders above the rest;* *How many lives would have been duller* *Had he not been here below?* *Here's to the whitest man I know –*
ACT FOUR: with a sarcastic twist at the end to make sure we catch the irony.	Though white is not my favourite colour.

Figure 8.2

line. If there are two narrators, a more dialectical interpretation is called for. The first narrator criticizes the second for submerging himself in others, effacing his interests for theirs in a way that turns him from an individual into a cliché: '*A decent chap, a real good sort*'. On the other hand, the second narrator has the middle stanza in which to mount, however self-deprecatingly ('It didn't work for them or me'), the case for the defence. The disproportion in the allocation of verses, two for the first narrator and one for the second, may load the dice in favour of self-ishness and against unselfishness, but the element of alterity makes this a less bitter reading of the poem than Hartley's.

There is a third option in which the critique is widened and the poem given an emancipitory value: for if there are two narrators, the second (Hartley's spoken subject) is assuredly male (*He devoted his life to others*) and probably white (as in 'White Major'); but the first narrator (Hartley's speaking subject) is neither raced nor sexed. If we retain the two-narrator model but race the first as non-white, then a poem in which a selfish narrator criticizes a second narrator's altruism is replaced by a poem of postcolonial liberation from imperial humbug (see Figure 8.3). This interpretation is the least parsimonious of the three we have considered. It is also the most responsive to the language of whiteness, of the British Raj and of Edwardian Music Hall parodies tantalizingly alluded to by Hartley.

The diction the first narrator applies to the second is deliberately platitudinous (Google gives approximately eight million entries for 'He devoted his life to others', mainly obituary notices) and Victorian in provenance. The *Oxford English Dictionary* quotes Gladstone in 1883 using the word 'displays' in the manner of the second verse 'Sort' is dated to 1880. 'Straight as a die' has been traced to the 1878 report of the Royal Society research expedition of HMS Challenger. A 'brick', meaning 'a loyal, dependable person', has been dated to 1840 and by 1857 was common enough currency to feature in Thomas Hughes' public school classic *Tom Brown's Schooldays* ('what a brick not to give us even twenty lines to learn'). The earliest citation I have found for 'head and shoulders above', meaning 'to far exceed', is Webster's *American Dictionary* (1865). Captain Wybrow, in George Eliot's *Scenes from Clerical Life* (1858), considers that his life 'would have been duller' had Caterina not been there. 'Sport' is slightly later, Partridge dating it to 1905. The expression 'the whitest man I know' is a declension of 'white man', which the *Penguin Dictionary of Historical Slang* dates to 1865 in the United States and 1887 in Britain, and which the *OED* defines as 'A man of honourable character such as one associates with a

LARKIN'S FOUR-ACT STRUCTURE

Sympathy in White Major

ACT ONE: A black narrator speaking of a white one.	When I drop four cubes of ice Chimingly in a glass, and add Three goes of gin, a lemon slice, And let a ten-ounce tonic void In foaming gulps until it smothers Everything else up to the edge, I lift the lot in private pledge: *He devoted his life to others.*
ACT TWO: The white narrator speaking of himself.	While other people wore like clothes The human beings in their days I set myself to bring to those Who thought I could the lost displays; It didn't work for them or me, But all concerned were nearer thus (Or so we thought) to all the fuss Than if we'd missed it separately.
ACT THREE: The black narrator speaking ironically of the white ...	*A decent chap, a real good sort, Straight as a die, one of the best, A brick, a trump, a proper sport, Head and shoulders above the rest; How many lives would have been duller Had he not been here below? Here's to the whitest man I know–*
ACT FOUR: with a sarcastic aside at the end.	Though white is not my favourite colour.

Figure 8.3

European (as distinguished from a Negro)'. The most famous uses of this terminology are those of Kipling in poems like 'A Song of the White Men' ('But well for the world when the White Men drink / To the dawn of the White Man's day') and 'The White Man's Burden'.[35]

That this imperial lexicon is being employed ironically is confirmed by the fact that the ideology at issue was already being viciously lampooned in the years before Larkin's birth, as illustrated within the poem at the level of citation. This is the opening of 'The Whitest Man I Know' (1914), a music hall parody with words by J. Milton Hayes and music by R. Fenton Gower:

> He's a'-cruisin in a pearler with a dirty nigger crew,
> A' buyin' pearls and copra for a stingy Spanish Jew,
> And his face is tann'd like leather 'neath a blazin' tropic sun,
> And he's workin' out a penance for the things he hasn't done.
> Round the Solomons he runs, tradin' beads and cast-off guns,
> Buyin' pearls from grinning niggers, loadin' copra by the ton;
> And he'll bargain and he'll smile, but he's thinkin' all the while
> Of the penance that he's workin' out for sins he hasn't done.
> We'd been round the Horn together, and I'd come to know his
> worth;
> The greatest friend I'd ever had, the whitest man on earth.

The joke, of course, is that our hero is far from white, not only in the moral sense (these opening lines have already established him as a racist arms-dealer) but also in terms of pigmentation ('his face is tann'd like leather' neath a blazin' tropic sun'). This lampoon was itself lampooned in 'The Tightest Man I Know' by Billy Bennett, 'Almost a Gentleman', which begins –

> The tightest man I know is an Irish Eskimo,
> He's selling grapes with whiskers on beneath a burning sun.
> And he's working night and day, though his feet are turning grey,
> Trying to straighten out bananas, and that's a thing he hasn't done!

– and ends:

> When they call the final rolls, and we just wear camisoles,
> In a land that's far away from earthly woe;
> When Jim hands in his cheque, if they don't include his neck,
> I'm sure he'll be the whitest man I know!

Probably the most charged parody is to be found in the Nighttown episode of Joyce's *Ulysses*. Afflicted by pangs of conscience over his past sexual cravings, Leopold Bloom hallucinates a trial before an anti-Semitic Irish mob – a voice from the gallery shouts 'Moses, Moses, king of the jews, / Wiped his arse in the Daily News'. Bloom's imaginary defense attorney, J.J. O'Molloy, makes a perceptive but comically ill-judged speech that moves from one sort of provocation of the Jew-baiters ('when in doubt persecute Bloom') to another: 'I regard him as the whitest man I know'.[36]

Other of the hackneyed eulogisms applied to the poem's butt also came to Larkin with decades of satirical spin. The term 'chaps', associated with a cocooned upper-class milieu, was savagely undercut in Hemingway's first masterpiece, *In Our Time* (1925): 'The Greeks were nice chaps too. When they evacuated they had all their baggage animals they couldn't take off with them so they just broke their forelegs and dumped them in the shallow water.'[37] Some terms had taken on new and scurrilous meanings in the interim between their Victorian heyday and the date of the poem's composition: by the 1920s the term 'sport' was underground slang for a prostitute (hence the 'Sporting-house girls' of 'For Sidney Bechet', a sporting-house being a brothel); 'brick' as a term of approbation had been supplanted by its usage as an insult ('as thick as a brick'); and the word 'trump', used by Dickens, Trollope and Du Maurier to mean (in the *OED*'s phrase) 'a person of surpassing excellence', was now best known as a synonym for 'fart'. It is part of Larkin's genius that he is able to exploit this semantic shift to register that what our protagonist stood for no longer means what it once did.

All these complexities, already in play with the first two interpretations, are altogether more vibrantly orchestrated in the third, bi-racial model. For a black narrator to follow '*Here's to the whitest man I know*' with 'Though white is not my favourite colour' is for the poem to drive a wedge between white as a symbol of moral purity and white as a racial signifier. Indeed, it is to bring white pigmentation into the racial debate it is assumed by whites to transcend. Other people are raced, we whites are just people, so that what makes us different is our potential to transcend our raced bodies.[38] *They* have to start sentences 'Speaking as a black person' or 'as an Asian', and be lumped together with other non-whites as 'people of colour'. As Richard Dyer has noted, 'The 1933 *Oxford English Dictionary* and the 1992 Collins English Dictionary both give "colourless" as one of the meanings of white'.[39] Race thus becomes the indelible mark of negative difference measured against a transcendent 'colourless' white. This is the ideology that is exploded at the end of the poem when the narrator categorically stipulates that 'white' *is* a 'colour' and one that he does not favour.

Gautier's 'Symphonie en blanc majeur' is a poem that takes inspiration from music and painting to offer an image of an alabastor swan-woman, beautiful, glacial, a 'Madonna of the snows' whose 'implacable whiteness' suggests both virginal purity and a Nordic sexuality which lures men to disaster by freezing rather than heat.[40] Larkin has regendered the poem, opened it to post-imperial and anti-racist readings, and in the process shattered the chromatic bias that would place white outside the spectrum of hues. Whether the poem is regarded as the interior monologue of a self-hating old colonial or a black narrator's critique of such a person – and Larkin's ellipsis prevents either option from routing its rival – the inviolable selfhood symbolized in the Gautier original is replaced by a more ambivalent, historically compromised sensibility akin to Gilroy's concept of the diasporic. Far more often than he has proposed a theory of nation, Larkin has dramatized the dissonances within the unisonant discourse of cultural belonging. Written between the notorious Smethwick election and Powell's 'rivers of blood' speech, this is a poem of emotional disinvestment from whiteness.

III   Being and nothingness

Almost all the poems in Larkin's three major collections were written in ports. The intrusion of docks into civic spaces, emblematizing the contiguity of the near and the remote, provides an appropriate setting for the analysis of deracinated identities. Larkin compounds the sense of displacement through ellipsis: the Belfast of 'Arrivals, Departures' is accurately described – 'This town has docks where channel boats come sidling' (*CP*, 65) – yet unnamed, geographically decontextualized, a symbolic port that may itself be transported. Hull lends itself particularly well to this elliptical treatment. Built on the confluence of two rivers, the tiny Hull and the two-mile wide Humber, the original city was further enclosed by a circlet of interconnecting docks which virtually severed it from the mainland and gave it a provisional, offshore, island identity. 'Friday Night in the Royal Station Hotel' faithfully depicts a local landmark without specifying the host city: what matters is not that the setting is Hull but that it is islanded from nation, mainland and indigenity:

> How
> Isolated, like a fort, it is –
> The headed paper, made for writing home
> (If home existed) letters of exile
>
> (*CP*, 163)

On the rare occasions when Hull is directly invoked, as in 'Here', it is not by name but by diasporic reference:

> Here domes and statues, spires and cranes cluster
> Beside grain-scattered streets, barge-crowded water ...
>
> Within a terminate and fishy-smelling
> Pastoral of ships up streets, the slave museum,
> Tattoo-shops, consulates
>
> (*CP*, 136)

When Liverpool's Merseyside Maritime Museum opened a permanent Transatlantic Slavery gallery in 1994, belatedly commemorating the fact the city had once controlled over eighty per cent of the British slave trade, it claimed it was the first such memorial in the country. However, in 1906 a port which had never been involved in the trade opened the first, and for most of the twentieth century the only British slave museum at the home of the late M.P. and emancipationist, William Wilberforce. This is the institution acknowledged in 'Here'. Larkin takes Hull's role in the abolition of 'the abominable slave trade' (*LJ*, 83) as its blazon.

Larkin's prose also emphasizes Hull's diasporic associations, its distance from the heart of Englishness, its intimacy with water:

> You alight with an end-of-the line sense of freedom. Signs in foreign languages welcome you. Outside is a working city, yet one neither clenched in the grip of the industrial revolution nor hiding behind a cathedral to pretend it is York or Canterbury. Unpretentious, recent, full of shops and special offers like a television commercial, it might be Australia or America, until you come upon Trinity House or the Dock Offices.
>
> (*FR*, 128)

Above all, Larkin's sense of ports like Belfast and Hull as sites of imperma-
nence is underwritten by their closeness to the littoral: 'As for Hull, I like
it because it's so far away from everywhere else. On the way to nowhere, as
somebody put it. It's in the middle of this lonely country, and beyond the
lonely country there's only the sea. I like that' (*RW*, 54). It is symptomatic
of the way Larkin is misread by anglicizing critics that Whitehead's *Hardy
to Larkin: Seven English Poets* quotes this passage thus: 'It's in the middle of
this *lovely* country, and beyond the *lovely* country there's only the sea' (my
emphases).[41] The significance of the substitution is not just that it misrep-
resents Larkin as cosy but also that it recruits him to the concept of nationality flagged up in Whitehead's subtitle. A uniquely disquieting poet of the
margins is replaced by a mainstream celebrant of the English landscape.

The larger point evaded by Whitehead is that Larkin's use of ports and
the littoral as sites of arrival and departure is symbolic of life's transience.
An uncollected poem posthumously published in *Metre* magazine exem-
plifies the matter.[42] In the first verse we look out from a coastline to
observe how 'The sea collapses, freshly'. In the second we look inland to
remark 'The hideous chapel' and 'A railed tomb of sailors'. These images
of ugliness and confinement are eluded in the third stanza when our gaze
returns seaward to catch 'Embedded in the horizon/A tiny sunlit ship'.
The poem closes with one of those single line exclamations familiar from
'Absences' and 'The Card-Players': 'O things going away!' Slight though
the poem is, that ending is fully freighted with diasporic meaning: it
could express the regret of the contented landlubber waving away loved
ones; it could express the envy of the entrapped for those who escaped;
or it could be an existential pang, prompted by the sight of a disappear-
ing ship, at the fugitive nature of life. If the first two meanings illustrate
the equivalency of immigration and emigration, the third implies that we
are all migrants, all *en route*, no sooner arrived than gone.

Once the connection is made between itinerancy and evanescence,
the address to death in such late grand poems as 'The Building', 'The
Old Fools' and, supremely, 'Aubade', may be seen to be implicit in
dozens of earlier poems not directly associated with the theme of mortality. The opening lines of 'Places, Loved Ones', for example, invest a
simple statement of the nomadic with intimations of mortality:

> No, I have never found
> The place where I could say
> *This is my proper ground,*
> *Here I shall stay.*
>
> (*CP*, 99)

Staying is not an option for Larkin; life's brevity makes the very concept otiose.

Again, 'Mr. Bleaney' begins with a landlady showing the narrator, a prospective lodger, round the recently vacated 'digs':

> 'This was Mr Bleaney's room. He stayed
> The whole time he was at the Bodies, till
> They moved him'.
>
> (*CP*, 102)

The manifest meaning is: Mr Bleaney worked at the local car body factory until the employers moved him on to another of their industrial sites. The (not so) latent meaning is less palatable: Mr Bleaney worked at something funereal – an undertakers, perhaps (Boddy's is a long-established Hull funeral parlour) – until he was himself carried out in a casket. The sinister subtext of the opening surfaces again at the poem's close when Mr Bleaney's room is referred to as a 'hired box', an expression associated with coffins. Despite the sparseness of the accommodation – 'no hook // Behind the door, no room for books or bags' – the narrator says, 'I'll take it'. Presumably he and Bleaney share the view that life is too fleeting to make a down payment on a house (or even on some books) worthwhile.

Life's brevity is scarcely a new theme in literature but few writers address it as unblinkingly as Larkin. In a brilliant interview with Miriam Gross, he said: 'If you assume you're going to live to be seventy, seven decades, and think of each decade as a day of the week, starting with Sunday, then I'm on Friday afternoon now. Rather a shock, isn't it? If you ask why does it bother me, I can only say I dread endless extinction' (*RW*, 55). Encroaching annihilation is directly addressed in minor poems like 'Heads in the Women's Ward' and masterpieces like 'Aubade':

> Unresting death, a whole day nearer now,
> Making all thought impossible but how
> And where and when I shall myself die.
>
> (*CP*, 208)

More unusual is Larkin's sense that the erasure that lies ahead is complemented by that which encroaches from behind, poems like 'The

Winter Palace' and 'The View' recording the amnesia that accompanies the aging process and which obliterates one's past:

> The view is fine from fifty,
>   Experienced climbers say;
> So, overweight and shifty,
>   I turn to face the way
>   That led me to this day.
>
> Instead of fields and snowcaps
>   And flowered lanes that twist,
> The track breaks at my toe-caps
>   And drops away in mist.
>   The view does not exist.

(CP, 195)

The sense of life as a match-spurt between two oblivions is reminiscent of both Heidegger's philosophy and this celebrated passage from the *History of the English Church and People* by the Venerable Bede:

> When we compare the present life of man with that time of which we have no knowledge, it seems to me like the swift flight of a lone sparrow through the banqueting-hall where you sit in the winter months. ... This sparrow flies swiftly in through one door of the hall, and out through another. ... Similarly, man appears on earth for a little while, but we know nothing of what went on before this life, and what follows.[43]

Sometimes this void that constitutes our past and our future also permeates our present. 'The Life with a Hole in It' uses the advertising slogan for polos, 'The Mint with a Hole', to imply that life is 'a hollow stasis' (*CP*, 202) like that confectionery that for half a century has been marketed for its core absence rather than its toroidal presence. Life, it would seem, is a case of nothing behind, nothing in front, nothing within.

Unsurprisingly, critics concur that for Larkin death is utterly obliterative, unreservedly bad, the one subject that does not lend itself to a deconstructive play with binary opposites. That the reality is more complex may be demonstrated by juxtaposing from nearly a quarter of a century apart two quotations centred upon the word 'oblivion'. The first excerpt beautifully encapsulates the position of late Larkin which the critics present as definitive:

> At death, you break up: the bits that were you
> Start speeding away from each other for ever
> With no one to see. It's only oblivion, true:
> We had it before, but then it was going to end,
> And was all the time merging with a unique endeavour
> To bring to bloom the million-petalled flower
> Of being here. Next time you can't pretend
> There'll be anything else.
>
> (*CP*, 196)

Even here one might remark the radicalism with which Larkin relocates the mystical rose of Dante's *Paradiso* from heaven to earth, from the afterlife to this one. His position is not dissimilar to that of Wittgenstein's *Tractatus*: 'not how the world is, but *that* it is, is the mystical'. However, the effect of regarding the world as an earthly paradise is simply to heighten the pain of leaving it. Certainly, 'The Old Fools' underscores the terror and absurdity of living in the shadow of 'Extinction's alp'.

Contrast this with the second strophe of 'Wants' in which it is possible to see, as in other 1950s poems like 'Absences', an attempt to embrace as an object of 'desire' the 'oblivion' that would later be so dreaded:

> Beneath it all, desire of oblivion runs:
> Despite the artful tensions of the calendar,
> The life insurance, the tabled fertility rites,
> The costly aversion of the eyes from death –
> Beneath it all, desire of oblivion runs.
>
> (*CP*, 42)

The early and late works agree that God is dead; but where the latter express the post-Nietzschean nihilism of Western philosophy, the former sometimes adopt a spirit of acceptance more akin to Eastern philosophies like Taoism and Buddhism.

This last might seem a preposterous suggestion to make of a poet who famously quipped, 'I wouldn't mind seeing China if I could come back the same day' (*RW*, 55). Often cited by the humourless as proof of Larkin's Little Englandism, the joke might better be approached as another of his booby-traps. In *A Thousand Pieces of Gold* (2002), a 'memoir of China's past through its proverbs', the celebrated Chinese writer Adeline Yen Mah recounts:

> When I was a medical intern at the London Hospital in the 1960s, I had the privilege of looking after the renowned British poet Philip Larkin. He once described Chinese proverbs as 'white dwarfs' of literature because each was so densely compacted with thoughts and ideas. He told me that 'white dwarfs' were tiny stars whose atoms were packed so closely together that their weight was huge compared to their size. He said that the enormous heat radiated by these small stars was like the vast knowledge and profound wisdom contained in these compact sayings gleaned from China.[44]

In an earlier work, *Watching the Tree to Catch a Hare* (2000), a personal interpretation of Chinese philosophy and spiritual beliefs, Yen Mah recalled Larkin asking her 'what's the best book you've ever read?'

> 'Shakespeare's *King Lear*', I answered without hesitation.'What's yours?'
> He started to laugh. 'It's almost too ironical. Here you are – a Chinese girl saying that the best book in the world, ever, is Shakespeare's *King Lear*. And here I am, an Englishman, telling you that it's the *Tao Te Ching* by Lao Zi. Every word in that book matters. Nothing is superfluous. It's a work of absolute genius! Are you familiar with it? No?! I almost feel like learning Chinese just to be able to read it to you in the original. You must get hold of a copy! Most British libraries carry the Arthur Waley translation.[45]

Yen Mah graciously concludes that Larkin's words from forty years earlier may have sown the seeds of her latest project:

> Looking back, his belief that the *Tao Te Ching* was the greatest book ever written must have influenced me subliminally over the years. It suggested the possibility that Chinese thought, if properly translated, can be of interest to other western minds besides that of one brilliant, gifted British poet. It may even have inspired me to base *Watching the Tree* on this very theme.[46]

I have repeatedly remarked that Larkin's readings in French, Irish and American literature make the dominant Anglocentric kenning of his *oeuvre* comically inept. Yen Mah's revelation that the Larkin she met in

1961 was well read in Chinese literature and philosophy and regarded the *Tao Te Ching* (rather than Hardy's *Collected Poems*, say, or a novel by Lawrence) as 'the best book in the world, ever', suggests that we need a model of his work as at least occasionally susceptible to influences from well outside the trans-Atlantic frame.[47]

According to Yen Mah, Taoism concerns the 'pervasive oneness of the universe ... the divine intelligence of non-being, from which all being has come'. When Buddhism arrived from India in the fourth century, it was correlated with this indigenous tradition: Ninian Smart notes that as early as the fifth century, Chinese writers were advancing 'the equivalence of the Buddhist pursuit of the void and the Taoist notion of non-existence'.[48] Something of the beauty of the Taoist concept of nothingness may be suggested by this short chapter from the *Tao Te Ching*:

> We put thirty spokes together and call it a wheel;
> But it is on the space where there is nothing that
>   the usefulness of the wheel depends.
> We turn clay to make a vessel;
> But it is on the space where there is nothing that
>   the usefulness of the vessel depends.
> We pierce doors and windows to make a house;
> And it is on these spaces where there is nothing that
>   the usefulness of the house depends.
> Therefore just us we take advantage of what is,
>   we should recognize the usefulness of what is not.[49]

As for 'the Buddhist pursuit of the void', it is worth reminding ourselves that Buddha challenged the Hindu and Jain belief in reincarnation, denying the existence of an eternal soul that is endlessly reborn in different bodies. Rebirth is rather the lighting of one candle from another, the flames fuelled by false values and cravings: 'the Buddha does not want immortality or everlasting life. To the contrary, Buddhism seeks to stop the afterlife. The goal of Buddhism is to be annihilated – to blow out one's flame.'[50] The term *nirvana*, often translated as a state of bliss, literally means the 'extinguishing' of a flame, and Buddha dismissed questions about the life after death as the equivalent to asking 'where does a flame go when it goes out?'[51] In short, neither Taoism nor Buddhism is theistic; in neither is one returned by death to the bosom of Abraham; in both, material reality is illusory and 'Beneath it all, desire of oblivion runs'.

The centrality of non-existence in Larkin's thought is apparent at the level of diction: the *Collected Poems* offers fifty usages of 'nothing' plus one of 'nothingness'; twenty-one of 'empty' plus three of 'emptiness'; four of 'absence', two of 'absences' and two of 'absent'; three of 'oblivion', one of 'oblivious'; one of 'void' ... and so on. Moreover, the terms are deployed in attention-seeking ways: the word 'nothing' occurs in one title and six first lines; 'Absences' forms the title and the last word of a single poem; and elsewhere these vocables accumulate like debris round a plug-hole:

> There is nothing to grasp; nothing to catch or claim;
> Nothing to adapt ...
>
> (*CP*, 6)

> Where much is picturesque but nothing good,
> And nothing can be found ...
>
> (*CP*, 264)

> Nothing so wild, nothing so glad ...
> (*CP*, 278)

> Absence with absence
> (*CP*, 96)

Like Shakespeare, Larkin makes much ado about nothing.

One consequence of this sustained interrogation of the discourse of nothingness is that the concept is shown to be ambiguous and paradoxical. It may, for instance, be said to have content, the capacity to generate rather than nullify meaning, perhaps even spiritual value. In poems like 'Water', 'Solar' and 'High Windows' sunlight, blue sky and water are unhoused from geographical and seasonal specificity to do service as earnests of spatial and temporal illimitability: 'the deep blue air' is 'endless' (*CP*, 165); the sun pours out light 'for ever' (*CP*, 159); while 'any-angled light' congregates 'endlessly' in 'A glass of water' (*CP*, 93).[52] This nothingness that is endless but not empty has affinities with the limitless void of Taoism and Buddhism, for the non-being from which all being has come and to which it will return is characterized by fecundity, even repletion. There are also affinities with current conceptions of the vacuum, the nothingness of contemporary physics, which is no longer defined as a complete void but as that which is left when everything that can be has been removed. This *ground state* or *vacuum state* is the lowest energy state possible. According to John D. Barrow, 'its presence can be felt and measured in the elementary-particle world, and without its powerful contribution, the unity of nature could not be sustained'.[53] The vacuum energy of the cosmos is now regarded as that from which the universe emerged and which drives its observable expansion.

Thus far we have divided Larkin's meditations upon nothingness into a binary opposition: poems in which oblivion is utter extinction ('Heads in the Women's Ward', 'The View', 'The Old Fools', 'The Building', 'Aubade'), and those in which oblivion is a spatialized energy field compatible with contemporary vacuum theory and Oriental philosophy ('Wants', 'Water', 'Solar', 'Absences', 'High Windows' and the end of 'Here'). In typical deconstructive style, Larkin sometimes brings the two together in a single poem, a single paronomastic phrase or word. The overall tenor of 'Ambulances' identifies it with the 'Aubade' group of poems bespeaking the unspeakability of death as complete annihilation. However, the pivotal moment of the poem hints at the 'desire of oblivion' motif of poems like 'Wants', for as the bystanders observe the patient being 'stowed' in the ambulance, they

> sense the solving emptiness
> That lies just under all we do,
> And for a second get it whole,
> So permanent and blank and true.
>
> (*CP*, 132)

The tension between a 'permanent' emptiness that must be dreaded and a 'solving' emptiness that may be welcomed is suspended in a complex pun: for the *solution* offered by oblivion plays upon a spectrum of meanings – resolution, dissolution, absolution, and is echoed two lines later in the whole/hole homophony.

This sort of punning continues into the late poems, adding spots of alterity to the deepening gloom. No doubt the verbal ambiguity arises in part from the sheer difficulty of conceptualizing nothingness. As Thomas Nagel observes, 'we can perhaps conceive of the disappearance of everything in the world, so that there are no things left in it, but even then we are not imagining nothing at all'; rather, we are picturing space as a kind of receptacle which happens, at this moment, to be unoccupied.[54] The 'empty vessel' conception of oblivion is repeatedly invoked in Larkin's poems, from 'The Angels Yawning in an Empty Heaven' of his teenage musings (*CP*, 245) to these lines from 'Aubade' nearly forty years later:

> the total emptiness for ever,
> The sure extinction that we travel to
> And shall be lost in always.
>
> (*CP*, 208)

In both cases we dizzy at the paradox of an 'emptiness' that is 'total' and yet occupied, whether by angels or 'we' lost mortals.

The difficulty in conceptualizing oblivion highlights the limits of language: the word 'nothing', like the numerical zero sign, betrays its meaning by occupying the place of emptiness. As the greatest analyst of oblivion in contemporary English letters, Larkin confronts the dualities of presence and absence, being and nothingness, through the *aporia* between language and silence. As always, the fascination of his verse turns on the way it encourages and contests dogmatic readings by holding extreme alternatives in tension. Consider the violently contradictory meanings rampaging through those fifty recurrences of the word 'nothing' in the *Collected Poems*. The following locutions simultaneously affirm and negate the possibility that oblivion has being: 'seeing nothing' (*CP*, 11), 'Strange to know nothing' (*CP*, 107), 'deep blue air, that shows/Nothing' (*CP*, 165), 'nothing to think with, / Nothing to love or link with' (*CP*, 208) and 'Then there will be nothing I know' (*CP*, 211). Hence, the narrator of the latter may be read as not knowing anything or as coming to know the nature of nothingness. This type of pun is akin to the following passage from *Through the Looking-Glass and what Alice found there*:

> 'I see nobody on the road', said Alice.
> 'I only wish *I* had such eyes', the King remarked in a fretful tone. 'To be able to see Nobody! And at that distance too! Why, it's as much as *I* can do to see real people, by this light!'[55]

What is at issue is whether or not non-existence has materiality. A related set of puns affirms and negates the possibility that nothingness has agency: 'Nothing, like something, happens anywhere' (*CP*, 82), 'there's nothing going on' (*CP*, 97), 'That nothing cures' (*CP*, 126), 'Nothing shows why ... (*CP*, 129), 'Nothing provides for' (*CP*, 151).

Do these last three locutions assert that nothing is an entity with cura-tive, demonstrative and provisionary powers; or, to the contrary, that there is not anything that is so empowered?

A further round of punning on nothingness occurs in the fifty uses of the word 'love', since in addition to its tender associations the term means nil, or zero, as in the scoring of tennis.[56] The line 'What will sur-vive of us is love', so often quoted as an expression of unqualified pos-itivity, actually carries an undercutting secondary meaning – Nothing of us will survive. Similarly, the exclamation 'Lozenge of love!' in the poem 'Sad Steps' at once apostrophizes the moon as a traditional romantic symbol and witheringly dismisses the notion: Lozenge of nothingness!

What Larkin achieves by such rampant linguistic play is not a resolu-tion of the binaries entailed but the reader's assent to accord nothing-ness the compliment of a protracted contemplation. We do not have to consider his meditations progressively, as though the later ones are nec-essarily superior: such is the last refuge of the late millennial bowdler that even when the biography is not explicitly used to determine the meanings of the poems, the *oeuvre* is still read as an expression of the chronology of the author's life. It is true that by the time of 'Aubade' Larkin's teasing deliberations upon the positive and negative inflections of nothingness had come to focus upon the irreducible fact of its power to nihilate selfhood. There is, however, a late paradox that further embarrasses critics like Easthope, Gregson and Duncan who regard him as 'fixing the Personality' and rendering it 'static';[57] for like those riven nations or feuding families whose internecine disputes are abandoned in the face of a common enemy, the multiple selves of Larkin's narra-tology *pull themselves together* in the shadow of the executioner – just in time to be exterminated. As Mark Rowe finely observes, 'Aubade' is 'the first occasion when death and the first person encounter one another'.[58] Unhoused from the essentializing metanarratives of race, sex, class, reli-gion and nationality, identity for Larkin is so fugitive and conflicted that only the unified shout of 'no!' at death's approach lends it some semblance of singularity. The death that nihilates selfhood first con-structs it. In one of Larkin's more veiled puns, the 'Aubade' of the title invokes selfhood's morning and (oh, bad!) its mourning.

Conclusion: Larkin and Postmodernism

Modernism in the arts is usually assigned a specific historical period, approximately 1890–1940. In the anglophone world it is often said to have peaked in the year 1922. This was the year that saw the publication of Eliot's *The Waste Land* (commonly considered the definitive Modernist poem in English), Joyce's *Ulysses* (often considered *the* Modernist novel in English), Cummings's *The Enormous Room*, Woolf's *Jacob's Room* and Wittgenstein's *Tractatus Logico-Philosophicus*. It was also the year in which Proust died, thereby ending, complete but incompletely revised, the greatest Modernist novel in French, *A la Recherche du Temps Perdu*.

Philip Larkin was born in 1922, when Modernism was at its apogee. Significantly, some of the acknowledged masters of Postmodernist theory and practice were also born in that year (John Fowles, Alain Resnais, Kurt Vonnegut, Alain Robbe-Grillet, Jack Kerouac, Richard Hamilton), shortly before (Charlie Parker, Betty Friedan, Joseph Beuys, Paul Celan) or shortly thereafter (John Ashbery, Diane Arbus, Frantz Fanon, Andy Warhol, Michel Foucault, Italo Calvino, Gunter Grass, Miles Davis, Naom Chomsky). If Postmodernism is a relational term, meaning *after* Modernism, then historically Larkin belongs to the later culture phase.

On its own this epochal approach is insufficient to endow Larkin with Postmodernist credentials, since it is always possible to work after Modernism in an idiom that preceded it. Indeed, 'Larkin is', Corcoran insists, 'the major case in post-war English poetry of a thoroughgoing resistance to Modernism'.[1] In *Contemporary Poetry and Postmodernism* (1996) Gregson goes further, claiming that Larkin's influence 'has worked powerfully against modernism and postmodernism in British poetry'.[2] However, in his most recent book, *Postmodern Literature* (2004),

Gregson offers an account of Postmodernism that accords well with the picture of Larkin that has emerged from these pages:

> The dominant attitude in postmodernism is disbelief. The dominant strategy of both postmodern philosophy and postmodern aesthetics is deconstruction, which is disbelief put into practice. Deconstruction is an anti-system, or a system that subverts systems; it is a mechanism that exposes mechanisms. Deconstruction unscrews belief systems and uncovers their whirring cogs.[3]

In Chapter Five we remarked that Larkin is more Modernist than many Modernists: where they retreated from the nuclear crisis of modernity, the death of God, he, like his hero Hardy, kept faith with his lack of faith. Moreover, Larkin perceived that once God is removed as transcendental guarantor, essentializing discourses lose legitimacy and assume their place in the panoply of competing relativisms. Hence his deconstruction of such valourized discourses as patriarchy, imperialism, heterosexism, monogamy, nationalism, totalizing identitarianisms, monotheism and, in the realm of aesthetics, the supremacy of 'high art'.

Throughout this study, Larkin's work has been found compatible with, often anticipative of, the theories of Structuralists (Saussure, early Barthes), Poststructuralists (Bakhtin, late Barthes), Deconstructionists (Derrida), Poststructuralist feminists (Kristeva), Postcolonialists (Said, Bhabha, Gilroy), Postmodernists (Baudrillard, Jameson, Lyotard), and Queer Theorists (Butler, Dyer). Like Gregson in the passage quoted above, I have placed particular emphasis upon Deconstruction; in my case, because Larkin's poetic procedures uncannily foreshadow the central mechanics of Derridean analysis. The point I wish to emphasize here is that similar results are obtained if other of these theoretical discourses are employed. In *The Postmodern Condition: A Report on Knowledge* (1979), for instance, Jean-Francois Lyotard takes it as axiomatic that

> In contemporary society and culture – postindustrial society, postmodern culture – the question of the legitimation of knowledge is formulated in different terms. The grand narrative has lost its credibility, regardless of what mode of unification it uses, regardless of whether it is a speculative narrative or a narrative of emancipation.[4]

In other words, knowledge in the Postmodern era can no longer be organized and validated in relation to the *grandes histoires* that have shaped knowledge since the Renaissance and, more particularly, since the eighteenth century: metanarratives like the concept of progress embedded in the Enlightenment; the concept of social liberation through history embedded in Marxism; or the Rationalist concept of a sovereign subject whose unanimity releases it from inner contradiction and permits it a progressive conquest of all it surveys. 'Lyotard regards such narratives as violent and tyrannical in their imposition of a "totalizing" pattern and a false universality on actions, events and things.'[5] Hence his celebrated pronouncement, 'I define *postmodern* as incredulity toward metanarratives', and its accompanying injunction, 'Let us wage a war on totality'.[6] This, I have been at pains to demonstrate, is precisely what Larkin does. He must therefore, *sensu stricto*, be accounted a Postmodernist.

This being so, the question arises as to why Larkin is routinely lauded or damned for a thoroughgoing resistance to twentieth-century ideologies and aesthetic developments. The answer would seem to be that commentators remark his use of inherited poetic forms, regular metres and descriptive verisimilitude but not the way in which these traditional elements are eviscerated by ellipsis, paronomasia, citationality, negative qualifiers and the four-act structure with closing reversal. They see the empiricist but not the deconstructionist. They see the Realism but not that it is being employed against itself, to undermine rather than endorse 'reality'. This is not to pretend that Larkin exhibits the playfulness, the fabulation, the extreme stylistic innovation of canonical Postmodernists like Nabokov, Vonnegut, Ashbery, Carter, Pynchon, Perec, Rushdie or Muldoon. But even if we accept that such drastic aesthetic experiments are constitutive and not merely decorative, we are still left with a Larkin who is a Postmodernist in Realist clothing – or, at the least, a Realist with a Postmodernist sensibility. One final both/and, perhaps, in Larkin's career-long insurrection against the despotism of either/or.

It may not have escaped the reader's notice that in these pages I have joined combat with a sizeable sector of the English professoriate: Barbara Everett excepted, the rule of thumb is, the more eminent the academic the more vulgarly biographical the approach. During Larkin's lifetime the response from his fellow poets followed a different, though no less paradoxical, rule of thumb, the perspective varying in inverse ratio to the size of the talent. What an index to literary vanity that whereas the colossal Eliot, Auden, Lowell, Walcott and Heaney praised his achievement roundly, middling talents like Tomlinson, Paulin and O'Brien are much more niggardly, and incontestably minor (almost, one might say, microscopic) poets like Alvarez, Scupham, Mottram, Nuttall and Duncan are openly contemptuous! In the other arts, such as music, the warmth of the response was from the start almost universal: Leonard Bernstein nominated Larkin the greatest poet of the twentieth century;[7] leading British Postmodernist composers Alexander Goehr, Robin Holloway, Thomas Ades and Errollyn Wallen have all set Larkin's poems to music; *Jerry Springer – the Opera* ends, as we have seen, citing 'An Arundel Tomb'; a plethora of pop stars have declared a love for his strong lines, from Sir Bob Geldof to the sublime Radiohead and leftist Welsh rockers The Manic Street Preachers; while 'This Be The Verse' has been recorded by Anne Clark, Sneaky Feelings and The Circus McGurkhas, among others. A similar list might be compiled of theatre and cinema greats, whether writers (Pinter, Stoppard, Bennett, Plater), directors (Patrick Garland, Anthony Minghella, Sam Mendes) or actors (Alan Bates, Tom Courtenay, Oliver Ford Davies). As for the visual arts, even as I write Damien Hirst's latest exhibition is about to open at the Gagosian Gallery, Beverly Hills, California, every painting in the show being titled after a late poem by Larkin.[8]

Most gratifying of all, perhaps, is the frequency with which new millennial fiction writers incorporate within their novels an acknowledgement of Larkin's liberating role: recent examples include Matt Haig, *The Last Family in England* (2004); David Mitchell, *Cloud Atlas* (2004); Ian McEwan, *Saturday* (2005) and *On Chesil Beach* (2007)[9]; Tony Parsons, *Stories We Could Tell* (2005); John Banville, *The Sea* (winner of the 2005 Man Booker Prize); Zadie Smith, *On Beauty* (winner of the Orange Prize for 2006); and Sam Taylor's *The Amnesiac* (2007). The man who instigated this delightful game is surely Julian Barnes, whose first three novels – *Metroland* (1980), *Before She Met Me* (1982), *Flaubert's Parrot* (1984) – are lightly spiced with Larkin allusions. Belated signs of a comparable development in poetry may be found in twenty-first century volumes from Carol Ann Duffy, Alan Jenkins, Kathleen Jamie, Paul Farley, Kathryn Gray, Nick Laird, Kate Clanchy and Colette Bryce.

That the foregoing are some of the most exciting artists of the era, the one we are going into, the one they are helping to create, is particularly instructive; for it obliges us to read Larkin in ways other than those established by the critical consensus. This is the author I have tried to delineate: the one whose radical site-clearing prepared the ground for a British Postmodernism; the favoured role model of the brilliant young; the Larkin in whose works, so often perceived as backward-looking and terminal, the future keeps breaking through.

Notes

Introduction: Radical Larkin and the Late Millennial Bowdler

1. Robert Hendrickson, *The Literary Life and Other Curiosities* (Penguin, Harmondsworth, 1982), 198.
2. Hendrickson, *The Literary Life*, 218.
3. Noel Perria, *Dr Bowdler's Legacy: A History of Expurgated Books in England and America* (Macmillan, Basingstoke, 1970), 76.
4. Hendrickson, *The Literary Life*, 217.
5. Perria, *Dr Bowdler's Legacy*, xii.
6. Perria, *Dr Bowdler's Legacy*, viii.
7. Perria, *Dr Bowdler's Legacy*, xv.
8. Dennis O'Driscoll, *Troubled Thoughts, Majestic Dreams: Selected Prose Writings* (Gallery, Loughcrew, 2001), 193.
9. Lawrence Ferlinghetti, *Beat Writers at Work: The Paris Review Interviews*, ed. George Plimpton (Harvill, London, 1999), 346–7.
10. James Campbell, *This is the Beat Generation: New York – San Francisco – Paris* (Secker & Warburg, London, 1999), 60.
11. My wording here is indebted to Campbell, 97. Though it crosses the line between biography and literary criticism more freely than I prefer, this is a wonderfully readable and perceptive study.
12. Allen Ginsberg, *Howl and Other Poems* (City Lights Books, San Francisco, 1971), 9.
13. Ginsberg, *Howl and Other Poems*, 15.
14. Ginsberg, *Howl, Original Draft Facsimile*, ed. Barry Miles (Viking, New York, 1986), 131.
15. Ann Charters, ed., *The Penguin Book of the Beats* (Penguin, Harmondsworth, 1992), 435.
16. Sylvia Plath, *Collected Poems*, ed. Ted Hughes (Faber, London, 1981), 223.
17. Henry Miller, *Tropic of Cancer* (Panther, London, 1968), 11.
18. Plath, *Collected Poems*, 246–7.
19. Ted Hughes, ed., *A Choice of Coleridge's Verse* (Faber, London, 1996), 117.
20. Henry Wadsworth Longfellow, *The Works of Henry Wadsworth Longfellow* (Wordsworth, Ware, 1994), 43.
21. Plath, *Collected Poems*, 221–2.
22. Roland Barthes, *Image – Music – Text*, ed. and trans. Stephen Heath (Fontana, London, 1984), 143.
23. Eliot, *Selected Prose*, ed. John Hayward (Penguin, Harmondsworth, 1953), 29.
24. James Joyce, *A Portrait of the Artist as a Young Man* (Penguin, Harmondsworth, 1964), 215.
25. David Lodge, ed., *20th Century Literary Criticism: A Reader* (Longman, London, 1972), 334.
26. Barthes, *Image – Music – Text*, 159–60.

27. Barthes, *Image – Music – Text*, 147.

28. Barthes, *Image – Music – Text*, 146.

29. Anthony Thwaite, ed., *Larkin at Sixty* (Faber, London, 1982), 11–12.

30. Peter Levi, 'The English Wisdom of a Master Poet', *An Enormous Yes: in memoriam Philip Larkin (1922–1985)*, ed. Harry Chambers (Peterloo Poets, Calstock, 1986), 33.

31. Clive James, 'Pretending To Be Him', *Times Literary Supplement*, 28 February 2003, 19.

32. B.J. Leggett, *Larkin's Blues: Jazz, Popular Music and Poetry* (Louisiana State University Press, Baton Rouge, 1999), 2.

33. Peter Ackroyd, 'Poet Hands on Misery to Man', *The Times*, 1 April 1993, 35.

34. Brian Appleyard, 'The Dreary Laureate of our Provincialism', *Independent*, 18 March 1993, 27.

35. Germaine Greer, 'A Very British Misery', *Guardian*, 14 October 1988, 27.

36. Tom Paulin, *Times Literary Supplement*, 6 November 1992, 15.

37. Four years later Paulin castigated T.S. Eliot in the *London Review of Books* as the author of an anti-Semitic review in the July 1936 issue of the *Criterion*, even claiming that Eliot had altered the journal's typography to 'mock' Jewish suffering. The poet's widow Valerie Eliot coolly disclosed that the review had actually been written by one Montgomery Belgion, as was evident from the index. The strange insinuation regarding typography was also without foundation. Squaring up to Eliot, David to Goliath, Paulin delivers a superfluous beating to the negligible Belgion, Giant-the-Jack-killer style. See Jason Harding, 'A useful irritant: Montgomery Belgion, T.S. Eliot and the *Criterion*', *Times Literary Supplement*, 25 August 2000, 14–15.

38. Jonathan Bate, 'Very Juvenile, This Juvenilia', *Sunday Telegraph*, 28 April 2003, 13; Andrew Duncan, *The Failure of Conservatism in Modern British Poetry* (Salt, Cambridge, 2003), 62–3; Christopher Bray, 'A Writer's Life: Clive James', the *Telegraph* arts supplement, 5 November 2005, 12.

39. Dámaso López Garcia, 'Post-Metropolitan Larkin', *Hungarian Journal of English and American Studies*, vol. 9, 2, 2003, 80.

40. Martin Amis, 'The Ending: Don Juan in Hell', *The War Against Cliché* (Cape, London, 2001), 155.

41. Lisa Jardine, 'Saxon Violence', *Guardian*, Section 2, 8 December 1992, 4. Four years later Jardine extended these tactics to the visual arts. On the Women's Page of the *Guardian*, 3 December 1996, she declared that 'it really is time we took down from the walls of our public buildings works of art, however sanctioned by the passage of time, which contain graphic representations of acts which violate, harm or mutilate *anybody*'. Citing the example of *The Rape of the Sabine Women* by Jacques-Louis David, Jardine claimed that it represented 'over-muscled Roman soldiers ... brutally attacking the womenfolk of their enemies, the Sabines' in a way that amounted to a 'vile and despicable' glorification of 'violence against women'. Actually the painting honours Hersilia, daughter of the Sabine leader and wife of the Roman one, who bravely stands between father and husband, morally obliging the contending armies to put away their weapons and embrace. The painting Jardine would ban celebrates peace, not war; woman's moral courage, not female degradation. See 'NB', *Times Literary Supplement*, 6 December 1996, 16.

42. David Timms, *Philip Larkin* (Oliver and Boyd, Edinburgh, 1973), 19.

43. James Booth, *Philip Larkin: Writer* (Harvester, Hemel Hempstead, 1992), 78–9.

44. Timms, *Philip Larkin*, 23, 26, 33, 100, 83, 111.
45. A.T. Tolley, *My Proper Ground: A Study of the Work of Philip Larkin and Its Development* (Edinburgh University Press, Edinburgh, 1991), 86.
46. Warren Hope, *Student Guide to Philip Larkin* (Greenwich Exchange, Holywood, 1997), 39.
47. Timms, *Philip Larkin*, 86.
48. John Whitehead, *Hardy to Larkin: Seven English Poets* (Hearthstone, Munslow, 1995), 219.
49. Arthur Rimbaud, *Collected Poems*, trans. Martin Sorrell (Oxford University Press, Oxford, 2001), xvii; Eliot, *Selected Prose*, 30; James Joyce, *Ulysses* (Penguin, Harmondsworth, 1971), 189; W.H. Auden, *Later Auden*, ed. Edward Mendelson (Faber, London, 1999), 360.
50. Q.D. Leavis, *Fiction and the Reading Public* (Penguin, Harmondsworth, 1972), 36.
51. Leavis, *Fiction and the Reading Public*, 188.
52. Christopher Hitchens, *Unacknowledged Legislation: Writers in the Public Sphere* (Verso, London, 2002), 250; James Wood, 'Want Not, Write Not', *Guardian*, 30 March 1993, 20.
53. Roger Day, *Larkin* (Open University Press, Milton Keynes and Philadelphia, 1987), 89.

1 Larkin and Modernism: Jazz

1. This chapter benefited from conversations with John Mowat and John White – jazz buffs, Larkin friends and fellow Americanists.
2. See, for example, Cedric Watts, 'Larkin and Jazz', *Philip Larkin: The Poems*, eds Linda Cookson and Bryan Laughrey (Longman, London, 1987), 20–8.
3. Duke Ellington and Billy Strayhorn regularly borrowed from Modernist composers like Debussy and Ravel. In *Arabesque Cookie* they rewrote the *Arabian Dance* from Tchaikovsky's *Nutcracker Suite* in a jazz style that also contained echoes of Ravel's *Bolero*. The *Jazzing The Classics* album (ASV CD, AJA 5339) offers a handy miscellany of shorter jazz rewrites of classical compositions, mainly recorded between the world wars. These include a Quintette du Hot Club de France swing arrangement of the *D minor Concerto for Two Violins* by Bach; *Elegie* by Jules Massenet given a virtuoso jazz piano treatment by Art Tatum; and *Moon Love*, Glenn Miller's take on the second movement of Tchaikovsky's *Fifth Symphony*.
4. There is a growing critical industry investigating each of these elements in the musical stew: for instance, Jeffrey Melnick's *A Right to Sing the Blues: Africa Americans, Jews and American Popular Song* (Harvard University Press, Cambridge, 1999) explores the predominance of Jews among America's 'blackface' performers – Al Jolson, Sophie Tucker and Eddie Cantor being prime examples.
5. Jackie Kay, 'Admirable horn blower', *Observer Review*, 29 November 1998, 14.
6. Eliot, *The Sacred Wood* (Methuen, London, 1928), 38.
7. Eliot, *Selected Prose*, 29–30.
8. John Chilton, *Sidney Bechet: The Wizard of Jazz* (Macmillan, Basingstoke, 1987), 116.
9. In *Brodie's Notes on Philip Larkin's Selected Poems* (Pan, London, 1991), Graham Handley gets this entirely the wrong way round claiming that Storyville was 'named after a member of the US Navy who tried to close the

brothels'. The entry on 'For Sidney Bechet' also states that New Orleans acquired the nickname 'the Crescent City' from the fact that it 'is often depicted with the moon shining over the water'; actually, the name derives from the city's location on a curve of the Mississippi River. Even the title of the volume seems calculated to confuse the tyros at whom it is aimed as no such edition of Larkin's *Selected Poems* has been published. For the Storyville magazine and jazz label see Leggett, *Larkin's Blues*, 72.

10. Langston Hughes, *The Collected Poems of Langston Hughes*, eds Arnold Rampersad and David Roessel (Knopf, New York, 1994), 60. Larkin refers to Hughes in *AWJ*, 161. The composer Peter Dickinson remarks that Larkin and Amis listened to recordings of Hughes reading his poems to a jazz accompaniment but were not convinced the combination succeeded. 'Larkin's Jazz', *About Larkin*, 19 (2005), 7.

11. In the present writer's opinion the best Bechet compilation is *The Sidney Bechet Story*, a four-CD set issued by Proper Records as Properbox 18, 2001. A good single record collection is *Sidney Bechet, Really the Blues*, ASV CD, AJA 5107, 1993. Both sets include *Maple Leaf Rag*.

12. For the Jelly Roll Morton quote see Paul Oliver, *The Story of the Blues* (Penguin, Harmondsworth, 1972), 76–7. For King Oliver's *Dippermouth Blues* (and, indeed, the *Riverside Blues* of 'Reference Back') see the compilation in the Naxos Jazz Legends series, *King Oliver: Oh Play That Thing!*, CD 8.120666, 2003. For *Gut Bucket Blues* see the first volume of the four-CD set *Louis Armstrong: Hot Fives and Sevens*, JSLOUISBOX 100.

13. V. Penelope Pelizzon, 'Oh, play that thing!', *About Larkin*, 5 (1998), 17–18.

14. Chilton, *Sidney Bechet: The Wizard of Jazz*, 121. James Weldon Johnson says something similar when endeavouring to explain European performers' lack of 'swing': 'The trouble is, they play the notes too correctly; and do not play what is not written down'. See *The Book of American Negro Spirituals* (1925); reprint Da Capo, New York, 1977), 28. According to Langston Hughes, Louis Armstrong answered the question did he read music with the crushing reply 'Not enough to hurt my playing' (Hughes, 498).

15. The distinction between the author and his narrator is doubly underlined at this point; for not only does Larkin know what his narrator does not, that Bechet loved Classical music, but the poet shared that enthusiasm. On the *Desert Island Discs* radio programme only three of Larkin's eight choices were jazz records and he described Handel as his 'favourite composer'. Moreover, his description of Handel's 'great roaring finales' as 'the musical equivalent of sunshine' is remarkably close in spirit to the words 'On me your voice falls as they say love should, / Like an enormous yes', suggesting once again a rejection of the either/or of his narrator. (*FR*, 103–11).

16. Leggett, *Larkin's Blues*, 79.

17. Eliot, *Selected Prose*, 86.

18. Unpublished letter to Sutton, 2 April 1942, Brynmor Jones Library, University of Hull.

19. Andrew Motion, *Philip Larkin: A Writer's Life* (Faber, London, 1993), 47.

20. Claude Luter, not Claud, as Motion has it, *Philip Larkin: A Writer's Life*, 223, 564.

21. Tolley's edition of the *Early Poems and Juvenilia* (Faber, London, 2005) includes pieces with such titles as 'Young Woman Blues', 'Hard Lines, or Mean Old W.H. Thomas Blues', 'Fuel Form Blues', 'Blues' and 'Blues Shouter'.

The editor notes that in October 1939 the seventeen-year-old Larkin compiled a no longer extant collection of his poems under the title *One O'Clock Jump* (*EPJ*, 349). The title is a nod towards the young Count Basie who composed and recorded a brilliant track of that name in 1937 (re-released in 1996 on the K-Tel label, ASIN BOOOOOORUK).

22. Chilton, *Sidney Bechet: The Wizard of Jazz*, 178.
23. Thus, British politicians refused to see the Mau Mau revolt in Kenya as having anything to do with the colonial appropriation of Kikuyu lands, African aspirations for political independence or justifiable campaigns for an improvement in living standards. Instead, Mau Mau was seen as an evil spell which rebels cast over the minds of a susceptible populace. In the very year of Larkin's poem Alan Lennox-Boyd, the Colonial Secretary, told the House of Commons that

> as the terrorists grew more brutalized, their moral degradation was reflected in the characteristics of the Mau Mau oath. This developed sexual and sadistic aberrations which, in the higher form of the oath, included murder and cannibalism. ... The taking of the oaths had such a tremendous effect on the Kikuyu mind as to turn quite intelligent young Africans into entirely different human beings, into sub-human creatures without hope and with death as their only deliverance.

What Lennox-Boyd neglected to mention was that whereas the 'sub-human' rebels were responsible for the deaths of 32 white settlers, the British colonial administration killed 12,000 of them and incarcerated a further 70,000 Kenyans without trial. See David Anderson, *Histories of the Hanged: Britain's Dirty War in Kenya and the End of Empire* (Weidenfeld & Nicolson, London, 2005), 280–1.
24. John Ramsden writes:

> 'Nigger' was the actual name of Gibson's dog, of course, and the filmmakers now stuck to it in the interests of accuracy, but it also gives some indication of the mores of 1950s Britain; such a name would have been unthinkable in the United States at that time. For the American version of the film, the dog became 'Trigger', despite its overtones of the Western, presumably because it was the easiest word to dub on the soundtrack. By the end of the century, Britain had belatedly caught up. When ITV showed the film in 1999 the network was apparently 'inundated with complaints', as a result of which the soundtrack was edited to remove the offending word.

See Ramsden, *The Dam Busters* (Tauris, London, 2003), 51. A remake of *The Dam Busters* is in production, with a script by Stephen Fry. It will be fascinating to see if the makers retain the dog's name as an index of the values of the period or follow ITV in sanitizing history.

A comparable indication of the gap between Britain and the USA in terms of racial awareness was the bewilderment of the *Black and White Minstrels* when Diana Ross and the Supremes objected to sharing a stage with them at the 1968 Royal Command Variety Performance. Astonishingly, the young star of *The Minstrels* in the show's last years was the black comedian Lenny

Henry. Even after the television series ended, *The Minstrels* successfully toured the UK with a live stage production until 1987 – two years after Larkin's death.

25. Of course, this same polyphony also works to unhouse gender certitudes, melding the narratives of heterosexual males (like Sidney Bechet), gay men (Langston Hughes) and women (the Memphis prostitutes).

26. Clement Greenberg, *Art and Culture* (Thames and Hudson, London, 1973), 28; Larkin, *Guardian*, 20 May 1965, 9.

27. Leggett, *Larkin's Blues*, 50.

28. The poem does refer to 'The trumpet's voice, loud and authoritative' (*CP*, 80), but this does not constitute proof that the music entailed is jazz. The biggest UK hit record of 1953, when 'Reasons for Attendance' was composed, was a dreadfully mawkish number called *Oh, my Papa* by Eddie Calvert, billed as 'The Man with the Golden Trumpet'. The record was especially popular with those who, like the dancers in the poem, were 'under twenty-five'; and two years later Calvert followed it up with another Top Ten hit, the equally sentimental *Cherry pink and appleblossom white*. If this was the kind of music being played in the poem's dance venue, it would give Larkin's protagonist another reason for beating a hasty retreat!

2 Larkin and Modernism: Poetry

1. Barbara Everett, 'Philip Larkin: After Symbolism', *Essays in Criticism*, XXX (1980), 227–42; reprinted in Everett, *Poets in Their Time: Essays on English Poetry from Donne to Larkin* (Faber, London, 1986), 230–44.

2. Charles Tomlinson, 'Poetry Today', *Pelican Guide to English Literature, vol. 7, The Modern Period*, ed. Boris Ford (Penguin, Harmondsworth, 1964), 458.

3. Tomlinson, 'Poetry Today', 471.

4. Andrew Swarbrick, *'The Less Deceived' and 'The Whitsun Weddings' by Philip Larkin* (Macmillan, Basingstoke, 1986), 73.

5. Hugh Kenner, *A Sinking Island: The Modern English Writers* (Barrie & Jenkins, London, 1988), 240.

6. Everett, *Poets in Their Time*, 238–9.

7. Everett, *Poets in Their Time*, 234.

8. Everett, *Poets in Their Time*, 241. The only critic who has successfully followed Everett's lead in investigating Larkin's indebtedness to the French is Graham Chesters. See: 'Larkin and Baudelaire's Damned Women', *Making Connections: Essays in French Culture and Society in Honour of Philip Thody*, ed. James Dolamore (Peter Lang, Bern, 1999), 81–92; 'Tireless Play: Speculations on Larkin's "Absences"', *Challenges of Translation in French Literature: Studies and Poems in Honour of Peter Broome*, ed. Richard Bales (Peter Lang, Bern, 2005), 47–59; 'Larkin's Books: Sidelining French Literature', *French Studies Bulletin*, LX, 100 (2006), 72–5.

9. Everett, *Poets in Their Time*, 240.

10. My phrasing here is indebted to Mary Orr, *Intertextuality: Debates and Contexts* (Polity, London, 2003), 41.

11. Everett, *Poets in Their Time*, 232.

12. Eliot, *Selected Prose*, 112.
13. According to Tolley 'there is little use of intertextuality (conscious or uncon-scious) in Larkin's work: the reference to other literatures as a dimension of understanding ... was anathema to him': *My Proper Ground*, 177. The ensuing partial documentation of Larkin's copious citations may serve to embarrass such slavish echoing of the poet's propaganda at the expense of his practice.
14. K. Narayama Chandran, 'Some Shakespearean Reminiscences in Philip Larkin's "The Old Fools"', *The Literary Half-Yearly*, XXXV, One (1994), 78–82.
15. I am indebted to the late Ted Tarling for pointing this out to me.
16. I drew this connection from Roger Craik's fascinating essay 'Some Unheard Melodies in Philip Larkin's Poetry', *About Larkin*, 12 (2001), 11–13.
17. Marginalia in Ted Tarling's personal copy of Larkin's *Collected Poems*.
18. Indeed, I have simplified matters by excluding multi-layered citations from my list. It is a critical commonplace to connect 'you were less deceived' in 'Deceptions' (*CP*, 32) to Ophelia's 'I was the more deceived' (*Hamlet*, III.i.120); however, Laurence Lerner has made an equally persuasive link to the 'Digression on Madness' in Swift's *A Tale of a Tub* (*Philip Larkin*, Northcote, Plymouth, 1997, 12). Similarly, the title 'Annus Mirabilis' is usu-ally regarded as a direct invocation of Dryden's poem of the same name which was published exactly three hundred years earlier, but can be as mean-ingfully read against a short prose work, usually attributed to Dr John Arbuthnot, and published in 1722 (two hundred years before Larkin's birth). Focussing upon a day when everyone changes sex, this 'Annus Mirabilis', like Larkin's, exposes the arbitrariness of sexual conventions by mocking rev-olutionary changes in the libidinal economy. As for 'High Windows', in spring 2005 the letters page of the *Times Literary Supplement* was abuzz with competing suggestions for the title's source. Candidates included J.H. Shorthouse's novel *John Inglesant* and Ursula Le Guin's *Planet of Exile*; though the list was far from exhaustive – no one advanced Raymond Chandler's *The High Window*, for example.
19. I am indebted to Don Lee of the Philip Larkin Society for this information.
20. *The Viking Portable Walt Whitman*, ed. Mark Van Doren (Viking, New York, 1966), 116.
21. Roman Jakobson, *A Concise Glossary of Contemporary Literary Theory*, ed. Jeremy Hawthorn (Arnold, London, 1998), 109.
22. Eliot, *Complete Poems and Plays* (Faber, London, 1969), 96, 72, 65.
23. Eliot, *Complete Poems and Plays*, 13–14.
24. Robert Conquest, 'A Proper Sport', *Larkin at Sixty* (Faber, London, 1982), 32.
25. Bell died in poverty in 1978, too soon to know the talismanic power of his work for a new generation of Postmodernist poets (including the splendid Peter Didsbury). How typical of the way Larkin's practice is skewed against stereotype that he should have offered the warmest affirmation in Bell's mis-erable last years. Seven years after Bell's death and a few months away from his own, Larkin was still extolling the 'swashbuckling' virtues of his 'unig-norable oeuvre' (*SL*, 731).
26. As late as 1972 Larkin was describing himself as 'the Laforgue of Pearson Park' (*SL*, 460), a formulation that brings two other Modernist luminaries into play by echoing Dylan Thomas's description of himself as 'the Rimbaud of Cwmdonkin Drive'.

27. B.C. Southam, *A Student's Guide to the 'Selected Poems' of T.S. Eliot* (Faber, London, 1994), 79.
28. Eliot, *Complete Poems and Plays*, 57.
29. Eliot, *Complete Poems and Plays*, 63, 70, 78, 74, 68.
30. Alfred Tennyson, *The poems of Alfred Tennyson* (Kegan Paul, London, 1882), 28.
31. John Betjeman, *Collected Poems*, ed. Earl of Birkenhead (John Murray, London, 1958), 213.
32. Jean Hartley, *Philip Larkin, the Marvell Press, and Me* (Carcanet, Manchester, 1989), 119.
33. Longfellow, *The Works of Henry Wadsworth Longfellow*, 135.
34. Motion, *Philip Larkin: A Writer's Life*, 288.
35. The name Eros may be an error but is hardly a misnomer. When the American sexologist Alfred Kinsey visited London he was astounded by the amount of street prostitution, homosexual as well as heterosexual, in the area around Piccadilly Circus, likening it to downtown Havana. Since Larkin, this aspect of the location has been celebrated in popular song by the likes of Dire Straits, the Sundays and Morrisey.
36. Eliot, *Complete Poems and Plays*, 66, 68.
37. Christopher Ricks, *Allusion to the Poets* (Oxford University Press, Oxford, 2002), 2.
38. Timms, *Philip Larkin*, 117; Lerner, *Philip Larkin*, 23; Tolley, *My Proper Ground*, 95; Swarbrick, *'The Less Deceived' and 'The Whitsun Weddings'*, 50; Stephen Regan, *Philip Larkin: The Critics Debate* (Macmillan, Basingstoke, 1992), 115; Whitehead, *Hardy to Larkin*, 230; Blake Morrison, *The Movement: English Poetry and Fiction of the 1950s* (Methuen, London, 1980), 258.
39. Greer, 'A Very British Misery', 27; John Newsinger, 'Dead Poet: the Larkin Letters', *Race and Class*, vol. 34, no. 4 (1993), 87; Stan Smith, *Inviolable Voice: History and Twentieth Century Poetry* (Gill & Macmillan, Dublin, 1982), 176; Sean O'Brien, *The Deregulated Muse* (Bloodaxe Books, Newcastle, 1998), 27; Neil Corcoran, *English Poetry Since 1940* (Longman, London, 1993), 94; Regan, *The Critics Debate*, 116; Gilbert Phelps, 'Literature and Drama', *The Cambridge Guide to the Arts in Britain, vol.9, Since the Second World War*, ed. Boris Ford (Cambridge University Press, Cambridge, 1988), 213.
40. See *The Second Book of American Negro Spirituals*, ed. James Weldon Johnson (1926; reprint, Da Capo, New York, 1977), 158–9.
41. Martin Luther King, 'I have a dream', *The Penguin Book of Historic Speeches*, ed. Brian MacArthur (Viking, London, 1995), 491.
42. Seamus Heaney, *Finders Keepers: Selected Prose, 1971–2001* (Faber, London, 2002), 95, 79–80, 94.
43. Heaney, *Finders Keepers*, 151.
44. Simon Petch, *The Art of Philip Larkin* (Sydney University Press, Sydney, 1981), 60.
45. Frederick Grubb, 'Dragons', *Phoenix*, vol. 11/12 (1973), 133.
46. Peter Hollindale, 'Philip Larkin's "The Explosion"', *Critical Survey*, I (1989), 142.
47. Hollindale, 145.
48. John Donne, *Devotions upon Emergent Occasions*, XVII, ed. A. Raspa (McGill-Queens University Press, Montreal, 1975), 87.
49. Longfellow, *The Works of Henry Wadsworth Longfellow*, 204.

50. Elias Lonnrot, *The Kalevala: An Epic Poem After Oral Tradition*, trans. Keith Bosley (Oxford University Press, Oxford, 1989), 1.
51. John Ashbery, *April Galleons* (Carcanet, Manchester, 1987), 14.
52. I am indebted to Jim Orwin for this information.
53. William Wootten, 'In the Graveyard of Verse', *London Review of Books*, 9 August 2001, 24.
54. Ronald Draper, 'The Positive Larkin', *Critical Essays on Philip Larkin: The Poems*, eds Linda Cookson and Bryan Loughrey (Longman, London, 1989), 103–4.
55. Hollindale, 144.
56. Longfellow, *The Works of Henry Wadsworth Longfellow*, 213.
57. Marcus Cunliffe, *The Literature of the United States* (Penguin, Harmondsworth, 1964), 148.
58. Lewis Carroll, *The Complete Illustrated Works of Lewis Carroll* (Chancellor Press, London, 1982), 818.
59. I.A. Richards quoted in Newton Arvin, *Longfellow: His Life and Work* (Little, Brown & Co, Boston, 1963), 154. Longfellow confessed of the *Hiawatha* parodies, 'the better they are done, the worse they are in their effects; for one cannot get rid of them, but ever after sees them making faces behind the original'. See 'Introduction', *The Song of Hiawatha*, ed. Daniel Aaron (Everyman, London, 1992), xv.
60. As a librarian, of course, Larkin was a guardian of historical taxonomies, a professional intertextualist.
61. Julia Kristeva, 'Le Texte et sa science', quoted in Orr, *Intertextuality: Debates and Contexts*, 30.
62. Orr, 24–32. Norman Fairclough, *Discourse and Social Change* (Polity, London, 1992), and Simon Dentith, *Bakhtinian Thought* (Routledge, London, 1995), are among those who have challenged Kristevan intertextuality for its failure to indicate the social constraints and power relations which condition discourse. Dentith (p. 98) claims that 'intertextuality' entails the 'deracination of the signifying process' so that 'the production of meaning itself happens as a result of purely textual operations'.
63. Ezra Pound, *The Cantos of Ezra Pound* (revised and collected edition, Faber, London, 1975), 520–1.
64. *Jerry Springer – the Opera*, music by Richard Thomas, lyrics by Stewart Lee and Richard Thomas, directed by Stewart Lee, 2CD set, Sony Music UK, 514792 2 (2003).

3   Larkin and Philosophy: Existentialism

1. Valentine Cunningham, ed., *The Penguin Book of Spanish Civil War Verse* (Penguin, Harmondsworth, 1980), 58.
2. Cunningham, *The Penguin Book of Spanish Civil War Verse*, 50.
3. This exercise has been repeated down the years, most recently with *Authors Take Sides on Iraq and the Gulf War*, eds Jean Moorcroft Wilson and Cecil Woolf (Cecil Woolf, London, 2004).
4. F. Scott Fitzgerald, *This Side of Paradise* (Penguin, Harmondsworth, 1965), 253; *The Crack-Up and other Pieces and Stories* (Penguin, Harmondsworth, 1965), 9.

5. O'Driscoll, *Troubled Thoughts*, 45.
6. George Orwell, *Inside the Whale and Other Essays* (Penguin, Harmondsworth, 1966), 37.
7. Eliot, *Complete Poems and Plays*, 201.
8. See 'The Passion of St Eatherly', Malcolm Muggeridge, *Tread Softly for You Tread on my Jokes* (Collins, London, 1968), 219–27. As recently as 2000, Zachary Leader was erroneously describing Eatherly as 'the pilot who dropped the atom bomb' (mis-spelling his name in the process). See *The Letters of Kingsley Amis*, ed. Zachary Leader (HarperCollins, London, 2000), 756.
9. 'A Song About Major Eatherly', *Weep Before God* (Macmillan, London, 1962), 45.
10. Anthony Thwaite, *Poetry Today: A Critical Guide to British Poetry, 1960–1984* (Longman, London, 1985), 47.
11. Harry Ritchie, *Success Stories: Literature and the Media in England, 1950–1959* (Faber, London, 1982), 18.
12. Patricia Waugh, *The Harvest of the Sixties: English Literature and Its Background, 1960–1990* (Oxford University Press, Oxford, 1995), 128.
13. Regan, *The Critics Debate*, 80.
14. Brian Appleyard, *The Pleasures of Peace: Art and Imagination in Post-War Britain* (Faber, London, 1990), 104; Jeff Nuttall, 'The Singing Ted', *Poetry Information*, 9/10 (1974), 25; Terry Eagleton, 'Larkin: A Left View', *About Larkin*, 9 (2000), 8; Andrew Duncan, *The Failure of Conservatism in Modern British Poetry*, 65.
15. On page 19, for example, the anthology *Poetry from Oxford in Wartime* (1944) is wrongly referred to as a solo collection by Larkin, and of the flashback sequence in *A Girl in Winter* we are told 'this episode occupies most of the novel' when it actually comprises less than half. If Larkin wrote as carelessly as Appleyard reads, he would deserve censure.
16. Graham Holderness, 'Philip Larkin: The Limits of Experience', *Critical Essays on Philip Larkin*, 112.
17. Holderness, 'Philip Larkin: The Limits of Experience', 106.
18. Holderness, 'Philip Larkin: The Limits of Experience', 112.
19. Iris Murdoch, *Sartre* (Collins, London, 1968), 66.
20. Alan Bennett, *Writing Home* (Faber, London, 1994), 569, 571. In a talk to the Philip Larkin Society, 27 May 2006, the Chinese writer Adeline Yen Mah remarked that Larkin introduced her to the writings of Kierkegaard. To this day she prizes a passage from the 'Diapsalmata' section of *Either/Or* that Larkin impressed upon her in 1961. See Jim Orwin and John Osborne, 'Adeline Yen Mah', *About Larkin*, 22 (2006), 17–19.
21. Walter Kaufmann, ed. *Existentialism: From Dostoevsky to Sartre* (Meridian, New York, 1975), 17.
22. Kaufmann, *Existentialism*, 349.
23. George Steiner, *Heidegger* (Fontana, Glasgow, 1978), 57.
24. John Macquarrie, *Existentialism* (Penguin, Harmondsworth, 1973), 89–90.
25. Dave Robinson and Oscar Zarate, *Introducing Kierkegaard* (Icon, Cambridge, 2003), 92.
26. *Kierkegaard's View of Christianity*, eds Niels Thulstrup and Marie Mikulova (Reitzels Forlag, Copenhagen, 1984), 161; *Kierkegaard and the Church in*

Denmark, eds Niels Thulstrup and Marie Mikulova (Reitzels Boghandel, Copenhagen, 1978), 147; *Kierkegaard's View of Christianity*, 160.
27. *Kierkegaard and the Church*, 243, 48.
28. J.R. Watson, 'The Other Larkin', *Critical Quarterly*, 17, 4 (1975), 354; R.N. Parkinson, 'To keep our metaphysics warm: A study of "Church Going"', *Critical Survey*, 5 (1971), 224, 231; Terry Whalen, *Philip Larkin and English Poetry* (Macmillan, Basingstoke, 1986), 17; Patrick Garland, 'An Enormous Yes: A Memoir of the Poet', *An Arundel Tomb*, ed. Paul Foster (Otter Memorial Paper Number 1, Chichester, 1987), 24–5.
29. Tolley, *My Proper Ground*, 81.
30. Whitehead, *Hardy to Larkin*, 226.

4   Larkin and Philosophy: Poststructuralism

1. Jonathan Culler, *Barthes* (Fontana, Glasgow, 1983), 15.
2. Barbara Johnson, 'Writing', *Critical Terms for Literary Study*, eds Frank Lentricchia and Thomas McLaughlin (University of Chicago Press, Chicago, 1990), 43.
3. Jacques Derrida, *Of Grammatology*, trans. Gayatri Chakravorty Spivak (John Hopkins University Press, Baltimore, 1997), 142.
4. Jacques Derrida, 'Plato's Pharmacy', *Dissemination*, trans. Barbara Johnson (Athlone, London, 1981). For an interesting critique of Derrida's essay see Sean Burke, *The Death and Return of the Author* (Edinburgh University Press, Edinburgh, 1998).
5. It is worth remembering that Stalin banned *Hamlet* because its protagonist's indecisiveness was incompatible with Soviet optimism, fortitude and clarity.
6. Bennett, *Writing Home*, 554.
7. Larkin claimed that Connolly's *The Condemned Playground* was his 'sacred book' (Motion, *Philip Larkin: A Writer's Life*, 202) and wrote an introduction to a reprint edition (see *FR*, 134–8).
8. Morrison, *The Movement*, 142.
9. Morrison, *The Movement*, 143.
10. Greer, 'A Very British Misery', 27.
11. Bennett, *Untold Stories* (Faber, London, 2006), 541.
12. Conquest, *Larkin at Sixty*, 34–5.
13. Maurice Rutherford, *Love is a Four-Letter World* (Peterloo, Calstock, 1994), 57. Rutherford's other books are *Slipping the Tugs* (Lincolnshire & Humberside Arts, Lincoln, 1982) and *This Day Dawning* (Peterloo, Calstock, 1989). The world would be a better place if poets as good as Rutherford enjoyed a fraction of the celebrity of the pundits reviewed in these pages.
14. Janice Rossen, *Philip Larkin: His Life's Work* (Harvester, Hemel Hemstead, 1989), 70.
15. Asked why he wrote plays, Tom Stoppard replied: 'Because writing dialogue is the only respectable way of contradicting yourself'. Stoppard is a Larkin admirer. See 'Life of Czechs and balances', Kiernan Ryan, *Times Higher Education Supplement*, 29 August 2003, 27.
16. Culler, *Barthes*, 82.

17. Michael Schmidt, *Lives of the Poets* (Weidenfeld & Nicolson, London, 1... 799.

18. Tom Paulin, 'She Did Not Change: Philip Larkin', *Minotaur: Poetry a... Nation State* (Harvard University Press, Cambridge, 1992), 238, 250.

19. As Larkin said in the Hamilton interview: 'Maybe the average reade... understand what I say, but the above-average often can't' (*FR*, 25).

20. Bennett, *Writing Home*, 561.

21. John Carey, 'The Two Philip Larkins', *New Larkins for Old: Critical Essay... James Booth (Macmillan, Basingstoke, 2000), 58.

22. Compare with Harry Graham's 'Grandpapa' –

> As yet upon his vast estates
>   No labour troubles had arisen;
> There were no beggars at his gates –
> He and his brother-magistrates
>   Had sent them all to prison,
> Knowing 'twas wiser to avoid
> Encouraging the Unemployed.

or Betjeman's 'In Westminster Abbey':

> Gracious Lord, oh bomb the Germans.
>   Spare their women for Thy Sake,
> And if that is not too easy
>   We will pardon Thy Mistake.
> But, gracious Lord, what e'er shall be,
> Don't let anyone bomb me.

> Keep our Empire undismembered
>   Guide our Forces by Thy Hand,
> Gallant blacks from far Jamaica,
>   Honduras and Togoland:
> Protect them Lord in all their fights,
> And, even more, protect the whites.

Graham, *When Grandma Fell Off the Boat: The Best of Harry Graham*, ed. N... Kington (Methuen, London, 1986), 21; Betjeman, *Collected Poems*, 91–2...

23. I am indebted to Jim Orwin for reminding me of this fact.

24. The word 'like' is used on one hundred and ninety-three occasions in... *Collected Poems*.

25. Alex Preminger, ed., *Princeton Encyclopedia of Poetry and Poetics* (Macmi... London and Basingstoke, 1975), 768.

26. Andrew Crozier, 'Thrills and Frills: poetry as figures of empirical lyric... *Society and Literature, 1945–70*, ed. Alan Sinfield (Methuen, London, 1... 220.

27. Conversation with the author, 1 March 1991.

28. Eliot, *Complete Poems and Plays*, 13.

29. Adeline Yen Mah, *Watching the Tree to Catch a Hare* (HarperCollins, Lon... 2000), 174.

30. Yen Mah, *Watching the Tree*, 175.
31. Peter Scupham, *Phoenix*, 11/12, 174.
32. Especially helpful were J.R. Watson, 'Probably Neither Works: Negative Signifiers in Larkin's Poetry', *About Larkin*, 6 (1998–9), 14–17; R.J.C. Watt, 'The Larkin Concordance', *About Larkin*, 3 (1997), 28; Anthony Thwaite, 'The Poetry of Philip Larkin', *Phoenix*, 11/12, 41–58; Edna Longley, 'Larkin, Edward Thomas and the Tradition', *Phoenix*, 11/12, 63–89. In my opinion Larkin was drawn to Hardy less for his Englishness, as many commentators claim, than for a fidelity to doubt encapsulated in his use of negative prefixes. Larkin dates his admiration to 'the morning I first read "Thoughts of Phena At News of Her Death"' (RW, 29–30), a poem that combines the commonplace 'unease' with the arresting 'Disennoble' and the altogether remarkable 'unsight'. Elsewhere Hardy offered 'why unblooms the best hope ever sown?'; 'I, unknowing you'; 'I sang that song in summer, / All unforeknowingly'; 'time untouched me'; 'The whole day long I unfulfil'; and, in the heartrending 'Tess's Lament', 'I'd have my life unbe'. Thomas Hardy, *The Complete Poems*, ed. James Gibson (Macmillan, London and Basingstoke, 1981), 62, 9, 235, 577, 578, 579, 177.
33. Lolette Kuby, *An Uncommon Poet for the Common Man: A Study of Philip Larkin's Poetry* (Mouton, The Hague and Paris, 1974), 139.
34. There are twenty-eight uses of 'lie', one of 'lied', seven of 'lying' and seven of 'lies' in the *Collected Poems*.
35. Samuel Taylor Coleridge, *Biographia Literaria*, II (Scolar, Menston, 1971), 21.
36. Peter Childs and Patrick Williams, *An Introduction to Postcolonial Theory* (Longman, Harlow, 1997), 66.
37. I owe the expression 'Bonfire of the Binaries' to Ivan Phillips, 'I sing the bard electric', *Times Literary Supplement*, 19 September 2003, 15.

5 Larkin and Englishness

1. Donald Davie, *Thomas Hardy and British Poetry* (Kegan Paul, London, 1973), 64.
2. Motion, *Philip Larkin: A Writer's Life*, 372.
3. Heaney, *Finders Keepers*, 94; Grubb, 'Dragons', 134; Alan Gardiner, *Critical Essays on Philip Larkin*, eds Cookson and Loughrey, 62; Whitehead, *Hardy to Larkin*, 235.
4. Corcoran, *English Poetry Since 1940*, 93; A. Alvarez, *The New Poetry* (Penguin, Harmondsworth, 1963), 20; Nigel Alderman, '"The Life with a Hole in it": Philip Larkin and the Condition of England', *Textual Practice*, 8, 2 (1994), 285; Paulin, *Minotaur*, 250.
5. Steve Clark, '"The Lost Displays": Larkin and Empire', *New Larkins for Old*, ed. James Booth (Macmillan, Basingstoke, 2000), 170.
6. Appleyard, *The Pleasures of Peace*, 103–4.
7. Everett, 'Larkin's Edens', *Poets in Their Time*, 248.
8. Timms, *Philip Larkin*, 127.
9. G.S. Fraser and I. Fletcher, eds, *Springtime, an Anthology of Young Poets and Writers* (Owen, London, 1953), 12. Larkin is placed in the category of 'Regionalists'.
10. Alan Brownjohn, ed., *Departure* (Departure, Oxford, 1955), 20; Brownjohn, 'Poet who reluctantly came to the point', *The Listener*, 13 February 1986, 16. Kingsley Amis was subject to similar confusion when conflated with his

characters. After the publication of *Lucky Jim* he was regularly taken for a Yorkshireman, though Jim Dixon is a Lancastrian and Amis was a Londoner. Later, living in Swansea, he was described as a Welshman by Doris Lessing. See Humphrey Carpenter, *The Angry Young Men: A Literary Comedy of the 1950s* (Penguin, Harmondsworth, 2002), 179.

11. John Clubbe, ed., *Selected Poems of Thomas Hood* (Harvard, Cambridge, 1970), 35–6.
12. Winthrop Mackworth Praed, *The Poems of Winthrop Mackworth Praed* (Moxon, London, 1864), II, 379.
13. William Wordsworth, 'My heart leaps up when I behold', *William Wordsworth*, eds Stephen Gill and Duncan Wu (Oxford University Press, Oxford, 1994), 122.
14. Edward Thomas, *Collected Poems* (Faber, London, 1981), 66.
15. D.H. Lawrence, *Sons and Lovers* (Penguin, Harmondsworth, 1964), 265, 282.
16. I am indebted to Jean Hartley for this information.
17. Lawrence, *Sons and Lovers*, 442.
18. Adam Piette, 'Childhood Wiped Out', paper delivered at the Larkin and the 40s conference, University of London, 16 July 1999.
19. Aldous Huxley, *Those Barren Leaves* (Chatto and Windus, London, 1925), 114–9.
20. Eliot, *Complete Poems and Plays*, 103.
21. Eliot, *Complete Poems and Plays*, 104.
22. Stella Gibbons, *Cold Comfort Farm* (Penguin, Harmondsworth, 2000), 193.
23. Gibbons, *Cold Comfort Farm*, 206.
24. James Thurber, 'Preface: My Fifty Years with James Thurber', *The Thurber Carnival* (Penguin, Harmondsworth, 1965), 15–16.
25. Joyce, *Portrait*, 203.
26. Joyce, *Portrait*, 247.
27. Thom Gunn and Ted Hughes, *Selected Poems* (Faber, London, 1962), 14–15.
28. Timms, *Philip Larkin*, 81.
29. This term neatly encapsulated the cross-party Keynesian consensus, combining as it did the names of successive chancellors of the exchequer, Labour's Hugh Gaitskell (1950–1) and the Conservative R.A.B. Butler (1951–5).
30. As I write an exhibition celebrating the legacy of Walter Hussey is taking place at the Pallant House Gallery, Chichester, to which he donated his magnificent private collection of twentieth-century art.
31. James Fenton, 'Philip Larkin: Wounded by Unshrapnel', *The Strength of Poetry* (Oxford University Press, Oxford, 2000), 52. In 'Philip Larkin's Lost Childhood', Carol Rumens offers a reading of Larkin's *oeuvre* as an expression of suppressed childhood trauma. The psychopathology is virtually identical to that of Fenton and Piette, though Rumens augments their claim that the central trauma concerns Sydney's Fascist sympathies with a selection of alternatives (his parents' unhappy marriage, the devastations of war, repressed homosexuality, corporal punishment whether inflicted at home or in school). However, the very nimiety of speculations militates against taking any of them seriously, Rumens interpreting different Larkin works in relation to each of these hypothetical traumas while candidly admitting the paucity of verifiable evidence. See Rumens, *Self into Song* (Bloodaxe Books, Newcastle, 2007), 28–47.

32. Louise Campbell, *Coventry Cathedral: Art and Architecture in Post-War Britain* (Oxford University Press, Oxford, 1996), 9.
33. 'A Coventry woman resisted tears when bombed out until she discovered that her small son's toys had been looted. "I could hate the Germans, but I did not want to hate my own countrymen."' Norman Longmate, *How We Lived Then: A history of everyday life during the Second World War* (Arrow, London, 1973), 134.
34. Canon Michael Sadgrove, *The Pitkin Guide to Coventry Cathedral* (Pitkin Unichrome, Andover, 1991), 6; A.J.P. Taylor, *English History, 1914–1945* (Penguin, Harmondsworth, 1970), 611.
35. That it was right so to do is borne out by Richard J. Evans's excellent *Telling Lies About Hitler: The Holocaust, History and the David Irving Trial* (Verso, London, 2002). In seeking to demonstrate that Irving's upper estimate of 250,000 for the Dresden bombing was spurious, Evans presents compelling evidence that the actual figure was nearer 25,000 (still nearly fifty times the Coventry death toll, of course). See Chapter 5, 'The Bombing of Dresden', 157–92. A more recent volume, *Dresden: Tuesday 13 February 1945* by Frederick Taylor (Bloomsbury, London, 2004), puts the fatalities between 25,000 and 40,000. Coventry and Dresden are now twinned cities.
36. The following paragraphs spatchcock information drawn from Basil Spence, *Phoenix at Coventry* (Collins, London, 1964) and Louise Campbell, *Coventry Cathedral: Art and Architecture in Post-War Britain*.
37. Herbert Read, *Contemporary British Art* (Penguin, Harmondsworth, 1964), 31–5.
38. Penelope Lively, *The Road to Lichfield* (Heinemann, London, 1977), 158. The novel was shortlisted for the 1977 Booker Prize. Larkin, the Chair of that year's selection committee, wanted it to win.

    Larkin was baptised in the old Coventry Cathedral, a fact of which he was privately proud according to his intimate friend Maeve Brennan. The latter also notes that Larkin bought his first car on the day *The Whitsun Weddings* was published, 28 February 1964, following her father's example in the choice of a Singer Gazelle. The fact that it was made in Coventry with the Rootes group emblem on the steering wheel was apparently an added incentive. See Brennan, *The Philip Larkin I Knew* (Manchester University Press, Manchester, 2002), 34, 69. That the narrator of 'I Remember, I Remember' is credited with no such warm feelings towards Coventry once again points up the reductiveness of conflating author and protagonist.

    For the sake of brevity I have focussed on Coventry Cathedral when discussing the post-war rebuilding of the city. That the Cathedral was neither the only nor the worst example the city had to offer of the compromised Modernism of the era is suggested by this description in the current *Lonely Planet Guide to Britain* (Lonely Planet, London, 2001), 457: 'Coventry was once one of Britain's most important towns, a centre for the wool industry in medieval times and more recently a dynamic manufacturing centre. However, between the aerial bombshells of the Luftwaffe and the architectural bombshells of the planners, much of historic Coventry disappeared under a mountain of concrete …' Larkin was equally categorical about the devastation caused by the Nazi bombers, concluding his short memoir 'Not The Place' Fault' with the words 'Coventry had been ruined by the German

Air Force, and I never went back to live there again' (*FR*, 11). As for the devastation to urban Britain caused by the Modernist utopias of the post-war planners, that is in part the subject of the poem 'Going, Going' with its account of a new lustreless world of 'concrete and tyres', 'split-level shopping' and 'bleak high-risers' (*CP*, 189–90).

39. The *Lonely Planet Guide to Britain* notes (457): 'Coventry was one of the most inventive of the Victorian industrial centres and claims to be the birthplace of the modern bicycle. The first car made in Britain was a Daimler built in Coventry in 1896, and in the early years of the 20th century Coventry was Britain's motor manufacturing capital as well as a major aircraft manufacturing centre. But steady growth switched to headlong decline in the 1970s and 1980s as Sunbeam, Hillman, Singer, Humber and Triumph cars all disappeared. Now only Jaguar cars remain of the home-grown models, although French Peugots are also assembled in Coventry.' Alas, in 2005 the Jaguar ceased production in Coventry and on 8 January 2007 the Peugot plant closed.

6 Larkin and Gender

1. Alan Travis, *Bound and Gagged: A Secret History of Obscenity in Britain* (Profile, London, 2001), 94.
2. Travis, *Bound and Gagged*, 25.
3. Travis, *Bound and Gagged*, 67.
4. Travis, *Bound and Gagged*, 147. In the previous decade Larkin 'bought for 12 gns a real 1ˢᵗ ed signed Lady C' (*SL*, 150).
5. Travis, *Bound and Gagged*, 158.
6. Travis, *Bound and Gagged*, 218.
7. Eliot, *Complete Poems and Plays*, 37; Ernest Hemingway, *For Whom The Bell Tolls* (Penguin, Harmondsworth, 1966), 32.
8. Quentin Tarantino, *Reservoir Dogs* (Faber, London, 1994), 4.
9. Needless to say, this ellipse is wasted on the critics: Booth refers to 'the man' dragging the girl in a 'courtship' frolic, Cooper to 'the girl's male lover', neither with support from the poem. Booth, *TWG*, x; Cooper, *Philip Larkin: Subversive Writer* (Sussex Academic Press, Brighton, 2004), 99.
10. Booth, *TWG*, vii.
11. Both poems were on the list of thirteen that the French imperial prosecutor had named as obscene or blasphemous in the successful prosecution of Baudelaire's *Fleurs du Mal* in 1857. It was not until 1946 that the French government passed a law that allowed Baudelaire's poems to be exonerated, three years after Larkin's translation. See Elisabeth Ladenson, *Dirt for Art's Sake* (Cornell University Press, Ithaca and London, 2007), 'Chapter Two, Charles Baudelaire: Florist of Evil', especially page 47.
12. Charles Baudelaire, *Fleurs du Mal/ Flowers of Evil*, eds Marthiel and Jackson Matthews (New Directions, Norfolk, 1955), 369.
13. Eliot, *Complete Poems and Plays*, 16, 23, 44, 56, 52–3.
14. Rossen, *Philip Larkin*, 66.
15. Rossen, *Philip Larkin*, 70–1, 76.
16. Tolley, *My Proper Ground*, 112.

17. Booth, *Philip Larkin: Writer*, 115.
18. Booth, *Philip Larkin: Writer*, 116.
19. This may be regarded as one of Larkin's double citations. In the early 1950s he discovered Flann O'Brien's novel *At Swim-Two-Birds*, and this remained a lifelong favourite – he was still enthusing about it in the year of his death (*SL*, 734). At one point the narrator's uncle says 'There are more things in life and death than you ever dreamt of, Horatio'. O'Brien, *At Swim-Two-Birds* (Penguin, Harmondsworth, 1975), 214.
20. Rossen, *Philip Larkin*, 85.
21. D.H. Lawrence, *Studies in Classic American Literature* (Mercury, London, 1965), 2.
22. Eliot, *Complete Poems and Plays*, 16.
23. Eliot, *Complete Poems and Plays*, 16.
24. Carey, 'The Two Philip Larkins', 51–65.
25. Carey, 'The Two Philip Larkins', 56.
26. Carey, 'The Two Philip Larkins', 65.
27. Carey, 'The Two Philip Larkins', 55.
28. Carey, 'The Two Philip Larkins', 61.
29. Carey, 'The Two Philip Larkins', 62, 63.
30. Vernon Watkins, *The Collected Poems of Vernon Watkins* (Golgonooza Press, Ipswich, 1986), 101–2.
31. Swarbrick, *'The Less Deceived' and 'The Whitsun Weddings'*, 64.
32. Swarbrick, *Out of Reach: The Poetry of Philip Larkin* (Macmillan, Basingstoke, 1995), 45.
33. Booth, *Philip Larkin: Writer*, 163.
34. Bradford's position is more complex – or muddled – than this graph suggests: 'When first we faced' is addressed to Betty with oblique references to Maeve; 'Morning at last' is addressed to Maeve but shadowed by Betty's presence; while 'The little lives ...' is 'directed towards Monica' but open to identification with (and by) Maeve. In sum, 'Larkin appears to have written into these poems a kind of signature which attaches each of them to one of his lovers ... but at the same time none of them is entirely exclusive to that woman; each carries a trace of at least one other.' I trust that is clear! Richard Bradford, *First Boredom, Then Fear* (Peter Owen, London, 2005), 244.
35. Booth, *Philip Larkin: Writer*, 167; Roger Day, *Larkin* (Open University Press, Milton Keynes, 1987), 81.
36. Motion, *Philip Larkin: A Writer's Life*, 290.
37. The radicalism of this strategy may be calibrated against the category certitudes, gender and otherwise, of the broadcast media of the day: think of the radio and television programmes *Housewife's Choice*, *Family Favourites*, *The Navy Lark*, *Workers' Playtime*, *Children's Hour*, *The Army Game*, *Woman's Hour*, *Dad's Army*. These are the hegemonic category restrictions Larkin, on our behalf, wrote his way out of.
38. Richard Davenport-Hines, *Auden* (Heinemann, London, 1995), 108. Charles Osborne reported the same incident in the American edition of *W.H. Auden: The Life of a Poet* (1979), but Betjeman had the passage suppressed from the English publication.
39. Schmidt, *Lives of the Poets*, 706–7.

7   Larkin and Politics

1. Heaney, *Finders Keepers*, 151.
2. James Simmons, 'The Trouble with Larkin', *Philip Larkin: A Tribute*, ed. George Hartley (Marvell, London, 1988), 232, 234.
3. Quoted in Hitchens, *Unacknowledged Legislation*, 250.
4. Hugh Calvert, *A History of Kingston upon Hull: From Earliest Times to the Present Day* (Phillimore, London and Chichester, 1978), 288. Even as I write a campaign is underway to save the façade of the National Picture Theatre on Hull's Beverley Road. A short walk from Larkin's Pearson Park flat, the cinema frontage is the last civilian bomb site with standing remains in the country. With awful irony, the cinema took a direct hit on the night of 18 March 1941 during a screening of Charlie Chaplin's *The Great Dictator*. See 'Blitzed cinema's status is recognized at last', *Hull Daily Mail, Flashback* supplement, 30 April 2007, 36.
5. Hitchens, *Unacknowledged Legislation*, 250. This enviable turn of phrase typifies the essay– indeed, the entire volume – which I thoroughly recommend.
6. Terry Eagleton, *The Eagleton Reader*, ed. Stephen Regan (Blackwell, Oxford, 1998), ix.
7. Eagleton, 'Larkin: A Left View', 4.
8. Hitchens, *Unacknowledged Legislation*, 250.
9. Corcoran, *English Poetry Since 1940*, 95.
10. The universal effacement by Larkin's leftist critics of his high regard for Cripps is instructive. Cripps was the nephew of Sidney and Beatrice Webb (Fabian Socialists, shapers of the Labour Party, pioneering historians of Trades Unionism and founders of the London School of Economics). Cripps was expelled from the Labour Party in 1939 for anti-appeasement agitation but later became Chancellor of the Exchequer in Attlee's Labour government (1947–51). His manifesto *Towards Christian Democracy* (1942) is a passionate advocacy of equality of opportunity, jobs for the employable, social security for the needy, the end of privilege for the few and the preservation of civil liberties. His tight control of fiscal policy in a period of post-war austerity gave Cripps a reputation as a puritan killjoy but for Larkin this was more honourable than the high-inflation consumerism of the Macmillan-Heath Tory Party or Harold Wilson's Labour government. Reassessment of this major figure has begun with Chris Bryant, *Stafford Cripps: The First Modern Chancellor* (Hodder and Stoughton, London, 2002) and Peter Clarke, *The Cripps Version: The Life of Sir Stafford Cripps, 1889–1952* (Penguin, Harmondsworth, 2002).
11. 'Bridge for the Living' – a brilliant execution of a public commission, though lacking the compulsion of Larkin's best work – presents the building of the Humber Bridge as an irrevocable historical intervention in the life of Hull and the Plain of Holderness. One line compares it to the moon landings by alluding to Neil Armstrong's 'giant step for mankind': 'And now this stride into our solitude, / A swallow-fall and rise of one plain line, / *A giant step* for ever to include / All our dear landscape in a new design.' (*CP*, 204. Emphases mine.)
12. Corcoran, *English Poetry Since 1940*, 93, 92, 95, 92.
13. Siegfried Sassoon, *Collected Poems, 1908–1956* (Faber, London, 1984), 75.

14. Brian Gardner, ed., *Up the Line to Death: The War Poets, 1914–1918* (Methuen, London, 1976), 135; Sassoon, *Collected Poems, 1908–1956*, 75.
15. Ezra Pound, 'Hugh Selwyn Mauberley', *Selected Poems*, ed. T.S. Eliot (Faber, London, 1954), 176.
16. Hugh Kenner, *The Pound Era* (Faber, London, 1975), 202.
17. Pound, *Selected Poems*, 175.
18. As Larkin wrote in a different context, 'The reader is left wondering ... whether there is a point beyond which innocence becomes culpable' (*RW*, 259).
19. Greer, 'A Very British Misery', 27.
20. Newsinger, 'Dead Poet: The Larkin Letters', 87.
21. Alvarez, *The New Poetry*, 20.
22. Quoted in Kenneth Allott, ed., *The Penguin Book of Contemporary Verse* (Penguin, Harmondsworth, 1962), 335.
23. Grubb, 'Dragons', 120.
24. The playlet is published in *About Larkin*, 13 (2002), 22–4.
25. Smith, *Inviolable Voice*, 176.
26. Regan, *The Critics Debate*, 140, 125.
27. Sean O'Brien, *The Deregulated Muse: Essays on Contemporary British and Irish Poetry* (Bloodaxe, Newcastle, 1998), 24.
28. Orwell, *Inside the Whale*, 64, 89, 90.
29. Motion, *Philip Larkin: A Writer's Life*, 419.
30. The Boothby story broke in *The Sunday Mirror*, 11 July 1964, the evidence including a photograph of the Peer with the homosexual gangster Ronnie Kray. The newspaper subsequently withdrew the story and paid £40,000 in compensation, but the case never went to court and the insinuations have never quite evaporated.
31. I am indebted to Derek Spooner, a professional geographer with a detailed knowledge of Larkin's poetry, for the explication of 'Grey area grants'.
32. Even the 'bleak high-risers' might invoke a specific Tory policy, the Conservative government in 1956 introducing legislation that made construction grants to local councils for rented accommodation proportionate to the height of the building.
33. Motion, *Philip Larkin: A Writer's Life*, 418.
34. D.H. Lawrence, *Kangaroo* (Penguin, Harmondsworth, 1963), 240.
35. Booth, *Philip Larkin: Writer*, 96.
36. Regan, *The Critics Debate*, 122.
37. John Wain, 'Engagement or withdrawal? Some notes on the work of Philip Larkin', *Critical Quarterly*, 17, 4 (1975), 347–60.
38. Harry Chambers, 'Some Light Views of A Serious Poem: A Footnote to the Misreading of Philip Larkin's "Naturally the Foundation Will Bear Your Expenses"', *Phoenix*, 11/12, 112.
39. Conquest, *Larkin at Sixty*, 36.
40 The ensuing information is drawn from several sources, quite the most useful of which was Correlli Barnett, *The Verdict of Peace* (Macmillan, Basingstoke, 2001), especially Chapter 17, 325–44.
41. Regan, *The Critics Debate*, 24.
42. Stevenson, *The Last of England?*, 171.

43. Douglas Dunn, *Under the Influence: Douglas Dunn on Philip Larkin* (Edinburgh University Press, Edinburgh, 1987), 3.

44. Steve Clark, '"Get Out As Early As You Can": Larkin's Sexual Politics', *Philip Larkin: A Tribute*, ed. George Hartley, 265.

45. Clark, 'The Lost Displays', offers a differently persuasive perspective on this terrain.

46. Macdonald Daly and Alexander George, eds, *Margaret Thatcher in Her Own Words* (Penguin, Harmondsworth, 1987), 42, 41.

47. *Margaret Thatcher in Her Own Words*, 59.

48. Motion, *Philip Larkin: A Writer's Life*, 436.

49. Motion, *Philip Larkin: A Writer's Life*, xviii–xix.

50. *Margaret Thatcher in Her Own Words*, 15.

51. *Margaret Thatcher in Her Own Words*, 72.

52. Motion, *Philip Larkin: A Writer's Life*, 395.

53. Whitehead, *Hardy to Larkin*, 234.

54. Booth, 'From Here to Bogland: Larkin, Heaney and the Poetry of Place', *New Larkins for Old*, 209.

55. Regan, *The Critics Debate*, 140.

56. Compare the 'price of stock' in 'Livings' I (*CP*, 186) and the 'horse-boxes' moving 'Towards the stock entrance' in 'Show Saturday' (*CP*, 200).

8 Larkin and Identity

1. Antony Easthope, 'How Good is Seamus Heaney?', *English*, 46, 184 (1997), 22, 21.

2. Easthope, *Poetry as Discourse* (Methuen, London, 1983), 76; 'How Good is Seamus Heaney?', 28.

3. Ian Gregson, *Contemporary Poetry and Postmodernism: Dialogue and Estrangement* (Macmillan, Basingstoke, 1996), 37.

4. Paulin, *Minotaur*, 238, 240.

5. Edna Longley, 'Larkin, Decadence and the Lyric Poem', *New Larkins for Old*, 37.

6. Clark, 'The Lost Displays', 94, 131.

7. *The Portable Whitman*, 311.

8. *The Portable Whitman*, 134.

9. At the very same moment Charles Olson was using the eyes/I's/ayes pun in *The Maximus Poems*. 'Letter 6' begins 'polis is / eyes' and ends 'There are no hierarchies, no infinite, no such many as mass, there are only / eyes in all heads / to be looked out of'. *The Maximus Poems*, ed. George Butterick (University of California Press, Berkeley and Los Angeles, 1983), 30, 33.

10. Booth, *Philip Larkin: Writer*, 167.

11. Everett, 'Larkin's Money', *New Larkins for Old*, 14.

12. Larkin's poem mentions no mirrors but its shadow text, Hardy's 'I Look Into My Glass', does. The Hardy begins 'I look into my glass, / And view my wasting skin …'. *The Complete Poems*, 81.

13. My wording here is indebted to Stuart Hall, 'Cultural Identity and Cinematic Representation', *Framework*, 36, 68.

14. This section benefited from conversations with Jaroslaw Kosciuszko, Motlalepula Matome and Dr Naz Wassim – Larkin lovers who came to these shores from three different continents.

15. Paulin, *Minotaur*, 249.
16. John Solomos, *Race and Racism in Britain* (Macmillan, Basingstoke, 2003), 219.
17. Solomos, *Race and Racism in Britain*, 218.
18. Solomos, *Race and Racism in Britain*, 173.
19. Paul Gilroy, *The Black Atlantic: Modernity and Double Consciousness* (Verso, London, 1998), 5.
20. Gilroy, *The Black Atlantic*, 3, 7, 3.
21. It is worth remarking Larkin's personal warmth to refugees of his acquaintance. According to Motion, 'some sort of near-paternal love' developed between Larkin and J.J. Graneek, Librarian at Queen's University, Belfast. Graneek was 'the son of Russian parents who had fled a pogrom' and was politically 'quite left-wing'. *Philip Larkin: A Writer's Life*, 201. Again, Larkin told Judy Egerton that the sculptor Willi Soukup 'has the charm and instinctive tolerant agreeableness of the refugee' (*SL*, 305).
22. That 'The Importance of Elsewhere', while not a major poem, has major implications for a consideration of Larkin's discussion of identity has only been fully grasped by Raphael Ingelbien, in *Misreading England: Poetry and Nationhood Since the Second World War* (Rodopi, Amsterdam, 2002). See especially Chapter 6.
23. 'Larkin: A Left View', 7.
24. Gilroy, *The Black Atlantic*, 120, 126–33, 161–3.
25. Gilroy, *The Black Atlantic*, 150.
26. Gilroy, The Black Atlantic, 5.
27. Booth, *Philip Larkin: Writer*, 28.
28. James Booth, *Philip Larkin: The Poet's Plight* (Macmillan, Basingstoke, 2005), 98, 97.
29. Eliot, *Complete Poems and Plays*, 14.
30. Eliot, *Complete Poems and Plays*, 21.
31. Compare with the opening page of Percival Everett's masterful novel *Erasure* (Faber, London, 2001): 'I have dark brown skin, curly hair, a broad nose, some of my ancestors were slaves and I have been detained by pasty white policemen in New Hampshire, Arizona and Georgia and so the society in which I live tells me I am black; that is my race. Though I am fairly athletic, I am no good at basketball. I listen to Mahler, Aretha Franklin, Charlie Parker and Ry Cooder on vinyl records and compact discs. I graduated *summa cum laude* from Harvard, hating every minute of it. I am good at math. I cannot dance.'
32. Let me be categorical: I am *not* countering the universal white narratology of Larkin scholarship with the claim that this or that narrator is black – such would simply reverse the racial binary in a manner that betrays Larkin's deconstructionism. I am at pains to say that, as the narrators' race is unspecified, black can only ever be one of the options we try out for its hermeneutical value.
33. George Hartley, 'Nothing To Be Said', *Philip Larkin: A Tribute*, 305–6.
34. Childs and Williams, *An Introduction to Postcolonial Theory*, 233.
35. Rudyard Kipling, *The Works of Rudyard Kipling* (Wordsworth, Ware, 1994), 282, 323.
36. Joyce, *Ulysses*, 446, 447.

37. Ernest Hemingway, *In Our Time* (Scribners, New York, 1996), 12.
38. As Toni Morrison says of a character in Hemingway's *To Have and Have Not*, 'Eddy is white, and we know he is because nobody says so'. By contrast, we learn that Wesley is a 'nigger' long before learning his name. Morrison, *Playing in the Dark: Whiteness and the Literary Imagination* (Picador, London and Basingstoke, 1993), 72.
39. Richard Dyer, *White* (Routledge, London, 1997), 46.
40. I quote from an unpublished translation of Gautier's poem by Professor Brian Rigby, who generously shared his knowledge of modern French literature with me on several occasions during the writing of this book.
41. Whitehead, *Hardy to Larkin*, 231.
42. David Wheatley and Justin Quinn, eds, *Metre*, 10 (2001), 7.
43. The Venerable Bede, *Ecclesiastical History of the English People*, trans. Leo Sherley-Price (Penguin, Harmondsworth, 1990), 129–30.
44. Adeline Yen Mah, *One Written Word is Worth a Thousand Pieces of Gold* (Harper Perennial, London, 2004), xxvii.
45. Yen Mah, *Watching the Tree*, 30.
46. Yen Mah, *Watching the Tree*, 32.
47. In what may be an unintended tribute to Oriental Larkin, Bodley Head published in 1981 an anthology for children, *Days Are Where We Live*. The first poem in the book, supposedly an excerpt from 'The World is Day-Breaking' by the Japanese poet Sekiya Miyoshi, provided the anthology's title: 'What are days for? / Days are where we live. / They come, they wake us / Time and time over. / They are to be happy in: / Where can we live but days?' This is, of course, the opening stanza of Larkin's 'Days' (*CP*, 67). The publisher and the compiler, Jill Bennett, deserve to be reprimanded for this howler; yet the fact that such an experienced team could make such a misattribution might suggest that Larkin's verse is neither as English, nor even as Occidental, as his explicators insist. See *Days Are Where We Live and Other Poems*, compiled by Jill Bennett, illustrated by Maureen Roffey (Bodley Head, London, 1981), 1.
48. Yen Mah, *Watching the Tree*, 33; Ninian Smart, *The Religious Experience of Mankind* (Collins, London and Glasgow, 1971), 233.
49. Arthur Waley, *The Way and the Power: A Study of the Tao Te Ching and Its Place in Chinese Thought* (George Allen & Unwin, London, 1934), 155.
50. Stephen T. Asma, *Buddha for Beginners* (Writers and Readers, New York and London, 1996), 70.
51. *Buddha for Beginners*, 99, 106.
52. See the excellent essay by the geographer-poet J. Douglas Porteous, 'Nowhereman', *About Larkin*, 8 (1999), 12–16.
53. John D. Barrow, *The Book of Nothing* (Cape, London, 2000), 237.
54. Thomas Nagel, 'Much ado', *Times Literary Supplement*, 7 May 2004, 3.
55. Lewis Carroll, *Alice's Adventures in Wonderland and Through the Looking-Glass* (Macmillan, London, 1966), 230–1.
56. Compare B.S. Johnson's poem 'Love All', with its punning conclusion that 'love was merely another means / of saying nil'. *Poems Two* (Trigram, London, 1972), 19.
57. Duncan, *The Failure of Conservatism in Modern British Poetry*, 64.
58. Mark Rowe, 'Larkin's "Aubade"', *Philosophy and Literature* (Ashgate, Aldershot, 2004), 203.

Conclusion: Larkin and Postmodernism

1. Corcoran, *English Poetry Since 1940*, 85.
2. Ian Gregson, *Contemporary Poetry and Postmodernism*, 213.
3. Ian Gregson, *Postmodern Literature* (Arnold, London, 2004), 1.
4. Jean-Francois Lyotard, *The Postmodern Condition: A Report on Knowledge* (Manchester University Press, Manchester, 1987), 37.
5. Tim Woods, *Beginning Postmodernism* (Manchester University Press, Manchester, 1999), 20–1.
6. Lyotard, *The Postmodern Condition*, xxiv, 82.
7. Dickinson, 'Larkin's Jazz', 4.
8. Damien Hirst, *Superstition*, Gagosian Gallery, 22 February – 6 April 2007. Each painting in the exhibition has two titles, one drawn from Larkin's late poems, especially the *High Windows* collection, and the other referencing religious texts and iconography.
9. As has already been remarked by Tim Adams (*Observer Review*, 25 March 2007, 24) and Peter Kemp (*Sunday Times, Culture* supplement, 1 April 2007, 39), *On Chesil Beach* may be read as an extended prose extrapolation of 'Annus Mirabilis'.

Bibliography

Ackroyd, Peter, 'Poet Hands on Misery to Man', *Times*, 1 April 1993, 35.

Alderman, Nigel, '"The Life with a Hole in it": Philip Larkin and the Condition of England', *Textual Practice*, 8, 2 (1994), 279–301.

Allott, Kenneth, ed. *The Penguin Book of Contemporary Verse* (Penguin, Harmondsworth, 1962).

Alvarez, A., ed. *The New Poetry* (Penguin, Harmondsworth, 1963).

Amis, Kingsley, *The Letters of Kingsley Amis*, ed. Zachary Leader (HarperCollins, London, 2000).

Amis, Martin, 'The Ending: Don Juan in Hell', *The War Against Cliché* (Cape, London, 2001), 153–72.

Anderson, David, *Histories of the Hanged: Britain's Dirty War in Kenya and the End of Empire* (Weidenfeld & Nicolson, London, 2005).

Appleyard, Brian, 'The Dreary Laureate of our Provincialism', *Independent*, 18 March 1993, 27.

Appleyard, Brian, *The Pleasures of Peace: Art and Imagination in Post-War Britain* (Faber, London, 1990).

Arvin, Newton, *Longfellow: His Life and Work* (Little, Brown & Co, Boston, 1963).

Ashbery, John, *April Galleons* (Carcanet, Manchester, 1987).

Asma, Stephen T., *Buddha for Beginners* (Writers and Readers, New York and London, 1996).

Auden, W.H., *Later Auden*, ed. Edward Mendelson (Faber, London, 1999).

Barnett, Correlli, *The Verdict of Peace* (Macmillan, Basingstoke, 2001).

Barrow, John D., *The Book of Nothing* (Cape, London, 2000).

Barthes, Roland, *Image – Music – Text*, ed. and trans. Stephen Heath (Fontana, London, 1984).

Bate, Jonathan, 'Very Juvenile, This Juvenilia', *Sunday Telegraph*, 28 April 2003, 13.

Baudelaire, Charles, *Fleurs du Mal/ Flowers of Evil*, eds Marthiel and Jackson Matthews (New Directions, Norfolk, 1955).

Bede, The Venerable, *Ecclesiastical History of the English People*, trans. Leo Sherley-Price (Penguin, Harmondsworth, 1990).

Bennett, Alan, *Untold Stories* (Faber, London, 2006).

Bennett, Alan, *Writing Home* (Faber, London, 1994).

Bennett, Jill, ed. *Days Are Where We Live and Other Poems* (Bodley Head, London, 1981).

Betjeman, John, *Collected Poems*, ed. Earl of Birkenhead (John Murray, London, 1958).

Booth, James, 'From Here to Bogland: Larkin, Heaney and the Poetry of Place', *New Larkins for Old*, ed. Booth (Macmillan, Basingstoke, 2000), 190–212.

Booth, James, *Philip Larkin: The Poet's Plight* (Macmillan, Basingstoke, 2005).

Booth, James, *Philip Larkin: Writer* (Harvester, Hemel Hempstead, 1992).

Bradford, Richard, *First Boredom, Then Fear* (Peter Owen, London, 2005).

Bray, Christopher, 'A Writer's Life: Clive James', *Telegraph arts supplement*, 5 November 2005, 12.

Brennan, Maeve, *The Philip Larkin I Knew* (Manchester University Press, Manchester, 2002).

Brownjohn, Alan, ed. *Departure* (Departure, Oxford, 1955).

Brownjohn, Alan, 'Poet Who Reluctantly Came to the Point', *The Listener*, 13 February 1986, 16.

Bryant, Chris, *Stafford Cripps: The First Modern Chancellor* (Hodder and Stoughton, London, 2002).

Burke, Sean, *The Death and Return of the Author* (Edinburgh University Press, Edinburgh, 1998).

Calvert, Hugh, *A History of Kingston upon Hull: From Earliest Times to the Present Day* (Phillimore, London and Chichester, 1978).

Campbell, James, *This is the Beat Generation: New York – San Francisco – Paris* (Secker & Warburg, London, 1999).

Campbell, Louise, *Coventry Cathedral: Art and Architecture in Post-War Britain* (Oxford University Press, Oxford, 1996).

Carey, John, 'The Two Philip Larkins', *New Larkins for Old: Critical Essays*, ed. James Booth (Macmillan, Basingstoke, 2000), 51–65.

Carpenter, Humphrey, *The Angry Young Men: A Literary Comedy of the 1950s* (Penguin, Harmondsworth, 2002).

Carroll, Lewis, *Alice's Adventures in Wonderland and Through the Looking-Glass* (Macmillan, London, 1966).

Carroll, Lewis, *The Complete Illustrated Works of Lewis Carroll* (Chancellor Press, London, 1982).

Chambers, Harry, 'Some Light Views of a Serious Poem: A Footnote to the Misreading of Philip Larkin's "Naturally the Foundation Will Bear Your Expenses"', *Phoenix*, 11/12 (1973–4), 110–4.

Chandran, K. Narayama, 'Some Shakespearean Reminiscences in Philip Larkin's "The Old Fools"', *The Literary Half-Yearly*, XXXV, One (1994), 78–82.

Charters, Ann, ed. *The Penguin Book of the Beats* (Penguin, Harmondsworth, 1992).

Chesters, Graham, 'Larkin and Baudelaire's Damned Women', *Making Connections: Essays in French Culture and Society in Honour of Philip Thody*, ed. James Dolamore (Peter Lang, Bern, 1999), 81–92.

Chesters, Graham, 'Larkin's Books: Sidelining French Literature', *French Studies Bulletin*, LX, 100 (2006), 72–5.

Chesters, Graham, 'Tireless Play: Speculations on Larkin's "Absences"', *Challenges of Translation in French Literature: Studies and Poems in Honour of Peter Broome*, ed. Richard Bales (Peter Lang, Bern, 2005), 47–59.

Childs, Peter and Patrick Williams, *An Introduction to Postcolonial Theory* (Longman, Harlow, 1997).

Chilton, John, *Sidney Bechet: The Wizard of Jazz* (Macmillan, Basingstoke, 1987).

Clark, Steve, '"Get Out As Early As You Can": Larkin's Sexual Politics', *Philip Larkin: A Tribute*, ed. George Hartley (Marvell, London, 1988), 237–71.

Clark, Steve, '"The lost displays": Larkin and Empire', *New Larkins for Old*, ed. James Booth (Macmillan, Basingstoke, 2000), 166–81.

Clarke, Peter, *The Cripps Version: The Life of Sir Stafford Cripps, 1889–1952* (Penguin, Harmondsworth, 2002).

Coleridge, Samuel Taylor, *Biographia Literaria* (Scolar, Menston, 1971).

Coleridge, Samuel Taylor, *A Choice of Coleridge's Verse*, ed. Ted Hughes (Faber, London, 1996).

Conquest, Robert, 'A Proper Sport', *Larkin at Sixty*, ed. Anthony Thwaite (Faber, London, 1982), 31–7.

Cooper, Stephen, *Philip Larkin: Subversive Writer* (Sussex Academic Press, Brighton, 2004).

Corcoran, Neil, *English Poetry Since 1940* (Longman, London, 1993).

Craik, Roger, 'Some Unheard Melodies in Philip Larkin's Poetry', *About Larkin*, 12 (2001), 11–13.

Crawford, Robert, *Devolving English Literature* (Oxford University Press, Oxford, 1992).

Crawford, Robert, *The Modern Poet: Poetry, Academia, and Knowledge since the 1750s* (Oxford University Press, Oxford, 2001).

Crozier, Andrew, 'Thrills and Frills: Poetry as Figures of Empirical Lyricism', *Society and Literature, 1945–70*, ed. Alan Sinfield (Methuen, London, 1983), 199–233.

Culler, Jonathan, *Barthes* (Fontana, Glasgow, 1983).

Cunliffe, Marcus, *The Literature of the United States* (Penguin, Harmondsworth, 1964).

Cunningham, Valentine, ed. *The Penguin Book of Spanish Civil War Verse* (Penguin, Harmondsworth, 1980).

Davenport-Hines, Richard, *Auden* (Heinemann, London, 1995).

Davie, Donald, *Thomas Hardy and British Poetry* (Kegan Paul, London, 1973).

Day, Roger, *Larkin* (Open University Press, Milton Keynes, 1987).

Dentith, Simon, *Bakhtinian Thought* (Routledge, London, 1995).

Derrida, Jacques, *Dissemination*, trans. Barbara Johnson (Athlone, London, 1981).

Derrida, Jacques, *Of Grammatology*, trans. Gayatri Chakravorty Spivak (John Hopkins University Press, Baltimore, 1997).

Dickinson, Peter, 'Larkin's Jazz', *About Larkin*, 19 (2005), 4–9.

Donne, John, *Devotions upon Emergent Occasions*, ed. A. Raspa (McGill-Quens University Press, Montreal, 1975).

Draper, Ronald, 'The Positive Larkin', *Critical Essays on Philip Larkin: The Poems*, eds Linda Cookson and Bryan Loughrey (Longman, London, 1989), 94–105.

Duncan, Andrew, *The Failure of Conservatism in Modern British Poetry* (Salt, Cambridge, 2003), 62–3.

Dunn, Douglas, *Under the Influence: Douglas Dunn on Philip Larkin* (Edinburgh University Press, Edinburgh, 1987).

Dyer, Richard, *White* (Routledge, London, 1997).

Eagleton, Terry, *The Eagleton Reader*, ed. Stephen Regan (Blackwell, Oxford, 1998).

Eagleton, Terry, 'Larkin: A Left View', *About Larkin*, 9 (2000), 4–8.

Easthope, Antony, *Poetry as Discourse* (Methuen, London, 1983), 76; 'How Good is Seamus Heaney?', 28.

Easthope, Antony, 'How Good is Seamus Heaney?', *English*, 46, 184 (1997), 21–36.

Eliot, T.S., *The Sacred Wood* (Methuen, London, 1928).

Eliot, T.S., *Selected Prose*, ed. John Hayward (Penguin, Harmondsworth, 1953).

Eliot, T.S., *Complete Poems and Plays* (Faber, London, 1969), 96, 72, 65.

Evans, Richard J., *Telling Lies About Hitler: The Holocaust, History and the David Irving Trial* (Verso, London, 2002).

Everett, Barbara, 'Larkin and Dockery: The Limits of the Social', *Philip Larkin: A Tribute*, ed. George Hartley (Marvell, London, 1988), 140–52.

Everett, Barbara, 'Larkin's Money', *New Larkins for Old*, ed. James Booth (Macmillan, Basingstoke, 2000), 11–28.

Everett, Barbara, *Poets in Their Time: Essays on English Poetry from Donne to Larkin* (Faber, London, 1986).

Everett, Percival, *Erasure* (Faber, London, 2001).

Fairclough, Norman, *Discourse and Social Change* (Polity, London, 1992).

Fenton, James, *The Strength of Poetry* (Oxford University Press, Oxford, 2000).

Fitzgerald, F. Scott, *The Crack-Up and Other Pieces and Stories* (Penguin, Harmondsworth, 1965).

Fitzgerald, F. Scott, *This Side of Paradise* (Penguin, Harmondsworth, 1965).

Fraser, G.S. and I. Fletcher, eds, *Springtime, An Anthology of Young Poets and Writers* (Owen, London, 1953).

Gardiner, Alan, 'Larkin's England', *Critical Essays on Philip Larkin: The Poems*, eds Linda Cookson and Bryan Loughrey (Longman, London, 1989), 62–71.

Gardner, Brian, ed. *Up the Line to Death: The War Poets, 1914–1918* (Methuen, London, 1976).

Garland, Patrick, 'An Enormous Yes: A Memoir of the Poet', *An Arundel Tomb*, ed. Paul Foster (Otter Memorial Paper Number 1, Chichester, 1987), 23–6.

Gibbons, Stella, *Cold Comfort Farm* (Penguin, Harmondsworth, 2000).

Gilroy, Paul, *The Black Atlantic: Modernity and Double Consciousness* (Verso, London, 1998).

Ginsberg, Allen, *Howl and Other Poems* (City Lights Books, San Francisco, 1971).

Ginsberg, Allen, *Howl, Original Draft Facsimile*, ed. Barry Miles (Viking, New York, 1986).

Graham, Harry, 'Grandpapa', *When Grandma Fell Off The Boat: The Best of Harry Graham*, ed. Miles Kington (Methuen, London, 1986), 20–4.

Greenberg, Clement, *Art and Culture* (Thames and Hudson, London, 1973).

Greer, Germaine, 'A Very British Misery', *Guardian*, 14 October 1988, 27.

Gregson, Ian, *Contemporary Poetry and Postmodernism: Dialogue and Estrangement* (Macmillan, Basingstoke, 1996).

Gregson, Ian, *Postmodern Literature* (Arnold, London, 2004).

Grubb, Frederick, 'Dragons', *Phoenix*, vol. 11/12 (1973), 119–36.

Gunn, Thom and Ted Hughes, *Selected Poems* (Faber, London, 1962).

Hall, Stuart, 'Cultural Identity and Cinematic Representation', *Framework*, 36 (1989), 68.

Handley, *Graham, Brodie's Notes on Philip Larkin's Selected Poems* (Pan, London, 1991).

Harding, Jason, 'A Useful Irritant: Montgomery Belgion, T.S. Eliot and the Criterion', *Times Literary Supplement*, 25 August 2000, 14–15.

Hardy, Thomas, *The Complete Poems*, ed. James Gibson (Macmillan, London and Basingstoke, 1981).

Hartley, George, 'Nothing To Be Said', *Philip Larkin: A Tribute*, ed. George Hartley (Marvell, London, 1988), 298–308.

Hartley, George, ed. *Philip Larkin: A Tribute* (Marvell, London, 1988).

Hartley, Jean, *Philip Larkin, the Marvell Press, and Me* (Carcanet, Manchester, 1989).

Hawthorn, Jeremy, *A Concise Glossary of Contemporary Literary Theory* (Arnold, London, 1998).

Heaney, Seamus, *Finders Keepers: Selected Prose, 1971–2001* (Faber, London, 2002).

Hemingway, Ernest, *For Whom the Bell Tolls* (Penguin, Harmondsworth, 1966).

Hemingway, Ernest, *In Our Time* (Scribners, New York, 1996).

Hendrickson, Robert, *The Literary Life and Other Curiosities* (Penguin, Harmondsworth, 1982).

Hitchens, Christopher, *Unacknowledged Legislation: Writers in the Public Sphere* (Verso, London, 2002).

Holderness, Graham, 'Philip Larkin the Limits of Experience', *Critical Essays on Philip Larkin: The Poems*, eds Linda Cookson and Bryan Loughrey (Longman, London, 1989), 106–18.

Hollindale, Peter, 'Philip Larkin's "The Explosion"', *Critical Survey*, I (1989), 139–48.

Hood, Thomas, *Selected Poems of Thomas Hood*, ed. John Clubbe (Harvard, Cambridge, 1970).

Hope, Warren, *Student Guide to Philip Larkin* (Greenwich Exchange, Holywood, 1997).

Hughes, Langston, *The Collected Poems of Langston Hughes*, eds Arnold Rampersad and David Roessel (Knopf, New York, 1994).

Huxley, Aldous, *Those Barren Leaves* (Chatto and Windus, London, 1925).

Ingelbien, Raphael, *Misreading England: Poetry and Nationhood Since the Second World War* (Rodopi, Amsterdam, 2002).

Jakobson, Roman, *A Concise Glossary of Contemporary Literary Theory*, ed. Jeremy Hawthorn (Arnold, London, 1998), 109.

James, Clive, 'Pretending To Be Him', *Times Literary Supplement*, 28 February 2003, 18–19.

Jardine, Lisa, 'Saxon Violence', *Guardian*, Section 2, 8 December 1992, 4.

Johnson, Barbara, 'Writing', *Critical Terms for Literary Study*, eds Frank Lentricchia and Thomas McLaughlin (University of Chicago Press, Chicago, 1990), 39–49.

Johnson, B.S., *Poems Two* (Trigram, London, 1972).

Johnson, James Weldon, *The Book of American Negro Spirituals* (Da Capo, New York, 1977).

Johnson, James Weldon, *The Second Book of American Negro Spirituals* (Da Capo, New York, 1977).

Joyce, James, *A Portrait of the Artist as a Young Man* (Penguin, Harmondsworth, 1964).

Joyce, James, *Ulysses* (Penguin, Harmondsworth, 1971).

Kaufmann, Walter, ed. *Existentialism: From Dostoevsky to Sartre* (Meridian, New York, 1975).

Kay, Jackie, 'Admirable Horn Blower', *Observer Review*, 29 November 1998, 14.

Kenner, Hugh, *A Sinking Island: The Modern English Writers* (Barrie & Jenkins, London, 1988).

Kenner, Hugh, *The Pound Era* (Faber, London, 1975).

King, Martin Luther, 'I have a dream', *The Penguin Book of Historic Speeches*, ed. Brian MacArthur (Viking, London, 1995), 487–91.

Kipling, Rudyard, *The Works of Rudyard Kipling* (Wordsworth, Ware, 1994).

Kuby, Lolette, An *Uncommon Poet for the Common Man: A Study of Philip Larkin's Poetry* (Mouton, The Hague and Paris, 1974).

Ladenson, Elisabeth, *Dirt for Art's Sake* (Cornell University Press, Ithaca and London, 2007).

Larkin, Philip, *A Girl in Winter* (Faber, London, 1975).

Larkin, Philip, *All What Jazz: A Record Diary, 1961–68* (Faber, London, 1970).

Larkin, Philip, 'Clouds Merge. The Coast Darkens', *Metre*, 10 (2001), 7.

Larkin, Philip, *Collected Poems*, ed. Anthony Thwaite (Marvell and Faber, London, 1988).

Larkin, Philip, *Early Poems and Juvenilia*, ed. A.T. Tolley (Faber, London, 2005).

Larkin, Philip, *Further Requirements: Interviews, Broadcasts, Statements and Book Reviews, 1952–1985*, ed. Anthony Thwaite (Faber, London, 2001; revised and expanded, 2002).

Larkin, Philip, *Jill* (Faber, London, 1975).

Larkin, Philip, *Larkin's Jazz: Essays and Reviews, 1940–85*, eds, Richard Palmer and John White (Continuum, London, 2001).

Larkin, Philip, 'Merry Christmas', *About Larkin*, 13 (2002), 22–4.

Larkin, Philip, *Required Writing: Miscellaneous Pieces, 1955–1982* (Faber, London, 1983).

Larkin, Philip, *Selected Letters*, ed. Anthony Thwaite (Faber, London, 1992).

Larkin, Philip, ed. *The Oxford Book of Twentieth Century English Verse* (Oxford University Press, Oxford, 1973).

Larkin, Philip, *Trouble at Willow Gables and Other Fictions* (Faber, London, 2002).

Lawrence, D.H., *Kangaroo* (Penguin, London, 1963).

Lawrence, D.H., *Sons and Lovers* (Penguin, Harmondsworth, 1964).

Lawrence, D.H., *Studies in Classic American Literature* (Mercury, London, 1965).

Leavis, Q.D., *Fiction and the Reading Public* (Penguin, Harmondsworth, 1972).

Leggett, B.J., *Larkin's Blues: Jazz, Popular Music and Poetry* (Louisiana State University Press, Baton Rouge, 1999).

Lerner, Laurence, *Philip Larkin* (Northcote, Plymouth, 1997).

Levi, Peter, 'The English Wisdom of a Master Poet', *An Enormous Yes: in memoriam Philip Larkin (1922–1985)*, ed. Harry Chambers (Peterloo Poets, Calstock, 1986), 33–5.

Lively, Penelope, *The Road to Lichfield* (Heinemann, London, 1977).

Lodge, David, *The Modes of Modern Writing: Metaphor, Metonymy, and the Typology of Modern Literature* (Arnold, London, 1977).

Lodge, David, ed. *20th Century Literary Criticism: A Reader* (Longman, London, 1972).

Longfellow, Henry Wadsworth, *The Song of Hiawatha*, ed. Daniel Aaron (Everyman, London, 1992).

Longfellow, Henry Wadsworth, *The Works of Henry Wadsworth Longfellow* (Wordsworth, Ware, 1994).

Longley, Edna, 'Larkin, Decadence and the Lyric Poem', *New Larkins for Old*, ed. James Booth (Macmillan, Basingstoke, 2000), 29–50.

Longley, Edna, 'Larkin, Edward Thomas and the Tradition', *Phoenix*, 11/12, 63–98.

Longley, Edna, 'Poete Maudit Manque', *Philip Larkin: A Tribute*, ed. George Hartley (Marvell, London, 1988), 220–31.

Longmate, Norman, *How We Lived Then: A History of Everyday Life during the Second World War* (Arrow, London, 1973), 134.

Lonnrot, Elias, *The Kalevala: An Epic Poem after Oral Tradition*, trans. Keith Bosley (Oxford University Press, Oxford, 1989).

López Garcia, Dámaso, 'Post-Metropolitan Larkin', *Hungarian Journal of English and American Studies*, vol. 9, 2 (2003), 81–9.

Lyotard, Jean-Francois, *The Postmodern Condition: A Report on Knowledge* (Manchester University Press, Manchester, 1987).

Macquarrie, John, *Existentialism* (Penguin, Harmondsworth, 1973).

Melnick, Jeffrey, *A Right to Sing the Blues: Africa Americans, Jews and American Popular Song* (Harvard University Press, Cambridge, 1999).

Miller, Henry, *Tropic of Cancer* (Panther, London, 1968).

Morrison, Blake, *The Movement: English Poetry and Fiction of the 1950s* (Methuen, London, 1980).

Morrison, Toni, *Playing in the Dark: Whiteness and the Literary Imagination (Picador, London and Basingstoke, 1993).*

Motion, Andrew, *Philip Larkin* (Methuen, London, 1982).

Motion, Andrew, *Philip Larkin: A Writer's Life* (Faber, London, 1993).

Muggeridge, Malcolm, 'The Passion of St Eatherly', *Tread Softly for You Tread on My Jokes* (Collins, London, 1968), 219–27.

Murdoch, Iris, *Sartre* (Collins, London, 1968).

Nagel, Thomas, 'Much ado', *Times Literary Supplement*, 7 May 2004, 3.

'NB', *Times Literary Supplement*, 6 December 1996, 16.

Newsinger, John, 'Dead Poet: The Larkin Letters', *Race and Class*, 34, 4 (April–June, 1993), 87–93.

Nuttall, Jeff, 'The Singing Ted', *Poetry Information*, 9/10 (1974), 23–30.

O'Brien, Flann, *At Swim-Two-Birds* (Penguin, Harmondsworth, 1975).

O'Brien, Sean, *The Deregulated Muse: Essays on Contemporary British and Irish Poetry* (Bloodaxe Books, Newcastle, 1998).

O'Driscoll, Dennis, *Troubled Thoughts, Majestic Dreams: Selected Prose Writings* (Gallery, Loughcrew, 2001).

Oliver, Paul, *The Story of the Blues* (Penguin, Harmondsworth, 1972).

Olson, Charles, *The Maximus Poems*, ed. George Butterick (University of California Press, Berkeley and Los Angeles, 1983).

Orr, Mary, *Intertextuality: Debates and Contexts* (Polity, London, 2003).

Orwell, George, *Inside the Whale and Other Essays* (Penguin, Harmondsworth, 1966).

Orwin, Jim and John Osborne, 'Adeline Yen Mah, *About Larkin*, 22 (2006), 17–19.

Parkinson, R.N., 'To Keep Our Metaphysics Warn: A study of "Church Going"', *Critical Survey*, 5 (1971), 224–33.

Paulin, Tom, letter, *Times Literary Supplement*, 6 November 1992, 15.

Paulin, Tom, 'She Did Not Change: Philip Larkin', *Minotaur: Poetry and the Nation State* (Harvard University Press, Cambridge, 1992), 233–51.

Pelizzon, V. Penelope, 'Oh, Play That Thing!', *About Larkin*, 5 (1998), 17–18.

Perria, Noel, *Dr Bowdler's Legacy: A History of Expurgated Books in England and America* (Macmillan, Basingstoke, 1970).

Petch, Simon, *The Art of Philip Larkin* (Sydney University Press, Sydney, 1981).

Phelps, Gilbert, 'Literature and Drama', *The Cambridge Guide to the Arts in Britain, vol. 9, Since the Second World War* (Cambridge University Press, Cambridge, 1988), 196–236.

Phillips, Ivan, 'I sing the bard electric', *Times Literary Supplement*, 19 September 2003, 15.

Piette, Adam, 'Childhood Wiped Out,' paper delivered at the Larkin and the 40s conference, University of London, 16 July 1999.

Plath, Sylvia, *Collected Poems*, ed. Ted Hughes (Faber, London, 1981).

Plimpton, George, ed. *Beat Writers at Work: The Paris Review Interviews* (Harvill, London, 1999).

Porteous, J. Douglas, 'Nowhereman', *About Larkin*, 8 (1999), 12–16.

Pound, Ezra, *Selected Poems*, ed. T.S. Eliot (Faber, London, 1954).

Pound, Ezra, *The Cantos of Ezra Pound* (revised and collected edition, Faber, London, 1975).

Praed, Winthrop Mackworth, *The Poems of Winthrop Mackworth Praed* (Moxon, London, 1864).

Preminger, Alex, ed. *Princeton Encyclopedia of Poetry and Poetics* (Macmillan, London and Basingstoke, 1975).

Quinn, Justin and David Wheatley, eds, *Metre*, vol. 14, Autumn, 2003.

Ramsden, John, *The Dam Busters* (Tauris, London, 2003).

Read, Herbert, *Contemporary British Art* (Penguin, Harmondsworth, 1964).

Regan, Stephen, *Philip Larkin: The Critics Debate* (Macmillan, Basingstoke, 1992).

Ricks, Christopher, *Allusion to the Poets* (Oxford University Press, Oxford, 2002).

Rimbaud, Arthur, *Collected Poems*, trans. Martin Sorrell (Oxford University Press, Oxford, 2001).

Ritchie, Harry, *Success Stories: Literature and the Media in England, 1950–1959* (Faber, London, 1982).

Robinson, Dave and Oscar Zarate, *Introducing Kierkegaard* (Icon, Cambridge, 2003).

Rossen, Janice, *Philip Larkin: His Life's Work* (Harvester, Hemel Hemstead, 1989).

Rowe, Mark, 'Larkin's "Aubade"', *Philosophy and Literature* (Ashgate, Aldershot, 2000), 182–219.

Rumens, Carol, *Self into Song* (Bloodaxe Books, Newcastle, 2007).

Rutherford, Maurice, *Love is a Four-Letter World* (Peterloo, Calstock, 1994).

Rutherford, Maurice, *Slipping the Tugs* (Lincolnshire & Humberside Arts, Lincoln, 1982).

Rutherford, Maurice, *This Day Dawning* (Peterloo, Calstock, 1994).

Ryan, Kiernan, 'Life of Czechs and Balances', *Times Higher Education Supplement*, 29 August 2003, 27.

Sadgrove, Canon Michael, *The Pitkin Guide to Coventry Cathedral* (Pitkin Unichrome, Andover, 1991).

Sassoon, Siegfried, *Collected Poems, 1908–1956* (Faber, London, 1984).

Schmidt, Michael, *Lives of the Poets* (Weidenfeld & Nicolson, London, 1998).

Scupham, Peter, 'A Caucus-race', *Phoenix*, 11/12, 173–82.

Simmons, James, 'The Trouble with Larkin', *Philip Larkin: A Tribute*, ed. George Hartley (Marvell, London, 1988), 232–36.

Smart, Ninian, *The Religious Experience of Mankind* (Collins, London and Glasgow, 1971).

Smith, Stan, *Inviolable Voice: History and Twentieth Century Poetry* (Gill & Macmillan, Dublin, 1982).

Solomos, John, *Race and Racism in Britain* (Macmillan, Basingstoke, 2003).

Southam, B.C., *A Student's Guide to the 'Selected Poems' of T.S. Eliot* (Faber, London, 1994).

Spence, Basil, *Phoenix at Coventry* (Collins, London, 1964).

Steiner, George, *Heidegger* (Fontana, Glasgow, 1978).

Stevenson, Randall, *The Last of England: The Oxford Literary History, vol 12, 1960–2000* (Oxford University Press, Oxford, 2004).

Swarbrick, Andrew, *'The Less Deceived' and 'The Whitsun Weddings' by Philip Larkin* (Macmillan, Basingstoke, 1986).

Swarbrick, Andrew, *Out of Reach: The Poetry of Philip Larkin* (Macmillan, Basingstoke, 1995).

Tarantino, Quentin, *Reservoir Dogs* (Faber, London, 1994).

Taylor, A.J.P., *English History, 1914–1945* (Penguin, Harmondsworth, 1970).

Taylor, Frederick, *Dresden: Tuesday 13 February 1945* (Bloomsbury, London, 2004).

Tennyson, Alfred, *The Poems of Alfred Tennyson* (Kegan Paul, London, 1882).

Thatcher, Margaret, *Margaret Thatcher in Her Own Words*, eds Macdonald Daly and Alexander George (Penguin, Harmondsworth, 1987).

Thomas, Edward, *Collected Poems* (Faber, London, 1981).

Thulstrup, Niels and Marie Mikulova, eds, *Kierkegaard and the Church in Denmark* (Reitzels Boghandel, Copenhagen, 1978).

Thulstrup, Niels and Marie Mikulova, eds, *Kierkegard's View of Christianity* (Reitzels Forlag, Copenhagen, 1984).

Thurber, James, *The Thurber Carnival* (Penguin, Harmondsworth, 1965).

Thwaite, Anthony, ed. *Larkin at Sixty* (Faber, London, 1982).

Thwaite, Anthony, *Poetry Today: A Critical Guide to British Poetry, 1960–1984* (Longman, London, 1985).

Thwaite, Anthony, 'The Poetry of Philip Larkin', *Phoenix*, 11/12, 41–58.

Timms, David, *Philip Larkin* (Oliver and Boyd, Edinburgh, 1973).

Tolley, A.T., *My Proper Ground: A Study of the Work of Philip Larkin and Its Development* (Edinburgh University Press, Edinburgh, 1991).

Tomlinson, Charles, 'Poetry Today', *Pelican Guide to English Literature, vol. 7, The Modern Period*, ed. Boris Ford (Penguin, Harmondsworth, 1964), 458–74.

Travis, Alan, *Bound and Gagged: A Secret History of Obscenity in Britain* (Profile, London, 2001).

Wain, John, 'A Song About Major Eatherly', *Weep Before God* (Macmillan, London, 1962), 40–5.

Wain, John, 'Engagement or Withdrawal? Some Notes on the Work of Philip Larkin', *Critical Quarterly*, 17, 4 (1975), 347–60.

Waley, Arthur, *The Way and the Power: A Study of the Tao Te Ching and Its Place in Chinese Thought* (George Allen and Unwin, London, 1934).

Watkins, Vernon, *The Collected Poems of Vernon Watkins* (Golgonooza Press, Ipswich, 1986).

Watson, J.R., 'Probably Neither Works: Negative Signifiers in Larkin's Poetry', *About Larkin*, 6 (1998–9), 14–17.

Watson, J.R., 'The Other Larkin', *Critical Quarterly*, 17, 4 (1975), 347–60.

Watt, R.J.C., *A Concordance to the Poetry of Philip Larkin* (Olms-Weidmann, Hildesheim, 1995).

Watt, R.J.C., 'The Larkin Concordance', *About Larkin*, 3 (1997), 28

Watts, Cedric, 'Larkin and Jazz', *Critical Essays on Philip Larkin: The Poems*, eds Linda Cookson and Bryan Loughrey (Longman, London, 1987), 20–8.

Waugh, Patricia, *The Harvest of the Sixties: English Literature and Its Background, 1960–1990* (Oxford University Press, Oxford, 1995).

Whalen, Terry, *Philip Larkin and English Poetry* (Macmillan, Basingstoke, 1986).

Whitehead, John, *Hardy to Larkin: Seven English Poets* (Hearthstone, Munslow, 1995).

Whitman, Walt, *The Viking Portable Walt Whitman*, ed. Mark Van Doren (Viking, New York, 1966).

Wood, James, 'Want Not, Write Not', *Guardian*, 30 March 1993, 20.

Woods, Tim, *Beginning Postmodernism* (Manchester University Press, Manchester, 1999).

Wootten, William, 'In the Graveyard of Verse', *London Review of Books*, 9 August 2001, 23–4.

Wordsworth, William, *William Wordsworth*, eds Stephen Gill and Duncan Wu (Oxford University Press, Oxford, 1994).

Yen Mah, Adeline, *One Written Word is Worth a Thousand Pieces of Gold* (Harper Perennial, London, 2002).

Yen Mah, Adeline, *Watching the Tree to Catch a Hare* (HarperCollins, London, 2000).

Index

Principal entries are cited in bold type.

Printed in the United States
148167LV00001B/4/P